SCIENCE AND PHILOSOPHY
IN THE WEST

PRENTICE HALL, UPPER SADDLE RIVER, NEW JERSEY 07458

Library of Congress Cataloging-in-Publication Data

Leon, Jeffrey C.
    Science and philosophy in the West / by Jeffrey C. Leon.
        p.   cm.
    Includes bibliographical references and index.
    ISBN 0-13-647439-X
    1. Science—Philosophy.   I. Title.
    Q175.L443   1998
    501—dc21   98-2872
                                                          CIP

Acquisitions Editor: Karita France
Editorial Assistant: Jennifer Ackerman
Editorial Director/EIC: Charlyce Jones Owen
Director of Marketing: Gina Sluss
Production Editor: Louise Rothman
Manufacturing Buyer: Tricia Kenny
Manufacturing Manager: Nick Sklitsis
Cover Design: Bruce Kenselaar

To Louis and Jacob .

This book was set in 11/13 Minion by Pub-Set
and was printed and bound by Courier-Westford.
The cover was printed by Phoenix Color Corp.

© 1999 by Prentice-Hall, Inc.
A Pearson Education Company
Upper Saddle River, NJ 07458

Printed in the United States of America

10 9 8 7 6 5 4 3 2 1

ISBN 0-13-647439-X

Prentice-Hall International (UK) Limited,London
Prentice-Hall of Australia Pty. Limited, Sydney
Prentice-Hall Canada Inc., Toronto
Prentice-Hall Hispanoamericana, S.A., Mexico
Prentice-Hall of India Private Limited, New Delhi
Prentice-Hall of Japan, Inc., Tokyo
Pearson Education Asia Pte. Ltd., Singapore
Editora Prentice-Hall do Brasil, Ltda., Rio de Janeiro

Contents

Preface

This book examines the history of the relationship between science and philosophy in the West. Conventional wisdom maintains that there is a division between the two and that science is the more contemporary and potent form of intellectual interpretation while philosophy is more antiquated and reflective. This book is designed to show that philosophy, science, and culture have a long and intimate relationship throughout history, and the story of this relationship is important for the present and the future of both science and philosophy. While the material is accessible for non-science majors, undergraduates and graduate students concentrating in the sciences should be well-served by this volume. Those students familiar with modern variants of particular scientists' works are probably unfamiliar with the commentary these scientists offer as to the philosophical and social import of their efforts. Such commentary is included here. And most science majors have at best a cursory acquaintance with philosophical issues in general. This book should give some insight into the philosophy of knowledge, reality, method, history, and society.

The scope of the material and the historical periods treated herein are indeed daunting, and many sacrifices as to content, precision, and analysis have been made. The hope is that by treating so much science and philosophy in one volume, some global themes will come to light. It is tempting to bias this study in favor of contemporary views. It is even perhaps justified by saying that contemporary views in science and philosophy are more complex and have built on their predecessors in such a way that necessitates more resources be devoted to recent theories. But such a bias would be simply that: a bias. Many philosophers have challenged the cumulative view of science. This text considers the issue of the growth of science—i.e., the question: does scientific knowledge grow progressively throughout history?—as an open one. Thus, to favor contemporary views as more sophisticated or as "containing" previous views would be to answer this question affirmatively. Instead, students and instructors are invited to consider this issue as part of our inquiry.

Chapters 1 and 2 survey some ancient Greek theories, from the Presocratic philosophers through Aristotle and Galen. Chapter 3 treats the seventeenth-century revolution in physical science, and Chapter 4 treats some metaphysical theories that accompanied this revolution. Here and in other places, I have avoided strictly historical presentations in favor of topical presentations; hence Descartes is in Chapter 4 while the later work of Newton is treated in Chapter 3. Chapter 5 focuses on modern, i.e., seventeenth-, eighteenth-, and nineteenth-century views of scientific method. Chapter 6 focuses on some modern developments in biology and medicine. Chapter 7 traces the evolution of classical mechanism from the seventeenth century to the beginning of its demise. Chapter 8 treats some later modern views on the status of scientific theory and its relation to metaphysics and religion. Chapter 9 treats other relationships between modern science, the analytic mindset that accompanies it, and social theory. Chapter 10 presents some twentieth-century developments in physical science: namely, special relativity, quantum theory, general relativity, and chaos theory. Chapter 11 deals with twentieth-century theories on scientific method, much as Chapter 5 deals with methodological theories that accompanied the seventeenth-century scientific revolution. Chapter 12 discusses, without the use of extensive citations, some contemporary areas of philosophy and science that remain fertile grounds for establishing new insights and relationships between the two disciplines.

Hence, the book can be divided into roughly four parts: (1) ancient science and philosophy, consisting of Chapters 1 and 2; (2) modern science and philosophy, consisting of Chapters 3, 4, 5, 6, and 7; (3) philosophy and science in transition to the postmodern and contemporary age, consisting of Chapters 8 and 9; and (4) science and philosophy in the postmodern and contemporary periods, consisting of Chapters 10, 11, and 12. Such organization may be useful in designing course syllabi or in deciding which sections to emphasize or omit.

Finally, I would like to acknowledge a few people who have helped in this effort, besides the publishers and the authors who have given permission to have their work reprinted and who are acknowledged throughout the text. I thank my wife Sara for her loving and enduring support; Bob Solomon for his early encouragement; Angie Stone at Prentice Hall, who first took an active interest in this project; Keith Burgess Jackson, University of Texas, Jesse Taylor, Appalachian State University, and Bob Dawden, California State University at Sacramento, for reviewing the manuscript; and the Department of Philosophy at the University of Texas at Austin.

Introduction

Imagine a world without science. Imagine a world without theoretical reflection. Imagine a world in the infancy of thinking. This world surely existed at one time, although where and when is a matter of considerable debate. Details of time and place aside, the student of intellectual history has the opportunity to observe and participate in the intellectual development of humanity in much the same way that a parent has the opportunity to be involved with the development of an infant. And in the same way that parents learn as much about themselves in the process of raising a child as the child learns about the world, students and historians learn as much as or perhaps more about their own consciousness—its basis, its legacy, and its direction—than they do facts of record.

What do we mean by "science" and "philosophy"? To say that science is experimental, or that it is mechanical, or that it involves mathematical theory is too narrow. Ancient Greeks and twentieth-century theorists would take issue with such a view. Science is the study of natural phenomena. It is the attempt to provide natural explanations for natural occurrences. This attempt is presumed to be in good faith and of a critical nature. That is, competing theories should be given equal weight, and debates should be judged on merit rather than extraneous criteria such as political or religious authority.

"Philosophy" is originally derived from Greek words meaning love and wisdom, and as such, philosophy is the love of wisdom. Philosophy is also taken to be critical and of good faith. Debate is encouraged and positions are judged by "philosophical" merit rather than extraneous criteria. Philosophy, however, does not focus exclusively on the natural but can delve into the supernatural. Philosophy also begins from a more basic stance; that is, some philosophers reject the very existence of an external world which could be the object of scientific study.

Philosophy traditionally contains three main fields of inquiry: the Real, the Good, and the Known. Studies of these are Metaphysics, Ethics, and Epistemology, respectively. Metaphysics includes such questions as: What sorts of things exist? What are the basic properties of such things? These two questions dealing with the "things" that constitute reality are the focus of a branch of metaphysics known as ontology. In addition, metaphysics includes speculations about the relationships among the constituents of reality, questions such as: Are there any universal laws of nature? Ethics is concerned with determinations of value, including questions such as: What constitutes a good act or virtuous character? What sorts of criteria can we use to adjudicate questions of value, that is, questions of good and bad, better and worse? How do these judgments relate to individual choice and responsibility, social organizations and institutions? Epistemology includes questions such as: What sorts of things can be known? How can we come to knowledge of them? What is the form of true knowledge?

Science can easily be seen to be involved with metaphysics and epistemology. In some periods of history, it is explicitly related to ethics. Some philosophers claim that science is always steeped in issues of value at least implicitly. In any case, all of these subdivisions are recognized relatively late in the sweep of human history. At its beginning, the story of science and philosophy recognizes no such distinctions. It is to this beginning that we now turn.

Ancient Dialogues

Thinking about the nature of the world seems to be an essential part of being human. Many cultures have advanced specific world-views through religious teachings, customs, or social organizations, and one of the earliest surviving philosophical or scientific dialogues about nature is found in early Greece.[1] In the period before Socrates, philosophers proposed views of the world based on observation, reflection, and critical analysis. The Presocratics and their successors carried on an extended dialogue about the fundamental entities of nature and reality, starting with Thales in the sixth century B.C.E.

In the first sections of this chapter, we treat the Presocratic doctrines of Thales, Anaximander, Heraclitus, Parmenides, and Zeno, as well as theories of the later Democritus and of the Pythagorean school. Their works, if any were written at all,[2] survive in fragmentary form, mostly through reports and commentary by philosophers and historians such as Aristotle, Sextus Empiricus, and Diogenes Laertius. Here we treat their writings as early commentary on the elements of nature. Scholars dispute whether or not this interpretation is valid, but philosophers and scientists throughout the ages have been inspired by the early Greeks, and for our purposes this is enough to warrant such examination.

Western medicine also traces its roots to ancient Greece, where the Hippocratic physicians founded a tradition of healing on which the modern Hippocratic oath is based. Galen, a later Greek philosopher, discussed some sophisticated issues in philosophy, medicine, and method. Much of his focus concerned scientific method, and he chronicled a debate between schools of thought we know as rationalism—the doctrine that rational argument and theoretical inquiry are the proper modes for scientific progress—and empiricism—the doctrine that science is better served by investigation using observation and tests drawn from experience. These methodological and philosophical themes are important throughout the subsequent history of philosophy and science.

Early Natural Ontologists

The birth of Western philosophy coincided with the birth of Western science. The Presocratic philosophers were interested in gleaning fundamental insights into the workings of nature. They presented rudimentary arguments, considered opposing positions, and challenged authoritative viewpoints from mythology, poetry, and earlier philosophers. Their interest in finding the basic elements of reality makes them ontologists, and their emphasis on evidence gleaned from observation makes them early natural scientists. Their methods and results differed dramatically from what later scientists would accept, and we will see reasons for this in the coming chapters. For one, they lacked a key development in the modern scientific revolution, namely, the articulation of a quantitative experimental technique. And another premodern feature is evident: the unification of value-oriented and factual inquiry. The Ancients explicitly included the search for the good with the search for the real and the true. Beginning in the sixth century B.C.E. and continuing through the works of Aristotle in ancient Greece and Augustine in the Middle Ages, investigation into the elements and order of the universe involved a quest for meaning and value. One early exception is found in the atomism of Democritus, who anticipated a more modern and mechanical view of the world.

Descartes, Galileo, and Newton together laid the groundwork for rejecting this unified approach, as we will see in Chapter 4. Such rejection is characteristic of the modern age of classical mechanics. The nineteenth and twentieth centuries saw challenges, both scientific and philosophical, to the mechanism of classical physics, and many of these challenges harken back to the Presocratics. Many twentieth-century philosophers and scientists see an emerging wholism in science—a unity of human affairs and physical reality—that is reminiscent of some of the themes emphasized in this section.

Thales: A World of Water

With Thales, the search for simple, natural, elemental explanation begins. He was born around 625 B.C.E. and lived until near 545. There are several anecdotes about Thales, probably apocryphal. He supposedly predicted an eclipse, which modern astronomers put at 585 B.C.E. This prediction established him as a sage, and he was also a noted mathematician and statesman. An ancient historian claims Thales discovered that the angles at the base of an isosceles triangle are equal. He is also said to have advocated the practicality of using constellations for navigation.

His most famous concepts are those associated with his assertion that water is the basic stuff of the world. Aristotle's *Metaphysics* (983b17–27) contains the following:

> There must be some entity—either one or more than one—from which the other things come to be. . . . Yet they do not all agree as to the number and the nature of these principles. Thales, the founder of this sort of philosophy, says the principle is water (for which reason he declared that the earth rests on water), getting the notion perhaps from seeing that the nutriment of all things is moist and that heat itself is generated from the moist and kept alive by it (and that from which they come to be is a principle of all things). He got his notion from this fact, and from the fact that the seeds of all things have a moist nature, and that water is the origin of the nature of moist things.

If Thales observed that life and other elements of nature are dependent on and transformed by water, then his natural philosophy was empirical. But regardless of his method, his postulate is not a poetic metaphor nor is it an element of mythology, and therein lies its significance. Thales offered a natural explanation for natural phenomena, and this explanation was intended to be clearly and explicitly understood. We do not need to be literary theorists, cultural anthropologists, or students of mythology to evaluate his theory.[3] His legacy teaches that the search for the basic truths of the universe need go no further than reasoned observation and interpretation of the world around us.

Thales further believed that such reasoning will evoke simpler, more basic truths until we discover one basic cause or building block for the universe. For Thales it was water. This faith in analysis and reason, characteristic of philosophy and science for millennia, has lately been labelled *reductionism*. The reductionist thesis is that science in the end reduces to a unified set of principles and physical entities on which all other natural phenomena depend. Such dependence is one-way in reductionism. Reductionists posit one fundamental entity, say the water of Thales or the solutions of a probability wave equation in quantum theory, which is a constituent or cause for everything else, and not vice-versa. A reductionist claims that traffic jams, earthquakes, and cell division must involve the basic entities of the universe, but these same entities can exist independently of such complex, derivative phenomena. Modern reductionists have much more sophisticated and, to some extent, weaker views of this dependence than the Presocratics did. We will return to modern and contemporary debates on reductionism in Chapter 12.

Since Thales is asking what the basic "stuff" of the world is, his focus is ontological. But his ontology is purely natural, and so natural science and philosophy are unified in this Presocratic world-view.

Anaximander: The Indeterminate Infinite

With Anaximander, the search for a primary element becomes more abstract. Anaximander was an associate of Thales, apparently younger. He was also interested in reasoning about the primary substance of the world, but concluded that it could not be any particular element found in nature. He believed that if one element, say water, were the basis of the universe, then the universe would eventually be subsumed by water and transformed into water. Therefore, according to Anaximander, the basic element is indeterminate. Such an element can be "eternal and ageless" and "encompass all worlds."[4]

For Anaximander the quest for a basic natural ontology ended in an abstract entity he called the indeterminate infinite. This foreshadows the esoteric turn ontology takes in the future. Many later philosophers abandon the natural world entirely when proposing a theory of reality.[5] But the basis for Anaximander's conclusion was intended to be empirical. He observed the change, growth, and death of natural entities and events and believed that nature cannot generate or sustain itself via concrete elements alone. He characterized nature as a destructive conflict of opposites. Anaximander's conclusion is not readily understandable in concrete terms, but we know that modern and contemporary scientists postulate theories that are no less abstract when they account for the behavior of the natural world.[6]

Anaximander had a notion of justice and balance in the structure of the world, and hence a place for values in a philosophy of nature. In his *History of Philosophy*, Frederick Copleston summarizes this aspect of Anaximander nicely when he says, "The encroachments of one element on another are poetically represented as instances of injustice, [e.g.,] the warm element committing an injustice in the summer and the cold in winter. The determinate elements make reparation for their injustice by being absorbed again into the Indeterminate Boundless. This is an instance of the extension of the conception of law from human life to the universe at large." (Vol. I, p., 25) This notion of justice and reparation in the universe as a whole shows an ethical dimension to nature.

If this style of reasoning resulted from a projection of human life onto the universe as a whole, then Anaximander's theory is anthropocentric. That is, he used humanity as a model for the universe without critically examining this premise. One version of the story of science throughout the ages is that it has been an effort to rid scientific theory of all vestiges of such bad-faith anthropocentrism. Some twentieth-century theorists believe that this effort has proved to be impossible. Such impossibility would yield new puzzles and insights for scientific theory and its relationship to humanity, as we will see.

Incidentally, Anaximander had hypotheses concerning evolution and the motion of the earth. He postulated that "in the beginning man was born from animals of another species." A version of the principle of sufficient reason is involved in Anaximander's discussion of the earth's motion or nonmotion. The principle of sufficient reason states that every phenomenon has an impetus that is sufficient to produce it—nothing happens without some reason. The Ancients were at odds to explain how the earth alone appears to be at rest—seemingly unsupported—unlike other bodies in the heavens. Instead of stipulating that something actually does support the earth, Anaximander hypothesized that the earth sits at the center of the universe, with no reason to wander from its privileged position. Without such a reason, it does not move. This is a controversial and converse version of the principle which states that everything that happens happens for a reason.

If such a principle is involved in Anaximander's philosophy, it is an example of how second-order reasoning enters his work. Instead of simply reasoning about the connections between observed phenomena, Anaximander engages in reasoning about reasoning. The principle of sufficient reason goes beyond empirical observation and fanciful speculation to try to determine how and why reasons and explanations themselves function. In this case, Anaximander finds that a lack of sufficient reason is enough to conclude that the earth does not move.

Similarly, his argument for an indeterminate substrata does not simply map one set of observations onto a basic explanation of the world as in Thales' world of water, but attempts to reason about how and why certain principles are adequate for basic explanations and others are not. Anaximander claimed that purely concrete elemental principles and substances cannot adequately account for the multiplicity of natural phenomena, and therefore more abstract postulates are necessary. He characterized different types of explanation as adequate and others as inadequate, and therefore engaged in a sort of meta-inquiry on the nature of inquiry. Like the principle of sufficient reason, this line of thinking goes beyond the stipulations of Thales.

Anaximander is widely regarded as advancing Thales' mission.[7] While the latter began a tradition of natural science, the former encompassed abstract and ethical dimensions as well. By uniting empirical observation, higher order reasoning, and the powers of abstraction, Anaximander brought a new level of sophistication to early science and philosophy.

Heraclitus: Fire, Change, and Motion

Heraclitus was born in Asia Minor and flourished around 500 B.C.E. His writings were obscure and difficult, which no doubt led to their reputation for profundity. Nevertheless, the natural philosophy of Heraclitus has been distilled to represent a sophisticated discussion of energy, change, motion, and unity.

Heraclitus, like his predecessors, was seeking a basic explanation for the natural world. But he understood perhaps more clearly the difficulties of this task. How could any one theory be adequate to account for the multiplicity of phenomena that surround us? For Heraclitean thought, the paradigm of the natural world was not some primary substance, as with the water of Thales, nor the law-like operation of cosmic justice as with Anaximander, but change and flux. Providing a unified description of this flux was the challenge Heraclitus tried to meet. The following fragments are reprinted from G.S. Kirk, Raven, and Schofield, *The Presocratic Philosophers*, and Jonathan Barnes, *Early Greek Philosophy*.

All things are an exchange for fire and fire for all things
The thunderbolt steers all things[8]

Plato transcribed:

Heraclitus somewhere says that all things are in process and nothing stays still.[9]

Heraclitus' most famous metaphor is captured in this report by Plutarch:

It is not possible to step twice into the same river, nor touch mortal substance twice . . . by the swiftness and speed of its change, it scatters and collects itself again.[10]

Like Anaximander, Heraclitus viewed the world as constantly changing. However, he was not led to a purely abstract explanation of this change, since there are concrete elements of the world that embody energy, change, and flux: namely, fire and lightning. Heraclitus noted that fire exists by consuming and transforming its material and itself. The continued existence of fire is dependent on its constant change into something new. This not only shows the coherence of this view but also the basis of Heraclitus' thought in observation.

There is a preliminary concept of energy in the notions of flux and fire. Twentieth-century physics can be viewed as confirming the hypothesis that a study of energy is the basic tool for understanding the world. In Chapters 10 and 12 we will see contemporary analogues of Heraclitean natural philosophy. Physicists such as Albert Einstein, Werner Heisenberg, and Ilya Prigogine cite the wisdom of Heraclitus as an inspiring force in their work. Although we may be engaged in inaccurate projection when we attribute a concept of energy to Heraclitus, his writings are significant not only as evidence of what was going through the mind of one man in ancient Greece, but also for the ways in which they echo throughout history.

Many casual students of ancient philosophical and scientific history may be familiar with Heraclitus' notion of flux, change, and fire, but it is also important to note that he emphasized these elements in order to bring a *unified* theory into concert with the natural world. This unity is what philosophers ancient and modern have called The One. Heraclitus declared, "it is wise to agree that all things are one." Here we see Presocratic reductionism again, although for Heraclitus this reductionism involved a radical translation from the world of experience, which seems to contain solid objects and other unchanging elements, to the basic substrata of fire and lightning characterized by constant flux. Parmenides provided a different interpretation of The One that is the antithesis of Heraclitean flux.

Parmenides: Being and The One

Parmenides lived in Southern Italy sometime in the late sixth century B.C.E. (differing evidence puts his period either around 540 or around 515). With Parmenides, we see Presocratic philosophy turn again to abstract reasoning. Like Anaximander, Parmenides did not believe that concrete, observable elements of nature could form the basis for a natural philosophy.

Parmenides was struck by the elegant, simple truths of abstract thinking. Through contemplation, Parmenides believed he could reduce the universe to a simple whole, a **One** both necessary and unchanging. For Parmenides the essential fact of the universe was existence. The fact that nonexistence is an elusive if not impossible concept to visualize provided evidence for Parmenides that all existence is necessary. Change is a form of creation and perishing, and thus involves states of nonexistence. For Parmenides, this was enough to dismiss change as illusory. The following passages reflect these themes.

What is for being and for thinking must be; for it can be and nothing can not.

Nothing either is or will be other than what is, since fate has fettered it to be whole and unmoving. Hence all things are a name which mortals lay down . . . coming into being and perishing . . . changing place and altering bright color. . . .

It never was nor will be, since it is now, altogether, one, continuous. For what birth will you seek for it? . . . I shall not allow you to say or to think from not being . . . And how could what is be in the future? How could it come to be? For if it came into being, it is not. . . . Thus coming into being is extinguished.[11]

This last passage is an argument for Parmenides' doctrine. This doctrine states It, i.e., The One or Being, is. It is one, whole, and unchanging. Where Heraclitus gave credence to change, flux, and becoming, Parmenides dismisses these as nominal, names "which mortals lay down." There is only Being, and Being is One.

His argument is that if becoming were the case, there are only two ways to account for it. Either something comes from nothing, which is impossible, or from something, in which case it already exists and then ceases to exist, which also cannot account for existence according to Parmenides. So there is no becoming, no change, and existence is eternal and final. Such a conclusion is far from apparent, and thus Parmenides' ideas promote notions of true being and mere seeming. For Parmenides, the realm of true being was found in contemplation, while the changing world of particular objects was nothing more than illusion.

This is another case of anthropocentrism in metaphysics and natural philosophy. Parmenides identifies reality with the act of contemplation: "What is for being and thinking must be." Without further argumentation, a sceptical inquirer should challenge this thesis. Why does contemplation, a human activity, reveal how the universe must be? Parmenides gave an enigmatic hint at his reasoning in his passage: "for it can be, and nothing cannot." Nevertheless, the belief that the external world mirrors the world of human thought is a direct example of anthropocentrism in metaphysics. We will see more versions, both explicit and tacit, of this idea.

Again we see an esoteric dimension to natural philosophy as in Anaximander. These turns de-emphasize observation, but are important for understanding the problems and complexities of attempting to formulate ideas of the world. We will revisit controversies between theories of immutability, unity, and flux in Chapter 12 when we look at some implications of the results obtained by Einstein, Podolski, and Rosen in the twentieth century (see Chapters 10 and 12). These twentieth-century results have become a focal point for debate about the status of twentieth-century science.

Parmenides can be regarded as the most fervent reductionist yet. Thales, Anaximander, and Heraclitus sought to analyze the natural world into its most basic elements or laws, hence they reduced nature to its fundamental essence in scientific and philosophical theory. The simpler this essence, the more the world is reduced. For Parmenides, this reduction leads to the ultimate simplicity: The changeless One.[12] Reductionism is a perennial theme in Western science, with various physical and metaphysical theories competing for recognition as the correct interpretation of nature's basic elements. Most attempt to square basic elemental theories of nature with ordinary experience by accounting for part of this experience as mere "seeming." The next section treats Zeno and his reasons for believing with Parmenides that the world is other than it appears.

Zeno of Elea

Zeno of Elea was a friend, follower, and contemporary of Parmenides. In defense of an unchanging One in the face of seeming change and multiplicity, Zeno presents various problems of place and motion. These puzzles serve as motivators for science as well as philosophy. Zeno's arguments were designed to support Parmenides' views, but more significantly, they show how naive, commonsense hypotheses on the nature of reality can be problematic.

Those who did not accept The One proposed various alternative theories, and Zeno presented problems with such alternatives. Moreover, according to Zeno, such theories failed to account for the very phenomena for which they were designed, and thus are inadequate on their own criteria. For example, the Pythagoreans and the atomists proposed that the world is composed of an infinite number of discrete units, not a continuous whole. This proposition is the target of Zeno's famous parable of Achilles and the tortoise. Aristotle gave the parable as follows:

Let us suppose that Achilles and a tortoise are going to have a race. Since Achilles is a sportsman, he gives the tortoise a start. Now, by the time that Achilles has reached the place from which the tortoise started, the latter has again advanced to another point; and when Achilles reaches that point, then the tortoise will have advanced still another distance, even if very short. Thus Achilles is always coming nearer to the tortoise, but never actually overtakes it—and never *can* do so, on the supposition that a line is made up of an infinite number of points.[13]

Zeno also proposed that traversing a stadium is impossible if space consists of an infinite number of points. This is so because one would need to traverse an infinite number of points in a finite time—the first half before the second, the first half of the first half before its second, and so on.

Another of Zeno's arguments was designed to show that the idea of spatial location is nonsensical. Zeno argued that if things were located, they must be located somewhere. But that location would also have to be located somewhere in space, and that location likewise. Thus we are led to an infinite regression of locations of locations, of space within space within space. In this way, Zeno argued that one of our commonsense notions relating the things in the world to each other is absurd.

These paradoxes and puzzles are taken to support two claims. One is that doctrines of the natural world which purport to account for multiplicity and change are inadequate. The second is that the Parmenidean One is not so outlandish given that our commonsense notions of motion, place, composition, and multiplicity are not straightforwardly acceptable. A third, stronger claim is absent, namely, that the Parmenidean One is correct.

Democritus: Atoms and Void

Atomism, the doctrine that indivisible units of material being are at the root of nature, arose in early Greece with Leucippus of Miletus. Leucippus was a genuine Presocratic, living just after Parmenides and continuing the latter's examination of being. Democritus was a contemporary of Socrates and further refined the notions of the Atomist School. We will focus on Democritus in this section.

Some aspects of the thought of Parmenides are apparent in Democritean atomism. The atoms, the indivisible units of which everything is composed, are "endowed with the properties of Parmenidean being."[14]

That is, the atoms themselves are unchanging and eternal; they are not subject to corruption or transformation any more than they are subject to division. While Parmenidean being is compelling for the atomists, they were also concerned to reconcile this rational theory with experience. With this in mind, Democritus posited an infinite number of such units of being.

Such units combine to form the objects of which the world is composed. These combinations are governed by the size, shape, and numbers of atoms involved. Atoms combine when the appropriately sized and shaped counterparts come into contact, and these combinations separate when an external force acts upon them. In this way, we see the emergence of an attempt at a "complete mechanism."[15] Mechanism is an important theme in ancient, modern, and contemporary physical theory and therefore warrants a bit of definition and elaboration.

We saw that Anaximander put forward notions of justice and balance in the world, and that Parmenides believed that the universe was a connected unity. Mechanism is a general mindset that rejects such ideas. A mechanical philosophy or science is one that explains everything in terms of direct contact and interaction between concrete elements. Specifically, there can be no action by unitary wholistic forces. Such global effects must be further explained by reducing them to their concrete components. For Democritus, they are the atoms. For modern mechanists such as Robert Boyle (see Chapter 8), they are corpuscles. Mechanistic notions also reject any type of explanation that focuses on value or purpose. We will see in Chapter 2 how Aristotle used a notion of purpose in his physical and metaphysical theories, a notion that is inherently forward-looking. Mechanistic explanations in terms of direct contact and combination do not look to the future in order to explain actions in the present. Mechanical systems operate via laws of *antecedent causation,* i.e., explanations that work from the past toward the present and future.

Atomistic ontology omits notions of justice or balance as forces in the world; or metaphorical references to fire; or any transcendent Parmenidean unity. The promise of a world-view that explains nature in such simple, elegant, and powerful terms, all within the grasp of objective, rational inquiry, is perhaps the most influential aspect of atomism. Isaac Newton and his successors, among them Boyle and Laplace (Chapters 3, 7, and 8), sought the goal of a fully mechanistic physical science. Later revolutionaries such as Ludwig Boltzmann, Niels Bohr, Max Planck, and Albert Einstein (Chapters 8, 10, and 12) have been directly influenced by the atomistic doctrine. Indeed, attempts to establish a mechanistic world-view, and the failures of these attempts as well as the reactions against them, have been driving forces for Western science after Aristotle.

None of Democritus' own writings on atomism survive. The following passages are references to the teachings of Democritus found in other sources.

Democritus thinks that the nature of eternal things consists in small substances, infinite in quantity, and for them he posits a place, distinct from them and infinite in extent. He calls place by the names 'void,' 'nothing,' and 'infinite'. . . . He thinks that the substances are so small that they escape our senses, and that they possess all sorts of forms and all sorts of shapes and differences in magnitude. From them . . . he was able to generate and compound visible and perceptible bodies. The atoms struggle and are carried about in the void because of their dissimilarities . . . and as they are carried about they collide and are bound together in a binding which makes them touch and be contiguous with one another but which does not genuinely produce any other single nature whatever. . . . He explains how the substances remain together in terms of the ways in which the bodies entangle with and grasp hold of one another, for some of them are uneven, some hooked, some concave, some convex, and others have innumerable other differences. So he thinks that they hold on to one another and remain together up to the time when some stronger force reaches them from the environment and shakes them and scatters them apart.[16]

Democritus seems to have been persuaded by appropriate and scientific arguments. . . . There is a difficulty if one supposes that there is a body or magnitude which is divisible everywhere. For what will there be that escapes the division? . . . [S]uppose it to have been so divided. What will be left? A magnitude? That is not possible; for then there will be something that has not been divided, but we supposed it divisible everywhere. . . . But if there is to be no body or magnitude left. . . . it will either consist of points and its components will have no magnitude, or else they will be nothing at all and so that it would come to be, and be composed, from nothing and . . . would be nothing. . . .

Similarly, if it is made of points it will not be a quantity . . . even if all the points are put together they will not make a single magnitude. . . .

So if it is impossible for magnitudes to consist of contacts or points, necessarily there are indivisible bodies and magnitudes.[17]

Democritus:

> By convention bitter, by convention hot, by convention cold, by convention colour: in reality, atoms and void. . . .
> We in reality know nothing firmly but only as it changes in accordance with the condition of the body and of the things which enter it and of the things which resist it. . . .
> And a man must recognize by this rule that he is removed from reality . . . in reality we know nothing about anything, but our belief in each case is a changing of shape. . . . Yet it will be clear that to know how each thing is in reality is a puzzle.[18]

The ancient atomism of Democritus was also bound up with theories of knowledge and methods of rational inquiry. Like Parmenides, Democritus proposed an ultimate reality based on changeless being. And like Parmenides and his disciples, Democritus had to bring such a metaphysical picture into reconciliation with a world of experience, which is characterized by change. This in turn led to another version of the separation between being and seeming. For Democritus, seeming was associated with conditions of the body, labelled simply "convention" in that most famous passage. Reality consisted of atoms and void.

Like Zeno, Democritus approached the reconciliation between being and seeming as a difficult one for any philosopher, not just a philosopher of unchanging being. In any rational metaphysics, a theory will be proposed that purports to tell us what it is to know things in reality. And yet ultimately we can only be guided by "conditions of the body." Indeed, under these circumstances, knowledge of reality in any scheme will be a puzzle.

Parmenides explicitly stated that there is a direct relationship between contemplation and reality. This led him to the conclusion that the nature of existence is One. Democritus did not make this strong claim about the relationship between thought and reality, and characterized any such relationship as enigmatic. Yet rational argument, according to Aristotle, convinced Democritus that reality is essentially unchanging, although unchanging through a permanent multiplicity of atoms. The puzzle of knowledge about reality is here made explicit; it resounds throughout history as sceptics, realists, rationalists, and empiricists tackle the issue. A sceptic is one who *withholds assent* about the truth of any theory. That is, the sceptic neither affirms nor denies the ultimate truth of any physical or metaphysical theory. A realist claims that a given theory—or set of observations, for that matter—really exists in nature, i.e., its elements are the actual elements of independent reality. Recall from the discussion in the introduction to this chapter that rationalists and empiricists differ about the method used to access knowledge. A rationalist claims that the insights of reason, e.g., theoretical laws or metaphysical unity, are the favored access to true knowledge. The empiricist claims that observation of particular events and experienced relationships are a more appropriate grounding for knowledge. These methodological positions, together with a view on scepticism or realism, have implications not only for the rules of scientific investigation but also for the results obtained. For example, a rationalist who is also a realist would claim that theoretical systems arrived at via a rational method of inquiry contain elements of independently existing reality. Further on in this chapter, we will see how Galen, who was familiar with Democritus,[19] argued for a sort of sceptical empiricism.

Although Democritus made some comments in the spirit of scepticism, e.g., his remark about knowledge as a "puzzle," it is also evident that he was a rationalist and a reductionist. The rationalism is found in Aristotle's report previously quoted. The reductionism is apparent in that Democritus attempted to understand nature by reducing it to its most basic ontological components, the fundamental atoms of reality. There is nothing more, according to this view, and all else is merely the combination of these atoms and the conditions of the body they effect, which we name by convention. The action for this combination is presumed to be purely mechanical, i.e., acting by direct contact with no animate force, spiritual direction, or higher purpose; neither any grand unity of being, cosmic balance, nor ultimate value. Such a thoroughgoing mechanism continued to be a goal of scientists and philosophers in the modern age.

The Pythagoreans: Mysticism and Number

Pythagoras lived in the early sixth century B.C.E. He founded a school of thought that thrived in Southern Italy through the next several generations. Pythagoreanism spanned metaphysical views on the transmigration of the soul; related ethical injunctions against eating animals; ontology and mysticism regarding numbers; and a social structure of secrecy and political insurrection. Although the association that first springs to mind with the mention of Pythagoras is one with numbers and geometry, Barnes reports that it is unlikely that the Pythagoreans made many technical contributions to mathematics.[20]

In this section, we will treat Pythagorean metaphysics, without regard to whether its origin was with Pythagoras or the later Pythagoreans. The following are selected fragments from some later philosophers who report the views of this mysterious sect.

Pythagoras acquired a great reputation. . . . What he said to his associates no one can say with any certainty; for they maintained no ordinary silence. But it became very well known to everyone that he said, first, that the soul is immortal; then, that it changes into other kinds of animals; and further, that at certain periods whatever has happened happens again, there being nothing absolutely new; and that all living things should be considered belonging to the same kind. . . .[21]

[T]he so-called Pythagoreans touched on mathematics: they were the first to bring it forward and, having been brought up in it, to think that its principles were the principles of all the things that exist. . . . Since they thought they observed in numbers many similarities to the things that exist and come into being (more so than in fire and earth and water)—for example, that justice is such and such a modification of numbers, soul and mind such and such, opportunity something else, and so on, for pretty well everything else (and they also saw that the modifications and ratios of harmonies depend on numbers): since, then, all other things appeared to have been modelled on numbers in their nature, while numbers seemed to be the first things in the whole of nature, they supposed that the elements of numbers were the elements of all the things that exist, and that the whole heaven was harmony and number. . . .[22]

Aristotle and others report on both mystical and *ad hoc* elements of Pythagorean reductionism. For example, the Pythagoreans apparently deduced the essential numbers behind particular species by placing stones in the shape of the animal and then counting them. They also held that ten was the essential number of the cosmos. However, the ancient Greeks only knew of nine significant cosmological bodies, including the earth, so the Pythagoreans invented another invisible planet, the counter-earth, to ensure that the heavenly bodies were ten in number. The Pythagoreans believed, unlike Thales, Anaximander, or Aristotle, that the earth moved around a central "fire." The counter-earth, they contended, moved around this same fire on the opposite side in a perfectly synchronized orbit, so that we could never actually see this tenth astronomical body. Such a postulate, while ingenious and fascinating for its use of a nongeocentric (in this case "fire centric") model, is an example of *ad hoc* theorizing. That is, in order to save a theory that contradicted known evidence, the Pythagoreans added an extra postulate designed solely to support the theory and which could not be substantiated or derived from any other known fact.

Like the Presocratics and Democritus, the Pythagoreans sought to identify first principles or fundamental entities in nature. And like Anaximander, they turned to abstraction. Pythagorean metaphysics, then, can be interpreted as a reductionism of nature to mathematics. Weaknesses and non-scientific elements notwithstanding, this is an important dimension to Pythagoreanism. Mainstream science and philosophy have taken similar reductionist turns in subsequent centuries. Philosophers and scientists from Plato to Descartes, Newton to Kant have been struck by the ability of mathematics to identify essential relations in the natural world. While some consider this an enigma and one of the central mysteries of philosophy, others such as Plato, Kant (see Chapter 5), and Roger Penrose (see Chapter 12) follow the Pythagoreans and claim that mathematical entities should be admitted as fundamental metaphysical components.

Other elements of Pythagoreanism, such as the idea of eternal recurrence, can be found in later scientific theories as well—for example, Boltzmann's statistical mechanics (see Chapter 8). Twentieth-century cosmological debates also include a position that shares some aspects of the idea of eternal recurrence. And Pythagoras was perhaps one of the first Western philosophers to emphasize the individual mind or soul as a fundamental metaphysical component (he is thought to have been influenced by the Egyptians in this regard) as opposed to thinking or rationality in general. While ideas of transmigration are not usually regarded as part of the mainstream Western tradition in science or philosophy of science, theories of the individual mind or consciousness play important roles in science and philosophy of science in the twentieth century (see Chapters 10 and 12).

The beginnings of rational inquiry into nature yield disparate views and sophisticated dialogues. In pursuing a reductionist account of the world, the early Greeks advanced views that sometimes emphasized abstract elements of rational inquiry and sometimes postulated that observable elements form the basis for the natural world. This differing emphasis on the abstract versus the concrete, rational versus the empirical, can be interpreted either metaphysically or methodologically. Indeed, we will see throughout this text that establishing a methodological position on empiricism or rationalism also entails a position on the status of scientific knowledge as well as the rules of investigation.

Debates on the status of scientific knowledge are attempts to answer questions such as: Is science invented or discovered? Are scientific laws and descriptions "real," or are they merely useful tools for predicting and manipulating the world of experience? In the next section we will see a similar issue in medical practice which foreshadows epistemological tensions in modern and contemporary science.

Clearly, at this stage, philosophy and science are not at all disparate. Furthermore, science, philosophy, and other modes of culture are unified, as demonstrated by the poetic nature of the writings of Anaximander and Parmenides. This is very much characteristic of early Greek thought, and even later philosophers such as Plato and Aristotle frequently cite poets as authorities on physics, metaphysics, politics, and other issues.

Galen: Medical Methodology

Galen was a physician and philosophical commentator who lived in the second half of the third century C.E. His theories were dominant in medical practice until the modern age (see Chapter 6). Once they became antiquated, however, Galen's own writings on medicine and philosophy did not receive much attention until the twentieth century. This is not due to their insignificance, however, since Galen presents a debate among medical practitioners of ancient Greece that is important throughout the history of science and philosophy.

The theory of scientific knowledge can be approached from two epistemological perspectives. Empiricists argue that the basis of knowledge is empirical observation and empirical corroboration. Rationalists argue that the rules of logic and reason form the basis for knowledge, which is ultimately, then, theoretical. Debates between these schools have been mediated by a number of reconciliatory views combining parts of each, but these basic positions form the counterpoints for an epistemological discussion that has the utmost import for a philosophical understanding of science.

In Galen's time, he presented the debate as one between Empiricists and Dogmatists, the latter representing the rationalist position. This debate was joined by medical practitioners, who disagreed on the basis and status of medical knowledge. We find Galen asking: Is there a true theoretical basis for this knowledge, or is the question irrelevant to the point of medicine, which is to cure the patient? This epistemological debate can be seen in *On The Sects for Beginners* and *An Outline of Empiricism*.[23]

FROM *ON THE SECTS FOR BEGINNERS*:

. . . to speak quite generally, the dogmatics and the empiricists draw on the same medicines for the same affections. What they disagree about is the way these remedies are discovered. For, in the case of the same manifest bodily symptoms, the dogmatics derive from them an indication of the cause, and, on the basis of this cause, they find a treatment, whereas the empiricists are reminded . . . of what they have observed often to happen in the same way.

. . . For example, in their inquiries concerning the discovery of things which are not manifest, one part praises anatomy, indication, and logical theory . . . The empiricists, on the other hand, do not grant that anatomy makes any discoveries, or that it would be necessary for the art, even if it did. Furthermore, they do not grant that there is such a thing as indication . . . Nor do they grant that there is such a thing as a sign of something which by its very nature is nonmanifest. Furthermore, they argue that no art has any need for logic.

FROM *AN OUTLINE OF EMPIRICISM*:

. . . empiricists give credence only to those things which are evident to the senses, and to those things of which, on the basis of the former, one has memory. The dogmatics, on the other hand, give credence not only to these things but also to those which are discovered by reason independently of observation, on the basis of the natural relationship of consequences. . . .

But the empiricist not only uses definitions and determinations, which rely solely on what is evident, but also makes use of causal accounts and proofs based on what has been ascertained antecedently . . . Let us assume, then, that the question has been raised, as indeed, it does get raised, what the art of medicine aims at. I claim that the empiricist who firmly holds to the line of his school will answer . . . I try to cure . . . and display my views by my deeds. Hence, it makes no difference to me whether one speaks of soundness, health . . . so long as I am in a position to display my views by my deeds. I . . . do not care to get concerned with long-winded, empty discourse, since I am fully occupied with the exercise of the art. . . .

This is the response I think the empiricist ought to give. For, if he should try to adjudicate the dispute, he would have to deal with the theorems of the dialectic which, as he himself says, he does not want to have anything to do with.

In these passages, Galen has a sophisticated understanding of a radical kind of empiricism. While rationalists admit to having at their disposal many devices for deducing causes, deriving treatments, and organizing observation and theory, the empiricist disavows such abstractions. Although this may seem to give the rationalist an advantage, it is a double-edged one. The empiricist would claim that the strengths of rationalism are undercut by the rationalist's strong positions on the reality of theoretical, or non-manifest, phenomenon. Entities such as indications, causes, anatomical theory, and logical and dialectical proofs are difficult to place in the practical art of medical science. These theories are furthermore always under dispute, which belies the rationalist's claim that they are true. Finally, if theoretical entities are as real as the medicines and bodies they describe, then the rationalist world-view is considerably more cluttered than that of the empiricists.

The empiricist position has the advantage of economy but has its own difficulties. The empiricist must completely disavow the tools of the rationalist, or at least claim to take no interest in them. While such a disposition might appeal to common sense, it provides little motivation or organization for research. A patient with fever might soon perish if a strict empiricist program for his cure were pursued; that is, the doctor could try any number of prescriptions—from jumping out of a tree to an olive oil enema—in the search for a previously unobserved cure. This is a difficult position to maintain, but Galen has a good deal more sympathy for this than the rationalism of the dogmatists.

Of course this debate transcends Hellenistic medicine. We will see differing positions on the status of theoretical versus empirical inquiry throughout the course of this book. Ancient, modern, and contemporary rationalists have strong views endowing theoretical results with a realistic status. Such a position has little difficulty explaining how science gets done but a good deal of difficulty defending an independently real status for theoretical entities that are nonmanifest and seemingly always under revision. Empiricists, on the other hand, have no such problem but have a corresponding difficulty explaining how science is systematic and progressive, and not a haphazard response to overwhelming empirical stimuli. Galen's treatises show how this debate is originally and fundamentally a part of the Western scientific tradition.

Summary

Ontological and epistemological issues concerning nature, knowledge, scientific method, and theoretical structure were raised in Ancient Greece. At this time, all of these issues were the proper focus for both science and philosophy. Most importantly, the inquiry was underway—open for conscious deliberation, discussion, reflection, and revision in the face of new evidence and new arguments. With the possible exception of the Pythagoreans, the philosophers in this chapter operated by exposing their ideas for criticism and attempted to take new evidence or argument to heart in formulating their theories. This set the stage for dramatic progress in understanding and controlling nature. The effects of such control permeate the entire history of Western culture and affect the very mindset of people in modern and contemporary society.

The theories in these sections have import beyond being the progenitors of a rich culture and tradition in the West. Scientists, philosophers, poets, and lay persons continue to hold views similar to those of the early Greeks. Reductionism, for example, is still a predominant theme in twentieth-century physics (see Chapter 12). Mechanism was de-emphasized by Aristotle (see Chapter 2) but was revived in the seventeenth century and beyond to supplant medieval Aristotelianism and provide a new framework for science and philosophy in the modern age (see Chapters 3, 4, and 5). The Parmenidean One finds adherents of late among physicists who seek to jolt twentieth-century science from the reductionism and mechanism that inspired classical mechanics. This same mechanism was overwhelmingly successful in the seventeenth, eighteenth, and nineteenth centuries, but eventually led to the quantum and relativistic revolutions in physics (see Chapters 10 and 12). If the physics that mechanism inspired has been overthrown by theoretical revolutions, then perhaps mechanism itself is in need of replacement.

In the next chapter we see a world-view inspired by Presocratic investigation as well as original genius. Aristotle had an eclectic approach that emphasized logic as well as observation, mechanism as well as mind. Aristotle's extensive writings and authoritative positions remained the focal point for scientific physics and religious cosmology for more than a thousand years.

Notes

1. See Introduction for some definitions and groundwork for this volume.
2. Thales, for example, apparently did not transcribe his thoughts. See Jonathan Barnes, *Early Greek Philosophy* (London: Penguin Books, 1987), 61.
3. Although some twentieth-century philosophers of science disagree (see Chapter 11).
4. Frederick Copleston, S.J. *A History of Philosophy* (New York: Image Books, 1985, Vol. I), 25.
5. For example, Parmenides, Plato, and the Pythagoreans (see below).
6. Quantum mechanics and contemporary cosmology are but two examples that will be discussed in later chapters. Constructions such as probability wave equations and multidimensional spaces are contemporary analogues of Anaximander's esoteria that are treated in Chapters 10 and 12.
7. This thesis can be challenged on the grounds that Anaximander was more of a poet than a scientist.

8. Kirk, Raven, and Schofield, *The Presocratic Philosophers* (New York: Cambridge University Press, 1983). All excerpts from this volume are used by permission of Cambridge University Press.

9. Ibid., 195.

10. Barnes, 117.

11. Kirk, Raven, and Schofield, *The Presocratic Philosophers*, 250.

12. This interpretation of Parmenides can be challenged on the grounds that Parmenides does not really reduce natural phenomena to one basic explanation, he merely dismisses all phenomena as illusory.

13. Aristotle, *Physics* 239b14, from Frederick Copleston, S.J., *A History of Philosophy* (New York: Image Books, 1985), 57.

14. Copleston, 75.

15. Ibid., 73.

16. Aristotle fragment, quoted in Simplicius, *Commentary on the Heavens*, from Barnes, 248.

17. Aristotle, *On Generation and Corruption*, in Barnes, 251.

18. Sextus Empiricus, *Against the Mathematicians* VII, in Barnes, 254.

19. Barnes, 255.

20. Ibid., 210.

21. Porphyry, in Barnes, 86.

22. Aristotle, *Metaphysics*, in Barnes, 209.

23. Reprinted from *Galen: Three Treatises on the Nature of Science*, translated by R. Walzer and M. Frede, 1985, by permission of Hackett Publishing Company. All rights reserved.

Suggestions for Further Reading

Barnes, Jonathan, *Early Greek Philosophy* (London: Penguin Books, 1987).

Barnes, *The Presocratic Philosophers* (1982).

Copleston, Frederick, S.J., *A History of Philosophy* (New York: Image Books, 1985), Volume I.

Galen: *Three Treatises on the Nature of Science*, R. Walzer and M. Frede, Transls. (Indianapolis: Hackett Publishing Company, 1985).

Hankinson, R.J., *Galen: On the Therapeutic Method* (New York: Oxford University Press, 1991).

Kirk, G.S., Raven, J.E., and Schofield, M., *The Presocratic Philosophers* (New York: Cambridge University Press, 1983).

Sambrusky, S., *Physical Thought from the Presocratics to the Quantum Physicists* (New York: Pica Press, 1975).

2

Greek and Medieval Aristotelian Science

By standing on the shoulders of his predecessors[1], Aristotle was able to use his visionary genius to unify Greek science and philosophy into a system of massive scope. His powers of abstraction, criticism, and reflection gave birth to entirely new disciplines of philosophy, mathematics, and science. Aristotle relied on observation and has been deemed a biologist for his systematic study of anatomy in *Parts of Animals*, but his lack of sophisticated experimental technique is still quite marked, as it was with the natural ontologists of the Presocratic period.

In this chapter we will see how Aristotle established a metaphysical basis for science that emphasized purpose. For Aristotle, nature was forward-looking. This process is analogous to human striving toward desired ends, and according to Aristotle nature aims at the highest of all ends, the ultimate good. This aspect of Aristotelian metaphysics is known as *final causation*. Final causation provided ways to describe a unified world of nature and human values.

We saw in the last chapter that Anaximander and Parmenides both had anthropocentric elements in their systems of natural philosophy. Final causation can be interpreted as Aristotle's anthropocentrism. If Aristotle projected a model of human behavior—namely, planning for desired ends and striving toward these goals—onto the universe as a whole, then the thesis that there are purposes in nature is anthropocentric. There are other interpretations of final causation, however, and in any case, Aristotle included other types of explanation in his natural philosophy.

Aristotle's scheme was adopted by the later Medievals. Middle Eastern scholars preserved the works of Aristotle after most of his writings had been lost in the West, and the rediscovery of Aristotle via Arab influences was cause for renewed scholarship. Observation was important for the Presocratics and for Aristotle, but for the Medievals, theories of the world became more literary—an exercise in textual evaluation and comparison. And in both Greek and medieval science, quantitative experimental methods were rarely employed.[2] This chapter sets the stage for understanding the dramatic nature of change ahead when the modern scientific revolution displaces the premodern world-view.

A Natural Purpose

Aristotle was born in Stageira about 384 B.C.E. and died in 322. He was the last of the most famous philosophical triumvirate in history: he was a student of Plato, who had been a student of Socrates. Aristotle was in turn the teacher of Alexander the Great. Aristotle entered Plato's Academy in Athens about 368 and became its most famous student. Plato was influenced by Heraclitus and adopted the latter's position that the observable world was one of constant change and flux. Plato, however, took this to be evidence that there was another realm of existence, which must be the object of knowledge. Hence he advocated a bifurcated theory of being and seeming, similar in style to some notions of Parmenides and Zeno. Plato's higher realm of being was inhabited by what he called *forms*: abstract, universal entities that were the source for all knowledge, order, and value in the world.

Aristotle is commonly regarded as opposing Plato's view with one that emphasized the particular as well as the universal, observation as well as abstraction, force and matter as well as form. Aristotle nevertheless shared a gift for metaphysical speculation, and hence his natural philosophy is of the metaphysical as well as the physical. Aristotle's view of causation is therefore both scientific and philosophical, and in this section we examine his four causes and his emphasis on the final cause. In nature, processes are forward-looking, design-oriented, and purposive, according to Aristotle. Furthermore, the overall goal and purpose of nature is to reach the highest good. We can also see quite clearly his incorporation of the presocratic mission to find the ultimate substance of which things are made. Aristotle has a cosmological theory as well, and we will see how this is an extension of his more basic physical and metaphysical concepts.

Physics

In the following selections from the *Physics*, Aristotle presents his four causes. He incorporates the idea of primary substance from the Presocratics into his material cause, continuing their dialogue and adding increased depth of explanation. His formal cause is regarded as a way of accommodating the concepts of his teacher, and the efficient cause is the one most readily identifiable as the sort of cause–effect scheme that science as we know it describes. His final cause is the ultimate end, purpose, or design of a process, and is usually regarded as Aristotle's most fundamental level of explanation.[3] The following passages are excerpted from *The Complete Works of Aristotle*, Princeton Revised Edition (Oxford).[4]

BOOK I

When the objects of an inquiry, in any department, have principles, causes, or elements, it is through acquaintance with these that knowledge and understanding is attained. For we do not think that we know a thing until we are acquainted with its primary causes or first principles ... Plainly, therefore, in the science of nature too our first task will be to try to determine what relates to its principles.

The natural way of doing this is to start from the things which are more knowable and clear to us and proceed ... towards those which are clearer and more knowable by nature.

The principles in question must be either one or more than one. If one, it must be either motionless, as Parmenides and Milessus assert, or in motion ... some declaring air to be the first principle,[5] others water. If more than one, then either a finite or infinite plurality. ...

Now to investigate whether what exists is one and motionless is not a contribution to the science of nature. To inquire ... whether what exists is one in this sense would be like ... refuting a merely contentious argument—a description which applies to the arguments of ... Parmenides.

We, on the other hand, must take for granted that the things that exist are, either all or some of them, in motion—which is indeed made plain by induction.

... "one" itself, no less than "is" is used in many ways, so we must consider what way the word is used when it is said that the universe is one. ...

There is, indeed, a difficulty about part and whole ... namely, whether the part and the whole are one or more than one, and in what way they can be one or many. ...

But if all things are one in the sense of having the same definition ... then it turns out that they are maintaining the Heraclitean doctrine, for it will be the same thing to be good and bad ... man and horse; in fact, their view will be, not that all things are one, but that they are nothing. . . .

What is may be many either in definition (for example to be white is one thing and to be musical another, yet the same thing may be both, so the one is many) or by division, as the whole and its parts ... as if there was any difficulty about the same thing being both one and many, provided these are not opposites; for what is one may be either potentially or actually one.

If, then, we approach the thesis in this way, it seems impossible for all things to be one. . . .

The ... argument holds good against Parmenides. ... His assumption that 'is' is used in a single way only is false, because it is used in several.

The physicists on the other hand have two modes of explanation.

The first set make the underlying body one ... then generate everything else from this.[6]

The second assert that the contraries are contained in the one and emerge from it by segregation, for example Anaximander.

. . . It is plain, then that they all in one way or another identify the contraries with the principles. And with good reason. For first principles must not be derived from one another nor from anything else, while everything has to be derived from them. But these conditions are fulfilled by the primary contraries, which are not derived from anything else because they are primary, nor from each other because they are contraries.

. . . some assume contraries which are prior, others contraries which are posterior; some those more knowable in order of explanation, others those more familiar to sense.

Things which come to be without qualification, come to be in different ways: by change of shape, as a statue; by addition, as things which grow; by taking away . . . ; by putting together, as a house; by alteration, as things which turn in respect of their matter.

It is plain that these are all cases of coming to be from some underlying thing.

Thus, from what has been said, whatever comes to be is always complex. There is, on the one hand, something which comes to be, and again, something which becomes that. . . .

Plainly then, if there are causes and principles which constitute natural objects ... everything comes to be from both subject and form. . . . For the musical man is composed in a way of man and musical. . . .

Now the subject is one numerically. . . . And the form is one.

BOOK II

Of things that exist, some exist by nature, some from other causes. By nature the animals and their parts exist, and the plants and the simple bodies. . . .

All the things mentioned plainly differ from the things which are *not* constituted by nature. For each of them has within itself a principle of motion and of stationariness. . . . On the other hand, a bed and a coat and anything else of that sort, *qua* receiving these designations ... have no innate impulse to change. . . . But insofar as they happen to be composed of stone or of earth ... they *do* have such an impulse, and just to that extent. . . .

Nature then is what has been stated. Things have a nature which have a principle of this kind. Each of them is a substance; for it is a subject. . . .

Some identify the nature or substance of a natural object with the immediate constituent of it which taken by itself is without arrangement, e.g., the wood is the nature of the bed and bronze is the nature of the statue. . . .

This then is one account of nature, namely that it is the primary underlying matter of things.

Another account is that nature is the shape or form which is specified in the definition of the thing.

... nature in the sense of a coming-to-be proceeds toward nature. . . .

The next point to consider is how the mathematician differs from the student of nature; for natural bodies contain surfaces and volumes, lines and points, and these are the subject-matter of mathematics.

Further, is astronomy different from natural science or a department of it? It seems absurd to suppose that the student of nature should be supposed to know the nature of sun or moon, but not know their essential attributes, particularly as the writers on the subject do discuss their shape and whether the earth and the world are spherical or not. . . .

Since two sorts of thing are called nature, the form and the matter, we must investigate its objects ... with which is the student of nature concerned?

If we look at the ancients, natural science would seem to be concerned with the *matter.* . . .

But if on the other hand art imitates nature ... it would be a part of natural science also to know nature in both its senses.

Again, that for the sake of which, or the end, belongs to the same department of knowledge as the means. But the nature is the end or that for the sake of which. For if a thing undergoes a continuous change toward some end, that last stage is actually that for the sake of which. . . .

Now that we have established these distinctions, we must proceed to consider causes, their character and number. . . .

In one way, then, that out of which a thing comes to be and which persists, is called a cause, e.g., the bronze of the statue, or the silver of a bowl. . . .

In another way, the form or the archetype, i.e., the definition of the essence and its genera, are called causes (e.g., ... generally number). . . .

Again, the primary source of the change or rest; e.g. the man who deliberated is a cause, the father is the cause of the child, and generally what makes of what is made and what changes of what is changed.

Again, in the sense of end or that for the sake of which a thing is done, e.g., health is the cause of walking about. ("Why is he walking about?" We say: "To be healthy," and having said that, we think we have assigned the cause.) . . .

This then perhaps exhausts the number of ways in which the term "cause" is used.

As things are called causes in many ways, it follows that there are several causes of the same thing (not merely accidentally), e.g., both the art of the sculptor and the bronze are causes of the statue ... the one being the material cause, the other the cause whence motion comes [these refer to the bronze and the art in reverse order—ed.]. . . .

All the causes now mentioned fall into four familiar divisions . . . the material [is the cause of] of artificial products ... in the sense of "that from which" ... one set are causes ... in the sense of essence— the whole and the combination and the form ... the maker [is] the source from which change originates ... others are causes in the sense of the end or the good of the rest; for that for the sake of which tends to be what is best and the end of the things that lead up to it. (Whether we call it good or apparently good makes no difference.)

A difficulty presents itself: why should not nature work, not for the sake of something, nor because it is better so, but just as the sky rains, not in order to make the corn grow, but of necessity? (What is drawn up must cool, and what has been cooled must become water and descend. . . .) . . .

Such are the arguments (and others of the kind) which may cause difficulty on this point. Yet it is impossible that this should be the true view . . . [A]ction for an end is present in things which come to be and are by nature.

Further, where there is an end, all the preceding steps are for the sake of that. Now surely as in action, so in nature . . . .

For those things are natural which, by a continuous movement originated from an internal principle, arrive at some end: the same end is not reached from every principle; nor any chance end, but always the same tendency in each is toward the same end, if there is no impediment . . . .

In natural products, the sequence is invariable, if there is no impediment.

It is absurd to suppose that purpose is not present because we do not observe the agent deliberating. Art does not deliberate. If the ship-building art were in the wood, it would produce the same result by nature. If, therefore, purpose is present in art, it is present also in nature. The best illustration is a doctor doctoring himself: nature is like that.

It is plain then that nature is a cause, a cause that operates for a purpose.

Aristotle's four causes are: The Material Cause, or "that from which"; The Formal Cause, identified with form, essence, and sometimes mathematical structure; The Efficient Cause, the "source from which change originates"; and The Final Cause, "that for the sake of which." Of these four, two are immediately familiar to a modern mind-set: the material and the efficient. The fundamental material of nature is the focus of both presocratic and modern physical study, while efficient causation can be identified with the study of causal properties and laws of motion which are the "primary source of change or rest." Aristotle includes the formal cause, which he identifies with mathematical form, and as such this is also a common element in both ancient and modern physical theory. It is Aristotle's final cause, which he views as most important, that is conspicuously absent from modern scientific world-views. We will see wide-ranging implications of this difference as our study proceeds. One that is immediately apparent pertains to the concept of good in nature. By claiming that natural processes occur for the sake of an end, Aristotle assumes that nature has a purpose or meaning. He identifies this with a theory of good in the *Physics* as well as in *The Nichomachean Ethics*, where he says, "Every art and every inquiry, and similarly every action and pursuit, is thought to aim at some good; and for this reason the good has rightly been declared to be that at which all things aim." (*Nichomachean Ethics*, Book I, Chapter 1)

Other parts of the *Physics* deal with the theory of motion. Aristotle not only argues against the Heraclitean and Parmenidean ideas of constant motion or eternal rest, but proposes more detailed explanations of why things in the world move as they do. We will see the Aristotelian purpose, or *telos*, also playing a role here. The following are selections on this theme.

BOOK VIII

[E]arth and all other bodies necessarily remain in their proper places and are moved from them only by violence; from the fact, then, that some of them are in their proper places it follows that in respect of place all things cannot be in motion.

. . . It is likewise impossible that all things should be in motion or should be always in motion and the remainder always at rest. We have sufficient ground for rejecting all these theories in the single fact that we *see* some things sometimes in motion and sometimes at rest. It is evident, therefore, that it is no less impossible that some things should be always in motion and the remainder always at rest than that all things should be at rest or that all things should be in motion continuously. . . .

When . . . things are in motion to positions the reverse of those they would properly occupy, their motion is violent: when they are in motion to their proper positions—the light thing up and the heavy thing down—their motion is natural; but in this case it is no longer evident, as it is when the motion is unnatural, whence their motion is derived. It is impossible to say that their motion is derived from themselves: this is a characteristic of life peculiar to living things. Further, if it were, it would have been in their power to stop themselves. . . .

. . . The activity of lightness consists in the light thing being in a certain place, namely high up; when it is in a contrary place, it is being prevented. . . . how can we account for the motion of light things and heavy things to their proper places? The reason for it is that they have a natural tendency towards a certain position; and this is what it is to be light or heavy, the former being determined by an upward, the latter by a downward, tendency. . . .

If then the motion of all things is either natural or unnatural and violent, and all things whose motion is violent and unnatural are moved by something, and something other than themselves, and again all things whose motion is natural are moved by something—both those that are moved by themselves and those that are not moved by themselves (e.g., light things and heavy things, which are moved either by that which brought the thing into existence and made it light and heavy, or by that which released what was hindering and preventing it); then all things that are in motion are moved by something. . . .

. . . We must consider whether it is or is not possible that there should be a continuous motion, and, if it is possible, which this motion is, and which is the primary motion. . . .

Let us now proceed to maintain that it is possible that there should be an infinite motion that is single and continuous, and that this motion is rotary motion. The motion of everything that is in the process of locomotion is either rotary or rectilinear or a compound of the two. . . .

It can now be shown plainly that rotation is the primary loco-motion. Every locomotion, as we said before, is either rotary or rec-tilinear or a combination of the two; and the former must be prior to the last . . . because it is more simple and complete. For the line traversed in rectilinear motion cannot be infinite; for there is no such thing as an infinite straight line; and even if there were it would not be traversed by anything in motion; for the impossible does not happen and it is impossible to traverse an infinite distance. On the other hand rectilinear motion on a finite line is composite if it turns back, i.e., two motions . . . Now rotary motion can be eternal; but no other motion . . . can be so, since in all of them rest must occur. . . .

. . . the original mover gives the power of being a mover either to air or to water or to something else of the kind . . . it causes something else consecutive with it to be in motion, and of this again the same may be said. . . .

There is a difficulty in supposing it to be possible for anything that is in motion to cause motion continuously and not merely in the way in which it is caused by something repeatedly pushing (in which the continuity amounts to no more than successiveness). Such a mover must either itself continue to push or pull or perform both of these actions, or else the action must be taken up by something else and be passed on from one mover to another (the process . . . occurring in the case of things thrown, since the air, being divisible, is a mover in virtue of the fact that different parts of the air are moved one after the other); and in either case the motion cannot be a single motion but only a consecutive series of motions.

Here Aristotle appeals to observation to refute the doctrines of Heraclitus and Parmenides with respect to motion. He further advances the study of mechanics by asking and answering far more specific questions than any of his predecessors. How can locomotion be decomposed analytically into its constituent elements? Why do heavy objects fall? What are the causes of particular motions, e.g., projectile? Is there an ultimate form and source for all motion? These questions shaped the course of Western history, and for this reason they may be regarded as far more significant than the now antiquated answers Aristotle gave.

His answers do have cogent arguments, however, inviting speculation as to how subsequent history might have been shaped had a lesser authority than Aristotle been the one to establish such a coherent (though mistaken) system of mechanics and cosmology. Several details of Aristotelian physics presented in this section and the next must be rejected. For one, the idea that rotary motion is natural and the idea that rectilinear motion naturally ceases must be replaced by a modern concept of inertia. Similarly, inertia obviates the need for continual contact in the case of continuing motion. Modern notions of gravity refute the idea that heavier objects fall faster, a thesis held by Aristotle as we will see in the next section. Seventeenth-century mechanism also rejects the idea that objects seek their natural resting places and thus obey the laws of final causation. Refutations of these concepts come two thousand years later, though, and only after the formidable task of overcoming the authoritative weight of the Catholic Church, divine and purposive physics, and Aristotle himself.

De Caelo

In *De Caelo*, or *On the Heavens*, Aristotle extends his physics to a system of cosmology. He argues in the *Physics* that natural motion is either rotary, towards the center, or away from the center. In *De Caelo*, he uses this thesis to argue that just as there are substances which naturally move upward and downward, namely fire and earth, respectively, there must also be a substance that exemplifies circular motion. And since circular motion is more perfect than linear motion, by virtue of the fact that it can continue unceasingly, the substance which possesses naturally circular motion is more perfect than terrestrial elements.

This coherent extension of his physical theory is also a continuation of the philosophical dialogue begun by Thales. Aristotle considers the question of the earth's motion or non-motion and examines the alternative theories on the shape and extent of the universe. He argues that the universe is finite, bounded by an outer sphere of divine heaven moving in an eternal and unchanging rotation. Later in this chapter we will see how Aristotelian cosmology is adopted by medieval and Renaissance Europe.

BOOK I

Now revolution about the centre is circular motion, while the upward and downward motions are in a straight line, "upward" meaning motion away from the centre, and "downward" motion towards it. All simple motion, then, must be motion either away from or towards or about the centre. This seems to be in exact accord with what we said above. . . .

Supposing, then, that there is such a thing as simple movement, and that circular movement is simple, and that both movement of a simple body is simple and simple movement is of a simple body. . . . Further, this circular motion is necessarily primary. For the complete is naturally prior to the incomplete, and the circle is a complete thing. . . .

. . . the prior movement belongs to the body which is naturally prior, and circular movement is prior to straight, and movement in a straight line belongs to simple bodies—fire moving straight upward and earthly bodies straight downward towards the centre—since this is so, it follows that circular movement also must be the movement of some simple body. . . . On all these grounds, therefore, we may infer with confidence that there is something beyond the bodies that are about us in this earth, different and separate from them; and that the superior glory of its nature is proportionate to its distance from this world of ours.

It is equally reasonable to assume that this body will be ungenerated and indestructible and exempt from increase and alteration, since everything that comes to be comes into being from a contrary and some substrate, and passes away likewise in a substrate by the action of a contrary into a contrary, as we explained in our opening discussions.[7] Now the motions of contraries are contrary. If then this body can have no contrary, because there is no contrary motion to the circular, nature seems justly to have exempted from contraries the body which was to be ungenerated and indestructible. . . .

Our theory seems to confirm the phenomena and be confirmed by them. . . . If then there is, as there certainly is, anything divine, what we have just said about the primary bodily substance was well said. The mere evidence of the senses is enough to convince us of this, at least within human certainty. For in the whole range of time past, so far as our inherited records reach, no change appears to have taken place either in the whole scheme of the outermost heaven or in any of its proper parts. The name, too, of that body seems to have been handed down right to our own day from our distant ancestors who conceived of it in the fashion which we have been expressing. The same ideas, one must believe, recur in men's minds not once or twice but again and again. And so, implying that the primary body is something else beyond earth, fire, air, and water, they gave the highest place the name of *aether*, derived from the fact that it "runs always" for an eternity of time. . . .

The body which moves in a circle must necessarily be finite in every respect, for the following reasons. If the body so moving is infinite, the radii drawn from the centre will be infinite. But the space between infinite radii is infinite . . . Now the infinite cannot be traversed, and if the body is infinite the interval between the radii is necessarily infinite: circular motion is therefore an impossibility. Yet we see that the heavens revolve in a circle. . . .

Now the whole included with the extreme circumference must be composed of all physical and sensible body, because there neither is nor can come into being any body outside the heaven. . . .

It is therefore evident that there is also no place or void in time outside the heaven ... in the absence of natural body there is no movement, and outside the heaven ... body neither exists nor can come to exist. It is clear then that there is neither place, nor void, nor time outside the heaven. Hence whatever is there, is of such a nature as not to occupy any place, nor does time age it; nor is there any change in any of the things which lie beyond the outermost motion; they continue through their entire duration unalterable and unmodified, living the best and most self-sufficient of lives.

BOOK II

... we must consider why there is more than one motion [in the heavens], though we have to pursue our inquiries at a distance—a distance created not so much by our spatial position as by the fact that our senses enable us to perceive very few of the attributes of the heavenly bodies. But let not that deter us. The reason must be sought in the following facts. Everything which has a function exists for its function, the activity of God is immortality, i.e., eternal life. Therefore the movement of God must be eternal. But such is the heaven, viz. a divine body, and for that reason to it is given a circular body whose nature it is to move always in a circle. Why, then, is not the whole body of the heaven of the same character as that part? Because there must be something at rest in the centre of the revolving body ... It could do so only if that body's natural movement were towards the centre ... Earth then has to exist; for it is earth which is at rest at the centre. (At present we may take this for granted. It will be explained later.)

The shape of the heaven is of necessity spherical; for that is the shape most appropriate to its substance and also by nature primary ... The sphere is among solids what the circle is among plane figures ... It is clear, then, that the sphere is first among solid figures.

[T]he movements of the several stars depend, as regards the varieties of speed which they exhibit, on their distances. It is established that the outermost revolution of the heavens is simple movement and the swiftest of all, and that the movement of all other bodies is composite and relatively slow, for the reason that each is moving on its own circle with the reverse motion to that of the heavens. . . .

With regard to the shape of each star, the most reasonable view is that they are spherical. It has been shown that it is not in their nature to move themselves, and since nature does nothing without reason or in vain, clearly she will have given things which possess no movement a shape particularly unadapted to movement. Such a shape is the sphere.... Again, what holds of one holds of all, and the evidence of our eyes shows us that the moon is spherical. For how else should the moon as it waxes and wanes show for the most part a crescent shaped ... figure, and only at one moment a half moon? And astronomical arguments give further confirmation; for no other hypothesis accounts for the crescent shape of the sun's eclipses....

Of many ... problems, one of the strangest is the problem why we find the greatest number of movements in the intermediate bodies, and not, rather, in each successive body a variety of movement proportionate to its distance from the primary motion. For we might reasonably expect, since the primary body shows one motion only, that the body which is nearest to it should move with the fewest movements, say two, and the one after that with three, or some similar arrangement. But the opposite is the case. The movements of the sun and moon are fewer than those of some of the planets. Yet these planets are farther from the centre and thus nearer to the primary body than they, as observation has itself in some cases revealed. For we have seen the moon, half-full, pass beneath the planet Mars, which vanished on its shadow side and came forth by the bright shining part....

A second difficulty which may with equal justice be raised is this. Why is it that the primary motion includes such a multitude of stars that their whole array seems to defy counting, while of the other stars each one is separated off, and in no case do we find two or more attached to the same motion?

... We think of the stars as mere bodies, and as units with serial order indeed but entirely inanimate; but we should rather conceive of them as enjoying life and action.... We must, then, think of the actions of the stars as similar to that of animals and plants. For on our earth it is man that has the greatest variety of actions—for there are many goods that man can secure; hence his actions are various and directed to ends beyond them—while the perfectly conditioned has no need of action, since it is itself the end.... For while it is clearly best for any being to attain the real end, yet, if that cannot be, the nearer it is to the best the better will be its state. It is for this reason that the earth moves not at all and the bodies near to it with few movements. For they do not attain the final end, but only come as near to it as their share in the divine principle permits. But the first heaven finds it immediately with a single movement, and bodies intermediate to it ... attain it indeed, but at the cost of a multiplicity of movement. ...

It remains to speak of the earth, of its position, of the question whether it is at rest or in motion, and of its shape.

As to its *position* there is some difference of opinion. Most people—all, in fact, who regard the whole heaven as finite—say it lies at the centre. But the ... Pythagoreans take the contrary view. At the centre, they say, is fire, and the earth is one of the stars, creating night and day by its circular motion about the centre.

... Others, again, say that the earth, which lies at the centre, is rolled, and thus in motion, about the axis of the whole heaven. So it stands written in [Plato's] *Timaeus*.

There are similar disputes about the shape of the earth. Some think it is spherical, others that it is flat and drum shaped. For evidence they bring the fact that, as the sun rises and sets, the part concealed by the earth shows a straight and not a curved edge, whereas if the earth were spherical the line of section would have to be circular. In this they leave out of account the great distance of the sun from the earth and the great size of the circumference, which, seen from a distance on these apparently small circles appears straight. ...

There are many different ways in which the movement or rest of the earth has been conceived. The difficulty must have occurred to everyone. It would indeed be a complacent mind that felt no surprise that, while a little bit of earth, let loose in mid-air, moves and will not stay still, and the more there is of it the faster it moves, the whole earth, free in mid-air, should show no movement at all. Yet here is this great weight of earth, and it is at rest. ... The difficulty, then, has naturally passed into a commonplace of philosophy. ...

[Some] say the earth rests upon water. This, indeed, is the oldest theory that has been preserved, and is attributed to Thales of Miletus. ... As if the same account had not to be given of the water which carries the earth as of the earth itself!

... there are some, Anaximander, for instance, among the ancients, who say that the earth keeps its place because of its indifference. Motion upward or downward or sideways were all, they thought, equally inappropriate to that which is set at the centre and indifferently related to every extreme point; and to move contrary directions is impossible: so it must needs remain still. This view is in-genious but not true. The argument would prove that everything which is put at the centre must stay there. Fire, then, will rest at the centre; for the proof turns on no peculiar property of earth. . . . The observed facts about the earth are not only that it remains at the cen-tre, but also that it moves to the centre. . . . The reason then is not in the fact that the earth is indifferently related to every extreme point; for this would apply to any body, whereas movement to the centre is peculiar to earth. . . .

We have now outlined the views held as to the shape, position, and rest or movement of the earth.

. . . the natural movement of the earth, part and whole alike, is to the centre of the whole—whence the fact that it is now actually situated at the centre . . . heavy bodies moving towards the earth do not move parallel but so as to make equal angles, and thus to a sin-gle centre, that of the earth. It is clear, then, that the earth must be at the centre and immovable. . . .

Its shape must necessarily be spherical. For every portion of the earth has weight until it reaches the centre, and the jostling of parts greater and smaller would bring about not a waved surface, but rather compression and convergence of part and part until the centre is reached. . . . Therefore earth in motion whether in a mass or in fragments, necessarily continues to move until it occupies the centre equally every way, the less being forced to equalize itself by the greater owing to the forward drive of the impulse.

. . . The evidence of the senses further corroborates this. How else would eclipses of the moon show segments shaped as we see them? . . . in eclipses, the outline is always curved; and, since it is the interposition of the earth that makes the eclipse, the form of this line will be caused by the form of the earth's surface, which is therefore spherical. Again, our observations of the stars make it evi-dent, not only that the earth is circular, but also that it is a circle of no great size. For quite small changes of position on our part to the south or north causes a manifest alteration of horizon. There is much change, I mean, in the stars which are overhead, and the stars seen are different, as one moves northward or southward. Indeed, there are some stars seen in Egypt and in the neighborhood of Cyprus which are not seen in the northerly regions. . . . Also, the mathematicians who try to calculate the size of the earth's circum-ference arrive at the figure 400,000 stades.[8]

BOOK III

The common error of all views which assume a single element is that they allow only one natural movement, which is the same for every body ... If then all bodies are one, all will have one movement. With this motion the greater their quantity the more they will move, just as fire, in proportion as its quantity is greater, moves faster with the upward motion which belongs to it. But the fact is that increase of quantity makes many things move faster downward. For these reasons, then, as well as from the distinction already established of a plurality of natural movements, it is impossible that there should be only one element.

BOOK IV

The shape of bodies will not account for their moving upward or downward in general, though it will account for their moving faster or slower. ... For the problem is raised why a flat piece of iron or lead floats upon water, while smaller and less heavy things, so long as they are round or long—a needle, for instance—sink down; ... since some continua are easily divided and others less easily, and things which produce division differ similarly in the ease with which they produce it, the explanation must be found in this fact. ... Thus, the reason why broad things keep their place is because they cover so wide a surface and the greater quantity is less easily disrupted. Bodies of the appropriate shape sink down because they occupy so little of the surface, which is therefore easily parted.

Aristotle appeals to a variety of kinds of evidence: observation, mathematical calculation, logical argument, history, and authority. Some of his conclusions are amazingly sound, such as the earth's shape and circumference, and the effects of shape on motion. Others seem bizarre, such as his theory that minds or spirits direct the planets. This thesis is an example of a type of theory known as *animism*.[9] Animistic theories postulate that spirits or minds are responsible for the behavior of what we would consider to be inanimate bodies. Planetary animism is a coherent extension of Aristotelian physics given that Aristotle used literal analogs of human consciousness in his reasoning about nature as a whole. Final causation is one example of such analogical reasoning, cosmological animism is another. And as with the *Physics*, the detailed level of analysis and uncompromising honesty in presenting reasoned evidence give Aristotelian cosmology a pivotal place in history.

Metaphysics

Aristotle's *Metaphysics* gave its name to the philosophical study of reality. It has been taken to mean beyond, or higher than, physics, but this could be a mistaken interpretation of a title that might simply have indicated that the work follows a work on physics.

BOOK V

We call a cause (1) that from which (as immanent material) a thing comes into being ... (2) the form or pattern. ... (3) That from which the change or the freedom from change first begins. ... (4) The end, i.e., that for the sake of which. ...

BOOK VII

[I]n one sense matter is said to be the nature of substratum, in another, shape, and in a third sense, the compound of these. By the matter I mean, for instance, the bronze, by the shape the plan of its form, and by the compound of these (the concrete thing) the statue. ...

We have outlined the nature of substance, showing that it is that which is not predicated of a subject, but of which all else is predicated ... on this view, *matter* becomes substance. For if this is not substance, it is beyond us to say what else is. When all else is taken away evidently nothing but matter remains. ... By matter I mean that which in itself is neither a particular thing nor of a certain quantity nor assigned to any of the other categories. ...

Here we see a movement from a discussion of four causes to the nature of a primary substance. Although he has stated in *De Caelo* that there is not one kind of fundamental matter, he believes that matter in general is the fundamental substance of nature. This view is opposed to some of the more spiritual and esoteric speculations of other philosophers, and it is influential in Western physics.

Aristotle's view of matter is far from the modern, however, and is more metaphysical than physical. In the *Metaphysics* and elsewhere, he gives an account of matter as pure potential, without form. This is in accord with his comments above. The antipode of matter is form, which is pure actuality. Aristotle claimed that substance moves from potential to actual, and the actualization of matter in form is its *telos*. This is a coherent extension of the ends-driven teleology which pervades the Aristotelian corpus. That which is pure form, pure actuality, is divine. This aspect of Aristotle's philosophy is not emphasized in our study of philosophy and science. But it is worth noting here for its similarity to the Platonic philosophy of forms and for its influence on medieval conceptions of God and the material world.

In ancient Greece there is an established dialogue in natural philosophy. Such a dialogue encourages criticism and advancement, and is largely the defining characteristic of Western thought at its most productive. This openness was interrupted by the rise of a medieval tradition which viewed study of the natural world as a distraction from more important tasks: preparation for judgment in the apocalypse and judgment at the end of individual life. Fortunately for the subsequent history of philosophy and science, Arabian and Islamic scholars preserved the legacy of Aristotle under the patronage of Byzantine and then Islamic rulers. In the next section, we see a more authoritarian approach to natural science, which deftly combines elements of Aristotelian physics and cosmology with Christian doctrine.

The Rebirth of Aristotelian Natural Philosophy

Aristotle's works on logic survived the intervening period between the fall of classical civilization and the rise of High Medieval culture in the tenth century, but his other major works fell out of fashion or were lost. St. Augustine was originally a Neoplatonist, and when he undertook the formidable task of synthesizing ancient wisdom with the prevailing moral and political scheme of Christianity in the fourth century C.E., he naturally emphasized elements of Neoplatonic philosophy. As such, Augustinian doctrines contain a bifurcated scheme of natural and supernatural, worldly and divine, creature and creator. And like the Neoplatonists (and Plato, for that matter), Augustine placed supreme value in the spiritual, eternal, and divine realm of God.

The works of Aristotle were reintroduced to the West via Islamic and Jewish writers in Spain. The Islamic empire, which extended to encompass the Iberian peninsula in 711 C.E., tolerated intellectual and ethnic diversity to some extent so long as political and military rule were secure. When the Islamic empire began to dissolve due to lack of internal cohesion, Spain was reconnected to the Medieval West. The Arabian and Jewish schools of philosophy, which thrived in Spain, sparked renewed interest in the works of Aristotle. In the twelfth and thirteenth centuries, Christian scholars began the task of synthesizing Aristotelian philosophy and Christian doctrine. This effort culminated with the works of St. Thomas Aquinas, and Dante's *Divine Comedy* provides evidence that this world-view was ubiquitous until the Renaissance.

Thomistic Unity of the Divine, Natural, and Human Worlds

Thomas Aquinas was born about 1225 in Southern Italy and died in 1274. He studied under Albertus Magnus, himself an interpreter of Aristotle. Sir William Cecil Dampier's *A History of Science* helpfully characterizes the driving force behind Aquinas' dedication to utilize Aristotelian philosophy. Dampier says that the works of St. Thomas "recognize two sources of knowledge: . . . Christian faith. . . , and the truths of human reason. . . . The two sources cannot be opposed, since they both flow from God as the one source."[10] Thus, Aquinas sought to emphasize mutually compatible elements in ancient philosophy and Christian doctrine.

An example of this compatibility is found in the Aristotelian geocentric universe and creation myths of Scripture. "As man was the object of creation, so the earth was the centre of the Universe, and round it revolved concentric spheres. . . . Medieval pictures of the Day of Judgement show how naturally this view led to the vision of heaven localized above the sky, and hell beneath the ground. Within the premises given by contemporary Christian dogma and Aristotelian philosophy, the scheme . . . held together in a consistent and convincing whole. . . ."

Aquinas found more compatibility in Aristotle's mechanics of motion: ". . . From the idea that all motion implies a continual exertion of force, Aquinas deduced results in accordance with the theology of his age. . . ." In particular, Aristotle's arguments could be used to show that the world is dependent on the continued intervention of God.

Dampier goes on to characterize the powerful influence of this synthesis: "The deductions being regarded as verified, the premises became strengthened, and thus the whole of natural knowledge was welded with theology into one rigid structure, the parts of which were believed to be interdependent, so that an attack on Aristotelian philosophy or science became an attack on the Christian faith."[11] The following are brief selections from *The Summa Theologica* illustrating these themes.

PART I QUESTION 2 ARTICLE 3

. . . God's existence can be proved in five ways, the first and clearest proof is the argument from motion. It is certain, and in accordance with sense experience, that some things in this world are moved. Now everything that is moved is moved by something else

... it is impossible ... that anything ... should move itself.... We are therefore bound to arrive at a first mover which is not moved by anything, and all men understand that this is God.

The second way is from the nature of an efficient cause. We find that there is a sequence of efficient causes in sensible things. But we do not find anything is the efficient cause of itself ... neither can the sequence of efficient causes be infinite.... We are therefore bound to suppose a first efficient cause. All men call this God.[12]

PART I QUESTION 3 ARTICLE 2
WHETHER THERE IS COMPOSITION OF FORM AND MATTER IN GOD

We proceed to the second article thus:

1. It appears that there is composition of form and matter in God. Anything which has a soul is composed of matter and form, since soul is the form of body....

2. Again, according to *De Anima*[13] ... anger, joy, and the like are passions of the composite. Scripture attributes such passions to God.... Hence God is composed of matter and form....

I answer: there cannot possibly be matter in God. In the first place, matter is characterized by potentiality,[14] and ... God is pure act.... Such things as anger are attributed to God metaphorically....

QUESTION 2 ARTICLE TEN
WHETHER REASON IN SUPPORT OF THE THINGS OF FAITH
DIMINISHES THE MERITS OF FAITH

We proceed to the tenth article thus:

1. It seems that a reason in support of the things of faith diminishes the merits of faith....

I answer: ... the act of faith can be meritorious inasmuch as it depends on the will, in respect of assent and not only of practice. Now human reason in support of faith may relate to the will of the believer ... things which encourage faith do not always diminish the readiness of the will to believe. Neither, therefore, do they always diminish the merit of faith.

Although Aquinas appeals to doctrines of Aristotle and dogma of the Church to support his conclusions, his method and style are intended to be analytic and dialectical. He used reason as a grounds for appeal (along with faith and revelation) and thereby laid the foundation for a new infusion of rational inquiry into science and philosophy.

The unity of Thomistic thought encompasses the divine, natural, and human in the sense that ultimate causes, natural order, and human virtues are all the subject of philosophic inquiry. This contrasts with the Neoplatonic bifurcation of philosophical theology into two distinct subject areas: one of heaven, the other of earth. Such a division disparaged inquiry into the human and natural realms. While the modern scientific revolution displaced the unity between human virtues and natural order, the initial re-unification of the study of ultimate principles with discussions of the natural world is important for the scientific revolution ahead.

Medieval and Renaissance Cosmology: The Paradise

The geocentric picture of the universe and the evaluative order of nature presented by Aquinas and Aristotle are further embodied in the religious literature of the Renaissance. Dante was a Florentine who lived from 1265 until 1321. Dante's *Divine Comedy*, a poetic work sometimes regarded as satirizing the Church, contains a picture of the world that is enlightening to those of us trying to understand a medieval mental matrix that seems so alien. In the poem, Dante the Pilgrim is depicted travelling through the passages of Hell in the *Inferno*, enduring limbo in the *Purgatory*, and reaching Heaven in the *Paradise*. The entire scheme shows the Aristotelian notion that "the superior glory of [heaven's] nature is proportionate to its distance from this world of ours."[15] It also shows the purposive nature of the Aristotelian and medieval view of the universe.

PARADISE

CANTO I

The Glory of the One Who moves all things
penetrates the universe . . .

I have been in His brightest shining Heaven . . .

I could not look for long, but my eyes saw the sun enclosed in
blazing sparks of light . . .

And suddenly it seemed as if one day
shone on the next . . .

And Beatrice stood there, her eyes fixed
　　on the eternal spheres, entranced . . .

the great sphere that spins . . . captured my mind with strains
　　of harmony tempered and tuned by You . . .

Among all things, however disparate
　　there reigns an order, and this gives the form
　　that makes the universe resemble God . . .

and in this order all created things,
　　according to their bent, maintain their place
　　disposed in proper distance from their Source . . .

This is what carries fire toward the moon,
　　this is the moving force in mortal hearts,
　　this is what binds the earth and makes it one . . .

The Providence that regulates the whole
　　becalms forever with its radiance
　　the heaven wherein revolves the swiftest sphere;

to there, to that predestined place, we soar,
　　propelled there by the power of that bow . . .

and just as fire can be seen as falling
　　down from a cloud, so too man's primal drive,
　　twisted by false desire, may bring him down . . .

CANTO II

Within the highest Heaven of God's peace
　　revolves a body in whose power lies
　　the essence of all things contained therein.

The next sphere which is lit with myriad eyes
　　divides this essence into many types,
　　distinct from it yet contained in it.

The other spheres, by various differences
　　direct their own distinctive qualities
　　to their own ends and fruitful operations.

These universal organs, you now see,
　　proceed from grade to grade, receiving the power
　　from those above, acting on those below.[16]

Dante described an ordered universe, full of religious and philosophical meaning and evaluative organization. This universe explicitly includes elements from *De Caelo*. For example, the outermost sphere of divine heaven is the swiftest, and the movement of the planets is attributed to the pursuit of "their own ends and fruitful operations." Dante's portrayal also includes the Aristotelian notion of proper place and natural end. *The Divine Comedy* further illustrates the connection between philosophy, science, and culture. Here we find an enduring work of Renaissance art shaped by Aristotle's scientific mind and Aquinas' religious interpretation.

Summary

Aristotle proposed a natural philosophy using an eclectic method. Some elements of this method as well as specific postulates of the resulting theory are anthropocentric, e.g., final causation and planetary animism. Other parts of Aristotelian natural philosophy are grounded in objective observation and logical theory. In all, Aristotle's legacy was a philosophical system of unparalleled scope and breadth of explanation, encompassing as it did cosmology, physics, human values, and metaphysical substance.

This philosophy contains an abstract framework and concrete elements that were adopted by medieval philosophers. The abstract framework includes concepts of purposive nature, divine motion, and a taxonomy of substance and causes. Among the elements of Aristotle's concrete picture of the world that were adopted by the Medievals were his concepts of the earth at rest in the center of the universe,[17] the spherical motion of divine heaven, and the teleological explanations of motion. Having established this premodern picture, we are now prepared to appreciate the modern scientific revolution and its monumental impact on philosophy and Western history.

Notes

1. To paraphrase Newton's acknowledgement of his debt to others: "If I have seen further than other men, it is because I stood on the shoulders of giants. . . ."

2. Archimedes (287–212 B.C.E.) was a notable counterexample. He made extensive experiments to determine specific gravities and densities of substances, and also determined a geometric formula for the operation of the lever. See William Cecil Dampier, *A History of Science* (New York: Macmillan, 1943), 45–47, for the significance of Archimedes in ancient science.

3. Some scholars downplay Aristotle's emphasis on final causation and argue that it is more a methodological rubric than a metaphysical principle. (See for example R.J. Hankinson, "Philosophy of Science," in *The Cambridge Companion to Aristotle*, Jonathan Barnes, ed., Cambridge University Press, 1995). For our purposes, we can

emphasize the final cause for historical reasons: the Medievals seized on Aristotelian teleology to forge a Christian science.

4. *The Complete Works of Aristotle: The Revised Oxford Translation*, Jonathan Barnes, ed. (Princeton, N.J.: Princeton University Press, 1984). Reprinted by permission of Princeton University Press.

5. This refers to Anaximenes, a successor of Anaximander. Other doctrines in this passage have been treated in Chapter 1.

6. For example, the water of Thales or the fire of Heraclitus.

7. See the *Physics* above.

8. Approximately 10,000 miles. This astoundingly accurate figure, off by little more than a factor of 2 (the actual circumference is 24,800 miles), is improved upon by other ancients, including Eratosthenes who gives the calculation at about 24,000 miles. (These figures cannot be attributed with absolute accuracy since the conversion from stades to modern units is uncertain.) Modern day cosmologists would do well to come within such acceptable margins when working from limited observation to theoretical calculation—the notoriously elusive figure for the mass of the universe is one example where contemporary physicists and astronomers are at a loss to come to a determinate estimate to within a factor of 10 at best.

9. This sort of theory is also referred to less perjoratively as *panpsychism*.

10. Dampier, 93.

11. Dampier, 96.

12. Both of these arguments originate from Aristotle, see *Physics*, Books 7 and 8.

13. Aristotle's treatise on the soul or mind.

14. See commentary on Aristotle above.

15. From *De Caelo*.

16. From Dante, *The Divine Comedy, Volume III: Paradise*, Mark Musa, transl. (Penguin Books: New York, 1986).

17. Ptolemy incorporated the geocentric picture into his detailed astronomical system (see next chapter) in the second century, predating medieval cosmology.

Suggestions for Further Reading

The Complete Works of Aristotle: The Revised Oxford Translation, Jonathan Barnes, ed. (Princeton, N.J.: Princeton University Press, 1984).

Dampier, Sir William Cecil, *A History of Science and its Relations with Philosophy and Religion*, 4th ed. (Cambridge, England: Cambridge University Press, 1948).

Barnes, Jonathan, ed., *The Cambridge Companion to Aristotle* (New York: Cambridge University Press, 1995).

The Seventeenth-Century Revolution in Physical Science

Ancient philosophers and scientists preserved and perpetuated a lively debate on the nature of the universe and the proper means for human beings to come to scientific understanding of it. In Chapter 1, we saw several influential theories of the natural world and scientific method. By the time of the Middle Ages, however, this pluralism succumbed to the authoritative doctrines of a few ancient figures and their medieval defenders. Aristotle's geocentric picture of cosmology was accepted by one of the greatest astronomical observers in history in the person of Ptolemy, a second-century C.E. Greek scientist who established the earth-centered world-view by Aristotelian arguments. His extensive calculations and observations provided the accurate system of prediction and explanation which bore his name. Aristotle's physical and metaphysical theories were further synthesized into Catholic dogma by St. Thomas, as we saw in the last chapter.

Such a monistic view made a revolution necessary in order to achieve any progress in scientific thinking. If dogmatic Aristotelian science necessitated revolution, other underlying assumptions of The Philosopher (as he was known to his medieval disciples) laid the groundwork for modernity. The analytic approach taken by Aristotle is fundamental for science as we know it today, and his hypothesis that the world is intelligible opposes the mysticism of other ancient and medieval philosophers.

Although the result of the seventeenth-century scientific revolution was a new methodology, the impetus for new development in science was still somewhat literary. Augustine and Aquinas undertook the monumental task of synthesizing ancient wisdom and Christian Scripture, but with the reintroduction of Aristotelian writings and the reconnection of Arab commentary on Aristotle with the West, it became apparent that ancient wisdom itself contained antithetical positions. Discovery of controversy among the Ancients gave rise to freedom of speculation.[1] Such speculation began conservatively, but resulted in drastic new world-views and a new experimental methodology. Elegance of explanation, concurrence with observation, and careful measurement became important criteria in the seventeenth century, and these criteria are no less important centuries later.

The seventeenth-century scientific revolution was bound up with a revival of mechanism.[2] A mechanistic explanation is one that relies solely on arrangement and contact of concrete material elements to produce subsequent effects according to determinate laws. A mechanical theory must first reduce natural phenomena to their constituent material elements. Predictions and explanations then involve only interaction by direct contact of these elements. Furthermore, effects are deduced according to determinate laws, i.e., a certain arrangement of elements produces one and only one effect that can be completely determined by the antecedent state of affairs.

Final causation is banished from this perspective, as are nonmaterial esoteria such as indeterminate substrata.[3] Similarly, any sort of animism is excluded from a mechanical theory. The stipulation that the physical world obeys objective, determinate laws puts physics at odds with the world of human affairs. While some philosophers, notably the Stoics, advocate a certain determinism and fatalism in human life, the most straightforward idea of human action depicts the human agent as free in some sense to determine his or her own destiny. Such freedom is also tied to notions of responsibility, since humans also must face the ethical consequences of right or wrong choices.[4] The determinism of the material world from antecedent causes is in stark contrast to the subjective world of human valuation and striving. We will see mechanical and quasi-mechanical elements of physical theory come forward in this chapter, as well as some notable exceptions to modern mechanism, e.g., Newton's theory of gravitation.

In this chapter we will examine some of the writings of Galileo on Astronomy and Mechanics. Then we will look at the work of the astronomer Johannes Kepler. This treatment omits the work of Copernicus, the modern founder of the view that the sun is at the center of the solar system while the earth in fact moves, in order to explore some of the relationships between Kepler's theories and Newton's. Isaac Newton's laws of motion and his theory of gravitation are the crowning achievements of the seventeenth-century scientific revolution and serve as the guiding force for physics in subsequent centuries.

Galileo the Scientist

Galileo was indeed one of the "giants" on whose shoulders Newton stood.[5] He was born in Pisa in 1564 and died in Florence in 1642. He was not only a brilliant observationalist, theoretical physicist, astronomer, inventor, and mathematician, but also a philosopher of the first order. His writings on knowledge and scientific method are significant contributions to philosophy in their own right. We will consider the philosophical side of Galileo in Chapter 5. In this chapter we treat his astronomical observations, his apparati and experiments with acceleration, and his refutation of Aristotelian ideas of motion.

Precise answers to quantitative questions require recognition that these questions can be asked and answered. Galileo advocated a theory of uniform acceleration due to gravity, i.e., equal acceleration for any body over equal time intervals. The notion of equal time intervals as a theoretical or practical construction required measuring technology in order to make the measurements meaningful. In order to conduct his experiments, Galileo devised entirely new ways to measure time.[6]

Astronomy

Although Galileo's specialties did not include optics, he employed the newly developed telescope in order to support a heliocentric view of the universe. He was not alone in probing the heavens with the new instrument, but he achieved remarkable success with the primitive devices available. He discovered the four Galilean moons of Jupiter, and he made sketches of the surface of Earth's moon. These sketches are a puzzling artifact of scientific history since several commentators point out that they do not match any known features of the lunar surface.[7]

Despite such flaws, Galileo's astronomical work was an important breakthrough for several reasons. For one, he was a persuasive advocate for the telescope as a valid means of scientific observation. Once this validity was established, Galileo's observations of details of planetary structure belied Aristotelian notions of heavenly perfection. Hence his studies laid the groundwork for laws of physics which treated heavenly material no differently than that of earth, as we will see. The following selections from *The Sidereal Messenger* illustrate these themes.[8]

... It is most beautiful and pleasing to the eye to look upon the lunar body ... so near ... so that the diameter of the same Moon appears as if it were thirty times ... larger than when observed only with the naked eye. Anyone will then understand with the certainty of the senses that the Moon is by no means endowed with a smooth and polished surface, but is rough and uneven, just as the face of the

Earth itself, crowded everywhere with vast prominences, deep chasms, and convolutions. . . .

[W]e have been led to the conclusion that we certainly see the surface of the Moon to be not smooth, even, and perfectly spherical, as the great crowd of philosophers have believed about this and other heavenly bodies, but, on the contrary, to be uneven, rough, and crowded with depressions and bulges. And it is like the face of the Earth itself, which is marked here and there with chains of mountains and depths of valleys. The observations from which this is inferred are as follows.

. . . [W]hen the Moon displays herself to us with brilliant horns, the boundary dividing the bright from the dark part does not form a uniformly oval line, as would happen in a perfectly spherical solid, but is marked by an uneven, rough, and very sinuous line. . . . Indeed, a great number of small darkish spots, entirely separated from the dark part, are distributed everywhere over almost the entire region already bathed by the light of the Sun. . . . We noticed, moreover, that all these small spots just mentioned always agree in this, that they have a dark part on the side toward the Sun while on the side opposite the Sun they are crowned with brighter borders like shining ridges. And we have an almost entirely similar sight on Earth, around sunrise, when the valleys are not yet bathed in light but the surrounding mountains facing the Sun are already seen shining with light. . . .

[O]n the seventh day of January of the present year 1610, at the first hour of the night, when I inspected the celestial constellations through a spyglass, Jupiter presented himself. And since I had prepared for myself a superlative instrument, I saw . . . that three little stars were positioned near him—small but very bright. Although I believed them to be among the number of fixed stars, they nevertheless intrigued me because they appeared to be arranged exactly along a straight line and parallel to the ecliptic. . . . I decided that henceforth they should be observed more accurately and diligently. . . . I . . . arrived at the conclusion . . . that in the heavens there are three stars wandering around Jupiter. . . . This was at length seen clear as day in many subsequent observations, and that there are not only three, but four wandering stars making their revolutions about Jupiter. . . .

We have, moreover, an excellent and splendid argument for taking away the scruples of those who, while tolerating with equanimity the revolution of the planets about the Sun in the Copernican system, are so disturbed by the attendance of one Moon around the Earth while the two together complete the annual orb around the Sun that they conclude that this constitution of the universe must be overthrown as impossible. . . . [O]ur vision offers us four stars wandering around Jupiter like the Moon around the Earth. . . .

In this last passage, Galileo referred with pride to his discovery of the four Galilean moons of Jupiter, which he dubbed the Medicean stars after the first family of Florence and Tuscany. He used this discovery as evidence against one argument for the geocentric world-view. Supporters of the idea that the sun, stars, and planets revolve around the Earth pointed to the fact that the moon clearly does so. And it seems theoretically economical to use this same model of revolution for the rest of the heavenly bodies. Indeed, it would seem strange if all planetary bodies revolved around the Sun except the Moon. Galileo claimed we need not face this anomaly, since other moons revolve around at least one other planet, and that it is not a cosmic aberration for the Earth and its companion to revolve around the Sun.

Galileo felt that he added positive evidence in favor of a heliocentric world-view. At the very least, he evinced many reasons to doubt the Aristotelian cosmology. Heavenly material, at least in the case of the moon, appeared to be more similar to that of the Earth than to the perfection predicted by Aristotle's theory. And Galileo's emphasis on instrumentation and observation as opposed to theoretical speculation paved the way for revolutionary change in cosmological as well as terrestrial physics.

In order to shift scientific inquiry from the theoretical to the experimental, however, supporters of empiricism had to counter doubts about the use of new instrumentation. And without a sophisticated theory of optics to provide reasons for believing in telescopic observation, many conservative cosmologists, philosophers, and theologians decided to disregard Galileo's observations as charlatanism. So, in fact, new theory was needed to bolster a new empiricism. This interdependence between theory and experiment in both the seventeenth and the twentieth centuries is treated in Chapter 11.

The Evolution of Objective Science

The philosophic method of Aristotle resulted in a world-view in which the actions and plans of human beings had an analogue in the fundamental causes of nature. Aristotle's final cause, or *telos*, gave a unified picture of human experience, including striving and valuing, and physical causation.

Such a picture was compatible with the evaluative orderings of the universe held by medieval and Renaissance figures, as we saw in the last chapter. The seventeenth century saw a physical and metaphysical rejection of this picture.

Galileo and Descartes[9] established a dichotomy between subjective and objective which makes for a dramatic shift in science, philosophy, and culture, and can largely be taken to define the modern mind-set. We will revisit this theme in Chapter 4 and throughout our study. The beginning of this dichotomy can be seen in the following selection from Galileo's *Assayer*, written in 1623.[10]

...I shall certainly state my ideas concerning the proposition "Motion is the cause of Heat," explaining in what way it appears to me to be true. But first it will be necessary for me to say a few words concerning that which we call "heat," for I strongly suspect that the commonly held conception of the matter is very far from the truth, inasmuch as heat is believed to be a true ... quality which actually resides in the material which we feel to be heated.

Now, whenever I conceive of any material or corporeal substance, I am necessarily constrained to conceive of that substance as bounded and as possessing this or that shape, as large or small in relationship to some other body, as in this or that place during this or that time, as in motion or at rest ... and by no stretch of the imagination can I conceive of any corporeal body apart from these conditions. But I do not at all feel myself compelled to conceive of bodies as necessarily conjoined with such further conditions as red or white, bitter or sweet, having sound or being mute, or possessing a pleasant or unpleasant fragrance. On the contrary, were they not escorted by our physical senses, perhaps neither reason nor understanding would ever, by themselves, arrive at such notions. I think, therefore, that these tastes, odors, colors, etc., so far as their objective existence is concerned, are nothing but mere names for something which resides exclusively in our sensitive body, so that if the perceiving creatures were removed, all of these qualities would be annihilated. ...

Sounds come to us indiscriminately, from above and below and from either side, since we are so constituted as to be equally disposed to every direction of the air's movement.... Sounds, then, are produced in us and felt when ... there is a rapid vibration of the air, forming minutely small waves, which move certain cartilages of a certain drum which is in our ear. The various external ways in which this wave-motion of the air is produced are manifold, but can in large part be reduced to the vibrating of bodies which strike the air and form waves which spread out with great velocity. High frequencies give rise to high tones; low frequencies give rise to low tones, but I cannot believe that there exists in external bodies anything, other than their size, shape, or motion (slow or rapid) which could excite in us our tastes, sounds, and odors. And indeed, I should judge that, if ears, tongues, and noses be taken away, the number, shape, and motion of bodies would remain, but not their tastes, sounds, and odors. The latter, external to living creatures, I believe to be nothing but mere names. . . .

. . . I confess myself to be very much inclined to believe that heat, too, is of this sort, and that those materials which produce and make felt in us the sense of heat and to which we give the general name "fire" consist of a multitude of tiny particles of such and such shape, and having such and such a velocity . . . and it is their contact, felt by us, which is the affection we call heat. . . . In sum, the operation of fire, considered in itself, is nothing but movement . . . that there exists in fire apart from shape, number, movement, penetration, and contact, some further quality we call "heat" I cannot believe. And again I judge that heat is altogether subjective. . . .

The importance of these ideas cannot be overemphasized. We saw that in the ancient and medieval periods, science and philosophy were unified within natural philosophy. Abstract reasoning, observed evidence, and philosophical argument were all employed in matters of physical science, ethical theory, cosmology, and metaphysics. Furthermore, these subjects were treated within unified and coherent systems of philosophy and human affairs. An example of this coherence is found in Aristotle's final causation, the doctrine that nature has purposes.

An important exception to these ancient themes is found in the teachings of Democritus. As we have seen, Democritus proposed that heat is a "convention," an affect of the body, and that in reality there is nothing but atoms and their collisions in the "void." Galileo had a similarly mechanistic explanation of heat. Despite the pluralism of ancient views, medieval interpretations of Aristotle formed the dominant world-view during Galileo's time.

Galileo challenged this manner of thinking in fundamental ways. Modernity denied that nature is purposive, and thus undercut one analogy that Aristotle used between nature and human beings. Galileo believed that nature was even further removed from any resemblance to human conscious operations. He stated that qualities such as heat are not in natural objects, but in the human subject. These came to be known as "secondary qualities," and include taste, sound, and color along with heat.

The modern period created a new world-view in which the affairs of mind and the affairs of matter become separate. The separation begins in the scientific and philosophical writings of Galileo, Descartes, and Newton, but later produces a situation in which science becomes increasingly separate from philosophy. Philosophy becomes the realm of epistemology, ethics, and mind. Science becomes the study of facts. Room for metaphysical speculation in philosophy becomes increasingly crowded out by the intrusion of scientific theories of reality into formerly philosophical domains, and eventually even the realm of mind is forsaken to science (see Chapter 8).

The world of values remained the subject matter for philosophy, and was seen to have little bearing on science. We will see some challenges to modern subjective/objective bifurcation in Chapters 8 through 12. Mechanism is subsequently challenged by wholistic metaphysical theories, as we will see in Chapters 10 and 12. In the twentieth century, philosophers uncovered epistemological dilemmas challenging the notion of objective knowledge, as we will see in Chapter 11. In addition, the story of science and philosophy continues to be influenced by attempts to synthesize science and human experience, as we will see in the final chapter.

Mechanics and Cosmology

In Galileo's popularly styled dialogues, he defended a Copernican picture of the world with scientific evidence and everyday observation. He also challenged the authority of Aristotle and poked fun at "slavish" defenders of Aristotle known as Peripatetics.[11] In these and other ways he contributed to the scientific and popular acceptance of his views. The character Salviati in the dialogue that follows expresses Galileo's views, while Simplicio is the voice of the Aristotelians, and Sagredo is an arbitrator.[12]

In defending heliocentric cosmology with everyday examples, Galileo brought the grand science of astronomy down to earth. This led to a unification of mechanics and cosmology that inspired Newton and succeeding physicists. We will see in Chapters 11 and 12 that some critics of twentieth-century physics believe that contemporary cosmology has forsaken such unity.

Galileo's troubles with the inquisition are well known, and his defense of the heliocentric system and his attack on Aristotle earned him inquisitional summons and house arrest. He was also made to recant his views, and the censure of Galileo by the church outlived the man by several centuries.

DIALOGUE CONCERNING THE TWO CHIEF WORLD SYSTEMS: THE SECOND DAY

Sagredo. . . . yesterday's discourse may be summarized as a preliminary examination of the two following opinions as to which is the more probable and reasonable. The first holds the substance of the heavenly bodies to be ingenerable, incorruptible, inalterable, invariant, and in a word free from all mutations except those of situation, and accordingly to be a quintessence most different for our generable, corruptible, alterable bodies. The other . . . considers the earth . . . to be a movable and a moving body no less than the moon, Jupiter, Venus, or any other planet. Later, many detailed parallels were drawn between the earth and the moon. . . . And having finally concluded this second opinion to have more likelihood than the other, it seems to me that our next step should be to examine whether the earth must be considered immovable. . . .

Simplicio. I confess that all last night I was meditating on yesterday's material, and truly I find it to contain many beautiful considerations which are novel and forceful. Still, I am much more impressed by the authority of so many great authors. . . .

Sagr. But what you say does not in the least diminish the absurdity of the Peripatetics' reply: who, as a counter to sensible experience, adduced no experiment or argument of Aristotle's, but just the authority of his bare *ipso dixit.*

Simp. Aristotle acquired his great authority only because of the strengths of his proofs and the profundity of his arguments. Yet one must understand him, and not merely understand him, but have such a thorough familiarity with his books that the most complete idea of them may be formed . . . one must have a grasp of the whole grand scheme, and be able to combine this passage with that, collecting together one text here and another very distant from it. There is no doubt that whoever has this skill will be able to draw demonstrations of all that can be known; for every single thing is in them.

Sagr. My dear Simplicio, since having things all over the place does not disgust you, and since you believe that by the collection and combination of the various pieces you can draw the juice out of them, then what you and the other brave philosophers will do with Aristotle's texts I shall do with the verse of Virgil and Ovid. . . . But why do I speak of Virgil, or any other poet? I have a little book, much briefer. . . . It is the alphabet, and no doubt anyone . . . can dig out of it the truest answers to every question. . . .

Simp. But if Aristotle is to be abandoned, whom shall we have for a guide in philosophy? Suppose you name some author.

Salviati. We need guides in forests and unknown lands, but on plains and in open places only the blind need guides. . . . Let the beginning of our reflections be the consideration that whatever motion comes to be attributed to the earth must necessarily remain imperceptible to us and as if nonexistent, so long as we look at terrestrial objects; for as inhabitants of the earth, we consequently participate in the same motion. But on the other hand, it is indeed just as necessary that it display itself generally in all other visible bodies. . . .

Now there is one motion which is most general and supreme over all, and it is that by which the sun, moon, and all other planets and fixed stars—in a word, the whole universe, the earth alone excepted—appear to be moved as a unit from east to west in the space of twenty-four hours. . . . [L]et us consider only the immense bulk of the starry sphere in contrast with the smallness of the terrestrial globe. . . . Now if we think of the velocity of motion required to make a complete rotation in a single day and night, I cannot persuade myself that anyone could be found who would think it the more reasonable and credible thing that it was the celestial sphere which did the turning, and the terrestrial globe which remained fixed.

Simp. The arrangement is not new; rather, it is most ancient, as is shown by Aristotle refuting it. . . .

. . . heavy bodies . . . falling from a height, go perpendicularly to the surface of the earth. Similarly, projectiles thrown vertically upward come down again perpendicularly by the same line, even though they have been thrown to an immense height. . . .

Salv. Aristotle says, then, that a most certain proof of the earth's being motionless is that things projected perpendicularly upward are seen to return by the same line to the same place. . . . Now, in order to begin to untie these knots, I ask Simplicio by what means he would prove that freely falling bodies go along straight and perpendicular lines directed toward the center. . . .

Simp. By means of the senses, which assure us that the tower is straight and perpendicular, and which show us that a falling stone goes along grazing it, without deviating a hairsbreadth. . . .

Salv. But if it happened that the earth rotated, and consequently carried along the tower, and if the falling stone were seen to graze the side of the tower just the same, what would its motion then have to be?

Simp. In that case one would have to say "its motions," for there would be one with which it went from top to bottom, and another needed for following the path of the tower ... It would have to be slanting, and different from the straight perpendicular line it would describe with the earth motionless.

Salv. Hence, just from seeing the falling stone graze the tower, you could not say for sure that it described a straight and perpendicular line, unless you first assumed the earth to stand still.

Simp. Exactly so. ...

THE THIRD DAY

Salv. We shall next consider the annual movement generally attributed to the sun, but then, first by Aristarchus of Samos and later by Copernicus, removed from the sun and transferred to the earth. ...

Simp. The first and greatest difficulty is the repugnance and incompatibility between being at the center and being distant from it. For if the terrestrial globe must move in a year around the circumference of a circle ... it is impossible for it at the same time to be at the center. ... But the earth is at the center, as is proved in many ways by Aristotle, Ptolemy, and others. ...

Salv. I might very reasonably dispute whether there is in nature such a center, seeing that neither you nor anyone else has so far proved whether the universe is finite and has a shape. ...

Simp. Aristotle gives a hundred proofs that the universe is finite, bounded, and spherical.

Salv. Which are later all reduced to one, and that to none at all. For if I deny him his assumption that the universe is movable all his proofs fall to the ground, since he proves it to be finite and bounded only if the universe is movable. But in order not to multiply our disputes, I shall concede to you for the time being that the universe is finite, spherical, and has a center. ...

Simp. How do you deduce that it is not the earth, but the sun, which is at the center of the revolutions of the planets?

Salv. This is deduced from most obvious and therefore most powerfully convincing observations. The most palpable of these ... is that we find all the planets closer to the earth at one time and farther from it at another.

Simp. But what are the signs that they move around the sun?

Salv. This is reasoned out from finding the three outer planets—Mars, Jupiter, and Saturn—always quite close to the earth when they are in opposition to the sun, and very distant when they are in conjunction with it.... Next, it is certain that Venus and Mercury must revolve around the sun, because of their never moving far away from it....

In the following selection from *Dialogues Concerning the Two New Sciences*,[13] we see the precise formulation of concept of acceleration over time and its relationship to distance.

THE THIRD DAY

Salv. ... At present it is the purpose of our Author merely to investigate and to demonstrate some of the properties of accelerated motion (whatever the cause of this acceleration might be)—meaning thereby a motion, such that the ... velocity ... goes on increasing after departure from rest, in simple proportionality to the time, which is the same as saying in equal time intervals the body receives equal increments in velocity....

Sagr. So far as I see it, the definition might have been put a little more clearly perhaps without changing the fundamental idea, namely, uniformly accelerated motion is such that its speed increases in proportion to the space traversed; so that, for example, the speed acquired by a body falling four cubits would be double that acquired by a body falling two cubits....

Salv. It is very comforting to me to have had such a companion in error; and moreover, let me tell you that the proposition seems so highly probable that our Author himself admitted, when I advanced this opinion to him, that he had for some time shared the same fallacy ... as false and impossible as that motion should be completed instantaneously; and here is a very clear demonstration of it. If the velocities are in proportion to the spaces traversed, or to be traversed, then these spaces are traversed in equal intervals of time; if, therefore, the velocity with which the falling body traverses a space of eight feet were double with which it covered the first four feet (just as the one distance is double the other) then the time-intervals required for these passages would be equal. But for one and the same body to fall eight feet and four feet in the same time is possible only in the case of instantaneous motion; but observation shows us that the motion of a falling body occupies time, and less of it in covering a distance of four feet than of eight feet; therefore it is not true that its velocity increases in proportion to the space. . . .

Sagr. You present these recondite matters with too much evidence and ease; this great fallacy makes them less appreciated than they would be had they been presented in a more abstruse manner. For, in my opinion, people esteem more lightly that knowledge which they acquire with so little labor than that acquired through long and obscure discussion.

Galileo resisted the doctrines of Aristotelians with observation and reason, but he acknowledged the debt science and philosophy owes to Aristotle himself. By displacing the earth from the center of the universe and discrediting the notion that mechanics and cosmology were disparate subject matters, Galileo posed a radical unity of physical science. He not only argued against a geocentric picture, but questioned the very idea of a universal center. This is coherent with and part of Galilean relativity. For Galileo, no place or point of view is privileged; location and motion are no more than relations between objects. What looks like straight vertical motion from the vantage point of the surface of the spinning earth could look like curvilinear motion from another perspective.

Galileo's open-minded, scientific, experimental approach allowed significant evolution in his own thought. When he initially formulated laws of naturally accelerated motion, Galileo employed a mistaken notion of acceleration as a function of distance. He later revised this notion to describe correctly the acceleration of falling bodies as equal increases of velocity in equal time.

Newton formalized the unity of Galilean physics in his laws of motion and gravitation, but he rejected Galilean relativity in favor of absolute space and time. Newton insisted that there is a fixed coordinate system in the universe (hence, in Galileo's terms, a "center"), and his notion of absolute space and time gave concrete meaning to this notion. Later developments proved that not only was Newton mistaken in this postulate but that Galilean relativity was not radical enough. Einstein proposed that not only are spacial measurements relative to points of view but that space and time are relative to each other.

Kepler

Johannes Kepler was born December 27, 1571, in what later came to be Germany. His work owes an immeasurable debt to two other European scientists. Nicholas Copernicus was the first post-ancient Western astronomer to defend the notion that the earth moves around the sun. He refrained from publishing his *On the Revolutions of the Heavenly Spheres* until shortly before his death in 1543 out of fear of persecution by religious and political leaders. While his ideas were indeed radical, there are several conservative elements to Copernican thought. Copernicus often hedged on how "true" he wanted his picture to be taken. He offered it as an alternative, not a replacement, theory. And most notably, Copernicus was unwilling to let go of the idea of the perfection of circular motion.

Copernicus laid the foundation for Kepler to construct a totally new theory of Astronomy. Another foundational element for Kepler was the observations of Tycho Brahe, a contemporary of Kepler. Tycho was a geocentrist, but his lifetime of observing and recording the movements of the stars and planets gave Kepler the experience and data needed for the latter's theory. Kepler was Tycho's assistant and successor as imperial mathematician at the observatory near Prague.

Kepler employed exact mathematical calculations to achieve a complete reformulation of cosmology. His laws of planetary motion describe the motions of the planets as elliptical, with varying velocities as they vary their distances from the sun. Such a system not only differed from its predecessors in quantitative accuracy but also in overall mission. William H. Donahue, the translator for the Cambridge edition of *Astronomia Nova*, points out that Kepler was a pioneer in the realm of physical modeling. Kepler's predecessors, including Tycho, Copernicus, and Aristotle, used geometric modeling to give an ideal, qualitative picture of astronomical motion. Kepler, as we see in the selections that follow, is keen to establish an accurate physical model which can quantitatively account for the actual planetary motions. In order to understand the revolutionary nature of this method, a brief digression into predecessor theories is warranted.

As we saw in the last chapter in the selection from Dante's *Paradise*, earlier figures were not interested in making ideas of heaven coherent with everyday human experience. The heavens were made of different stuff, obeyed different laws, and were bound to fool merely human senses. Therefore, the best science could do was to save appearances, that is, to qualitatively describe in some geometric fashion how the planets moved. This description was not at all intended to reflect the actual workings of planetary motion. Witness the predominance of the theory of epicycles, or compounded circular motions, to represent the noncircular shape of planetary orbits. According to Ptolemaic and Copernican theory, planets moved according to the paths of circles compounded with other circles. Serious thought was not really given to the existence of these circles, how they are circumscribed, their physical laws, or what their causes were. It was enough that a sufficient number of epicycles could approximately describe any motion, no matter how complex.[14] Such was the method of geometric modeling, as opposed to Kepler's goal of discovering the actual movements of the planets themselves.

In this section, we present Kepler's work in Astronomy from *Astronomia nova*, and *On The Principle Parts of the World*,[15] as well as his curious obsession with mysticism—*The Dream*, which is a work of imaginative fiction with astrological and magical themes.

ASTRONOMIA NOVA

The power that extends from the sun to the planets moves them in a circular course around the immovable body of the sun. This cannot happen, or be conceived in thought, in any other way than this, that the power traverses the same path along which it carries the other planets. . . .

But this *species* (of power) is immaterial, proceeding from its body out to this distance without the passing of any time. . . .

Therefore, since this *species* of the source, or the power moving the planets, rotates about the centre of the world, I conclude with good reason, following this example, that that of which it is the *species*, the sun, also rotates.

Further, we see that the individual planets are not carried along with equal swiftness. . . . Nevertheless, it follows from what has been said that every orb of power emanating from the sun is twisted around with a whirl equal to that which spins the solar body. . . . It is consequently clear that the planets are not so constituted as to emulate the swiftness of the motive power.

. . . as the sun forever turns itself, the motive force or the outflowing of the *species* from the sun's magnetic fibres, diffused through all the distances of the planets, also rotates in an orb. . . .

The example of the magnet I have hit upon is a very pretty one, and entirely suited to the subject; indeed, it is little short of being the very truth. So why should I speak of the magnet as if it were an example? For, by the demonstration of the Englishman William Gilbert, the earth itself is a big magnet. . . . I am therefore entirely within my rights to state that the moon is carried along by the rotation of the earth.

. . . It is therefore plausible . . . that the sun is a magnetic body.

BOOK FOUR OF *EPITOME OF COPERNICAN ASTRONOMY*: ON THE PRINCIPAL PARTS OF THE WORLD

Aristotle . . . is the man who in *On the Heavens* asks: "For what reason are there many movements?" . . . So I ask: "Why is any planet moved with so much speed, no more, no less?" . . . In Chapter 12 he asks: "Why in the descent from the upper to the lower planets are not the movements of the single planets found to be more manifold?" . . . But I myself, led on by this same praiseworthy thirst for philosophy, first wiped away from the eyes of astronomy those mists of the multiplicity of movements in the single planets: then I gave a demonstration of the following: that the movement of the planets is not uniform throughout its whole circuit—as Aristotle argued in Chapters 6 and 7; but that in reality the movement is increased and decreased at places in its period which are fixed and are opposite to one another; and I explained the efficient or instrumental causes of this increase as the lessening of the interval between the planet and the sun, from which as from a source that movement arises.

. . . That same Aristotle . . . sends his students to the astronomers and who defers to the astronomers in respect to their . . . testimony. . . . For he orders his students "to read through both" . . . and today that would be Ptolemy and Tycho: "but to follow" not, he says, the more ancient, but "the more accurate."

Why do you call them the proper movements of the planets?
1. Because the apparent daily movement—with which the doctrine of the sphere is concerned and which is common to both the planets and stars, and so to the whole world, is seen to travel from the east to the west; but the far slower single movements of the single planets travel in the opposite direction from west to east; and therefore it is certain that these movements . . . should be assigned to the planets themselves. . . .

What are the hypotheses or principles wherewith Copernican astronomy saves the appearances in the proper movements of the planets?
They are principally: (1) that the sun is located at the centre of the sphere of fixed stars—or approximately at the centre—and is immovable in place; (2) that the single planets move really around the sun in their single systems, which are compounded of many perfect circles revolved in absolutely uniform movement; (3) that the Earth is one of these planets, so that ... it describes its orbital circle between the orbital circles of Mars and Venus; ... (5) that the moon is arranged around the earth as its centre. ...

What in turn do you substitute for the second principle. . . ?
... even though the planets really are eccentric to the centre of the sun: nevertheless there are not smaller circles called epicycles, which by their revolution vary the intervals between the planet and the sun; but the bodies themselves of the planets ... furnish the occasion for this variation. ...

Are there solid spheres whereon the planets are carried? And are there empty spaces between the spheres?
Tycho Brahe disproved the solidity of the spheres by ... the movement of comets. ...

Then what is there in the planetary regions besides the planets?
Nothing except the ether which is common to the spheres and to the intervals; it is very limpid and yields to the moveable bodies no less readily than it yields to the lights of the sun and the stars, so that the lights can come down to us.

BOOK FIVE

... what remains for our imagination concerning the figure of the route of the planet?
The orbit remains a perfect ellipse in a true and most regular plane inclined to the plane of the ecliptic at constant angles. ... The planet moves in this orbit with unequal speed through its parts.

Kepler's posthumously published *The Dream*[16] is often overlooked by historians and philosophers, but it adds dimension to our picture of one of the great minds of the scientific revolution.

THE DREAM

... It happened then on a certain night that after watching the stars and moon, I stretched out on my bed and fell sound asleep. In my sleep I seemed to be reading a book I had got from the market. This was how it went:

My name is Duracotus. My home is Iceland, which the ancients called Thule.... In my early childhood, my mother often would lead me ... to Hekla's lower slopes.... Gathering various herbs there, she took them home and brewed them with elaborate ceremonies, stuffing them afterward into little goatskin sacks which she sold in the nearby harbor to sailors as charms.... Once, out of curiosity, I cut open a pouch.... Angry with me for cheating her out of payment, she gave me to the captain.....And he, setting out unexpectedly next day with a favorable wind, headed as if for Bergen in Norway.... [B]lown off course between Norway and England, he headed for Denmark ... since he had a letter from a Bishop of Iceland for Tycho Brahe, the Dane.... After the boat reached shore, the captain left me and the letter....

Brahe, greatly delighted with the letter I gave him, ... imposed upon his students the task of talking with me frequently ... I told them many new things about my homeland in return for the marvels they related to me....

The astronomical exercise pleased me greatly. Brahe and his students passed whole nights with wonderful instruments fixed on the moon and stars. This reminded me of my mother because she, too, used to commune constantly with the moon....

After I had passed several years ... I was seized with a desire to see my home again.... I was most happy to find my mother still alive, still engaged in the same pursuits as before. And the sight of me, unharmed and thriving, brought an end to her prolonged regret at having rashly sent her son away.... She delighted in the knowledge I had acquired about the sky. She compared my reports with her discoveries she herself had made about it....

By nature eager for knowledge, I asked about her arts.... One day when there was time for conversation she told me everything from the beginning, much as follows:

Duracotus, my son, ... there are at present among us very wise spirits.... Nine of these spirits are especially worthy of note. One, particularly friendly to me, most gentle and purest of all, is called forth by twenty-one characters. With his help, I am transported in a moment of time to any foreign shore I choose, or, . . . I learn as much by asking him as I would by going there myself. . . . I should like you to go with me now to a region she has talked about many times. . . . She called it Levania.

. . . My mother withdrew from me, . . . and then, performing some ceremonies, she returned. . . . Scarcely had we got our heads covered with our robes (as was the agreement) when there arose a hollow indistinct voice, speaking in Icelandic to this effect:

THE DAEMON FROM LEVANIA

Fifty thousand German miles up in the air the island of Levania lies. The road to it from here, or from it to the earth, seldom lies open for us. . . . No Germans are suitable, but we do not despise the lean hard bodies of the Spaniards.

The whole of the journey is accomplished in the space of four hours at most. . . . On such a headlong dash, we can take a few human companions. . . . Then comes a . . . difficulty: terrific cold and difficulty breathing. . . .

Many further difficulties arise which would be too numerous to mention. . . . If the shadow of the earth strikes the moon with its sharp point, as generally happens, we, too, attack the earth. . . . This can be done at no other time than when the men see the sun go into eclipse; it is for this reason that men so greatly fear eclipses of the sun.

So much for the trip to Levania. Now let me tell you about the place itself, starting, as the geographers do, with those things which are determined by the heavens.

Although all of Levania has the same view of the fixed stars as we have, it has, nevertheless, such a different view of the motions and sizes of the planets that it must surely have a wholly different system of astronomy.

Just as our geographers divide the earth's circle into five zones with respect to heavenly phenomena, so Levania consists of two hemispheres: one Subvolva, the other Privolva. The former always enjoys Volva, which is to it what our moon is to us; while the latter is forever deprived of the sight of Volva. . . . Now at both poles the sun, balancing between day and night, circles around the mountains of the horizon, half of it hidden and half of it shining. For Levania seems to its inhabitants to be stationary, while the stars go around it. . . .

All Levania does not exceed fourteen hundred German miles in circumference, only a fourth part of our earth. Nevertheless, it has very high mountains, and very deep and broad valleys. . . .

Whatever is born from the soil or walks on the soil is of prodigious size. Growth is very quick; everything is short lived, although it grows to such enormous bodily bulk. . . . A race of serpents predominates in general. It is wonderful how they expose themselves in the sun at midday as if for pleasure, but only just inside the mouths of caves in order that there might be a safe and convenient retreat. . . .

When I had arrived at this point in my dreaming, a wind accompanied by the sound of rain came along and dissolved my sleep and destroyed with it the last part of that book. . . . And so, having taken leave of that Daemon who was speaking, and of the audience, Duracotus the son with his mother Fioxhilde, even as they had their heads covered, so I came to my senses to find my head in fact covered by a pillow, my body wrapped in bedclothes.

Kepler combines an active imagination, an interest in mysticism, and his knowledge of astronomy in this remarkable work. As a piece of literature, it is open to great depth of interpretation. *The Dream* illustrates how scientific theory can be used to open new avenues of speculation outside the bounds of analytic reason. As a clue to Kepler's human story, we can perhaps glean that he yearned for more than scientific access to wisdom. He grants here, albeit fictionally, various means to knowledge of the universe.

Kepler's mystical side was not an impediment to his mathematical acumen. In fact, there are many examples of mathematical and mystical emphasis in the same school of thought. The Pythagoreans of ancient Greece who served as an inspiration for Kepler's *Dream* and his *Harmonicus Mundi* were famous for their mixture of mathematical brilliance and mystical doctrines. Coincidentally, they also thought the earth moved around a central "fire" (see Chapters 1 and 2). Kepler also gave serious voice to his imaginative speculations, and wrote in a letter to Galileo upon reading Galileo's *Sidereal Messenger* that the Moon's "inhabitants" may "construct giant projects" that are visible through telescopic observation.[17]

Kepler also held less than accurate views about the causes of the orbital motion of the planets. He believed that the spinning of the sun on its axis somehow provided the impetus for planetary motion. It will not be until the end of the seventeenth century that a proper theory of gravitation will be worked out by Newton, as we see in the next section. Kepler's calculations and observations are distilled into his laws of planetary motion. These equations describe planetary motion in an ellipse with the sun as one focus. The unequal speeds Kepler describes are elegantly given by the equal areas principle: a planet sweeps out an equal area of elliptic section in equal time intervals.

Newton

Isaac Newton was born in 1642, the year Galileo died in Florence under house arrest. His contributions to the landscape of intellectual history are monumental, and most historians see his work as the pinnacle of the modern scientific revolution.[18] His most enduring work is *The Mathematical Principles of Natural Philosophy*, or *Principia*, first published in 1687. In addition to his theoretical achievements in physics and mathematics, he practiced philosophy and theology, and served as President of the Royal Society. Newton died in 1727.

He is credited with inventing calculus, an achievement he shares with Leibniz. Indeed, the new mathematics was necessary for the new physics, and such a mathematical advance would have been difficult without the specific impetus provided by physical inquiry. Newton relied on mathematical abstraction like Kepler and Galileo before him, and he viewed experiment as a derivative, imperfect tool for the advancement of physical theory. Such a view allowed Newton to defend some of his controversial positions regarding absolute space and time from a decidedly nonempirical standpoint.

Newton's theory of gravitation came under attack during his time for its seeming occult properties. The action-at-a-distance description given by Newton and the lack of mechanistic underpinnings was deemed contrary to the more concrete, elemental explanations modern philosophers and scientists sought. We will see throughout the course of our study that gravity remains a rogue phenomenon with respect to physics and philosophy of science for centuries.

The Unification of Mechanics and Cosmology

Galileo proposed that the earth and the heavens are made of similar stuff and obey similar laws. Newton's famous Three Laws gave us these formulas that apply to both heavenly and earthly motion. The specifics of Newtonian mechanics finally disposed of the ideas of natural circular motion and the violent nature of other types of motion. They also formalized the notion of inertia. Newton is indebted to Galileo for this idea and is anticipated by Descartes[19] (see Chapter 4 for a discussion of Cartesian philosophy). Newton's Laws make no reference to final causation, and hence are another step away from Aristotelian physics. The following selections from the *Principia* establish these themes.[20]

PREFACE

Since the ancients (as we are told by Pappus) esteemed the science of mechanics of the greatest importance in the investigation of natural things, and the moderns, rejecting substantial forms and occult qualities, have endeavored to subject the phenomena of nature to the laws of mathematics, I have in this treatise cultivated mathematics as far as it relates to philosophy.... [R]ational mechanics will be the science of motions resulting from any forces whatsoever, and of the forces required to produce any motions, accurately proposed and demonstrated.... I offer this work as the mathematical principles of philosophy, for the whole burden of philosophy seems to consist in this—from the phenomena of motions to investigate the forces of nature, and then from these forces to demonstrate the other phenomena; and to this end the general propositions in the first and second books are directed. In the third book I give an example of this in the explication of the System of the World; for by the propositions mathematically demonstrated in the former books in the third I derive from the celestial phenomena the forces of gravity.... I wish we could derive the rest of the phenomena of Nature by the same kind of reasoning from mechanical principles, for I am induced by many reasons to suspect that they may all depend upon certain forces by which the particles of bodies, by some cause hitherto unknown, are either mutually impelled toward one another, and cohere in regular figures, or are repelled and recede from one another.

DEFINITIONS

Definition I. The quantity of matter is the measure of the same, arising from its density and bulk conjointly.

Thus air of a double density, in a double space, is quadruple in quantity.... It is this quantity that I mean hereafter everywhere under the name of body or mass. And the same is known by the weight of each body, for it is proportional to the weight....

Definition II. The quantity of motion is the measure of the same, arising from the velocity and the quantity of matter conjointly.

The motion of the whole is the sum of the motions of all the parts; and therefore in a body with double quantity, with equal velocity, the motion is double; with twice the velocity, it is quadruple.

Definition III. The *vis insita*, or innate force of matter, is a power of resisting, by which every body, as much as in it lies, continues in its present state, whether it be of rest, or of moving uniformly forward in a right line.

This force is always proportional to the body whose force it is and differs nothing from the inactivity of the mass, but in our manner of conceiving it. A body, from the inert nature of matter, is not without difficulty put out of its state of rest or motion. Upon which account, this *vis insita* may, by a most significant name, be called inertia or force of inactivity. But a body only exerts this force when another force, impressed upon it, endeavors to change its condition; and the exercise of this force may be considered as both resistance and impulse; it is resistance so far as the body, maintaining its present state, opposes the force impressed; it is impulse so far as the body, by not easily giving way to the impressed force of another endeavors to change the state of that other. Resistance is usually ascribed to bodies at rest, and impulse to those in motion; but motion and rest, as commonly conceived, are only relatively distinguished; nor are those bodies always truly at rest, which commonly are taken to be so.

Definition IV. An impressed force is an action exerted upon a body, in order to change its state, either of rest, or of uniform motion in a right line.

This force consists in action only, and remains no longer in the body when the action is over. For a body maintains every new state it acquires, by its inertia only. But impressed forces are of different origins....

AXIOMS, OR LAWS OF MOTION

Law I. Every body continues in its state of rest, or of uniform motion in a right line, unless it is compelled to change that state by forces impressed upon it.

Projectiles continue their motions, so far as they are not retarded by the resistance of the air, or impelled downwards by the force of gravity. A top, whose parts by their cohesion are continually drawn aside from rectilinear motions, does not cease its rotation, otherwise than as it is retarded by the air. The greater bodies of the planets and comets, meeting with less resistance in freer spaces, preserve their motions both progressive and circular for a much longer time.

Law II. The change of motion is proportional to the motive force impressed, and is made in the direction of the right line in which that force is impressed.

If any force generates a motion, a double force will generate double the motion, a triple force triple the motion, whether that force be impressed altogether at once, or gradually and successively. And this motion (being always directed the same way with the generating force), if the body moved before, is added to or subtracted from the former motion, according as they directly conspire with or are directly contrary to each other; or obliquely joined, when they are oblique, so as to produce a new motion compounded from the determination of both.

Law III. To every action there is always opposed an equal reaction; or, the mutual actions of two bodies upon each other are always equal, and directed to contrary parts.

Whatever draws or presses another is as much drawn or pressed by that other. If you press a stone with your finger, the finger is also pressed by the stone.

Corollary I. A body, acted on by two forces simultaneously, will describe the diagonal of a parallelogram in the same time as it would describe the sides by those forces separately. . . .

Newton's simple, elegant, formal, quantitative system here described is astoundingly useful as an abstract modeling tool for all kinds of motion. It completely reversed the status of straight-line motion. Instead of uniform rectilinear motion needing an explanation, its cessation now requires a reason. Projectile motion can be described as inertial motion affected by gravity and air resistance instead of needing a continuous moving impetus as in Aristotelian dynamics. Furthermore, the "natural" component of motion in a projectile is not the downward motion caused by the force of gravity, it is the continuity of rectilinear motion described by the principle of inertia.

Newton's laws of motion are here purely mechanical. Changes occur only via "impression," and forces are imparted only during contact. Thus, we speak of Newton's three laws of motion as Newtonian Mechanics. Newton's theory of gravitation, however, did not yield so readily to a mechanistic interpretation, as we will see.

Postulates of Absolute Space, Time, and Motion

Galileo viewed location and motion as relative phenomena. In the tower argument, he talks of how a stone's motion when dropped from a tower can seem straight from one frame of reference, curved from another. Galileo's relativity, unlike special relativity treated in Chapter 12, only postulates that spatial measurements are relative to other spatial aspects of a frame of reference. He does not make the twentieth-century claim that space and time are relative to each other.

Newton, however, viewed space as an absolute dimension. Unlike Galileo, who left aside such issues as an absolute center of the universe, Newton claimed that space does have an absolute perspective. This selection from the *Principia* actually falls within the previous passages, but is treated separately here since Newtonian absolute space is independent of his laws of motion.

SCHOLIUM

Hitherto I have laid down the definitions of such words as are less known, and explained the sense in which I would have them to be understood in the following discourse. I do not define time, space, place, and motion as being well-known to all. Only I must observe, that the common people conceive those quantities under no notions but from the relation they bear to sensible objects. And thence arise certain prejudices, for the removing of which it will be convenient to distinguish them into absolute and relative, true and apparent, mathematical and common.

I. Absolute, true, and mathematical time, of itself, and from its own nature, flows equably without relation to anything external, and by another name is called duration: relative, apparent, and common time, is some sensible and external (whether accurate or unequable) measure of duration by the means of motion, which is commonly used instead of true time: such as an hour, a day, a month, a year.

II. Absolute space, in its own nature, without relation to anything external, remains always similar and immovable. Relative space is some movable dimension or measure of the absolute spaces; which our senses determine by its position to bodies; and which is commonly taken for immovable space; such is the dimension of a subterraneous, an aerial, or celestial space, determine by its position in respect of the earth. Absolute and relative space are the same in figure and magnitude; but they do not remain always numerically the same. For if the earth, for instance, moves, a space of our air, which relatively in respect of the earth remains always the same, will at one time be a part of the absolute space into which the air passes; at another time it will be another part of the same, and so absolutely understood, it will be continually changed.

III. Place is a part of space which a body takes up, and is according to the space, either absolute or relative. . . .

IV. Absolute motion is the translation of a body from one absolute place into another; and relative motion, the translation from one relative place into another. Thus in a ship under sail, the relative place of a body is that part of the ship which that body possesses; or that part of the cavity which the body fills, and which therefore moves together with the ship: and relative rest is the continuance of the body in the same part of the ship, or of its cavity. But real, absolute rest, is the continuance of the body in the same part of immovable space, in which the ship itself, its cavity, and all that it contains, is moved. Wherefore, if the earth is really at rest, the body, which relatively rests in the ship, will really and absolutely move with the same velocity which the ship has on the earth. But if the earth also moves, the true and absolute motion of the body will arise, partly from the true motion of the earth, in immovable space, partly from the relative motion of the ship on the earth. . . .

Wherefore relative quantities are not the quantities themselves whose names they bear, but those sensible measures of them (either accurate or inaccurate), which are commonly used instead of the measured quantities themselves. And if the meaning of words is to be determined by their use, then by the names of time, space, place, and motion, their measures are properly to be understood; and the expression will be unusual, and purely mathematical, if the measured quantities themselves are meant. On this account, those violate the accuracy of language, which ought to be kept precise, who interpret these words for the measured quantities. Nor do those less defile the purity of mathematical and philosophical truths, who confound real quantities with their relations and sensible measures.

It is indeed a matter of great difficulty to discover, and effectually to distinguish, the true motions of particular bodies from the apparent; because the parts of immovable space, in which those motions are performed, do by no means come under the observation of our senses. Yet the thing is not altogether desperate; for we have some arguments to guide us, partly from the apparent motions; partly from the forces, which are the causes and effects of the true motions. For instance, if two globes kept at a given distance one from the other by means of a cord that connects them, were revolved about their common centre of gravity, we might from the tension of the cord, discover the endeavor of the globes to recede.... And thus we might find both the quantity and the determination of this circular motion, even in an immense vacuum, where there was nothing external or sensible with which the globes could be compared. But now, if in that space some remote bodies were placed that kept always at a given position to one another, as the fixed stars do in our regions, we could not indeed determine whether from the motion did belong to the globes or to the bodies. But if we observed the cord, and found that its tension was that very tension which the motions of the globes required, we might conclude the motion to be in the globes.... But how we are to obtain the true motions from their causes, effects, and apparent differences, and the converse, shall be explained more at length in the following treatise. For to this end it was that I composed it.

These passages are significant both for their explicit conclusions and for the implicit method used to justify them. Notions of absolute space and time continue to dog physics until they are overthrown by Einstein.[21] We can also see that Newton was a rationalist. He sought to define space and time in themselves, apart from their relation to "sensible objects." In this, he sought to render his system "mathematical" as opposed to "common." Although he was not insensitive to experimental difficulties in determining absolute motion, and he proposed some apparati for measuring motion in absolute space, his emphasis was on defining true mathematical notions independent of observation.

The Theory of Gravitation

Newton also formulated a theory of gravitation that endured for centuries. We have already seen that Newton defined the quantitative measure of matter, its mass, with respect to inertia. Newton also proposed that matter attracts other matter in proportion to the quantity of masses involved and the inverse square of the distances between them. These laws of gravitation gave formal, mathematical ways to account for both the motions of the planets and of falling bodies. Kepler's idea of attraction—without the magnet—is preserved, but his concepts of the spinning sun and its whirlpool effect are jettisoned in favor of mathematical relations.

The concept of inertia is crucial for Newton's explanation. Since Newton proposed that continuous motion is an innate force of matter, he does not need, as Kepler did, a mechanical impetus that keeps the planets moving. Once Newton described the effects of gravity, he could dispense with the vague analogies used by Kepler.

PRINCIPIA, BOOK III

PROPOSITIONS

PROPOSITION IV. THEOREM IV

That the moon gravitates towards the earth, and by the force of gravity is continually drawn off from rectilinear motion, and retained in its orbit. . . .

The demonstration of this Proposition may be more diffusely explained in the following manner. Suppose several moons to revolve about the earth. . . . Now, if the lowest of these were very small, and were so near the earth as almost to touch the tops of the highest mountains, the centripetal force[22] thereof, retaining it in its orbit, would be nearly equal to the weights of any terrestrial bodies that should be found on the tops of those mountains. . . . Therefore, if the same little moon should be deserted by its centrifugal force[23] . . . and be disabled from going onward therein, it would descend to the earth. . . . Therefore since both these forces, that is, the gravity of heavy bodies, and the centripetal forces of the moons, are directed to the centre of the earth, are similar and equal between themselves, they will . . . have one and the same cause. And therefore the force which retains the moon in its orbit is that very force which we commonly call gravity. . . .

PROPOSITION VI. THEOREM VI

That all bodies gravitate towards every planet; and that the weights of bodies towards any one planet, at equal distances from the centre of the planet, are proportional to the quantities of matter which they severally contain.

It has been shown for a long time, observed by others, that all sorts of heavy bodies ... descend to the earth *from equal heights* in equal times....

Cor. V. The power of gravity is of a different nature from the power of magnetism; for the magnetic attraction is not as the matter attracted. Some bodies are attracted more by the magnet, others less. ...

PROPOSITION VII. THEOREM VII

That there is a power of gravity pertaining to all bodies, proportional to the several quantities of matter which they contain. ...

PROPOSITION VIII. THEOREM VIII

In two spheres gravitating towards the other, if the matter in places on all sides round about and equidistant from the centers is similar, the weight of either sphere towards the other will be inversely as the square of the distance between their centers. ...

HYPOTHESIS I.

That the centre of the system of the world is immovable. ...

PROPOSITION XIII. THEOREM XIII

The planets move in ellipses which have their common focus in the centre of the sun; and, by radii drawn to that centre, they describe areas proportional to the times of description.

Newton was at a loss to explain the exact mechanism for gravitational attraction, however. Inertia is an innate force of matter, according to Newton, but not gravity. He said in a letter to his friend Bentley, who subscribed to the notion that gravity was an active quality of matter, "You sometimes speak of gravity as essential and inherent to matter. Pray, do not ascribe that notion to me; for the cause of gravity is what I do not pretend to know, and therefore would take more time to consider of it."[24] He goes on to state in another letter:

It is inconceivable, that inanimate and brute matter should, without the mediation of something else, which is not material, operate upon, and affect other matter without mutual contact; as it must do, if gravitation ... be essential and inherent in it. And this is one reason, why I desire you would not ascribe innate gravity to me. That gravity should be innate, inherent and essential to matter, so that one body may act on another at a distance through a *vacuum*, without the mediation of anything else ... is to me so great an absurdity, that I believe no man who has in philosophical matters a competent faculty of thinking, can ever fall into it. Gravity must be caused by an agent acting constantly ... but whether this agent be material or immaterial, I have left to the consideration of my readers."[25]

This shows Newton's desire for a fully mechanical system, as well as an important incompleteness. It was for this omission that many of Newton's contemporaries criticized him. Newton also failed to connect the inertial properties of matter with the gravitational properties, a step Einstein takes in general relativity centuries later. Until then, the dual inertial and gravitational properties of mass remain mysteriously connected yet unexplained.

Newton's powers of abstraction gave modern physics to the world. His predilection for precise, mathematical method resulted in the most powerful system of mechanics yet seen. Furthermore, Newton's Three Laws make no reference to anything but antecedent causes of motion, in this case forces which result from contact between masses. His mathematical model for natural philosophy rejects purposive, final causes as necessary postulates of mechanical motion. In this way Newton rejected anthropocentric reasoning in physical science.

Newton's abstract postulates did not stop at the physical, however, and despite his desires to the contrary, Newton delved into arenas where empirical science could find no footing. His postulates of absolute space and time are nonempirical constructions that cohere well with Newton's focus on a purely mathematical physics, but which remain at odds with much of the empiricism fostered by the new scientific revolution. Newton also speculated on issues of divine creation and governance, another element of Newtonian physics and metaphysics. Newton attempted to justify his efforts with methodological arguments in science and philosophy, as we will see in Chapter 4.

Summary

In this chapter we have witnessed the banishment of final causation from physics, the rise of a mechanistic world-view, and the triumph of quantitative formulation and observation. Philosophy also embraced these scientific developments as we see in the next chapter. Notably, the banishment of secondary qualities from nature serves as a transition to our study of Cartesianism. Throughout, however, modern science is still based on the Aristotelian notion that the world is intelligible.

It is worth noting that all of the figures in this chapter attend to the sentiments which make undertaking our study worthwhile. That is, the previous selections, many of which are taken from popularized, non-technical writings, are explicitly intended to inform and otherwise influence the state of Western culture as a whole. By interpreting their works for uninitiated, traditional, and skeptical readers of Europe at the dawn of the modern age, Kepler, Galileo, Newton, and many other figures of their time wrought an unprecedented revolution not merely in physics and philosophy but in the mental matrix of the Western human being. The strange, labyrinthine feeling one experiences trying to unravel medieval views; the mixture of recognition and alienation one feels in reading the Ancients; and the affinity we can have with the ideas of modernity all attest to the deep effects of the scientific, philosophical, and cultural revolution of the seventeenth century.

This revolution has sometimes been sanitized for presentation as a road of simple discovery. Kepler's *New Astronomy* belies this to anyone who would care to look at the pages of false starts, rejected approaches, backtracks, and missteps. The observations of Tycho were brilliant and necessary for the new astronomy, but they were not sufficient to overcome the geocentrism of Tycho himself. And Galileo, Newton, Leibniz, and their contemporaries disagreed about many fundamental principles. Through all this important dialogue, the diligence and creative insights of the age shine forth. As Butterfield says in *The Origins of Modern Science*, "the course of the seventeenth century . . . represents one of the great episodes in human experience . . . amongst the epic adventures that have helped to make the human race what it is. It represents one of those periods when new things are brought into the world and into history out of [our] own creative activity."[26]

Seventeenth-century mechanism resulted from the successful application of reductionism to natural science. Galileo reduced the number of properties and materials required for a scientific explanation of nature. All material, both heavenly and earthly, were now seen to be of similar makeup in opposition to the multiplicity of types of bodies in the Aristotelian cosmos. Qualitative experiences such as heat were reduced to objective motions and interactions of tiny particles, thus reducing the number of properties essential in nature. Newton reduced the number of universal laws to three mechanical laws of motion and one theory of gravity. Thus, natural phenomena were reduced to an essentially mechanical system of basic laws, properties, and materials. We will see in the next chapter some philosophical counterparts to the reductionism, mechanism, and analytic rationalism used by these seventeenth-century scientists. Cartesian metaphysics and rival theories that accompanied it spawned centuries of progress and controversy in both science and philosophy.

Notes

1. Sir Herbert Butterfield, *The Origins of Modern Science* (New York: Macmillan, 1949).

2. A.N. Whitehead, in *Science and the Modern World*, accuses scientists of being perennially vague about what they mean by mechanism, and the definition herein is not explicitly found in any specific scientific treatise.

3. See Anaximander, Chapter 1.

4. There are some philosophers who attempt to reconcile free will and determinism. Such doctrines are known as compatibilism, and we will see one example of a compatibilist philosophy in studying the work of J.S. Mill in Chapter 9. On the surface, however, there are tensions between the idea that human beings are free decision makers while the universe is governed by purely deterministic laws.

5. See note 1, Chapter 2.

6. Galileo first began experimenting with rudimentary clocks in order to measure pulse rates as a student at the University of Pisa in 1581. He went on to formalize mathematical laws of pendulum behavior and to develop practical models for a pendulum clock. He maintained an interest in measuring time throughout his life and continued to correspond with other interested parties on the subject even under house arrest after his condemnation by the Church. (Bern Dibner, "Galileo the Innovator," in *A Letter from Galileo*, Burndy Library, Norwalk, Connecticut, 1967.)

7. See Paul Feyerabend, *Against Method* (London: New Left Books, 1975) 130, for example.

8. Reprinted with permission of The University of Chicago Press from Galileo, *Sidereus Nuncius*, Albert van Helden, trans. (Chicago: The University of Chicago Press, 1989).

9. See Chapter 4 for a treatment of Descartes' philosophy. Descartes was also a scientist, and could be given a section in this chapter. Historical accuracy would favor this, since Descartes preceded Newton, but Descartes is most famous for his philosophical writings, and so a topical organization such as the current one dictates that Cartesian metaphysics be presented with the other metaphysical systems of the next chapter.

10. From *Introduction to Contemporary Civilization in the West*, Vol. I (second edition). Copyright © 1954, Columbia University Press. Reprinted with permission of the publisher.

11. This label was given to Aristotle's own followers who discoursed with the master while walking.

12. Galileo, *Dialogues Concerning the Two Chief World Systems: The Ptolemaic and Copernican*, second revised edition, translated/edited by Drake, Stillman. Copyright © 1952, 1962, 1967, Regents of the University of California.

13. Galileo, *Dialogues Concerning the Two New Sciences* (New York: Macmillan, 1914). Copyright 1914 by the Macmillan Company.

14. Various results in subsequent mathematical history, e.g., work by Fourier, actually prove that any path can be arbitrarily closely approximated with a finite number of circles.

15. Reprinted with permission from *The Great Books of the Western World* (Chicago: Encyclopaedia Britannica, Inc., 1952). Copyright 1952, 1990 Encyclopaedia Britannica, Inc.

16. Johannes Kepler, *The Dream*, John Lear, ed., Patricia Frueh Kirkwood, transl., (Berkeley: University of California Press, 1965).

17. Reprinted in Albert Van Helden, "Conclusion" to Galileo's *Sidereus Nuncius*, 1989.

18. See Michael Matthews, *The Scientific Background to Modern Philosophy* (Indianapolis: Hackett, 1989), 133, for example.

19. Descartes developed his views on inertia before Newton, e.g., this passage from Descartes' *The World*: ". . . each individual part of matter continues always to be in the same state so long as collision with others does not force it to change that state . . . if it is brought to rest in some place, it will never leave that place unless others drive it out; and if it has once begun to move, it will always continue with an equal force until others stop or retard it." Descartes' other lasting contributions to science include the Cartesian coordinate system and the law of conservation of momentum.

20. Reprinted from Isaac Newton, *Mathematical Principles of Natural Philosophy and His System of the World*, Florian Cajori, ed., trans./ed. by Andrew Motte. Copyright 1934 and 1962 by the Regents of the University of California. Used by permission.

21. Some philosophers argue that Einstein only changed the character of spatial geometry. While he earlier favored rejection of any notion of absolute space, in his later years Einstein had doubts about the possibility of physical theory without some kind of independently existing space. Nevertheless, the most straightforward interpretation of special relativity is that it is intended to transcend ideas of absolute space (see Chapter 10).

22. That is, the force drawing the body toward the center of its orbit.

23. Which is no more than the effect of its inertia.

24. Second of the "Letters to Dr. Bentley," in *Opera quae Exstant Omnia*, V. IV, 437; also quoted in Cajori's appendix to *Principia*, Volume II, 633.

25. Third Letter to Bentley, *Opera*, V. IV, 439.

26. Butterfield, 179.

Suggestions for Further Reading

Armitage, *The World of Copernicus* (New York: Mentor Books, 1961).

Burtt, Edwin Arthur, *The Metaphysical Foundations of Modern Physical Science* (New York: Harcourt, Brace, 1925).

Butterfield, Sir Herbert, *The Origins of Modern Science* (New York: Macmillan, 1958).

Feyerabend, Paul, *Against Method* (New York: New Left Books, 1975).

Chapter

4

Seventeenth- and Eighteenth-Century Transformations in Metaphysics

The seventeenth-century revolution in science was bound up with transformations in philosophy. Galileo and Newton were as much philosophers as scientists, and we will see that René Descartes was a scientist as well as the founder of modern philosophy. Descartes, for example, proposed laws of inertia before Newton. Philosophical and scientific thinking intermingled and converged in the seventeenth century, emphasizing the same themes and producing some of the same results. Both scientists and philosophers used reductionist techniques in analyzing the material substance of the world. Such abstraction and analysis concerning matter yielded the postulates of inertia, among other developments. Natural philosophers developed theories concerning the status of qualitative experience and the use of human centered analogistic reasoning, e.g., final causation. And the seventeenth-century scientific revolution was both inspired by and productive of new mathematical modes of thought—both Leibniz and Newton share credit for the invention of the calculus, for instance. In this chapter we will explore this serendipitous relationship between philosophy and science in the early modern period.

Both Descartes and Galileo helped banish secondary qualities from nature. Descartes constructed a philosophy of subject and object, equating the physical with the objective, the mental with the subjective. What many of the ancients considered qualities in nature were relegated to subjective status.

While Descartes came to the conclusion that certainty and metaphysical priority can be found in the mental, or subjective, realm, science takes the opposite tack. This allowed science to proceed in the realm of the physical and quantitative. Cartesian dualism led to a division of labor between science and philosophy, between the world of objective material reality and essential human nature, which some twentieth-century philosophers and scientists have come to lament. And in purely physical theory, this bifurcation has led to an impasse that only a radical transformation in the classical mechanics inspired by dualism has been able to overcome. This transformation takes place in the form of quantum theory, which in some interpretations breaks down a strictly dualistic world-view.

Analytic philosophy and epistemology came to the fore on the continent while empiricism took hold in Britain. Immanuel Kant, Germany's great enlightenment philosopher, continued to emphasize the certainty found in analytic reasoning and like Descartes was concerned with demonstrability and method. The British empiricist David Hume used modern philosophy to attack a form of scientific realism. We will focus in this chapter on the philosophical systems of modernity that cohere with the scientific systems of the previous chapter, and in the next chapter we will continue the examination of scientific and philosophical interaction by considering what practitioners of each have to say about method.

Descartes

René Descartes was born in 1596 at La Haye near Tours, France, and died in 1650 at Stockholm. He lived for much of his professional life in Holland, a haven for unconventional thinkers. This was especially important at the time, since Descartes was working contemporaneously with Galileo, whose political troubles were discussed briefly in the previous chapter. Indeed, Galileo's condemnation by the church made Descartes reluctant to publish some of his works—*The World*, an excerpt of which follows, was published posthumously. His untimely death is reputed to have been a result of Queen Christina of Sweden's insistence that he rise early in the cold northern climate to tutor.

Scientific Philosophy

Descartes published treatises on optics, biology, and cosmology, but is primarily remembered for his writings on traditional philosophical subjects. His work did contain some basic scientific content, however, and in this section we will see how Descartes the philosopher approached the same problems that the scientists in the previous chapter tackled. The following excerpts are from *The World, Principles of Philosophy, Rules for Direction of the Mind,* and *Discourse of the Method.*[1]

THE WORLD OR TREATISE ON LIGHT

The subject I propose to deal with in this treatise is light, and the first point I want to draw to your attention is that there may be a difference between the sensation we have of light (i.e., the idea of light which is formed in our imagination by the mediation of our eyes) and what it is in the objects that produces this sensation (i.e., what it is in a flame or the sun that we call by the name "light"). For although everyone is commonly convinced that the ideas we have in our mind are wholly similar to the objects from which they proceed, nevertheless I cannot see any reason which assures us that this is so. . . .

When flame burns wood or some other similar material, we can see with the naked eye that it sets the minute parts of the wood in motion. . . . Others may, if they wish, imagine the form of fire, the quality of heat, and the process of burning to be completely different things in the wood. For my part, I am afraid of mistakenly supposing there is anything more in the wood than what I see must necessarily be in it, and so I am content to limit my conception to the motion of its parts. . . .

[A]mong the qualities of matter, we have supposed that its parts have had various different motions from the moment they were created. . . . And it is easy to accept that God, who is, as everyone must know, immutable, always acts in the same way. But without involving myself further in these metaphysical considerations, I shall set out two or three of the principal rules according to which it must be thought that God causes the nature of this new world to operate. . . .

The first is that each individual part of matter continues always to be in the same state so long as collision with others does not force it to change that state . . . if it is brought to rest in some place, it will never leave that place unless others drive it out; and if it has once begun to move, it will always continue with an equal force until others stop or retard it. . . .

I suppose as a second rule that when one body pushes another it cannot give the other any motion unless it loses as much of its own motion at the same time; nor can it take away any of the other's motion unless its own is increased by that much. . . .

PRINCIPLES OF PHILOSOPHY

Part Two

The Principles of Material Things

. . . we have a clear understanding of . . . matter as something that is quite different from ourselves or our mind; and we appear to see clearly that the idea of it comes to us from things located outside ourselves, which it wholly resembles. . . .

It will be enough, for the present, to note that sensory perceptions . . . normally tell us of the benefit or harm that external bodies may do . . . and do not, except occasionally and accidentally, show us what external bodies are like in themselves. If we bear this in mind, we will easily lay aside the preconceived opinions acquired from the senses, and in this connection make use of the intellect alone. . . .

If we do this, we shall perceive that the nature of matter, or body considered in general, consists not in its being something which is hard or heavy or coloured, or which affects the senses in any way, but simply in its being something which is extended in length, breadth, and depth. . . .

From God's immutability we can know certain rules or laws of nature. . . . The first of these laws is that each thing, in so far as it is simple and undivided, always remains in the same state, as far as it can, and never changes except as a result of external causes. . . . If it is at rest, we hold that it will never begin to move unless it is pushed into motion by some cause. And if it moves, there is equally no reason for thinking it will ever lose this motion of its own accord and without being checked by something else. . . . But we live near the Earth, whose composition is such that all motions occurring near it are soon halted, often by causes undetectable by our senses. Hence from our earliest years we have judged that such motions . . . come to an end of their own accord. . . .

The second law is that every piece of matter, considered in itself, always tends to continue moving, not in any oblique path but only in a straight line. . . .

These selections show that Descartes agrees with Galileo that the concept of physical matter must be abstracted from our qualitative notion of sensible things. For example, they agree that heat is a qualitative bodily affect, not an objective phenomenon of nature. Descartes originally formulated the concept of inertia. Such a formula crucially rejects Aristotelian circular motion and final causation. Circular motion is not natural, according to Descartes; rather, curved motion of any kind must be explained by analyzing external causes. And these causes are not teleological: no notion of proper place or end is employed. These concepts are obviously fundamental for scientific thinking in the seventeenth century, and they are originally found within philosophical discourses on method, existence, certainty, and theology. We will see Descartes' notions of these in the following sections.

Analytic, Sceptical Method

Descartes himself believed that his most important contribution to philosophy was his method. Unfortunately, he never explicitly and unequivocally laid out a schema for this method, even in his promisingly titled *Discourse on the Method*. He chose to proceed mostly by example, and the attempts at description he does provide are often vague and conflicting. Nevertheless, it is at least clear that his method was one of doubt and analysis. The following selections from *Rules for Direction of the Mind*, the *Discourse*, and *Principles* highlight Cartesian methodology.

RULES FOR DIRECTION OF THE MIND

RULE FOUR

We need a method if we are to investigate the truth of things.

So blind is the curiosity with which mortals are possessed that they often direct their minds down untrodden paths, in the groundless hope that they will chance upon what they are seeking....

When I first applied my mind to mathematical disciplines, ... I paid special attention to arithmetic and geometry, for these were said to be the simplest and, as it were, to lead into the rest. But in neither subject did I come across writers who fully satisfied me ... they did not seem to make sufficiently clear to my mind why these things should be so and how they were discovered....

RULE FIVE

The whole method consists entirely in the ordering and arranging of the objects on which we must concentrate our minds' eye if we are to discover some truth. We shall be following this method exactly if we first reduce complicated and obscure propositions step by step to simpler ones, and then, starting with the intuition of the simplest ones of all, to ascend through the same steps to a knowledge of all the rest.

This one Rule covers the most essential points in the whole of human endeavor. . . .

DISCOURSE
ON THE METHOD

PART ONE

Regarding philosophy, I shall say only this: seeing that it has been cultivated for many centuries by the most excellent minds and yet there is still no point in it which is not disputed and hence doubtful, I was not so presumptuous as to hope to achieve any more in it than others had done. And, considering how many diverse opinions learned men may maintain on a single question—even though it is impossible for more than one to be true—I held as well-nigh false everything that was merely probable.

As for the other sciences, in so far as they borrow their principles from philosophy I decided that nothing solid could have been built upon such shaky foundations. . . .

That is why, as soon as I was old enough to emerge from the control of my teachers, I entirely abandoned the study of letters. . . . I spent the rest of my youth travelling . . . And it was always my most earnest desire to learn to distinguish the true from the false in order to see clearly into my own actions and proceed with confidence in this life.

It is true that, so long as I merely considered the customs of other men, I found hardly any reason for confidence, for I observed in them almost as much diversity as I had found previously among the opinions of philosophers. . . . I learned not to believe too firmly anything of which I had been persuaded only by example and custom.

PRINCIPLES OF PHILOSOPHY

PART ONE

THE PRINCIPLES OF HUMAN KNOWLEDGE

1. *The seeker after truth must, once in the course of his life, doubt everything as far as it is possible. . . .*
2. *What is doubtful should even be considered as false. . . .*

Descartes' method of doubt is crucial for modernity, both in science and philosophy, which as we have seen struggled to emerge from the medieval period. The Medievals were encumbered by at least two traditions: religious doctrine and the philosophical teachings of the ancients. Moderns such as Descartes and Galileo gave Western intellectual culture the courage and ammunition to attack both.

Descartes elaborated somewhat on his method, enjoining the seeker after truth to consider all preconceptions regarding the subject matter at hand as false. Furthermore, we are encouraged to follow an analytic prescription: reduce complex propositions to simple ones suitable for recognition by "intuition." It is this last step that is perhaps the most controversial, and Descartes' belief that human reason can recognize truths in this way makes his philosophy a rationalist one. We will see the specific results of Cartesian rationalism in the next section.

The Meditations

Descartes' *Meditations on First Philosophy*, published in 1641, is perhaps the most influential work in Western Philosophy. It has inspired students of metaphysics, epistemology, mind, and reason for centuries. It also lends itself to numerous interpretive techniques, since its organization and fictional presentations can be approached from literary, religious, or philosophical perspectives. Its elegance and accessibility all add to its impact.

Descartes also added to its moment by publishing the *Meditations* along with objections and replies. Most of the conclusions of the *Meditations* can be found in his earlier works, however, and serious study of his philosophy must be accompanied by study of these other treatises. Nevertheless, the most succinct and beautiful descriptions of Cartesian doubt, rationalism, analysis, and modern dualism are contained in the *Meditations*.

The theses of dualism—that mind and matter are fundamentally separate substances; that the essence of human existence is found in the subjective ego which is fundamentally a thinking thing; that the objective world of physical substance is wholly other than mind and essentially extensive and quantitative; and that certainty is the only basis for philosophy or science— transform all of Western culture from science to philosophy, politics to literature, theology to economics.

MEDITATION I[2]

OF THE THINGS OF WHICH WE MAY DOUBT

1. SEVERAL years have now elapsed since I first became aware that I had accepted, even from my youth, many false opinions for true, and that consequently what I afterward based on such principles was highly doubtful; and from that time I was convinced of the necessity of undertaking once in my life to rid myself of all the opinions I had adopted, and of commencing anew the work of building from the foundation, if I desired to establish a firm and abiding superstructure in the sciences. But as this enterprise appeared to me to be one of great magnitude, I waited until I had attained an age so mature as to leave me no hope that at any stage of life more advanced I should be better able to execute my design. On this account, I have delayed so long that I should henceforth consider I was doing wrong were I still to consume in deliberation any of the time that now remains for action. To-day, then, since I have opportunely freed my mind from all cares [and am happily disturbed by no passions], and since I am in the secure possession of leisure in a peaceable retirement, I will at length apply myself earnestly and freely to the general overthrow of all my former opinions.

2. But, to this end, it will not be necessary for me to show that the whole of these are false—a point, perhaps, which I shall never reach; but as even now my reason convinces me that I ought not the less carefully to withhold belief from what is not entirely certain and indubitable, than from what is manifestly false, it will be sufficient to justify the rejection of the whole if I shall find in each some ground for doubt. Nor for this purpose will it be necessary even to deal with each belief individually, which would be truly an endless labor; but,

as the removal from below of the foundation necessarily involves the downfall of the whole edifice, I will at once approach the criticism of the principles on which all my former beliefs rested.

3.   All that I have, up to this moment, accepted as possessed of the highest truth and certainty, I received either from or through the senses. I observed, however, that these sometimes misled us; and it is the part of prudence not to place absolute confidence in that by which we have even once been deceived.

4. But it may be said, perhaps, that, although the senses occasionally mislead us respecting minute objects, and such as are so far removed from us as to be beyond the reach of close observation, there are yet many other of their informations (presentations), of the truth of which it is manifestly impossible to doubt; as for example, that I am in this place, seated by the fire, clothed in a winter dressing gown, that I hold in my hands this piece of paper, with other intimations of the same nature. But how could I deny that I possess these hands and this body, and withal escape being classed with persons in a state of insanity, whose brains are so disordered and clouded by dark bilious vapors as to cause them pertinaciously to assert that they are monarchs when they are in the greatest poverty; or clothed [in gold] and purple when destitute of any covering; or that their head is made of clay, their body of glass, or that they are gourds? I should certainly be not less insane than they, were I to regulate my procedure according to examples so extravagant.

5. Though this be true, I must nevertheless here consider that I am a man, and that, consequently, I am in the habit of sleeping, and representing to myself in dreams those same things, or even sometimes others less probable, which the insane think are presented to them in their waking moments. How often have I dreamt that I was in these familiar circumstances, that I was dressed, and occupied this place by the fire, when I was lying undressed in bed? At the present moment, however, I certainly look upon this paper with eyes wide awake; the head which I now move is not asleep; I extend this hand consciously and with express purpose, and I perceive it; the occurrences in sleep are not so distinct as all this. But I cannot forget that, at other times I have been deceived in sleep by similar illusions; and, attentively considering those cases, I perceive so clearly that there exist no certain marks by which the state of waking can ever be distinguished from

sleep, that I feel greatly astonished; and in amazement I almost persuade myself that I am now dreaming.

6. Let us suppose, then, that we are dreaming, and that all these particulars—namely, the opening of the eyes, the motion of the head, the forth-putting of the hands—are merely illusions; and even that we really possess neither an entire body nor hands such as we see. Nevertheless it must be admitted at least that the objects which appear to us in sleep are, as it were, painted representations which could not have been formed unless in the likeness of realities; and, therefore, that those general objects, at all events, namely, eyes, a head, hands, and an entire body, are not simply imaginary, but really existent. For, in truth, painters themselves, even when they study to represent sirens and satyrs by forms the most fantastic and extraordinary, cannot bestow upon them natures absolutely new, but can only make a certain medley of the members of different animals; or if they chance to imagine something so novel that nothing at all similar has ever been seen before, and such as is, therefore, purely fictitious and absolutely false, it is at least certain that the colors of which this is composed are real. And on the same principle, although these general objects, viz. [a body], eyes, a head, hands, and the like, be imaginary, we are nevertheless absolutely necessitated to admit the reality at least of some other objects still more simple and universal than these, of which, just as of certain real colors, all those images of things, whether true and real, or false and fantastic, that are found in our consciousness (cogitatio), are formed.

7. To this class of objects seem to belong corporeal nature in general and its extension; the figure of extended things, their quantity or magnitude, and their number, as also the place in, and the time during, which they exist, and other things of the same sort.

8. We will not, therefore, perhaps reason illegitimately if we conclude from this that Physics, Astronomy, Medicine, and all the other sciences that have for their end the consideration of composite objects, are indeed of a doubtful character; but that Arithmetic, Geometry, and the other sciences of the same class, which regard merely the simplest and most general objects, and scarcely inquire whether or not these are really existent, contain somewhat that is certain and indubitable: for whether I am awake or dreaming, it remains true that two and three make five, and that a square has but four sides; nor does it seem possible that truths so apparent can ever fall under a suspicion of falsity [or incertitude].

9. Nevertheless, the belief that there is a God who is all powerful, and who created me, such as I am, has, for a long time, obtained steady possession of my mind. How, then, do I know that he has not arranged that there should be neither earth, nor sky, nor any extended thing, nor figure, nor magnitude, nor place, providing at the same time, however, for [the rise in me of the perceptions of all these objects, and] the persuasion that these do not exist otherwise than as I perceive them? And further, as I sometimes think that others are in error respecting matters of which they believe themselves to possess a perfect knowledge, how do I know that I am not also deceived each time I add together two and three, or number the sides of a square, or form some judgment still more simple, if more simple indeed can be imagined? But perhaps Deity has not been willing that I should be thus deceived, for he is said to be supremely good. If, however, it were repugnant to the goodness of Deity to have created me subject to constant deception, it would seem likewise to be contrary to his goodness to allow me to be occasionally deceived; and yet it is clear that this is permitted.

10. Some, indeed, might perhaps be found who would be disposed rather to deny the existence of a Being so powerful than to believe that there is nothing certain. But let us for the present refrain from opposing this opinion, and grant that all which is here said of a Deity is fabulous: nevertheless, in whatever way it be supposed that I reach the state in which I exist, whether by fate, or chance, or by an endless series of antecedents and consequents, or by any other means, it is clear (since to be deceived and to err is a certain defect) that the probability of my being so imperfect as to be the constant victim of deception, will be increased exactly in proportion as the power possessed by the cause, to which they assign my origin, is lessened. To these reasonings I have assuredly nothing to reply, but am constrained at last to avow that there is nothing of all that I formerly believed to be true of which it is impossible to doubt, and that not through thoughtlessness or levity, but from cogent and maturely considered reasons; so that henceforward, if I desire to discover anything certain, I ought not the less carefully to refrain from assenting to those same opinions than to what might be shown to be manifestly false.

11. But it is not sufficient to have made these observations; care must be taken likewise to keep them in remembrance. For those old and customary opinions perpetually recur—long and familiar usage

giving them the right of occupying my mind, even almost against my will, and subduing my belief; nor will I lose the habit of deferring to them and confiding in them so long as I shall consider them to be what in truth they are, viz, opinions to some extent doubtful, as I have already shown, but still highly probable, and such as it is much more reasonable to believe than deny. It is for this reason I am persuaded that I shall not be doing wrong, if, taking an opposite judgment of deliberate design, I become my own deceiver, by supposing, for a time, that all those opinions are entirely false and imaginary, until at length, having thus balanced my old by my new prejudices, my judgment shall no longer be turned aside by perverted usage from the path that may conduct to the perception of truth. For I am assured that, meanwhile, there will arise neither peril nor error from this course, and that I cannot for the present yield too much to distrust, since the end I now seek is not action but knowledge.

12. I will suppose, then, not that Deity, who is sovereignly good and the fountain of truth, but that some malignant demon, who is at once exceedingly potent and deceitful, has employed all his artifice to deceive me; I will suppose that the sky, the air, the earth, colors, figures, sounds, and all external things, are nothing better than the illusions of dreams, by means of which this being has laid snares for my credulity; I will consider myself as without hands, eyes, flesh, blood, or any of the senses, and as falsely believing that I am possessed of these; I will continue resolutely fixed in this belief, and if indeed by this means it be not in my power to arrive at the knowledge of truth, I shall at least do what is in my power, viz, [suspend my judgment], and guard with settled purpose against giving my assent to what is false, and being imposed upon by this deceiver, whatever be his power and artifice. But this undertaking is arduous, and a certain indolence insensibly leads me back to my ordinary course of life; and just as the captive, who, perchance, was enjoying in his dreams an imaginary liberty, when he begins to suspect that it is but a vision, dreads awakening, and conspires with the agreeable illusions that the deception may be prolonged; so I, of my own accord, fall back into the train of my former beliefs, and fear to arouse myself from my slumber, lest the time of laborious wakefulness that would succeed this quiet rest, in place of bringing any light of day, should prove inadequate to dispel the darkness that will arise from the difficulties that have now been raised.

MEDITATION II

OF THE NATURE OF THE HUMAN MIND;
AND THAT IT IS MORE EASILY KNOWN THAN THE BODY

1. The Meditation of yesterday has filled my mind with so many doubts, that it is no longer in my power to forget them. Nor do I see, meanwhile, any principle on which they can be resolved; and, just as if I had fallen all of a sudden into very deep water, I am so greatly disconcerted as to be unable either to plant my feet firmly on the bottom or sustain myself by swimming on the surface. I will, nevertheless, make an effort, and try anew the same path on which I had entered yesterday, that is, proceed by casting aside all that admits of the slightest doubt, not less than if I had discovered it to be absolutely false; and I will continue always in this track until I shall find something that is certain, or at least, if I can do nothing more, until I shall know with certainty that there is nothing certain. Archimedes, that he might transport the entire globe from the place it occupied to another, demanded only a point that was firm and immovable; so, also, I shall be entitled to entertain the highest expectations, if I am fortunate enough to discover only one thing that is certain and indubitable.

2. I suppose, accordingly, that all the things which I see are false (fictitious); I believe that none of those objects which my fallacious memory represents ever existed; I suppose that I possess no senses; I believe that body, figure, extension, motion, and place are merely fictions of my mind. What is there, then, that can be esteemed true? Perhaps this only, that there is absolutely nothing certain.

3. But how do I know that there is not something different altogether from the objects I have now enumerated, of which it is impossible to entertain the slightest doubt? Is there not a God, or some being, by whatever name I may designate him, who causes these thoughts to arise in my mind? But why suppose such a being, for it may be I myself am capable of producing them? Am I, then, at least not something? But I before denied that I possessed senses or a body; I hesitate, however, for what follows from that? Am I so dependent on the body and the senses that without these I cannot exist? But I had the persuasion that there was absolutely nothing in the world, that there was no sky and no earth, neither minds nor bodies; was I not, therefore, at the same time, persuaded that I did not exist? Far from

it; I assuredly existed, since I was persuaded. But there is I know not what being, who is possessed at once of the highest power and the deepest cunning, who is constantly employing all his ingenuity in deceiving me. Doubtless, then, I exist, since I am deceived; and, let him deceive me as he may, he can never bring it about that I am nothing, so long as I shall be conscious that I am something. So that it must, in fine, be maintained, all things being maturely and carefully considered, that this proposition (pronunciatum) I am, I exist, is necessarily true each time it is expressed by me, or conceived in my mind.

4. But I do not yet know with sufficient clearness what I am, though assured that I am; and hence, in the next place, I must take care, lest perchance I inconsiderately substitute some other object in room of what is properly myself, and thus wander from truth, even in that knowledge (cognition) which I hold to be of all others the most certain and evident. For this reason, I will now consider anew what I formerly believed myself to be, before I entered on the present train of thought; and of my previous opinion I will retrench all that can in the least be invalidated by the grounds of doubt I have adduced, in order that there may at length remain nothing but what is certain and indubitable.

5. What then did I formerly think I was? Undoubtedly I judged that I was a man. But what is a man? Shall I say a rational animal? Assuredly not; for it would be necessary forthwith to inquire into what is meant by animal, and what by rational, and thus, from a single question, I should insensibly glide into others, and these more difficult than the first; nor do I now possess enough of leisure to warrant me in wasting my time amid subtleties of this sort. I prefer here to attend to the thoughts that sprung up of themselves in my mind, and were inspired by my own nature alone, when I applied myself to the consideration of what I was. In the first place, then, I thought that I possessed a countenance, hands, arms, and all the fabric of members that appears in a corpse, and which I called by the name of body. It further occurred to me that I was nourished, that I walked, perceived, and thought, and all those actions I referred to the soul; but what the soul itself was I either did not stay to consider, or, if I did, I imagined that it was something extremely rare and subtile, like wind, or flame, or ether, spread through my grosser parts. As regarded the body, I did not even doubt of its nature, but thought I distinctly knew it, and if I had wished to describe it according to the notions I then entertained, I should have explained myself in this manner: By

body I understand all that can be terminated by a certain figure; that can be comprised in a certain place, and so fill a certain space as therefrom to exclude every other body; that can be perceived either by touch, sight, hearing, taste, or smell; that can be moved in different ways, not indeed of itself, but by something foreign to it by which it is touched [and from which it receives the impression]; for the power of self-motion, as likewise that of perceiving and thinking, I held as by no means pertaining to the nature of body; on the contrary, I was somewhat astonished to find such faculties existing in some bodies.

6. But [as to myself, what can I now say that I am], since I suppose there exists an extremely powerful, and, if I may so speak, malignant being, whose whole endeavors are directed toward deceiving me? Can I affirm that I possess any one of all those attributes of which I have lately spoken as belonging to the nature of body? After attentively considering them in my own mind, I find none of them that can properly be said to belong to myself. To recount them were idle and tedious. Let us pass, then, to the attributes of the soul. The first mentioned were the powers of nutrition and walking; but, if it be true that I have no body, it is true likewise that I am capable neither of walking nor of being nourished. Perception is another attribute of the soul; but perception too is impossible without the body; besides, I have frequently, during sleep, believed that I perceived objects which I afterward observed I did not in reality perceive. Thinking is another attribute of the soul; and here I discover what properly belongs to myself. This alone is inseparable from me. I am—I exist: this is certain; but how often? As often as I think; for perhaps it would even happen, if I should wholly cease to think, that I should at the same time altogether cease to be. I now admit nothing that is not necessarily true. I am therefore, precisely speaking, only a thinking thing, that is, a mind (mens sive animus), understanding, or reason, terms whose signification was before unknown to me. I am, however, a real thing, and really existent; but what thing? The answer was, a thinking thing.

7. The question now arises, am I aught besides? I will stimulate my imagination with a view to discover whether I am not still something more than a thinking being. Now it is plain I am not the assemblage of members called the human body; I am not a thin and penetrating air diffused through all these members, or wind, or flame, or vapor, or breath, or any of all the things I can imagine; for I supposed that all these were not, and, without changing the supposition, I find that I still feel assured of my existence. But it is true, perhaps, that those

very things which I suppose to be non-existent, because they are un-known to me, are not in truth different from myself whom I know. This is a point I cannot determine, and do not now enter into any dispute regarding it. I can only judge of things that are known to me: I am conscious that I exist, and I who know that I exist inquire into what I am. It is, however, perfectly certain that the knowledge of my existence, thus precisely taken, is not dependent on things, the existence of which is as yet unknown to me: and consequently it is not dependent on any of the things I can feign in imagination. Moreover, the phrase itself, I frame an image (effingo), reminds me of my error; for I should in truth frame one if I were to imagine my-self to be anything, since to imagine is nothing more than to con-template the figure or image of a corporeal thing; but I already know that I exist, and that it is possible at the same time that all those images, and in general all that relates to the nature of body, are merely dreams [or chimeras]. From this I discover that it is not more reasonable to say, I will excite my imagination that I may know more distinctly what I am, than to express myself as follows: I am now awake, and perceive something real; but because my perception is not sufficiently clear, I will of express purpose go to sleep that my dreams may represent to me the object of my perception with more truth and clearness. And, therefore, I know that nothing of all that I can embrace in imagination belongs to the knowledge which I have of myself, and that there is need to recall with the utmost care the mind from this mode of thinking, that it may be able to know its own nature with perfect distinctness.

8. But what, then, am I? A thinking thing, it has been said. But what is a thinking thing? It is a thing that doubts, understands, [conceives], affirms, denies, wills, refuses; that imagines also, and perceives.

9. Assuredly it is not little, if all these properties belong to my na-ture. But why should they not belong to it? Am I not that very being who now doubts of almost everything; who, for all that, understands and conceives certain things; who affirms one alone as true, and de-nies the others; who desires to know more of them, and does not wish to be deceived; who imagines many things, sometimes even de-spite his will; and is likewise percipient of many, as if through the medium of the senses. Is there nothing of all this as true as that I am, even although I should be always dreaming, and although he who gave me being employed all his ingenuity to deceive me? Is there also any one of these attributes that can be properly distinguished from

my thought, or that can be said to be separate from myself? For it is of itself so evident that it is I who doubt, I who understand, and I who desire, that it is here unnecessary to add anything by way of rendering it more clear. And I am as certainly the same being who imagines; for although it may be (as I before supposed) that nothing I imagine is true, still the power of imagination does not cease really to exist in me and to form part of my thought. In fine, I am the same being who perceives, that is, who apprehends certain objects as by the organs of sense, since, in truth, I see light, hear a noise, and feel heat. But it will be said that these presentations are false, and that I am dreaming. Let it be so. At all events it is certain that I seem to see light, hear a noise, and feel heat; this cannot be false, and this is what in me is properly called perceiving (sentire), which is nothing else than thinking.

10. From this I begin to know what I am with somewhat greater clearness and distinctness than heretofore. But, nevertheless, it still seems to me, and I cannot help believing, that corporeal things, whose images are formed by thought [which fall under the senses], and are examined by the same, are known with much greater distinctness than that I know not what part of myself which is not imaginable; although, in truth, it may seem strange to say that I know and comprehend with greater distinctness things whose existence appears to me doubtful, that are unknown, and do not belong to me, than others of whose reality I am persuaded, that are known to me, and appertain to my proper nature; in a word, than myself. But I see clearly what is the state of the case. My mind is apt to wander, and will not yet submit to be restrained within the limits of truth. Let us therefore leave the mind to itself once more, and, according to it every kind of liberty [permit it to consider the objects that appear to it from without], in order that, having afterward withdrawn it from these gently and opportunely [and fixed it on the consideration of its being and the properties it finds in itself], it may then be the more easily controlled.

11. Let us now accordingly consider the objects that are commonly thought to be [the most easily, and likewise] the most distinctly known, viz, the bodies we touch and see; not, indeed, bodies in general, for these general notions are usually somewhat more confused, but one body in particular. Take, for example, this piece of wax; it is quite fresh, having been but recently taken from the beehive; it has not yet lost the sweetness of the honey it contained; it still retains

somewhat of the odor of the flowers from which it was gathered; its color, figure, size, are apparent (to the sight); it is hard, cold, easily handled; and sounds when struck upon with the finger. In fine, all that contributes to make a body as distinctly known as possible, is found in the one before us. But, while I am speaking, let it be placed near the fire—what remained of the taste exhales, the smell evaporates, the color changes, its figure is destroyed, its size increases, it becomes liquid, it grows hot, it can hardly be handled, and, although struck upon, it emits no sound. Does the same wax still remain after this change? It must be admitted that it does remain; no one doubts it, or judges otherwise. What, then, was it I knew with so much distinctness in the piece of wax? Assuredly, it could be nothing of all that I observed by means of the senses, since all the things that fell under taste, smell, sight, touch, and hearing are changed, and yet the same wax remains.

12. It was perhaps what I now think, viz, that this wax was neither the sweetness of honey, the pleasant odor of flowers, the whiteness, the figure, nor the sound, but only a body that a little before appeared to me conspicuous under these forms, and which is now perceived under others. But, to speak precisely, what is it that I imagine when I think of it in this way? Let it be attentively considered, and, retrenching all that does not belong to the wax, let us see what remains. There certainly remains nothing, except something extended, flexible, and movable. But what is meant by flexible and movable? Is it not that I imagine that the piece of wax, being round, is capable of becoming square, or of passing from a square into a triangular figure? Assuredly such is not the case, because I conceive that it admits of an infinity of similar changes; and I am, moreover, unable to compass this infinity by imagination, and consequently this conception which I have of the wax is not the product of the faculty of imagination. But what now is this extension? Is it not also unknown? for it becomes greater when the wax is melted, greater when it is boiled, and greater still when the heat increases; and I should not conceive [clearly and] according to truth, the wax as it is, if I did not suppose that the piece we are considering admitted even of a wider variety of extension than I ever imagined, I must, therefore, admit that I cannot even comprehend by imagination what the piece of wax is, and that it is the mind alone which perceives it. I speak of one piece in particular; for as to wax in general, this is still more evident. But what is the piece of wax that can be perceived only by the [understanding

or] mind? It is certainly the same which I see, touch, imagine; and, in fine, it is the same which, from the beginning, I believed it to be. But (and this it is of moment to observe) the perception of it is neither an act of sight, of touch, nor of imagination, and never was either of these, though it might formerly seem so, but is simply an intuition (inspectio) of the mind, which may be imperfect and confused, as it formerly was, or very clear and distinct, as it is at present, according as the attention is more or less directed to the elements which it contains, and of which it is composed.

13. But, meanwhile, I feel greatly astonished when I observe [the weakness of my mind, and] its proneness to error. For although, without at all giving expression to what I think, I consider all this in my own mind, words yet occasionally impede my progress, and I am almost led into error by the terms of ordinary language. We say, for example, that we see the same wax when it is before us, and not that we judge it to be the same from its retaining the same color and figure: whence I should forthwith be disposed to conclude that the wax is known by the act of sight, and not by the intuition of the mind alone, were it not for the analogous instance of human beings passing on in the street below, as observed from a window. In this case I do not fail to say that I see the men themselves, just as I say that I see the wax; and yet what do I see from the window beyond hats and cloaks that might cover artificial machines, whose motions might be determined by springs? But I judge that there are human beings from these appearances, and thus I comprehend, by the faculty of judgment alone which is in the mind, what I believed I saw with my eyes.

14. The man who makes it his aim to rise to knowledge superior to the common, ought to be ashamed to seek occasions of doubting from the vulgar forms of speech: instead, therefore, of doing this, I shall proceed with the matter in hand, and inquire whether I had a clearer and more perfect perception of the piece of wax when I first saw it, and when I thought I knew it by means of the external sense itself, or, at all events, by the common sense (sensus communis), as it is called, that is, by the imaginative faculty; or whether I rather apprehend it more clearly at present, after having examined with greater care, both what it is, and in what way it can be known. It would certainly be ridiculous to entertain any doubt on this point. For what, in that first perception, was there distinct? What did I perceive which any animal might not have perceived? But when I distinguish the wax from its exterior forms, and when, as if I had stripped

it of its vestments, I consider it quite naked, it is certain, although some error may still be found in my judgment, that I cannot, nevertheless, thus apprehend it without possessing a human mind.

15. But finally, what shall I say of the mind itself, that is, of myself? for as yet I do not admit that I am anything but mind. What, then! I who seem to possess so distinct an apprehension of the piece of wax, do I not know myself, both with greater truth and certitude, and also much more distinctly and clearly? For if I judge that the wax exists because I see it, it assuredly follows, much more evidently, that I myself am or exist, for the same reason: for it is possible that what I see may not in truth be wax, and that I do not even possess eyes with which to see anything; but it cannot be that when I see, or, which comes to the same thing, when I think I see, I myself who think am nothing. So likewise, if I judge that the wax exists because I touch it, it will still also follow that I am; and if I determine that my imagination, or any other cause, whatever it be, persuades me of the existence of the wax, I will still draw the same conclusion. And what is here remarked of the piece of wax, is applicable to all the other things that are external to me. And further, if the [notion or] perception of wax appeared to me more precise and distinct, after that not only sight and touch, but many other causes besides, rendered it manifest to my apprehension, with how much greater distinctness must I now know myself, since all the reasons that contribute to the knowledge of the nature of wax, or of any body whatever, manifest still better the nature of my mind? And there are besides so many other things in the mind itself that contribute to the illustration of its nature, that those dependent on the body, to which I have here referred, scarcely merit to be taken into account.

16. But, in conclusion, I find I have insensibly reverted to the point I desired; for, since it is now manifest to me that bodies themselves are not properly perceived by the senses nor by the faculty of imagination, but by the intellect alone; and since they are not perceived because they are seen and touched, but only because they are understood [or rightly comprehended by thought], I readily discover that there is nothing more easily or clearly apprehended than my own mind. But because it is difficult to rid one's self so promptly of an opinion to which one has been long accustomed, it will be desirable to tarry for some time at this stage, that, by long continued meditation, I may more deeply impress upon my memory this new knowledge.

Modern dualism is born. Philosophers seize on different parts of the Cartesian cogito, the "*cogito, ergo sum*" found in the *Discourse*, to form vastly different philosophical doctrines. For our purposes at present, we can see how Descartes' ideas fit in with quantification and objectification as a goal of physical science.

It is also clear that philosophy and science were struggling to rid themselves of the evaluative encumbrances of religious and ancient doctrines. Descartes placed qualitative experience, including valuing and striving, in the subjective ego. Mental existence was completely separate from the extended world of objects. Thus, scientists and philosophers were free to say that the world of things does not have ends and purposes like the world of mind. Aristotle's analogical reasoning from human to physical was no longer warranted. His answer "To be healthy" to the question "Why is he walking about?" was not relevant to the physical world in a modern dualistic system. This is crucial for understanding how modern science attempted to banish values from its discourse and its objects.

While Descartes locates certainty in the subjective ego who thinks, other inheritors of dualism place such certainty in the objective world of quantitative measurement. In this way, science gradually sets itself up as the prime arbitrator of certainty in the physical world. Philosophy becomes increasingly focused on issues in ethics and epistemology, both of which explicitly involve a human, and thus mental, component. This division of labor is not universally (nor even overwhelmingly) accepted, however, and philosophical metaphysicians continue to delve into issues of physical reality, as we will see in the next section. Such speculations are increasingly taken to be irrelevant by scientists and the world at large, however, as we will see in later chapters.

An Analytic Metaphysics

Gottfried Wilhelm Leibniz was born at Leipzig in 1646. A contemporary of Newton, he took a great interest in the mathematical ideas of the British natural philosopher. Leibniz independently developed calculus, and although scholarly debate puts Newton's unpublished system of calculus slightly ahead of Leibniz's published efforts, the notation of the latter developed into the one more commonly used by mathematicians and engineers. Leibniz was a. major player in mathematics and science who continued to delve into speculative philosophy. In this section we examine his *Monadology*,[3] a study in atomistic metaphysics. Herein we find issues of determinism, relativity (*contra* Newton), and a single category of substance opposed to Cartesian dualism. This singular category is what is referred to by the term *monism*. Modern science influenced Leibniz's thought, as is apparent in the mechanical and analytic tone of the system. Leibniz also used Newton and Galileo as a point of departure, as is exemplified in Leibniz's monism as opposed to Descartes' dualism and in the metaphysical nature of *The Monadology* in general, in contrast to increasing focus on scientific and physical inquiries.

THE MONADOLOGY

1. The Monad, of which we will speak here, is nothing else than a simple substance, which goes to make up composites; by simple, we mean without parts.

2. There must be simple substances because there are composites; for a composite is nothing else than a collection . . . of simple substances.

3. Now, where there are no constituent parts there is possible neither extension, nor form, nor divisibility. These Monads are the true Atoms of nature, and, in fact, the Elements of things.

4. Their dissolution, therefore, is not to be feared and there is no way conceivable by which a simple substance can perish through natural means.

5. For the same reason there is no way conceivable by which simple substance might, through natural means, come into existence, since it can not be formed by composition.

6. We may say then, that the existence of Monads can begin or end only all at once, that is to say, the Monad can begin only through creation and end only through annihilation. . . .

7. There is also no way of explaining how a Monad can be altered or changed in its inner being by any other created thing, since there is no possibility of transposition within it, nor can we conceive of any internal movement which can be produced, directed, or increased or diminished there within the substance, such as can take place in the case of composites where a change can occur among the parts. The Monads have no windows through which anything may come in or go out. The Attributes are not liable to detach themselves and make an excursion outside the substance. . . . In the same way neither substance nor attribute can enter from without into a Monad.

8. Still Monads must needs have some qualities, otherwise they would not even be existences. And if simple substances did not differ at all in their qualities, there would be no means of perceiving any change in things. . . .

9. Each Monad, indeed, must be different from every other. For there are never in nature two beings which are exactly alike, and in which it is not possible to find a difference either internal or based on an intrinsic property.[4] . . .

10. It follows from what has just been said, that the natural changes of the Monad come from an internal principle, because an external cause can have no influence upon its inner being. . . .

13. . . . since every natural change takes place by degrees, there must be something which changes and something which remains unchanged,[5] and consequently there must be in the simple substance a plurality of conditions and relations, even though it has no parts.

14. The passing condition which involves and represents a multiplicity in . . . the simple substance, is nothing else than what is called Perception. This should be carefully distinguished from Apperception or Consciousness. . . . In this matter the Cartesians have fallen into a serious error, in that they treat as non-existent those perceptions of which we are not conscious. It is this also which has led them to believe that spirits alone are Monads and that there are no souls of animals. . . . They have thus adopted the Scholastic error that souls can exist entirely separated from bodies. . . .

17. It must be confessed, however, that Perception, and that which depends upon it, are inexplicable by mechanical causes, that is to say, by figures and motions. Supposing that there were a machine whose structure produced thought . . . we could conceive of it as increased in size . . . until one was able to enter into its interior, as he would a mill. Now, on going into it he would find only the pieces working on one another, but never would he find anything to explain Perception. It is accordingly in the simple substance, and not in the composite that the Perception is to be sought. Furthermore, there is nothing besides perceptions and their changes to be found in simple substance. . . .

19–21. If we wish to designate as soul everything which has perceptions and desires in the general sense . . . all simple substances or created monads could be called souls. But . . . we may reserve the term Soul for those whose perception is more distinct and accompanied by memory. . . .

When . . . there are a great number of weak perceptions where nothing stands out distinctively, we are stunned; . . . Among animals, death can occasion this state for quite a period.

22. Every present state of a simple substance is a natural consequence of its preceding state, in such a way that its present is big with its future. . . .

28. Men act in like manner as animals, in so far as the sequence of their perceptions is determined only by the law of memory, resembling the *empirical physicians*[6] who practice simply, without any theory, and we are empiricists in three-fourths of our actions. For instance, when we expect that there will be day-light to-morrow, we do so empirically. . . . It is only the astronomer who uses his reason in making such an affirmation.

29. But the knowledge of eternal and necessary truths is that which distinguishes us from mere animals and gives us reason and the sciences. . . .

31. Our reasoning is based upon two great principles: first, that of Contradiction, by means of which we decide that to be false which involves contradiction and that to be true which contradicts the false.

32. And second, the principle of Sufficient Reason, in virtue of which we believe that no fact can be real or existing and no statement true unless it has a sufficient reason why it should be thus and not otherwise. Most frequently, however, these reasons cannot be known by us.

33. There are also two kinds of Truths: those of Reasoning and those of Fact. The Truths of Reasoning are necessary, and their opposite impossible. Those of Fact, however, are contingent, and their opposite is possible. When a truth is necessary, the reason can be found by analysis in resolving it into simpler ideas and into simpler truths until we reach those which are primary.

36–39. . . . there must be . . . a sufficient reason for contingent truths of fact . . . There is [for example] an infinity of figures and movements, present and past, which enter into the efficient cause of my writing. . . . And as all this detail again involves other and more detailed contingencies . . . no real advance has been made. Therefore, the sufficient reason or ultimate reason must needs be outside the sequence. . . .

It is thus that the ultimate reason for things must be a necessary substance, in which the detail of the changes shall be present merely potentially, as in the fountainhead, and this substance we call God.

Now, since this substance is a sufficient reason for all the above mentioned details . . . *there is but one God, and this God is sufficient.* . . .

61. . . . [A]ll space is filled up; therefore, all matter is connected; and in a plenum or filled space every movement has an effect upon bodies. . . . Consequently every body responds to all that happens in the universe, so that he who saw all, could read in each one what is happening everywhere, and even what has happened and what will happen.

62. Thus although each created Monad represents the whole universe, it represents more distinctly the body which especially pertains to it. . . .

63. . . . every Monad is a mirror of the universe according to its own fashion. . . .

78. . . . The soul follows its own laws, and the body has its laws. They are fitted to each other in virtue of the pre-established harmony between all substances, since they are all representations of one and the same universe.

79. Souls act in accordance with the laws of final causes through their desires, purposes and means. Bodies act in accordance with the laws of efficient causes or of motion. . . .

87. As we established above that there is a perfect harmony between the two natural realms of efficient and final causes, it will be in place here to point out another harmony. . . .

88. This harmony brings it about that things progress themselves toward grace along natural lines, and that this earth, for example must be destroyed and restored by natural means at those times when the proper government . . . demands it. . . .

This esoteric work is the product of a mathematical genius, and it shows an application of analytic, atomistic, mathematical concepts to metaphysics. Here we see explicitly some notions of modern determinism. For Leibniz, all physical and spiritual phenomena are determined in every possible detail. For each monad, "its present is big with its future." Furthermore, this future is determined from creation by the pre-established harmony engendered by God, who is the sufficient reason for all existence.

There is a distinct tension in Leibniz between his monism, his thesis that there is only one type of simple substance, and his division of causes and entities into spiritual and physical. He claims that final causation rules the realm of souls, efficient causation rules the realm of bodies. This is consistent with the banishment of final causation from science and reserves a place for teleology in the moral, spiritual, and psychical realm. However, the harmony between final and efficient causation contributes to an evaluative explanation of cosmic evolution reminiscent of Aristotle and Anaximander. When Leibniz says that "things progress themselves toward grace along natural lines," this sounds very much like Aristotle's claim that Nature aims at a final good or Anaximander's idea that the universe maintains a just balance.

Leibniz, like Descartes and Newton, placed the utmost import on the truths of reason. This makes him a rationalist. In the next section, we treat the philosophy of Hume, which serves as a counterpoint to scientific and philosophical rationalism.

Hume's Sceptical Empiricism

David Hume was born in 1711 in Edinburgh, Scotland. He was a historian as well as a philosopher, and his publications circulated widely. His first major philosophical work was *A Treatise on Human Nature: An Attempt to Introduce the Experimental Method of Reasoning into Moral Subjects*, published in 1739.[7] This was perhaps his most ambitious work both in size and scope. In it he criticizes some of the rationalist doctrines regarding scientific method and the status of scientific law. Hume died in 1776.

A TREATISE ON HUMAN NATURE

Introduction

'Tis evident, that all the sciences have a relation, greater or less, to human nature; and that however wide any of them may seem to run from it, they still return back by one passage or another. Even *Mathematics*, *Natural Philosophy*, and *Natural Religion*, are in some measure dependent on the science of Man; since they lie under the cognizance of men, and are judged by their powers and faculties. . . .

And as the science of man is the only solid foundation for the other sciences, so the only solid foundation we can give to this science itself must be laid on experience and observation.

Book I. Of the Understanding

Part III

To begin regularly, we must consider the idea of *causation*, and see from what origin it is deriv'd. 'Tis impossible to reason justly, without understanding perfectly the idea concerning which we reason; and 'tis impossible perfectly to understand any idea, without tracing it up to its origin, and examining that primary impression, from which it arises. . . .

Let us therefore cast our eye on any two objects, which we call cause and effect, and turn them on all sides, in order to find that impression, which produces an idea of such prodigious consequence. At first sight I perceive, that I must not search for it in any of the particular *qualities* of the objects; since, which-ever of these qualities I pitch on, I find some object, that is not possessed of it, and yet falls under the denomination of cause or effect . . . 'tis plain there is no one quality, which universally belongs to all beings, and gives them a title to that denomination.

The idea, then, of causation must be derived from some *relation* among objects. I find in the first place, that whatever objects are consider'd as causes or effects, are *Contiguous*. . . . We may therefore consider the relation of **contiguity** as essential to that of causation. . . .

The second relation I shall observe as essential to causes and effects, is . . . that of **priority** of time in the cause before the effect. Some pretend that it is not absolutely necessary a cause shou'd precede its effect. . . . The consequence of this wou'd be no less than the destruction of that succession of causes, which we observe in the world; and indeed, the utter annihilation of time. For if one cause were cotemporary with its effect, and this effect with *its* effect, and so on, 'tis plain there would be no such thing as succession.

Having thus discover'd or suppos'd the two relations of *contiguity* and *succession* to be essential to causes and effects, I find I am stopt short. . . .

Shou'd any one . . . pretend to define a cause, by saying it is something *productive*, 'tis evident he would be saying nothing. For what does he mean by *production*? . . .

Shall we rest contented with these two relations . . . as affording a compleat idea of causation? By no means. An object may be contiguous and prior to another, without being consider'd as its cause. There is a **necessary connexion** to be taken into consideration. . . .

... When I cast my eye on the *known qualities* of objects, I immediately discover that the relation of cause and effect depends not in the least on *them*.

We must, therefore, proceed like those searching for any thing, that lies concealed, and ... beat about all the neighboring fields.... 'Tis necessary for us to leave the direct survey of this question concerning the nature of that *necessary connexion* ... and endeavor to find some other questions....

First, For what reason we pronounce it *necessary*, that every thing whose existence has a beginning, should also have a cause?

Secondly, Why we conclude, that such particular causes must *necessarily* have such particular effects; and what is the nature of that *inference* we draw from the one to the other, and of the *belief* we repose in it?

SECTION III

... 'Tis a general maxim in philosophy, that *whatever begins to exist, must have a cause of existence*.[8] This is commonly taken for granted in all reasonings, without any proof given or demanded. 'Tis suppos'd to be founded on intuition.... But if we examine this maxim ... we shall discover in it no mark of any such intuitive certainty; but on the contrary shall find, that 'tis of a nature quite foreign to that species of conviction.

All certainty arises from the comparison of ideas, and from the discovery of such relations as are unalterable.... These relations are ... none of which ... imply'd in this proposition, *Whatever has a beginning has also a cause of existence*. That proposition therefore is not intuitively certain.

... We can never demonstrate the necessity of a cause to every new existence, or new modification of existence, without shewing at the same time the impossibility there is, that any thing can ever begin to exist without some productive principle; and where the latter proposition cannot be prov'd, we must despair of ever being able to prove the former.

Since it is not from knowledge or any scientific reasoning, that we derive the opinion of the necessity of a cause ... that opinion must necessarily arise from observation and experience. The next question, then, should naturally be, *how experience gives rise to such a principle?* But as I find it more convenient to sink this question in the following, *Why we conclude, that such particular causes must necessarily have such particular effects, and why we form an inference from one to another?* ...

SECTION VI

'Tis easy to observe, that in tracing this relation, the inference we draw from cause to effect, is not derived merely from a survey of these particular objects, and from such a penetration into their essences as may discover the dependence of one upon the other. . . .

Therefore by **experience** only, that we can infer the existence of one object from that of another. The nature of experience is this. We remember to have had frequent instances of the existence of one species of objects; and also remember, that the individuals of another species of objects have always attended them, and have existed in regular order of contiguity and succession. . . . Thus we can remember to have seen that species of object we call *flame*, and to have felt that species of sensation we call *heat*. . . . Without any further ceremony, we call the one the *cause* and the other *effect*, and infer the existence of one from the other. . . .

. . . It may be thought that what we learn not from one object, we can never learn from a hundred, which are all of the same kind, and are perfectly resembling in any circumstance. . . . From mere repetition of any past impression, even to infinity, there will never arise any new original idea, such as that of necessary connexion. . . . But tho' this reasoning seems just and obvious; yet as it wou'd be folly to despair too soon, we shall continue . . . and having found, that after the discovery of the constant conjunction of any objects, we always draw an inference from one object to another. . . . Perhaps 'twill appear in the end, that the necessary connexion depends on the inference, instead of the inference's depending on the necessary connexion. . . .

Thus not only our reason fails us in the discover of the *ultimate connexion* of causes and effects, but even after experience has informed us of their *constant conjunction*, 'tis impossible for us to satisfy ourselves by our reason, why we should extend that experience beyond those particular instances. . . .

Hume claims that our ascription of causal relations to objects is suspect. He suggests that the necessary connection between cause and effect lies not within the objects themselves, but within our ideas and inferences.

Such a connection furthermore must be discovered by experience, and cannot be discovered by reason, according to Hume. This put him at odds with the rationalism of Descartes and Leibniz. Hume's philosophy originates with human nature, not with reason. Hume claimed we must consider ideas by examining their origin, that is, an "impression" or sensation. This is a clear case of empiricism. From this stance, Hume challenged the ideas of universal laws and necessary causation. This challenge represents a motivating force in philosophical discussions of science from this period onward.

Kant's Revival of Rationalism

Immanuel Kant was born in 1724 in Germany. He was well aware of the various opposing views on the status of scientific reasoning proposed by his predecessors. Hume's *Treatise* posed a dilemma which Hume solved by adopting a sceptical stance on causation and scientific law. Kant was interested in carrying forward the work of Descartes and Newton, but understood the difficulties of doing so given Hume's critique.[9] One interpretation of the *Critique of Pure Reason*, published in 1765, is that it is an effort to propose an alternative solution to Hume's sceptical empiricism.

Kant was educated in the rationalist tradition and thus was thoroughly acquainted with the work of Descartes and Leibniz. Leibniz's bold, speculative use of reason to construct a metaphysical system can be seen as a model for Kant's method. But Kant's work in the *Critique of Pure Reason* is obscure, difficult, turgid, and more ambitious than that of Leibniz. In order to facilitate the selection that follows, a few preliminary definitions and guidelines will be helpful.

Kant distinguished statements into four categories based on two dimensions of analysis. The first dimension is one of experience. Statements which can be known to be true or false prior to experience are *a priori*, those which can be known only by appeal to experience are *a posteriori*. The second dimension is one of conception or definition. Statements which can be known to be true or false by definition are *analytic*, those which cannot are *synthetic*. There is a natural categorical association between a priori and analytic statements as well as between a posteriori and synthetic statements. If a statement is true or false by definition, then it can be known to be so prior to experience. For example, the statement that all bachelors are unmarried is analytic and a priori, while the statement that Bill Clinton is not a bachelor is synthetic and a posteriori. Kant, however, proposed that some truths are synthetic a priori truths.

The synthetic a priori is especially important to our study, since Kant placed some laws of science in this category. Laws of science, e.g., the laws of inertia proposed by Descartes and Newton, are not analytic, and thus are not true by definition. But Kant claimed that these synthetic truths can be known prior to experience. If this is so, then reason and pure metaphysical theory can be said to precede experience. The following excerpt from the *Critique of Pure Reason*[10] deals with the significance of the synthetic a priori.

V.2

The Science of Natural Philosophy (Physics) contains in itself synthetic judgements *a priori* as principles. I shall adduce two propositions. For instance, the proposition, "in all changes of the material world, the quantity of matter remains unchanged"; or, that, "in all communication of motion, action and re-action must always be equal."[11] In both of these, not only is the necessity, and therefore their origin *a priori* clear, but also they are synthetical propositions. For in the conception of matter, I do not cogitate its permanency, but merely its presence in space. . . .

3. As to Metaphysics, even if we look upon it merely as an attempted science, yet, from the nature of human reason, an indispensable one, we find that it must contain synthetic propositions *a priori* . . . we must avail ourselves of such principles as add something to the original conception—something not identical with, nor contained in it. . . .

VI

. . . The proper problem of pure reason, then, is contained in the question, "How are synthetical judgements *a priori* possible?" . . . Upon the solution of this problem, or upon sufficient proof of the impossibility of synthetical knowledge *a priori*, depends the existence or downfall of the science of metaphysics. Among philosophers, David Hume came nearest of all to this problem; yet it never acquired in his mind sufficient precision. . . . On the contrary, he stopped short at the synthetical proposition of the connection of the effect with its cause . . . insisting that such a proposition *a priori* was impossible. According to his conclusions, then, all that we term metaphysical science is a mere delusion, arising from the fancied insight of reason into that which is in truth borrowed from experience, and to which habit has given the appearance of necessity. . . .

In the solution of the above problem is at the same time comprehended . . . the answer to the following questions:

> How is pure mathematical science possible?
> How is pure natural science possible?
>
> Respecting the sciences, as they do certainly exist, it may with propriety be asked, *how* they are possible?—for that they must be possible, is shown by the fact of their really existing.[12]

Kant's solutions to these problems are complex and difficult, and the summary that follows is necessarily lacking in many respects. Kant accepted Hume's criticism of the rationalist project as laid out by Descartes, Leibniz, and Newton, but he proposed a different approach to salvage the foundations of natural science and metaphysics, and to rehabilitate the truths of pure reason. Instead of asking how objective knowledge is possible given the subjective status of experience and inference, he proposed that even subjective awareness—such as Descartes' *cogito*—actually presupposes a knowledge of existences outside the subject. This method of reasoning from given facts to presupposed and hence proven theory is known as Kant's transcendental argument.

In this way, Kant tried to salvage the principles of science and metaphysics. He outlined several principles of metaphysics and science, which he claimed were synthetic a priori judgments established by transcendental deduction. The details of these principles will not concern us here, but it is important to note that scientific results and philosophical discussions of the status of scientific theory were important for Kant, and the apt criticisms levelled by Hume make the project of defining a rationalist, objectively certain foundation for scientific knowledge difficult even in the eighteenth century. These difficulties continue throughout the history of science and philosophy.

Summary

In this chapter, we have dealt with some of the most difficult works in all of philosophy. Many scholars study the systems presented herein as high philosophy and metaphysics, independent of any scientific or historical developments. In this volume, however, we can see the influence of modern science on philosophy as well as the influence of modern philosophy on science. And furthermore, it is evident that the subject matter taken on by science and philosophy changes in the modern period due to the mutual interaction of both.

The seventeenth century begins with philosophy firmly intertwined with science. The eighteenth century finds philosophers more as spectators and commentators than practitioners with respect to science. Philosophy has found its modern niche: commentary and interpretation of science along with the examination of the "subjective": qualities, values, consciousness, and knowledge.

Notes

1. Reprinted with the permission of Cambridge University Press from René Descartes, *Philosophical Writings*, Vols. I and II, John Cottingham, Robert Stoothoff, and Dugald Murdoch, eds. (New York: Cambridge University Press, 1985). Reprinted with the permission of Cambridge University Press.

2. John Veicht translation, 1901, copyright 1904 by the Free Press.

3. Reprinted by permission of Open Court Publishing Company, a division of Carus Publishing Company, Peru, IL, from *Discourse on Metaphysics/Correspondence with Arnauld/Monadology* by Gottfried Wilhelm Leibniz, trans. George Montgomery. Copyright 1988.

4. This passage employs the principle of the identity of indiscernibles, which Leibniz emphasized throughout his work.

5. This thesis can be found in Aristotle.

6. See Chapter 1 on Galen. Italics in original.

7. David Hume, *A Treatise on Human Nature* (Oxford: Oxford University Press, 1888 and 1978).

8. See Leibniz's principle of sufficient reason.

9. Norman Kemp Smith, *Commentary to Kant's Critique of Pure Reason*, 2nd ed. (London, Macmillan and Co., Ltd., 1923) xxv–xxviii.

10. Immanuel Kant, *Critique of Pure Reason*, J.M.D. Meilkejohn, transl. (London: J.M. Dent & Sons, Ltd., 1934).

11. See excerpts from Newton's *Principia*.

12. As to the existence of pure natural science, or physics, perhaps many may still express doubts. But we have only to look at . . . the *vis inertiae*, the equality of action and reaction, etc.—to be soon convinced that they form a science of pure physics. . . . [note in original]

Suggestions for Further Reading

Buchdahl, Gerd. *Metaphysics and the Philosophy of Science* (Cambridge, MA: MIT Press, 1969).

Descartes, René, *The Philosophical Writings*, vols. 1 & 2, John Cottingham, Robert Stoothoff, & Dugald Murdoch, eds. (New York: Cambridge University Press, 1985).

Hume, David. *An Enquiry Concerning Human Understanding*, Antony Flew, ed. (LaSalle, IL: Open Court Publishing Co., 1988).

Leibniz, G.W. *Discourse on Metaphysics/Correspondence with Arnauld/Monadology* (LaSalle, IL: Open Court Publishing Co., 1988).

Rescher, Nicholas, ed. *Leibnizian Inquiries: A Group of Essays* (Lanham: University Press of America, 1989).

Rescher, Nicholas. *Leibniz: An Introduction to His Philosophy* (Totowa, N.J.: Rowman and Littlefield, 1979).

Modern Views on Scientific Method

Scientists and philosophers began a new age in intellectual history during the seventeenth century. Modern science and philosophy transformed classical and medieval paradigms into a revolutionary new world-view that held great promise for the future success of human intellectual endeavor. Science immediately began delivering on this promise, expanding the scope, precision, and clarity of its inquiry. While this transformation was taking place and for centuries afterward, philosophers, scientists, and historians sought to describe how and why this discipline succeeded. Modern science relied on experiment, induction, mathematical demonstration, and theoretical reasoning, but the importance of any one of these elements, their interaction, and the status of scientific results were and are the subject of much debate. In this chapter, we will consider some figures from early modern history who pose different theories on scientific method.

Francis Bacon, a contemporary of many of the scientists discussed in Chapter 3, emphasized observation and induction. Galileo emphasized mathematical demonstration. Later philosophers adopted a position known as positivism. This school of thought was first articulated in its modern form by Auguste Comte, who advocated that positive, observable, given, and demonstrative proof is the sole arbiter for bona fide scientific knowledge. Each of these views can be seen to be one-sided in light of the actual history of science as presented in this volume and via the apt criticisms we will study in Chapter 11.

Bacon

Francis Bacon was born in 1561 in London. He was a successful member of the civil service until his discredit in 1621, and had risen to the rank of Lord Chancellor under James I when a bribery scandal ended his government career. He died in 1626. He had a rich public life, contributing to government, literature, science, and philosophy, and is best known for his philosophical empiricism. He inspired such later British empiricists as Hume (see the previous chapter), J.S. Mill (see Chapter 9), and Bertrand Russell.

Like the scepticism employed by Descartes, Bacon's empiricism was a purge that aided future progress. Michael R. Matthews, in the introduction to his chapter on Bacon in *The Scientific Background to Modern Philosophy*, summarizes well the straightforward empiricism of Bacon: "His epistemology was developed on the assumption that there is an external world that a perceiving subject confronts and gains knowledge of through sense impressions. The less the subject contributes, the more truthfully nature can speak."[1] Bacon disparaged the human contribution to science, and advocated a passive role for the scientific observer. Such a view is one-sided at best, and Bacon lacked appreciation for the power of speculation, imagination, and abstraction. The following are aphorisms from *The New Organon* (1620).[2]

XL

The formation of ideas and axioms by true induction is no doubt the proper remedy to be applied for the keeping off and clearing away of idols. To point them out, however, is of great use; for the doctrine of Idols[3] is to the interpretation of nature what the doctrine of the refutation of sophisms is to common logic.

XLVI

The human understanding when it has once adopted an opinion (either as being the received opinion or as being agreeable to itself) draws all things else to support and agree with it. And though there be a greater number and weight of instances to be found on the other side, yet these it either neglects and despises, or else by some distinction sets aside and rejects; in order that by this great and pernicious predetermination the authority of its former conclusions may remain inviolate. And therefore it was a good answer that was made by one who when they showed him hanging in a temple a picture of those who had paid their vows as having escaped shipwreck, and would have him say whether he did not now acknowledge the power of the gods,—"aye," asked he again, "but where are they painted that were drowned after their vows?" And such is the way of all superstition, whether in astrology, dreams, omens, divine judgements, or the like; wherein men, having a delight in such vanities, mark the events where they are fulfilled, but where they fail, though this happen much oftener, neglect and pass them by. But with far more subtlety does this mischief insinuate itself into philosophy and the sciences; in which the first conclusion colors and brings into conformity with itself all that come after, though far sounder and better. Besides, independently of that delight and vanity which I have described, it is the peculiar and perpetual error of the human intellect to be more moved and excited by affirmatives than by negatives; whereas it ought properly to hold itself indifferently disposed towards both alike. Indeed in the establishment of any true axiom, the negative instance is the more forcible of the two.

XCV

Those who have handled sciences have been either men of experiment or men of dogmas. The men of experiment are like the ant, they only collect and use; the reasoners resemble spiders, who make cobwebs out of their own substance. But the bee takes a middle course: it gathers its material from the flowers of the garden and of the field, but transforms and digests it by a power of its own. Not unlike this is the true business of philosophy: for it neither relies solely or chiefly on the powers of the mind, nor does it take the matter which it gathers from natural history and mechanical experiments and lay it up in the memory whole, as it finds it, but lays it up in the understanding altered and digested. Therefore from a closer and purer league between these two faculties, the experimental and the rational (such as had never yet been made), much may be hoped.

XCVI

We have as yet no natural philosophy that is pure: all is tainted and corrupted: in Aristotle's school by logic; in Plato's by natural theology; in [others] ... by mathematics, which only ought to give definiteness to natural philosophy, not generate or give it birth. . . .

We see here a modern discussion of some of the same themes treated in Chapter 1 by Galen. Bacon has no sympathy for rationalism, which he and Galen both called dogmatism. Bacon advocated empiricism as an antidote for many problems of human psychology which hinder scientific progress. Idolatry and myth-making, according to Bacon, thrive on positive theorizing, spinning "cobwebs out of their own substance." Bacon correctly recognized that honest science should always be on the lookout for negative instances, since in the search for universal axioms, a single counter example is more noteworthy than an abundance of supporting evidence.[4]

Bacon's epistemology is empirical and inductive. His view is not entirely devoid of rationalism, however, since he notes that better progress is afforded by some form of analysis that renders scientific knowledge "altered" and "digested." Nevertheless, he views mathematics and speculative theorizing as potentially dangerous. Bacon's prescription could not even be followed in his own time, though, and in the next section we see how Galileo forged modern science, taking a different tack.

Galileo and Method

We have already seen that Galileo developed sophisticated arguments to make his case for some less than obvious conclusions. Chapter 3 contains arguments for the earth's motion and for the notion that qualities in nature are not so much present in observed objects as in the observer. Both of these ideas run contrary to simple observation of natural phenomena. In order to argue for these conclusions, Galileo employed philosophical reasoning and mathematical demonstration.

In this section, we will see that Galileo held that mathematical speculation, analysis, and demonstration were really more important than observation and experiment. Nonetheless, Galileo had a gift for devising experimental apparati and procedures, and will ever be remembered for his experimental side. The following selections show Simplicius, the Aristotelian foil, embracing experimental method and Salviati, Galileo's representative, using mathematical demonstration.

DISCOURSES CONCERNING TWO NEW SCIENCES

Salviati. I . . . call to mind what I learned from our Academician[5] who . . . according to his custom had demonstrated everything by geometrical methods so that one might fairly call this a new science.

For, although some of his conclusions had been reached by others, first of all by Aristotle, these are not the most beautiful, and, what is more important, they had not been proven in a rigid manner from fundamental principles. . . . I wish to convince you by demonstrative reasoning rather than to persuade you by mere probabilities. . . .

Simplicius. I am all at sea. . . . The arguments and demonstrations which you have advanced are mathematical, abstract, and far removed from concrete matter; and I do not believe that when applied to the physical and natural world these laws will hold.

Salv. [T]hese geometrical demonstrations . . . carry with them distinct gains. . . .

Simp. Aristotle . . . supposes bodies of different weights to move in the same medium . . . so that, for example, a body which is ten times as heavy as another will move ten times as rapidly as the other.

Salv. I greatly doubt that Aristotle ever tested by experiment whether it be true that two stones, one weighing ten times as much as the other, if allowed to fall, at the same instance, from a height of, say, 100 cubits, would so differ in speed that when the heavier had reached the ground, the other would not have fallen more than ten cubits.

Simp. His language would seem to indicate that he had tried the experiment, because he says: *We see the heavier;* now the word *see* shows that he had made the experiment.

Sagredo. But I, Simplicio, who have made the test can assure you that a cannon ball weighing one or two hundred pounds, or even more, will not reach the ground by as much as a span ahead of a musket ball weighing only half a pound. . . .

Salv. But, even without further experiment, it is possible to prove clearly, by means of a short and conclusive argument, that a heavier body does not move more rapidly than a lighter one provided both bodies are of the same material. . . . But tell me, Simplicio, whether you admit that each falling body acquires a definite speed fixed by nature, a velocity which cannot be increased or diminished except by the use of force. . . .

Simp. There can be no doubt. . . .

Salv. If then we take two bodies whose natural speeds are different, it is clear that on uniting the two, the more rapid one will be partly retarded by the slower, and the slower will be somewhat hastened by the swifter. . . .

> *Simp.* You are unquestionably right.
>
> *Salv.* But if this is true, and if a large stone moves with a speed of, say, eight while a smaller moves with a speed of four, then when they are united, the system will move with a speed less than eight; but the two stones when tied together make a stone larger than that which before moved with a speed of eight. Hence the heavier body moves with less speed than the lighter; an effect which is contrary to your supposition. Thus you see how, from your assumption that the heavier body moves more rapidly than the lighter one, I infer that the heavier body moves more slowly.

Although Salviati and Sagredo chastised Aristotle for failing to try the experiment Simplicio refers to, Galileo ultimately used a proof by contradiction to argue definitively for his conclusion that heavier bodies and lighter bodies do not naturally attain different speeds due to the force of gravity. Galileo used Salviati to show that by accepting the premise that a heavier body falls more quickly, he can derive the opposite conclusion that a heavier body falls more slowly. Thus, the original premise must be wrong. This abstract, logical form of demonstration is favored by Galileo in this passage and others.

Such a method, characterized by logical and mathematical proof, is another example of early modern rationalism. We have seen that Descartes favored the rational, intuitive powers of the mind in his mission to overcome scepticism. Galileo's geometrical method, which seeks proof "in a rigid manner from fundamental principles," coheres well with the sort of approach taken by other founders of modern science and philosophy. Francis Bacon, as seen in the previous section, is a notable detractor.

Newtonian Method

Newton realized his physics had the ammunition to answer many questions formerly reserved for metaphysics. Modern physics proposed mathematical theories of the sources of motion; the innate principles of matter; and cosmological laws. Furthermore, these theories were more determinate and useful than the metaphysical speculations of ancient, medieval, and modern philosophers, including Leibniz's *Monadology* (see Chapter 4). The following selections from Newton's *Principia* propose that the method and material of Newtonian physics are replacements for philosophical reasoning.

PRINCIPIA

BOOK III   RULES OF REASONING IN PHILOSOPHY

RULE I

We are to admit no more causes of natural things than such as are both true and sufficient to explain their appearances.

To this purpose the philosophers say Nature does nothing in vain, and more is in vain when less will serve; for Nature is pleased with simplicity, and affects not the pomp of superfluous causes.

RULE II

Therefore to the same natural effects we must, as far as possible, assign the same causes.

As to the respiration in a man and in a beast; the descent of stones in *Europe* and in *America*; the light of our culinary fire and of the sun; the reflection of light in the earth, and in the planets.

RULE III

The qualities of bodies, which admit neither intensification nor remission of degrees, and which are found to belong to all bodies within the reach of our experiments, are to be esteemed universal qualities of all bodies whatsoever.

For since the qualities of bodies are only known to us by experiments, we are to hold for universal all such as universally agree with experiments. . . . We are certainly not to relinquish the evidence of our experiments for the sake of dreams and vain fictions of our own devising. . . . [B]ecause we perceive extension in all that are sensible, therefore we ascribe it universally to all others also. . . . That all bodies are movable, and endowed with certain powers (which we call inertia) of preserving in their motion, or in rest, we only infer from the like properties observed in the bodies which we have seen. . . .

Lastly, if it universally appears, by experiments and astronomical observations, that all bodies gravitate towards the earth, and that in proportion to the quantity of matter which they severally contain . . . we must, in consequence of this rule, universally allow that all bodies whatsoever are endowed with a principle of mutual gravitation.

Rule IV

In experimental philosophy we are to look upon propositions inferred by general induction from phenomena as accurately or very nearly true, notwithstanding any contrary hypotheses that may be imagined, till such time as other phenomena occur, by which they may either be made more accurate, or liable to exceptions.

This rule we must follow, that the argument of induction may not be evaded by hypotheses.

The tensions here are manifold. Newton regards the new mathematical approach to physical science and natural philosophy pioneered by Galileo and himself as the way to gain true access to knowledge of fundamental reality. This emphasis on mathematical modes of reasoning is apparent in both the content and organization of the *Principia* as well as the *Optics* and other works. Newton not only formulates his natural philosophy in mathematical abstractions but also organizes his work into an axiomatic presentation reminiscent of Euclid's *Elements*, the ancient classic of geometry. However, in order for mathematical science to do the job Newton assigns it, we must have a way to bridge the gap from experienced phenomena, with their limited scope and imperfect presentation, to abstract reasoning and universal laws. The Rules are intended for this purpose.

We have seen in Chapter 4 that these rules are challenged subsequently by Hume. Specifically, Rules II, III, and IV refer to causation as a regular, law-like phenomenon existing in the external objective world that can be determined by induction. Each piece of this came under Hume's attack. Subsequent scientists and mathematicians sometimes regarded such critiques as retrograde throwbacks to an era in which indeterminate philosophical speculations were more highly regarded than scientific thinking. In the next section we will see how Comte carries this torch for Newtonian science.

Positivism

Auguste Comte was a French philosopher born in 1798. He is credited with founding the scientific study of social structures as well as founding the school of thought known as *positivism*. His best known philosophical work, *Cours de Philosophie Positive*, was published in six volumes from 1830 to 1842. He died in 1857.

Positivism embraced the progress attained by empirical science and sought to establish science as the only method for obtaining knowledge. Scientific method as seen by Comte was closer to the empiricism of Bacon than the rationalism of Descartes or Galileo. According to the positivist view, philosophical metaphysics must be abandoned in favor of scientific inquiry. The positivist is charged with expanding the scope of science into areas formerly reserved for philosophy, such as studies of mind and of politics. Philosophy should only comment on the practices and results of science in their generalities and as they relate to human life.

The following selections from *Cours de Philosophie Positive* treat some methodological prescriptions of Comte's positivism.[6]

INTRODUCTION

CHAPTER 1

From the study of the development of human intelligence, in all directions, and through all times, the discovery arises of a great fundamental law. . . . The law is this: that each of our leading conceptions—each branch of our knowledge—passes successively through three different theoretical conditions: the theological, or fictitious; the metaphysical, or abstract; and the scientific, or positive. . . .

In the theological state, the human mind, seeking the essential nature of beings, the first and final causes (the origin and purpose) of all effects—in short, absolute knowledge—supposes all phenomena to be produced by the immediate action of supernatural beings.

In the metaphysical state, which is only a modification of the first, the mind supposes, instead of supernatural beings, abstract forces, veritable entities (that is, personified abstractions) inherent in all beings, and capable of producing all phenomena. What is called the explanation of phenomena is, in this stage, a mere reference of each to its proper entity.

In the final, the positive, state, the mind has given over the vain search after absolute notions, the origin and destination of the universe, and the causes of phenomena, and applies itself to the study of their laws—that is, their invariable relations of succession and resemblance. Reasoning and observation, duly combined, are the means of this knowledge. What is now understood when we speak of explanation of facts is simply the establishment of a connection between single phenomena and some general facts, the number of which continually diminishes with the progress of science.

The theological system arrived at the highest perfection of which it is capable when it substituted the providential action of a single Being for the varied operations of the numerous divinities that had been before imagined. In the same way, in the last stage of the metaphysical system, men substitute one great entity (Nature) as the cause of all phenomena, instead of the multitude of entities at first supposed. In the same way, again, the ultimate perfection of the positive system would be (if such perfection could be hoped for) to represent all phenomena as particular aspects of a single general fact—such as gravitation, for instance. . . .

The progress of the individual mind is not only an illustration, but an indirect evidence of that general mind. The point of departure of the individual mind and of the race being the same, the phases of the mind of man correspond to the epochs of the mind of the race. Now, each of us is aware, if he looks upon his own history, that he was a theologian in his childhood, a metaphysician in his youth, and a natural philosopher in his manhood. . . .

Besides the observation of these facts, we have theoretical reasons in support of this law.

The most important of these reasons arises from the necessity that always exists for some theory to which to refer our facts, combined with the clear impossibility that, at the outset of human knowledge, men could have formed theories out of the observation of facts. All good intellects have repeated, since Bacon's time, that there can be no real knowledge but that which is based on observed facts. This is incontestable, in our present advanced stage; but, if we look back to the primitive stage of human knowledge, we shall see that it must have been otherwise then. If it is true that every theory must be based on observed facts, it is equally true that facts cannot be observed without the guidance of some theory. Without such guidance, our facts would be desultory and fruitless; we could not retain them: for the most part we could not even perceive them.

Thus, between the necessity of observing facts in order to form a theory, and having a theory in order to observe facts, the human mind would have been entangled in a vicious circle were it not for the natural opening afforded by theological conceptions. . . . It is remarkable that the most inaccessible of questions—those of the nature of beings and the origin and purpose of phenomena—should be the first to occur in a primitive state, while those that are really within our reach are regarded as almost unworthy of serious study. The reason is evident enough: that experience alone can teach us the measure of our powers; and if men had not begun with an exaggerated estimate of what they can do, they never would have done all that they are capable of. Our organization requires this. . . .

The law of human development being thus established, let us consider what is the proper nature of the positive philosophy.

. . . the first characteristic of positive philosophy is that it regards all phenomena as subjected to invariable natural *laws*. Our business is—seeing how vain is any research into what are called *causes*, whether first or final—to pursue an accurate discovery of these laws, with a view to reducing them to the smallest possible number. . . . The best illustration of this is in the case of the doctrine of gravitation. We say that the general phenomena of the universe are *explained* by it, because it connects under one head the whole immense variety of astronomical facts . . . while the general fact itself is a mere extension of one that is perfectly familiar to us and we therefore say that we know—the weight of bodies on the surface of the earth. As to what weight and attraction are, we have nothing to do with that, for it is not a matter of knowledge at all. . . .

In mentioning . . . the four principle categories of phenomena—astronomical, physical, chemical, and physiological—there was an omission which will have been noticed. Nothing was said of social phenomena. Though involved with physiological, social phenomena demand a distinct classification. . . . They are the most individual, the most complicated, the most dependent on all others; and therefore they must be the latest—even if they had no special obstacle to encounter. This branch of science has not hitherto entered into the domain of positive philosophy. . . .

As knowledge accrues, the sciences part off; and students devote themselves each to some branch. . . . We all acknowledge that the divisions established for the convenience of scientific pursuit are radically artificial; and yet there are very few who can embrace in idea the whole of any one science: each science, moreover, being itself only a part of a great whole. . . . We must not be blind to the evil in seeking a remedy. We must not forget that this is the weakness of the positive philosophy. . . . As to the remedy, it certainly does not lie in a return to the ancient confusion of pursuits. . . . It lies in perfecting the division of employment itself—in carrying it one degree higher—in constituting one more speciality from the study of scientific generalities. Let us have a new class of students, suitably prepared, whose business it shall be to take the respective sciences as they are, determine the spirit of each, ascertain their relations and mutual connection, and reduce their respective principles to the smallest number of general principles, in conformity with the fundamental rules of the positive method. . . . It is time to complete the vast intellectual operation begun by Bacon, Descartes, and Galileo, by constructing a system of general ideas that must henceforth prevail among the human race. . . .

The consideration of all phenomena as referable to a single origin is by no means necessary to the systematic formation of science, any more than to the realization of the great and happy consequences that we anticipate from the positive philosophy. The only necessary unity is that of method, which is already in great part established. As for the doctrine, it need not be *one*; it is enough that it should be *homogeneous*. It is, then, under double aspect of unity of method and homogeneousness of doctrine that we shall consider different classes of positive theories. . . . While pursuing the philosophical aim of all science, the lessening of the number of general laws requisite for the explanation of natural phenomena, we shall regard as presumptuous every attempt, in all future time, to reduce them rigorously to one.

BOOK III

PHYSICS

Astronomy was a positive science, in its geometrical aspect, from the earliest days of the School of Alexandria; but physics, which we are now to consider, had no positive character at all till Galileo made his great discoveries on the fall of heavy bodies. . . .

Positive philosophy requires that we should draw off altogether from the study of *agents*, to which it may be imagined phenomena are to be referred. Any number of persons may discover a supposed agent—as, for instance, the universal ether of modern philosophers, by which a variety of phenomena may be supposed to be explained—and we may not be able to disprove such an agency. But we have no more to do with modes of operation than with the nature of the bodies acted upon. We are concerned with phenomena alone, and what we have to ascertain is their laws. In departing from this rule, we leave behind us all the certainty and consistency of real science. . . .

I have deferred till now what I have to offer on the important subject of the rational construction of scientific *hypotheses*, regarded as a powerful and indispensable auxiliary to our study of nature. . . .

There are only two methods by which we can get at the law of any phenomenon ... by induction or deduction. Neither of these methods would help us ... if we did not begin by anticipating the results, by making a provisional supposition, altogether conjectural in the first instance.... Hence the necessary introduction of hypotheses into natural philosophy.... But the employment of this instrument must always be subjected to one condition.... This condition is to imagine such hypotheses only as admit, by their nature, of a positive and inevitable verification.... In other words, philosophical hypotheses must always have the character of simple anticipations of what we might know at once, by experiment and reasoning....

... I must offer the observation that the philosophy of the sciences cannot properly be studied apart from their history, and conversely, that the history apart from the philosophy would be idle and unintelligible.

Comte's positivism prescribes a unity of method and an end to the "vain search after absolute notions, the origin and destination of the universe, and the causes of phenomena." Instead, we should be content to relate particular phenomena to general laws. We should strive to reduce the number of these laws as scientific investigation and positive philosophy progress. Such is the proper course for science and philosophy in our maturity.

Comte wanted to leave metaphysical inquiry behind as a relic of the youth of humanity. He specifically targeted "personified abstractions," that is, anthropocentric notions. Aristotle's final causation, Leibniz's grace and pre-established harmony, and Anaximander's universal justice are all metaphysical notions that Comte would regard as unwarranted personifications of nature. In addition, Leibniz's idea that the seeds of consciousness are in every basic element of being, or Aristotle's claim that the planets are moved by minds or souls, or Descartes' stipulation that thinking substance is a basic component of reality, could each be understood as anthropocentric projections from human qualities to the universe at large. Comte believed that science and philosophy were ready to move beyond these notions.

Comte understood the necessity of the use of hypotheses, but cautioned against the extravagant formulations employed in the past. Although he was vague on many of the characteristics of his unitary method, this feature stands out: he warned the positive philosopher "to imagine such hypotheses only as admit, by their nature, of a positive and inevitable verification.... In other words, philosophical hypotheses must always have the character of simple anticipations of what we might know at once, by experiment and reasoning." The four causes of Aristotle, the solar vortex of Kepler, the absolute space and time of Newton—all were excluded by Comte.

These hypotheses indeed prove untenable in the end, but nevertheless served as guiding forces in the scientific quest. And subsequent scientific doctrine contains many hypotheses that violate the positive condition. Atomic theory, genetics, and the increasingly mathematical physics of the twentieth century all propose causes and agents that defy immediate recognition and straightforward positive verification. Nevertheless, positivism was explicitly embraced by many practicing scientists of the nineteenth and twentieth centuries, including Ernst Mach and Albert Einstein in his early years. And the simple assurances given by positivism as to the uncontroversial status of scientific results remain a part of Western thinking until the present day.

Comte was a modern in that he supported the division of labor begun by Galileo and Newton. He advocated that science and philosophy separate, and that science itself become further specialized. He included one more puzzling specialty, however, and a brief examination into the division charged with "constructing a system of general ideas" will help illuminate further tensions within Comte's positivism.

Comte proposed several ambivalent themes with respect to reductionism. In support of the reductionist mission, he calls for a unity of method and homogeneity of doctrine. He further wanted to reduce the number of general laws as far as possible. Our selection includes his claim that "the ultimate perfection of the positive system would be (if such perfection could be hoped for) to represent all phenomena as particular aspects of a single general fact—such as gravitation, for instance."

Comte did not believe that such perfection was required, however, and thought the positivist should "regard as presumptuous every attempt, in all future time, to reduce [explanation] rigorously to one." So although Comte may have been a reductionist in spirit, he stops short of claiming that this spirit must be manifest in scientific discovery or in natural phenomena.

Summary

Although we have astounding progress in the sciences at the beginning of the modern period, scientists and philosophical commentators disagree on what it is that scientists do or should do. Bacon advocated the use of observation purged from logic, theology, and mathematics. Galileo modeled many of his demonstrations after geometrical, logical deductions. Comte allowed a combination of hypotheses and experiment, but only under strict limitations on the positive verifiability of such hypotheses. More than a century before Comte, Newton anticipated the positivistic sentiment: "the proper method for inquiring after the properties of things, is to deduce them from experiments. . . . And therefore I could wish all objections suspended, taken from hypotheses."[7] A famous passage from the *Principia* is also telling:

> whatever is not deduced from the phenomena is to be called an hypothesis; and hypotheses, whether metaphysical or physical, whether of occult qualities or mechanical, have no place in experimental philosophy. In this philosophy, particular propositions are inferred from the phenomena, and afterwards rendered general by induction.[8]

Comte's understanding of the interaction between hypothesis and experiment was slightly more sophisticated than that of Bacon or Newton, since the latter apparently believed scientists could operate without hypothetical devices at all. Comte's belief in positive verifiability nevertheless proved naive and too limiting in the face of subsequent scientific and philosophical developments. Alfred North Whitehead, in his seminal work *Process and Reality*, characterizes the limits of Bacon's methodology in ways that also describe positivism: "the . . . method of induction . . . if consistently pursued, would have left science where it found it. What Bacon omitted was the play of a free imagination. . . ."[9]

The disagreement over method foreshadows a disagreement over the status of scientific results. While all the scientists and philosophers cited here attached the utmost import to the results of scientific inquiry, their dispute concerning method shows that this status is not well understood. Are the results of science straightforward discovery and recognition of particular and general facts, as the methods of Bacon and Comte suggest? Or is science more like mathematics, which aims at axiomatic systems culminating in abstract formalizations, as Galileo's examples would indicate? Although each of these methodologists regard scientific results as true, real, and necessary, their disagreement about the specific reasons for this led later figures to more radical speculations. Critics of scientific realism claim that to regard scientific theory as fact is misguided. We will continue to explore these themes in later chapters.

Notes

1. Michael R. Matthews' excellent volume is to some extent a major inspiration for the present work. If the reader is interested in a similar treatment of themes within a narrower historical and scientific context, see his *The Scientific Background to Modern Philosophy* (Indianapolis: Hackett, 1989). The reduced scope yields a more manageable work in many ways, and the sacrifice made herein trades compact coherence for more comprehensiveness, a sometimes questionable bargain. The quote can be found on page 46.

2. *New Organon* by Bacon: Library of Liberal Arts by Fulton H. Anderson, ed., copyright 1960. Reprinted by permission of Prentice-Hall, Inc., Upper Saddle River, NJ.

3. In a previous aphorism, Bacon formalizes his doctrine of Idols as a classification of false ideas which "beset men's minds."

4. This theme is taken up again in Chapter 11 in the selection and discussion on Sir Karl Popper, an heir of British empiricism.

5. This is Galileo's way of referring to himself.

6. From *Auguste Comte and Positivism.* Copyright © 1975 by Gertrud Lenzer. (New York: Harper & Row, 1975). Reprinted by permission of Georges Borchardt, Inc. for the author.

7. Newton, *Opera quae Exstant Omnia,* quoted in Burtt, 121.

8. *Principia,* Volume II (Berkeley: The University of California Press, 1934) 547.

9. Whitehead, *Process and Reality,* Corrected Edition (New York: The Free Press, 1978), 5.

Suggestions for Further Reading

Burtt, E.A., *Metaphysical Foundations of Modern Science* (London: Routledge & Kegan Paul, 1942).

Lenzer, Gertrud, *Auguste Comte and Positivism: The Essential Writings* (New York: Harper and Row, 1975).

Matthews, Michael R., *The Scientific Background to Modern Philosophy* (Indianapolis: Hackett, 1989).

Modern Transformations in Biology and Medicine

As we saw in Chapter 1, basic issues in the philosophy of science arise in areas other than the narrowly physical sciences. Medical, social, and more recently computer sciences have their own contributions to philosophy (and conversely). Traditionally, however, the history of philosophy and science is predominantly tied to discussions of the physical sciences, and this predominance is reflected in the balance of the material in previous chapters. In this chapter, we will treat some developments in biology from the modern period in order to understand some parallel themes outside of this physical–philosophical tradition.

Physical science, metaphysics, and methodology in both science and philosophy emerged from the ancient period by replacing Aristotelian notions of final causation with mechanistic and positivistic models of interaction. Instead of proposing, for instance, that free-falling objects and projectiles move as they do because they seek their proper place, Newton and Comte were content with a law of gravity that relates specific to general facts, while they ignored metaphysical notions of agency and purpose. And though Aristotle's optimism regarding the accessibility of the natural world to the human intellect was a vital part of the modern mind-set, the method used to achieve this access evolved tremendously. Reflection and speculation were de-emphasized in favor of mathematical modeling and empirical test.

All of these developments required overcoming authoritative traditions, and in biology these obstacles were even greater. In the seventeenth century, William Harvey completed an effort to advance anatomy and physiology beyond ancient understanding by employing modern methods repugnant to medieval superstitions. The use of dissection on humans and the applications of mechanistic theories to physiology were antithetical to traditional views. Taboos against dissecting the human body had recurred throughout the West since ancient Greece, and the biblical creation myth was an impediment to scientific theories of anatomy. Harvey's theory regarding the circulation of the blood stands as a crowning achievement to efforts by Renaissance scientists and artists to understand the human structure.

The work of Louis Pasteur in the mid-nineteenth century continued that of Harvey in that he propelled medicine fully into the modern period. Although Harvey had achieved a modern theory of circulatory anatomy and physiology two centuries earlier, general theories of human function underwent several regressions during succeeding periods. It finally took Pasteur—equipped with laboratory methodology and a mechanistic mindset—to exorcise spiritual and mystical elements from infectious theory.

In the nineteenth century, Charles Darwin challenged final causation in developmental biology, and his theories eventually won over the scientific community. While teleology had been effectively challenged in physics and metaphysics by Darwin's time, theists and deists[1] still believed that the origin and development of life depended on guidance from God. The inexplicable complexities of macrobiology were seen as comforting evidence that modern science was not up to the task of refuting traditional religious and philosophical beliefs on the beginnings of life. Darwin's *Origin of Species* provided a mechanistic explanation for the evolution of life on earth that seemingly required no purpose or design. The following sections sketch the theories of Harvey, Pasteur, Darwin, and a few others whose work led to modern transformations in biological science.

Medicine

A brief look at some developments in medical science demonstrates that physics and cosmology were not the only disciplines encumbered by authoritative traditions and premodern methodology. William Harvey was very much a part of the modern scientific revolution, practicing contemporaneously with Galileo and Newton. He maintained some animistic theories of bodily function, believing in a life force that caused some activities in the body, but his primary contribution to medicine was his purely mechanical theory of circulatory anatomy. Pasteur finally expunged the remnants of mysticism and animism from biological science by developing a theory and technique that could be used to control the spread of agents of infection.

The Anatomy and Physiology of Blood Circulation

William Harvey was the seventeenth century's medical analogue to Newton and Galileo. He applied mechanistic hypotheses and experimental methods to revolutionize anatomy and medicine. The following exposition and commentary on the life and work of William Harvey is compiled from several secondary sources, including Butterfield's *The Origins of Modern Science* and Dampier's *A History of Science*.

William Harvey was a British physician born in 1578. He was educated at Cambridge and continued his studies abroad at Padua, where Galileo also worked, returning home to treat such famous personages as Francis Bacon and the kings James I and Charles I. He died in 1657. Harvey's time at Padua was crucial for his development, since it exposed him to Italian Renaissance artistic and scientific studies of human physiology as well as the beginnings of modern scientific thinking.

That anatomy and mathematics were part of art in the Renaissance is exemplified in the works of Michelangelo and Leonardo da Vinci, among others. Butterfield further notes that "the artists, much as they owed the ancient world, were the first to cry out against mere subservience to authority—the first to say that one must observe nature for oneself."[2]

This authority included Galen as well as Aristotle, and prevailing notions of blood circulation were derived from both. The notion that the chest was the seat of intellect and higher human function was derived from Aristotle. The idea that there were two separate circulatory systems and two types of blood was derived from Galen. One type was presumed to be flowing in the veins, and the venous system was regarded as centered in the liver; the other type was presumed to be flowing in the arteries, which centered around the heart. Medieval superstitions about dissection and medical experiment shielded these hypotheses until they became doctrinaire. Even after the practice of dissection became more common in the fifteenth and sixteenth centuries, observation was heavily biased[3] toward the teachings of Galen and Aristotle.

In addition, religious doctrine was antithetical to the application of mechanism to humanity. For example, the book of Genesis states that God created man in His image. Hence, a purely mechanical explanation of human structure, with no animistic or spiritual dimension, seemed contrary to the notion that humanity was a reflection of divinity. To be sure, there are many interpretations of these and other passages in Genesis that render an objective analysis of physiology compatible with religious tradition. Nevertheless, traditional views had a strong cultural grip on the minds of sixteenth- and seventeenth-century anatomists and physiologists.

Besides the mental encumbrances of early modern medical theorists, there was a technical difficulty that Harvey would uncover about methods of dissection. It was easy to draw mistaken inferences from many specimens since they had been bled to death, thus emptying the arterial system and the left ventricle of the heart. Thus, the fact that blood is expelled from the heart was obscured. Galen and his followers held that the heart draws in the venous blood, but that both venous and arterial blood are distributed by an "ebb and flow."[4] And the passage of blood from the right ventricle to the lungs and then to the left ventricle was unknown. The entire notion of one centrally activated system for circulating the same blood was overlooked in this way.

One by one, these errors were questioned and slowly corrected by anatomists in Italy.[5] And though much of the evidence was available before Harvey's work, it took the modern mind-set of Harvey to synthesize it into a cogent new theory. While contemporary theories made use of vital spirits, Harvey viewed the phenomenon of blood distribution with a mechanical eye. Harvey's book, *Exercitatio Anatomica de Motu Cordis et Sanguinis*, published in 1628, contains his modern theory that blood is pumped from the right ventricle of the heart to the lungs, then into the left ventricle, where it is pumped through the arteries and drawn back through the veins. He came to this knowledge through examination and analysis of the intricate valves in the parts of the heart and the veins, a comparative analysis with other animals that do not have lungs, and observation of wounds and surgery in live specimens. He also calculated the pumping capacity of the heart to be so great that the only way so much blood could be disposed of would be if it were in continual circulation throughout the entire body.

His achievement is monumental in the history of medicine. He gathered new evidence and arguments, synthesized new findings with old data, utilized mechanistic and analytic thinking, and proposed a correct theory. While Harvey mentioned some notions of vital spirits, he avoided the use of animistic explanations, e.g., a living force in the blood or a natural purpose inherent in the circulatory anatomy. His theory was one of a mechanical agent, the heart, causing the material of the blood, sans vital spirits, to flow around the body. This is a description based on antecedent causation and objective analysis.

This theory was heretical with respect to the Western tradition. For the purposes of circulatory study, Harvey regarded the human body as a machine. This contradicted religious and philosophical viewpoints that posited a divine or at least a nonmaterial dimension to the human organism. We have seen that dismissing analogous elements from physical science flew in the face of religious and philosophical dogma, landing Galileo under house arrest. Challenging purposive causation and animistic explanation in the human body was even more drastic.[6] Harvey's discovery is furthermore a *sine qua non* for the rest of medical science. Without a proper theory of circulation, modern progress in anatomical theory, as well as treatment of injury and illness, would have been impossible.

The Germ Theory of Life

Although Harvey expunged mystical and nonmechanical elements from their pivotal place in the anatomy of the heart, the battle with traditional forces in medicine was far from over until the nineteenth century. The vital spirits deemphasized by Harvey found their way back into other parts of medical theory, and indeed medical theory underwent several regressions before fully emerging into the modern age. It was not until the nineteenth century that medicine became the modern science that changed the face of human society.

Ancient and Medieval theories of spontaneous generation, the idea that life could originate from inanimate matter more or less spontaneously, were recurrently popular in the seventeenth and eighteenth centuries. In the seventeenth century, Francesco Redi demonstrated that dead animal flesh could not generate maggots if it were protected from insects, and in the eighteenth century, Abbé Spallanzani showed that boiling and enclosing fluids would protect them from even smaller infestations. The necessity of these demonstrations shows that medical science was still grappling with premodern theories until quite recently.

Louis Pasteur was a French physician who lived from 1822 until 1895. In 1864, he presented his findings that bacteria caused specific organic phenomena—from the souring of milk to the putrification of meat to disease—and showed that they did not arise spontaneously. His results were obtained with modern laboratory experimental techniques, and his apparati were simple. Using swan-necked flasks in which heat-sterilized liquid was kept from direct contact with outside air, he showed that the liquid remained sterile indefinitely, while a similar flask allowed to come in contact with microbes from the outside air was quickly contaminated. The following passage from Pasteur's 1864 presentation is quoted in René Dubos' *Pasteur and Modern Science.*[7]

I could point to that liquid and say to you, I have taken my drop of water from the immensity of creation, and I have taken it full of the elements appropriated to the development of the microscopic organisms. And I wait, I watch, I question it!—begging it to recommence for me the beautiful spectacle of the first creation. But it is dumb, dumb since these experiments were begun several years ago; it is dumb because I have kept from it the only thing the human mind does not know how to produce: from the germs which float in the air. . . . Never will the doctrine of spontaneous generation recover from the mortal blow of this simple experiment.

Pasteur paved the way for antiseptics and heat sterilization, thence-forward known as pasteurization, to be used effectively to eliminate agents of infection from processes as disparate as food production and distribution, surgery,[8] and child care. The humane effects of these developments are inestimable.

Once vital spirits and theories of spontaneous generation were overcome, a mechanical approach to medical science was underway. Mechanism, as we have stated in Chapter 3, is a viewpoint which claims that phenomena are dependent on the arrangement and interaction of elements in a determinate fashion governed by concrete laws. Such laws are specific formulations of antecedent causation. Furthermore, most mechanical explanations seek direct contact of physical bodies to produce subsequent results. Pasteur's theory proposed that germs in the air caused contamination only when they came into direct contact with a substance. He also stated that mechanistic agents operating within the body were the cause of health and illness. These postulates were crucial for the development of infectious theory. Otherwise, spiritual and other mystical approaches would still have been a part of the medical canon.

The Theory of Evolution and Antecedent Causation

With Darwin's *Origin of Species*, one of the last bastions of teleology is subsumed under modern scientific antecedent causation.[9] Instead of a purposive, divine creator for life, species, and humanity, Darwin postulated a theory of preexisting hardships which drive competition and selective adaptation in a mechanical way. Darwin himself postulated no agency for this mechanism, and in fact explicitly described his position as analogous to that of Newton, who refused to speculate on the agents of gravitation. Nonetheless, twentieth-century biology subsequently uncovered the mechanism for evolution in genetic science.

Charles Darwin was born in 1809 and died in 1882. He was a British naturalist who had biology in his lineage, being the son of a British country doctor and the grandson of Erasmus Darwin, a naturalist and philosopher who espoused a prototypical theory of evolution. Indeed, evolutionary ideas were in the wind, and Darwin's insight and observation were the catalysts for a new theory whose time had come. This is not to diminish the creative and exhaustive efforts of Darwin the individual. Darwin's work as a naturalist aboard the *Beagle* among the tropical islands of South America and his brilliant theoretical work were crucial for the development of the theory of evolution.

While mechanistic explanation held sway in the physical sciences for some time, developmental biology seemed to defy explanation in terms of modern antecedent causation. The mysteries of the origins of life and the extraordinary intricacies of individual, species, and ecological structure lent credence to a view that nature is designed for a purpose. Such arguments for design posited a variety of architects, from a personified God to more Aristotelian notions of purposive nature striving to achieve a final good. Although Darwin can be criticized for importing some teleological notions into his theory, such as a sufficiently loaded notion of "survival of the fittest" would suggest, he is successful in placing emphasis on antecedent causes and removing a conscious plan from nature. And even if some parts of evolutionary theory can be interpreted as ends-driven, neither individuals nor species have an internal *telos* of their own, nor does nature possess a deliberate purpose under Darwin's theory.

The following selections are from the last chapter of *On the Origin of Species* (1859).[10]

CHAPTER XV

RECAPITULATION AND CONCLUSION

... That many serious objections may be advanced against the theory of descent with modification through variation and natural selection, I do not deny. I have endeavored to give them their full force. Nothing at first can appear more difficult to believe than that the more complex organs and instincts have been perfected, not by means superior to, though analogous with, human reason, but by the accumulation of innumerable slight variations, each good for the individual possessor. ...

It is, no doubt, extremely difficult even to conjecture by what gradations many structures have been perfected, more especially among broken and failing groups of organic beings, which have suffered much extinction; but we see so many strange gradations in nature that we ought to be extremely cautious in saying that any organ or instinct, or any whole structure, could not have arrived at its present state by many graduated steps.

Turning to geographical distribution, the difficulties encountered on the theory of descent with modification are serious enough. All the individuals of the same species, and all the species of the same genus, or even higher groups, are descended from common parents; and therefore, in however distant and isolated parts of the world they may now be found, they must have in the course of successive generations have travelled from some one point to all the others. We are often wholly unable to conjecture how this could have been effected. Yet, as we have reason to believe that some species have retained the same specific form for very long periods ... too much stress ought not to be laid on the occasional wide diffusion of the same species; for during very long periods, there will always have been a good chance for wide migration.... A broken or interrupted range may often be accounted for by the extinction of species in intermediate regions....

As according to the theory of natural selection an interminable number of intermediate forms must have existed ... it may be asked, Why do we not see these linking forms all around us? Why are not all the organic beings blended together in an inextricable chaos? ... [W]e have reason to believe that only a few species of a genus ever undergo change; the other species becoming extinct ... only a few within the same country change at the same time; and all modifications are slowly affected. I have also shown that the intermediate varieties which probably at first existed ... would be liable to be supplanted by the allied forms....

I can answer ... questions and objections only on the supposition that the geological record is far more imperfect than most geologists believe. The number of specimens in all our museums is absolutely as nothing compared with the countless generations of countless species which certainly existed....

In the survival of favored individuals and races, during the constantly recurring Struggle for Existence, we see a powerful and everacting form of Selection. The struggle for existence inevitably follows from the high geometrical ratio of increase which is common to all organic beings. This high rate of increase is proved by calculation.... More individuals are born than can possibly survive.... The slightest advantage in certain individuals, at any age or during any season, over those with which they come into competition, or better adaptation in however slight a degree to the surrounding physical conditions, will, in the long run, turn the balance. ...

If, then, animals and plants do vary, let it be ever so slightly or slowly, why should not variations or individual differences, which are in any way beneficial, be preserved and accumulated through natural selection, or the survival of the fittest? ... I can see no limit to this power, in slowly and beautifully adapting each form to the most complex relations of life. The theory of natural selection, even if we look no further than this, seems to be in the highest degree probable. . . . On this same view we can understand how it is that in a region where many species of a genus have been produced, and where they now flourish, the same species should present many varieties; for where the manufactory of species has been successful, we might expect, as a general rule, to find it still in action. . . .

. . . This tendency in the large groups to go on increasing in size and diverging in character, together with the inevitable contingency of much extinction, explains the arrangement of all the forms of life in groups subordinate to groups, all within a few great classes. . . . This grand fact of the grouping of all organic beings . . . is utterly inexplicable on the theory of creation.

Many other facts are, as it seems to me, explicable on this theory [of natural selection]. How strange it is that a bird, under the form of a woodpecker, should prey on insects on the ground; that upland geese, which rarely or never swim, should possess webbed feet.

The similar framework of bones in the hand of a man, wing of a bat, fin of the porpoise, and leg of the horse—the same number of vertebrae forming the neck of the giraffe and of the elephant— and innumerable other such facts, at once explain themselves on the theory of descent with slow and successive modifications. . . . We may cease marvelling at the embryo of an air-breathing mammal or bird having bronchial slits and arteries running in loops, like those of a fish. . . .

CONCLUSION

I have now recapitulated the facts and considerations which have thoroughly convinced me that species have been modified, during a long course of descent. This has been effected chiefly through the natural selection of numerous successive, slight, favorable variations; aided in an important manner by the inherited effects of the use and disuse of parts. . . .

It can hardly be supposed that a false theory would explain, in so satisfactory a manner as does the theory of natural selection, the several large classes of facts above specified. It has recently been objected that this is an unsafe method of arguing; but it is a method used in judging the common events of life, and has often been used by the greatest natural philosophers . . . it is no valid objection that science as yet throws no light on the far higher problem of the essence or origin of life. Who can explain what is the essence of the attraction of gravity? No one now objects to following out the results consequent on this unknown element of attraction; notwithstanding that Leibniz formerly accused Newton of introducing "occult qualities and miracles into philosophy."

I see no good reason why the views given in this volume should shock the religious feelings of any one. . . . A celebrated author and divine writes that "he has gradually learned to see that it is just as noble a conception of the Deity to believe that He created a few original forms capable of self development into other needful forms, as to believe that He required a fresh act of creation to supply the voids caused by the action of His laws."

. . . The belief that species were immutable productions was almost unavoidable as long as the history of the world was thought to be of short duration. . . . The mind cannot grasp the full meaning of the term of even a million years; it cannot add up and perceive the full effects of many slight variations, accumulated during an almost infinite number of generations.

. . . It is so easy to hide our ignorance under such expressions as the "plan of creation," "unity of design," etc. and to think that we give an explanation when we only restate a fact. Any one whose disposition leads him to attach more weight to unexplained difficulties than to the explanation of a certain number of facts will certainly reject the theory. . . .

The day will come when this will be given as a curious illustration of the blindness of preconceived opinion. These authors seem no more startled at a miraculous act of creation than at an ordinary birth. . . . Do they believe that at each supposed act of creation one individual or many were produced? Were all the infinitely many numerous kinds of animals and plants created as seeds, or as full grown? and in the case of mammals, were they created bearing the false marks of nourishment from their mother's womb? . . . and certainly we ought not to believe that innumerable beings within each great class have been created with plain, but deceptive, marks of descent from a single parent. . . .

[W]hen analogous views on the origin of species are generally admitted . . . [t]he other and more general departments of natural history will rise greatly in interest. The terms used by naturalists, of affinity, relationship, community of type, paternity, morphology, adaptive characters, rudimentary and aborted organs, etc., will cease to be metaphorical, and will have a plain signification. When we no longer look at an organic being as a savage looks at a ship, as something wholly beyond his comprehension; when we regard every production of nature as one which has had a long history; when we contemplate every complex structure and instinct as the summing up of many contrivances, each useful to the possessor, in the same way as any great mechanical invention is the summing up of the labor, the experience, the reason, and even the blunders of numerous workmen; when we thus view the organic being, how far more interesting—I speak from experience—does the study of natural history become!

... Thus, from the war of nature, from famine and death, the most exalted object which we are capable of conceiving, namely, the production of the higher animals, directly follows.

Darwin's prophetic views on the importance of his works were by no means overstated. Not only did his theory spawn new fields of study and new interest and importance within existing fields of natural history, but the reluctance of the scientific community to accept his views is indeed a monument to the power of scientific and cultural prejudice.

Part of the difficulty Darwin faced was not entirely willful closed-mindedness, but a misunderstanding of the scope of geologic time. Darwin realized that the span of time during which life had been inhabiting the earth had been grossly underestimated and that consequently the completeness of the fossil record had been overestimated. Once scientists grasped the true range of natural history, a new theory could take hold. Such a change in scope facilitating a change in world-views has been witnessed many times in the course of scientific history. One of the most important discoveries of early modern astronomy was Copernicus' assertion that the orbits of the planets and their distances from the sun were orders of magnitude greater than the sizes of the planets themselves. A naive preconception of astronomical dimension had been thwarting a more modern view of planetary motion prior to this development. In the next chapter we will see how a similar change in scope, the realization of the magnitude of cosmic time, facilitates a new statistical explanation of time itself.

Darwin's position on teleology is ambiguous. He claims that traditional teleological explanation is a shield for ignorance, and that an appeal to nature's design is a restatement of the obvious rather than a scientific contribution to human understanding. However, the notions of "survival of the fittest" and accumulation of beneficial adaptations can be interpreted as ends-driven processes which strive for some good. Nevertheless, Darwin criticized a view of nature as deliberate and purposive. He claimed that theories which posit conscious acts of creation are less adequate to organic phenomena than his own theory of gradual modifications "summing up . . . many contrivances." And certainly no species or individual has an internal *telos* as a simplistic interpretation of natural purposiveness would have it.

Darwin's theory is meant to serve as a law-like explanation of some characteristics of nature. He admitted that the broader, more general questions of why these laws operate and what the agents of these laws might be are unanswered, and that those more persuaded by "unexplained difficulties than . . . the explanation of a certain number of facts" would reject his theory. He also understood that his manner of argument was far from conclusive. He posited no agency or overall explanation for the origins of life but instead appealed to the fact that disparate phenomena could be understood and related to each other in cogent ways by his theory. Darwinian evolution was in this way like Newtonian gravitation. Darwin saw this as a strength rather than a weakness.

Darwin left aside issues regarding the nature and beginning of a world that fosters evolutionary growth. Why do we live in such a world? Where did it come from? Later scientists and philosophers attempt to answer this question by further removing ideas of purpose or design from the universe. Although the development of complexity and intelligence in the living realm suggested to some a purpose or at least an astounding predilection for organization within nature, later scientists dismissed evolution as a random blip in the cosmic unfolding of entropic processes. This blip is explained by chance initial conditions, and tends to be overemphasized due to the fact that we live within it. In the next chapter, we will see some physical scientists who explicitly endorse this view.

Notions of survival of the fittest and natural selection were, of course, applied broadly outside the bounds of the biological sciences. Social Darwinism[11] became a popular method for understanding human cultural phenomena. Social Darwinism takes Darwin's model of selective adaptation and applies it to human society. Societies and cultures survive and dominate because they have been subjected to a struggle for survival, and the fittest have prevailed, according to the social Darwinist.

The way in which this mode of explanation was and still is employed belies the teleological parts of the theory. When a culture or society prospers or is extinguished by selective evolutionary forces, an appeal to survival of the fittest is often made. In making this appeal, it is assumed that grander forces are at work, and we have no way to question or criticize them. Furthermore, such forces work to achieve some greater good, according to some social Darwinists, and so survival of the fittest is taken to have not only a factual but a moral content.

This sort of reasoning has been accused of committing what philosophers call "the naturalistic fallacy." A fallacy is committed, according to philosophers, when a simple identification is made between the natural and the good. Once this equation is tacitly admitted, further philosophic study of value is obviated. Although Aristotle and his followers, as we saw, regarded nature as moving toward some good, the Aristotelian premise regarding final causes, purposes, and values in nature was not simply assumed but explicitly called out and supported. By simplistically and unconsciously identifying the natural with the good, sociologists and other scientists are at least impoverishing cultural dialogue, if not committing a full-blown fallacy.

Summary

In this chapter we have seen the rise of mechanistic explanation in biology. Harvey and Pasteur left aside questions of purpose when they made their discoveries. While Darwinian theory avoids explicit use of final causation, its drive for adaptation may conceal a more subtle teleology. However, the intended displacement of teleology is a sign of another, perhaps deeper transformation in philosophy and science. Science established itself as an autonomous area, independent of metaphysics, at least on the surface. Newton, Comte, and Darwin all shared a positivistic reluctance to delve into metaphysics, and the success of science under these auspices fuels further separation between philosophy and science. No longer the descendent of philosophical theories of nature, logic, or values, science can be pursued for its own sake.

This autonomy empowered theorists in biology and medicine. No longer constrained by metaphysical notions of humanity, biologists and physiologists strove to bring the study of the living being into the modern age. By proposing purely mechanical theories of physiology, infection, and development, the theorists in this chapter not only brought objective science to bear on new areas, they also further undercut the hold that traditional philosophy had on access to knowledge.

Notes

1. See Chapter 8. Modern, specifically Enlightenment (eighteenth century), deism was a popular metaphysical view proposing that the universe was governed by a supreme yet disinterested designer.
2. Butterfield, *The Origins of Modern Science*, 39.
3. For a general discussion of this sort of phenomenon, see Chapter 11 on Thomas Kuhn.
4. Ibid.
5. Vesalius, the brilliant anatomical illustrator at Padua; Colombo, his successor; and Miguel Serveto, the heretic; all contributed to this story. (See Butterfield, Chapter III.)

6. Harvey was not under the political influence of the papacy, however, since the Church of England had already separated from the Catholic Church by Harvey's time.

7. René Dubos, *Pasteur and Modern Science* (New York: Doubleday, 1960), 47.

8. Lister first applied Pasteur's results to surgery (Dampier, 282).

9. This interpretation of Darwinian natural selection can be challenged by appeal to Darwin's own conceptions, as we will see.

10. From Charles Darwin, *On the Origin of Species* (New York: Macmillan, 1927, 1962).

11. By some accounts, Herbert Spencer was a social Darwinist before Darwin. Marx also used components of social evolutionary theory along Darwinistic lines. And capitalistic political theory relies on such a principle to argue for the positive results of *laissez-faire* economics. (See Chapter 9.)

Suggestions for Further Reading

Butterfield, Herbert. *The Origins of Modern Science* (New York: Macmillan, 1958).

Dampier, Sir William Cecil. *A History of Science and its Relations with Philosophy and Religion*, 4th ed. (Cambridge, England: Cambridge University Press, 1948).

Darwin, Charles. *The Descent of Man* (New York: The Modern Library, 1936).

Dubos, René. *Louis Pasteur: Free Lance of Science* (New York: Charles Scribner's Sons, 1950).

Huxley, T.H. *Science and Culture* (London: Macmillan, 1882).

Watson, James. *The Double Helix: A Personal Account of the Discovery of the Structure of DNA* (New York: Athaneum, 1968).

The Refinement and Evolution of Mechanical Physics

In this chapter we will follow some developments in modern science from the seventeenth to the nineteenth centuries. Chemists and physicists used philosophical and scientific ideas to advance their understanding of the physical world,[1] and their theories in turn spawned new scientific and philosophical ideas that eventually replaced the world-view of Descartes, Galileo, Newton, and Leibniz. In particular, physical and chemical theories turned toward field-oriented, unitary descriptions instead of mechanical postulates. And a new discipline, statistical mechanics, had grave implications for our commonsense notion of time. Both field theory and statistical modeling foreshadow twentieth-century developments in physics. Einstein's general relativity posits that a space-time field is the fundamental substratum of the universe. Quantum theory posits that statistical methods are the fundamental access to physical knowledge.

We will see how chemistry, electromagnetism, and a new approach to mechanics both complement and undercut classical physical science. Robert Boyle's work was straightforwardly part of the modern revolution in science. As a contemporary of Newton and Robert Hooke, Boyle was important in forming a coherent world-view that successfully replaced that of the Medievals. Michael Faraday and James Maxwell each worked in the nineteenth century to expand the domain of physics to include electricity and magnetism. Josiah Gibbs and Ludwig Boltzmann staged a quiet revolution at the end of the nineteenth century in their development of statistical mechanics.

Faraday and Maxwell were building a mathematical and physical system which rejected some of the analytic techniques of their precedessors. Maxwell's electromagnetic equations do not rely on a mechanistic account, although he included some speculations concerning the "aether" that serve as his putative mechanical agents. His introduction of a sophisticated, mathematically sound system of fields foreshadowed the overthrow of classical mechanics by general relativity. Nevertheless, electromagnetic theory expanded the domain of classical physics and used alternative explanations in complementary areas. That is, Newton's laws remained valid for bodies in motion outside the influence of electrical or magnetic fields, while electromagnetic theory explained behavior within electrical or magnetic fields. Thus, the new modes of explanation found in Maxwell's theory were not yet threatening to established theories.

The construction of statistical mechanics and its success in replacing classical thermodynamics is an analogous situation. New modes of explanation and new mathematical techniques appeared on the scene to augment the power of modern science. Statistical techniques were basic to a new model of chemical interaction, and became basic to all of physics in the coming century. Quantum Theory uses statistical explanation in such fundamental ways that the very structure of the universe is described as probabilistic, not deterministic. And by attempting to explain the flow of time, statistical mechanics cannot take the doctrine of antecedent causation for granted but must probe its foundations. Thus the groundwork is again laid for a revolutionary paradigm shift[2] in physics, but this shift takes place in a specialized niche at the outset.

Thus, these new systems had the effect of accumulating more theoretical and practical apparati for explaining, predicting, and controlling the physical world. Human understanding seemed to be moving toward a final goal of ultimate knowledge. Subsequent scientific and philosophical history illustrates a breakdown of this faith in progress, as we will see in Chapter 11.

Corpuscularian Chemistry

Robert Boyle (1627–1691) was an English scientist who founded modern chemistry. He rejected Aristotelian causes, Greek elements, and other previous systems of chemistry. He advanced a "corpusculerian, mechanical, anti-Aristotelian world view."[3] We call such a system corpuscular because it posits that particles are the basic physical elements, but unlike the atoms of Democritus[4] corpuscles are not indivisible. This system is an application of mechanical causation and analytical method. Effects are mechanically produced from antecedent causes for Boyle—he rejected ethereal forms, final causes, and other animistic or mystical constructions. The only type of cause, theory, or explanation which is helpful to us must be material and mechanical, not spiritual or metaphysical.

Boyle anticipated some of the prescriptions of positivism,[5] and he emphasized some of the same themes as Newton. He was not concerned with metaphysical speculations on the essential attributes of his mechanical agents. Like Newton, Darwin, and other pioneering scientists, Boyle was able to propose general laws and principles while leaving aside philosophical debate on issues such as ultimate substance, agency, or cause. He admonished us to look not so much at what agents are but at what effects they produce, and how effects are produced. Yet Boyle believed the trend in scientific inquiry would lead to entities of smaller and smaller spacial dimension. In Boyle's analysis, scientific method proceeds from phenomena of larger scale to explanatory elements of smaller dimension. Thus, Boyle was an empirical reductionist with positivist leanings. The following are selections from *The Excellency and Grounds of the Corpuscular or Mechanical Philosophy*,[6] first published in 1674.

... if the principles of the Aristotelians and chymists are thus obscure, it is not to be expected the explications made by the help of such principles should be intelligible. And, indeed, many of them are so general and slight, or otherwise so unsatisfactory, that, granting their principles, 'tis very hard to understand or admit their applications of them to particular phenomena. And, methinks, even in some of the more ingenious and subtle of the peripatetic [Aristotelian] discourses, the authors, upon their superficial and narrow theories, have acted more like painters than philosophers; and only shown their skill in making men fancy they see castles, cities, and other structures, that appear solid, magnificent, and extensive; when the whole piece is superficial, artificial. ...

I next observe that there cannot be fewer principles than the two grand ones of our philosophy, matter and motion; for matter alone, unless it be moved, is wholly unactive; and whilst all the parts of a body continue in one state, without motion, that body will not exercise any action, or suffer any alteration; though it may, perhaps, modify the action of other bodies that move against it. ...

The next thing which recommends the corpuscular principles is their extensiveness. The genuine and necessary effect of the strong motion of one part of matter against another is either to drive it on, in its entire bulk, or to break and divide it into particles of a determinate motion, figure, size, posture, rest, order or texture. The first two of these, for instance, are each of them capable of numerous varieties: for the figure of a portion of matter may either be one of the five regular geometrical figures, some determinate species of solid figures, or irregular, as the grains of sand, feathers, branches, files, etc. And, as the figure, so the motion of one of these particles may be exceedingly diversified, not only by the determination to a particular part of the world but by several other things: as by almost infinitely different degrees of celerity; by the manner of its progression, with or without rotation, etc. and more yet by the line wherein it moves. . . .

Now, since a single particle of matter, by virtue of only two mechanical properties that belong to it, may be diversified so many ways; what a vast number of variations may we suppose capable of being produced by the compositions, and recompositions of myriads of single invisible corpuscles, that may be contained and concreted in one small body; and each of them be endued with more than two or three of the fertile, universal principles above-mentioned? And the aggregate of those corpuscles may be further diversified by the texture resulting from their convention into a body; which, as so made up, has its own magnitude, shape, pores, and many capacities of acting and suffering, upon account of the place it holds among other bodies, in a world constituted like ours: so that, considering the numerous diversifications that compositions and recompositions may make of a small number, those who think the mechanical principles may serve, indeed, to account for the phenomena of some particular part of natural philosophy, as statics, the theory of planetary motions etc. but prove unapplicable to all the phenomena of things corporeal seem to imagine, that by putting together the letters of the alphabet one may, indeed, make up all the words to be found in Euclid or Virgil, or in the Latin or English language, but that they can by no means supply words to all the books of a great library; much less, to all the languages in the world.

There are other philosophers, who, observing the great efficacy of magnitude, situation, motion, and connection in engines are willing to allow those mechanical principles a great share in the operations of bodies of a sensible bulk and manifest mechanism; and therefore to be usefully employed, in accounting for the effect and phenomena of such bodies: though they will not admit that these principles can be applied to the hidden transactions among the minute particles of bodies; and, therefore, think it necessary to refer these to what they call nature, substantial forms, real qualities, and the unmechanical agents. But this is not necessary: for the mechanical properties of matter are to be found, and the laws of motion take place, not only in the great masses and the middle-sized lumps, but in the smallest fragment of matter. . . .

When, to solve the problem of nature, agents are made use of which, though they involve no contradiction in their notions . . . yet are such that we conceive not how they operate to produce effects; such agents I mean, as the soul of the world, the universal spirit, the plastic power, etc., the curiosity of an inquisitive person is not satisfied hereby; who seeks not so much to know what is the general agent that produces a phenomenon, as by what means, and after what manner, it is produced. . . .

I come now to consider that which I observe most alienates other sects from the mechanical philosophy; viz. a supposition, that it pretends to have principles so universal and mathematical that no other physical hypothesis can be tolerated by it.

This I look upon as an easy, indeed, but an important mistake: for the mechanical principles are so universal, and appliable to so many purposes, that they are rather fitted to take in, than to exclude, any other hypothesis founded on nature. And such hypotheses, if prudently considered, will be found, as far as they have truth on their side, to be either legitimately deducible from the mechanical principles or fairly reconcileable to them. For such hypotheses will, probably, attempt to account for the phenomena of nature, either by the help of a determinate number of material ingredients, . . . or by introducing some general agents, such as the Platonic soul of the world, and the universal spirit. . . .

Now, the chief thing that a philosopher should look after, in explaining difficult phenomena, is not so much what the agent is or does, as what changes are made in the patient, to bring it to exhibit the phenomena proposed; and by what means, and after what manner, those changes are effected. So that the mechanical philosopher being satisfied, one part of matter can act upon another, only by virtue of local motion, or the effects and consequences thereof; he considers, if the proposed agent be not intelligible and physical, it can never physically explain the phenomena; and if it be intelligible and physical, it will be reducible to matter and some or other of its universal properties. And the indefinite divisibility of matter, the wonderful efficacy of motion, and the almost infinite variety of coalitions and structures that may be made of minute and insensible corpuscles being duly weighed; why may not a philosopher think it possible to make out, by their help, the mechanical possibility of any corporeal agent, how subtle, diffused, or active soever, that can be solidly proved to have a real existence in nature? . . .

The solidity, taste, etc. of salt may be fairly accounted for by the stiffness, sharpness, and other mechanical properties of the minute particles whereof salt consists. . . .

. . . if, besides rational souls, there be any immaterial substances . . . they can only help to constitute and effect things, but will very little help us to conceive how things are effects; so that, by whatever principles natural things are constituted, 'tis by the mechanical principles that their phenomena must be clearly explained. For instance . . . to explain the stations, progressions, and retrogradations, and other phenomena of the planets, we must have recourse . . . to theories wherein motion, figure, situation, and other mathematical, or mechanical properties are chiefly employed. . . .

. . . when this philosophy is more scrutinized and farther improved, it will be found applicable to the solutions of still more phenomena of nature. And 'tis not always necessary that he who advances an hypothesis . . . be able, a priori, to prove it true, or demonstratively to show that the other hypothesis proposed about the same subject must be false. . . . Thus, in physical hypotheses, there are some that, without falling foul upon others, peacably obtain the approbation of discerning men only by the fitness to solve the phenomena for which they were devised . . . and therefore, if the mechanical philosophy shall continue to explain corporeal things . . . in time unprejudiced persons will think it sufficiently recommended, by its being consistent with itself and applicable to so many phenomena of nature.

We can isolate the salient features of Boyle's system by classifying them as to specific postulates and methodological prescriptions. Boyle's specific postulates are that the intelligible, physical world is determined by actions of minute particles of "indefinitely divisible" matter. There are further only two types of principles which make this determination: matter and motion. A physical phenomenon, such as the taste of salt, can be completely explained by the matter involved and the motions of particles during tasting. These postulates exemplify modern notions of antecedent causation. We are to look at preceding causes, in the form of minute particular motions and compositions, for subsequent effects. In addition, the macroscopic world of visible objects is entirely dependent on the actions of mechanical corpuscles. Hence, we have a purely mechanical reductionism in Boyle's system.

Boyle also claimed that causation is exclusively material. This brings us to a discussion of his general, methodological prescriptions. We have seen in Chapter 1 in our discussion of Galen; Chapters 4 and 5 with our discussions of Galileo, Newton, Hume, and Bacon; and again in this chapter that scientists and philosophers take different sides of the empiricism/rationalism debate. Boyle's empiricism is no exception. He explicitly avoided rational argument concerning other possible theories or other philosophical systems, and looked to "peacably" establish his own corpuscular theory by its effectiveness in the arena for which it is intended. As we saw, he prescribed that science concern itself with effects and not preoccupy itself with metaphysical discussions of nature, essence, or agency. This concept can be applied to Boyle's theory itself. That is, he chose not to argue for the essential truth or meaning of his theory, but asked us to evaluate it by its predictive and explanatory power. Thus, a natural philosophy of mechanical cause and effect justifies itself by its own effectiveness. On a deep level, then, Boyle's theory is indeed "consistent with itself."

The Theory of Electromagnetism: Classical Physics Expands and Evolves

Although Galileo, Boyle, and Newton disagreed on several important physical and philosophical issues, including the status of absolute space, the role of hypothesis in scientific investigation, and the basic principles of physical science, they all shared a mechanical interpretation of the world. Newton's theory of gravitation was his most controversial proposal because it notably lacked a strictly mechanical account of its effects. Nevertheless, the modern preoccupation with mechanism and particles was pronounced, and proponents of modern science saw these principles as central for banishing the ethereal, spiritual, and philosophical baggage that science had inherited from the ancients and medievals.

As the nineteenth century dawned, scientists were preoccupied with electromagnetic phenomena. Such phenomena seemed to defy direct interpretation along mechanistic lines. In 1820, Hans Christian Oersted demonstrated that electric current could deflect a magnetized substance. This discovery was incorporated into a device, the galvanometer, which measured current through the slight deflection of a magnetic needle.

Michael Faraday (1791–1867), a British experimenter of humble origins, showed that magnetic fields could produce electricity. Faraday's *Experimental Researches in Electricity* outlines his "hope of obtaining electricity from ordinary magnetism." His apparatus includes "several feet of copper wire stretched in wide zigzag forms.... One of these wires was connected with a galvanometer, the other with ... a battery...." He proceeds to see if current is generated by a motion of these wires, and discovers that "[a]s the wires approximated, the induced current was in the contrary direction to the inducing. As the wires receded, the induced current was in the same direction. . . ."[7]

Thus, he shows that current flowing through one wire will induce current in another wire by means of an intermediate magnetic field. The galvanometer acts as a measure of this field. Faraday's result demonstrated that electromagnetism is indeed a unitary system of forces, and opens the possibility of converting mechanical work to electricity.

Faraday and James Clerk Maxwell inaugurated a major transition in physics, since they introduced the concept of fields of force, which supplemented and in some ways replaced the mechanistic visions of Galileo, Boyle, and Newton. The situation Faraday described is difficult for a mechanist like Newton or Boyle to explain. Boyle wanted us to rely on simple mechanical collisions and arrangements of particles like those which comprise "middle-sized lumps" of matter. Faraday's induction experiments provided a sound experimental basis for producing a phenomenon which acts at a distance through invisible lines of force. Faraday's zigzags of wire do not seem to be acting by collision, and the induction produced depends strangely on geometry in ways that do not seem to correspond to the phenomena of particles as we know them. To be sure, Boyle emphasized motion, arrangement, and mathematical properties, but the mechanism of Newton and Boyle was the more important and tangible replacement for ethereal substances, forms, and causes found in earlier natural philosophies. Maxwell elegantly formalized a decidedly nonmechanical model for electromagnetic theory, although he favored an underlying mechanical explanation.

James Clerk Maxwell was a Scottish physicist with broad interests and accomplishments who lived from 1831 until 1879. He worked in physics, astronomy, and chemistry, but his best-known contributions to scientific theory are his equations of the electromagnetic field. In Maxwell's work, we see the completion of a series observed in earlier great advances in modern physics: careful observation followed by mathematical formalization. We saw in Chapter 3 how Tycho Brahe's precise astronomical observations were essential for Kepler's mathematical model of the heliocentric solar system. In the nineteenth century, Farady and Maxwell played analogous roles. Faraday provided the experimental insights; Maxwell provided the unifying mathematical formula to incorporate the experimental results into physical theory.

While Maxwell's introduction of fields into the world-view of physics was new, at this point the world-view described by field theory complemented the mechanistic, corpuscular one of classical physics. Furthermore, Maxwell was not willing to part with a mechanical explanation for the action of the electromagnetic field. He proposed an aetherial medium filling space, and argued for its existence via the phenomena of light and heat.

Maxwell thus explicitly connected light, heat, and electromagnetism. The following selections are from *Matter and Motion*, (1877)[8] and *A Dynamical Theory of the Electromagnetic Field* (1895).[9]

MATTER AND MOTION

Physical Science, which up to the end of the eighteenth century had been fully occupied in forming a conception of natural phenomena as the result of forces acting between one body and another, has now fairly entered on the next stage of progress—that in which the energy of a material system is conceived as determined by the configuration and motion of that system.

84. ACTION AT A DISTANCE

In the case of two magnets there is no visible substance connecting the bodies between which the stress exists. The space between the magnets may be filled with air or with water. . . . We may even place a solid plate of glass or metal or wood between the magnets, and still we find that their mutual action depends simply on their relative position. . . . Hence the action between the magnets is commonly spoken of as *action at a distance.*

Attempts have been made, with a certain amount of success, to analyse this action at a distance into a continuous distribution of stress in an invisible medium [see below—ed.]; but still the general fact that . . . changes of configuration are accompanied by stresses or internal forces . . . remains an ultimate fact which has not been explained as the result of any more fundamental principle.

A DYNAMICAL THEORY OF THE ELECTROMAGNETIC FIELD

(1) The most obvious mechanical phenomenon in electrical and magnetical experiments is the mutual action by which bodies in certain states set each other in motion while still at a sensible distance from each other. The first step, therefore, in reducing these phenomena into scientific form, is to ascertain the magnitude and direction of the force acting between the bodies. . . . [I]t seems at first sight natural to explain the facts by assuming the existence of something either at rest or in motion in each body . . . capable of acting at a distance according to mathematical laws.

... the force acting between the two bodies is treated with reference only to the condition of the bodies and their relative position, and without any express consideration of the surrounding medium.

The theories assume, more or less explicitly, the existence of substances the particles of which have the property of acting on one another at a distance....

(2) ... I have ... preferred to seek an explanation of the facts in another direction, by supposing them to be produced by actions which go on in the surrounding medium as well as in the excited bodies, and endeavoring to explain the action between distant bodies without assuming the existence of forces capable of acting directly at sensible distances.

(3) The theory I propose may therefore be called a theory of *Electromagnetic Field*, because it has to do with the space in the neighborhood of the electric or magnetic bodies ... it assumes that in that space there is matter in motion, by which the observed electromagnetic phenomena are produced.

(4) The electromagnetic field is that part of space which contains or surrounds bodies in electric or magnetic conditions.

It may be filled with any kind of matter, or we may attempt to render it empty of all gross matter....

There is, however, enough of matter left to receive and transmit the undulations of light and heat, and ... we are obliged to admit that the undulations are those of an aetherial substance....

We have therefore some reason to believe, from the phenomena of light and heat, that there is an aethereal medium filling space.

(6) We may therefore receive, as a datum derived from a branch of science independent of that with which we have to deal, the existence of a pervading medium ... capable of being set in motion, and of transmitting motion from one part to another with great, but not infinite, velocity....

(10) According to the theory which I propose ... "electromotive force" is the force called into play during the communication of motion from one part of the medium to another, and it is by means of this force that the motion of one part causes motion in another part....

(11) When electromotive force acts on a dialectric, it produces a state of polarization of its parts similar to ... the influence of a magnet.

(16) Thus, then, we are led to the conception of a complicated mechanism capable of a vast variety of motion, but at the same time, so connected that the motion of one part depends, according to the definite relations, on the motion of other parts. ... Such a mechanism must be subject to the general laws of Dynamics. ...

(18) ... In order to bring these relations within the power of symbolical calculation, I then express them in the form of the General Equations of the Electromagnetic Field. ... There are twenty of these equations in all, involving twenty variable quantities.

(20) ... it is shewn that the only disturbance [propogated through a non-conducting field] ... are those which are transverse to the direction of propagation and that the velocity ... is so nearly that of light that it seems we have strong reason to conclude that light itself is an electromagnetic disturbance in the form of waves propagated through the electromagnetic field.

Maxwell was led by the brilliant experiments of Oersted and Faraday to theorize in new ways about physical systems. Instead of focusing on how material bodies collide and react, he proposed an interconnected system of forces and fields producing "a vast variety of motion." This system was mediated by an aetherial material for Maxwell, an assumption that Michelson and Morley refuted and later Einstein replaced entirely (see Chapter 10). However mistaken Maxwell may have been concerning the aether, his systemic, field-oriented approach to a mysterious "action-at-a-distance" phenomenon was tremendously fruitful, for it yielded his equations unifying electricity and magnetism.

Maxwell's result paved the way for the conversion of mechanical energy into electrical current. His formalization of the effects of disturbances within the electromagnetic field permitted the production and control of electricity. Electricity and magnetism were, according to Maxwell's theory, different aspects of the same phenomenon. The forces of electricity and magnetism coexist in perpendicular directions within one electromagnetic field. Since the speed at which changes in the field propagate is so close to the speed of light, Maxwell boldly speculated that light is an electromagnetic phenomenon. His conjecture would prove correct.

Physicists in the twentieth century were inspired by the unification of two disparate forces into one theory. Electromagnetic theory, stripped of the misguided mechanism Maxwell proposed, is an example of nonmechanical reductionism. Two effects, electrical and magnetic, are explained by one theory. Thus, we have a reductionism from two sorts of forces to one unified field. Twentieth-century reductionists, from Einstein's work in his last years to contemporary grand unificationists, continued in the reductionist spirit of Maxwell.

Statistical Mechanics

Josiah Gibbs and Ludwig Boltzmann pioneered statistical mechanics in the later nineteenth century. Historically, the impetus for the application of statistics to mechanics was in order to explain the second law of thermodynamics.[10] This law states that disorder, or entropy, in a closed system always remains the same or increases over time. This has also been interpreted to say that time is asymmetrical, that is, not reversible. A convenient term for this phenomenon is *time's arrow*. Such a postulate is not explained by or derived from a deterministic, mechanistic world-view, but rather from an empirical fact. The mathematical formulae of Newton, Laplace,[11] and Maxwell postulate no special direction for the flow of time. Strictly mechanical systems, such as projectile motion, are completely reversible—to see the reverse of a cannonball's path, simply fire the same projectile from its ending point toward its starting point. If the world were completely mechanical and deterministic in this way, then all events should have their time reversal counterparts. That is, we should see processes such as mixtures becoming unmixed and vapor flowing back into a bottle.[12] Since this conflicts with observation, the second law of thermodynamics is imposed upon classical physics. Physicists strove to explain this with a more coherent theory.

Such a theory must be a radical departure from traditional classical explanations. Since the goal is to explain the flow of time, time flow cannot be assumed as given. A basic armament of the modern mind-set, antecedent causation, takes for granted this very assumption. Antecedent causation postulates that in order to understand subsequent effects one must look to preceding causes. Such a postulate has time flow built into it. Therefore, using antecedent causation to explain time's arrow would beg the question. Time itself can have no special role in this new inquiry. So we see how a scientific investigation makes a methodological shift away from modern philosophical presuppositions. Eventually this investigation yields new philosophical and scientific insights on the status of time in our world.

Josiah Gibbs (1839–1903) was one of the first American scientists of international repute. The following is a selection from the "Preface" to *Elementary Principles in Statistical Mechanics.*[13]

The usual point of view in the study of mechanics is that where the attention is mainly directed to the changes which take place in the course of time in a given system. . . .

For some purposes, however, it is desirable to take a broader view of the subject. We may imagine a great number of systems of the same nature, but differing in configurations . . . so as to embrace every conceivable combination of configuration. . . . And here we may set the problem, not to follow a particular system through its succession of configurations, but to determine how the whole number of systems will be distributed. . . .

Such inquiries have been called by Maxwell *statistical.* . . .

But although, as a matter of history, statistical mechanics owes its origins to investigations in thermodynamics, it seems eminently worthy of independent development. . . . Moreover, the separate study of this branch of mechanics seems to afford the best foundation for the study of rational thermodynamics and molecular mechanics.

The laws of thermodynamics, as empirically determined, express the approximate and probable behavior of systems of a great number of particles . . . as they appear to beings who have not the fineness of perception to enable them to appreciate quantities of the order of magnitude of those which relate to single particles. . . . The laws of thermodynamics may be easily obtained from the principles of statistical mechanics, of which they are an incomplete expression, but they make a somewhat blind guide in our search. . . .

Moreover, we avoid the gravest difficulties when, giving up the attempt to frame hypotheses concerning the constitution of material bodies, we pursue statistical inquiries. . . . Difficulties of this kind have deterred the author from attempting to explain the mysteries of nature, and have forced him to be contented with the more modest aim of deducing some of the more obvious propositions relating to the statistical branch of mechanics.

Here again we have an example of an empiricist and positivistic approach to science. In fact, the statistical approach itself is born from a desire to give up the "difficulties" of discovering specific agents, causes, and other essential attributes of material bodies, according to Gibbs. Thus, Gibbs sought the general laws and large-scale behavior of systems, a pursuit worthy of science in its "maturity," according to Comte.[14]

Ludwig Boltzmann was a brilliant Austrian chemist with a wide range of achievements. His suicide in 1906 at age sixty-two may have been related to the reluctance of the scientific community to accept his controversial views. The following is excerpted from Boltzmann's *Application of the Second Law of Thermodynamics to the Universe as a Whole.*[15]

Is the apparent irreversibility of all known natural processes consistent with the idea that all natural events are possible without restriction? Is the apparent unidirectionality of time consistent with the infinite extent or apparent cyclical nature of time? He who tries to answer these questions in the affirmative must use as a model of the world a system whose ... positive and negative directions of time are equivalent, and by means of which the appearance of irreversibility over long periods of time is explicable by some special assumption. But this is precisely what happens in the atomic view of the world.

One can think of the world as a mechanical system of an enormously large number of constituents, and of an immensely long period of time, so that the dimensions of that part containing our own "fixed stars" are minute compared to the extension of the universe; and times that we call eons are likewise minute. . . . Then in the universe, which is in thermal equilibrium throughout and therefore dead, there will occur here and there relatively small regions of the same size as our galaxy . . . which, during the relatively short time of eons, fluctuate noticeably from thermal equilibrium. . . . For the universe, the two directions of time are indistinguishable, just as in space there is no up or down. However, just as at a particular place on the earth's surface we call "down" the direction toward the centre of the earth, so will a living being in a particular time interval of such a single world . . . distinguish the direction of time. . . . This method seems to me to be the only way in which one can understand the second law—the heat death of each single world. . . .

Obviously no one would consider such speculations as important discoveries, or even—as did the ancient philosophers—as the highest purpose of science. However, it is doubtful that one should despise them as completely idle. Who knows whether they may not broaden the horizon of our circle of ideas, and by stimulating thought, advance the understanding of the facts of experience?

... From the numerical data on the inconceivably great rareness of transition from a probable to a less probable state in observable dimensions during an observable time, we see that such a process within ... our ... world ... is so unlikely that its observability is excluded.

In the entire universe, the aggregate of all individual worlds, there will, however, in fact occur processes going in the opposite direction. But the beings who observe such processes will simply reckon time as proceeding from the less probable to the more probable states, and it will never be discovered whether they reckon time differently from us, since they are separated by eons of time and spatial distances $10^{10^{10}}$ times the distance of Sirius. ...

I have not avoided philosophical questions here, in the firm hope that philosophy and science will add new nourishment to each of these branches of learning. ...

Gibbs and Boltzmann here explained the statistical approach to thermodynamics in non-technical terms. Gibbs advocated the study of a vast number of systems representing every possible configuration in order to explain phenomena that were formerly explained by attempting to trace the development of one particular system through time. Both these scientists hint that a driving force of modern science, the theory of antecedent causation, had run its course of usefulness as a guide to investigation. New, non-intuitive approaches were needed.

Boltzmann spoke of the flow of time as an isolated phenomenon local to our region of a vast universe. Such a region is by chance highly organized initially, and time is observed as a disorganization. He speaks of the improbability of observing processes which appear to flow backward in time, i.e., toward organization, within any given region. These phenomena, such as vapor flowing back into a bottle, mixtures becoming unmixed, and so forth, are highly improbable because the number of states in which particles are distributed randomly is so much higher than ones in which they are not, e.g., localized into a bottle or separated into different substances. The amount of time one would have to wait before such an unlikely event would be remotely probable within a given region exceeds the age of the known universe.

Roughly, this is because of two aspects of states of high entropy, i.e., extreme disorganization. First, the general character, and thus overall appearance and behavior, of disorganized systems is the same no matter which components of the system are found where. Every highly disorganized system of, say, air molecules in a room looks the same. The air is distributed evenly throughout in all of these systems, whether molecule number 1 or molecule number 2,356,874,213 happens to be nearest the center of the room. And second, the number of possible systems with an even distribution is vastly greater than the number of systems that are organized. Consider one example of organization, say, a system in which all of the air molecules inside a room are within six inches of the floor. Such an organization entails some systemic relationship that constrains the number of systems that satisfy this relationship. This is the case in all instances of high organization, and so the likelihood of low entropy, i.e., high organization, is small.

Boltzmann and Gibbs explained time and the second law of thermodynamics by utilizing atomistic mechanics and advanced mathematical technique. Statistical mechanics provides a way to derive the second law of thermodynamics from conventional mechanics. This achieved greater coherence within physics and chemistry since external postulates were no longer needed to make physical theory fit observable experience. The time symmetry found in Newton's and Maxwell's laws is compatible with the irreversibility of experience. This compatibility is achieved by taking a statistical approach that does not follow the flow of time but considers all possible distributions of a given system.

The achievement of statistical mechanics is one of great vision, which undoubtedly served to stimulate thought and advance understanding, as Boltzmann hoped it would. One of the results of this inspiration is the discovery that statistical models are basic to atomic phenomena even when they are considered in isolation, apart from systems and distributions. In Chapter 10, we will see how quantum mechanics postulates that statistical, probabilistic phenomena are basic elements of even simple systems.

Summary

While some of the views put forward by physicists in the nineteenth century can be seen as new paradigms, for example, field theory and statistical approaches, the subject matter dealt with in these views complemented rather than replaced classical mechanics. Modern science since the seventeenth century successively progressed by experiment and mathematical formalization to achieve new successes. Scientific knowledge, while refined and evolved since Newton's time, seemed to grow cumulatively. This growth was made possible by a modern mind-set which included analytic technique, experimental method, mathematical theory, and mechanistic views of causation.

However, the new views in the form of statistics and fields were crucial in twentieth-century physical revolutions that outright displaced classical views. These revolutions, furthermore, displaced some of the philosophical underpinnings of modern science. Quantum theory and general relativity criticized corpuscular, mechanistic approaches to science like those discussed in Chapters 3 and 4. In philosophy, mechanistic constructions were augmented by the metaphysical theories of Alfred North Whitehead and others who drew inspiration from relativity and quantum theory. Twentieth-century physical theory depicts a world of interrelatedness, probability, and relativity, and hence many philosophers believed that an accurate metaphysical theory should accommodate such notions as well.

The theoretical advances in chemistry and electricity treated in this chapter contributed to the Industrial Revolution. The engines of the industrial age did not derive purely from the works of theoreticians, however. In fact, most innovations of the Industrial Revolution were contrived by those unfamiliar with the work of Newton. Yet both the industrial and scientific revolutions were engendered by similar mind-sets, that is, attitudes that fostered objective, quantitative inquiry designed to expand the scope of human influence, both speculative and practical. The Industrial Revolution in turn brought new problems to philosophy, science, and the world. Environmental, ethical, and political issues arose in the industrialized age which affected the framework of philosophy, as we will see in Chapters 9 and 10.

Notes

1. See the first section of Chapter 8, for example, which could be read in conjunction with the first section of this chapter to give both physical and metaphysical views on mechanism.
2. See Chapter 11 for an elaboration of the idea of paradigms in scientific practice.
3. Matthews, 110.
4. See Chapter 1.
5. See Chapters 5 and 8.
6. Excerpted from Marie Boas Hall, ed., *Nature and Nature's Laws* (New York: Harper and Row, 1970).
7. Michael Faraday, *Experimental Researches in Electricity*, reprinted in *The World of Physics*, Volume 1, Jefferson Hane Weaver (New York: Simon & Schuster, 1987).
8. James Clerk Maxwell, *Matter and Motion* (New York: Macmillan, 1920).
9. James Clerk Maxwell, *A Dynamical Theory of the Electromagnetic Field* (1895), reprinted in Jefferson Hane Weaver, *The World of Physics*, Volume 1 (New York: Simon & Schuster, 1987).
10. Formulated by Clausius in 1865.
11. See Chapter 8.

12. And, for that matter, all the King's horses and all the King's men would have no trouble putting Humpty together again.

13. Josiah Gibbs, *Elementary Principles in Statistical Mechanics* (New Haven: Yale University Press, 1902).

14. See Chapter 5.

15. Ludwig Boltzmann, *Application of the Second Law of Thermodynamics to the Universe as a Whole*. Reprinted in *Physical Thought from the Presocratics to the Quantum Physicists*, ed. Schmuel Sambursky (New York: Pica Press, 1975), 451. Reproduced by permission of Thieme Publishers.

Suggestions for Further Reading

Matthews, Michael R., ed. *The Scientific Background to Modern Philosophy* (Indianapolis: Hackett, 1989).

Weaver, Jefferson Hane. *The World of Physics*, Volume I Chapter 3 (New York: Simon & Schuster, 1987).

Science and the Obsolescence of Metaphysics and Religion

Modern scientists and philosophers were so impressed by the power, efficacy, and beauty of the new science that several of them declared philosophy and religion to be dead. This represents a very powerful form of exclusive scientific realism. Such a realism has the typical characteristic of stating that the objects and laws of science really exist independently of the human mind and describe the true way in which the universe operates; and contains the additional strong claim that as far as fundamental reality, scientific entities are the only sorts of things which exist. This view will be referred to as *scientism*, although the authors discussed in this chapter do not use such a term. We have seen some elements of scientism in our discussions of positivism, and in this chapter we deal with these elements explicitly.

Newton held a form of scientism and viewed his method of formulation and exposition, combining mathematical reasoning, experiment, induction, and axiomatic presentation, as the one true approach to discovering fundamental reality. He believed that this singular access is dictated by the fundamental character of Nature, since "Nature is pleased with simplicity." (*Principia*, Book III, Rule I) Newton's method is outlined in Book II of the *Principia*, as we saw in Chapter 5. Pierre Simon de Laplace was a mathematician and philosopher who enthusiastically supported the system of Newton in the late eighteenth and early nineteenth centuries. Laplace drew some additional conclusions from the success of Newtonian physics—he proposed that Newton's laws of motion and gravitation were sufficient to determine all phenomena, thereby eliminating the need for God as well as the role of chance and free will. Ernst Mach continued the positivist tradition of Comte, holding that a positive study of sensation could replace the critical speculations of the metaphysician.

This chapter also focuses on the early development of modern psychology through the work of William James and Sigmund Freud. While neither of these thinkers can be accused of scientism, their contribution to a new science of psychology added to the idea that philosophy was becoming more antiquated and impotent, even in the domain of mind. And their particular views undercut traditional Cartesian dualism, thus undermining another preeminent feature of philosophy that had become embedded in the modern culture. James rejected dualism explicitly in favor of an empirical philosophy based on a unity of experience. Freud undercut the rationalism of Descartes and the Cartesian tenet that the thinking self is a simple substance that can be known and understood with certainty. Both of these themes contributed to the demise of modern philosophy as it had been practiced in the seventeenth, eighteenth, and nineteenth centuries. Consequently, this situation left science and philosophy poised on the brink of revolution.

The Determinism of Laplace

Pierre Simon de Laplace was a French mathematician and philosopher. Born in 1749, he wrote his major works around the beginning of the nineteenth century and was a founder of the mathematics of probability. He died in 1827. Laplace proposed that Newtonian physics was sufficient to model the behavior of the solar system and could account for the long-term formation and stability of cosmological phenomena. He was one of the first to pioneer the theory that the solar system was formed out of a vast nebula. These results led Laplace to his most controversial declaration.

In a famous line from a letter to Napoleon, Laplace declared that he had no need for the hypothesis of a deity: *"Je n'ai pas besoin de cet hypothèse."* Previous modern deists had gradually depersonified God, eventuating in a popular Enlightenment theory that the deity was merely a disinterested first cause, a mechanical creator and observer. Laplace was one of the few to be so bold as to declare God unnecessary. This is another form of the positivism and strong scientific realism we find in Newton, Comte, and others.

Laplace took scientism a step further by postulating a deterministic universe of Newtonian mechanics. Newton's Laws are used to calculate the behavior of objects based on their antecedent positions and momenta. Laplace contended that if such information could be obtained about everything in the universe at some one time, all future and past events would be revealed. The entity which comes to obtain such knowledge has been dubbed "Laplace's demon." We can treat this as another component of scientism—since final causation, free will, creativity, and pure chance find no room in physical laws, Laplace assumed they are not real.

The following passages are excerpted from *A Philosophical Essay on Probabilities.*[1]

CHAPTER II.

CONCERNING PROBABILITY.

All events, even those which on account of their insignificance do not seem to follow the great laws of nature, are a result of it just as necessarily as the revolutions of the sun. In ignorance of the ties which unite such events to the entire system of the universe, they have been made to depend upon final causes or upon hazard, according as they occur and are repeated with regularity, or appear without regard to order; but these imaginary causes have gradually receded with the widening bounds of knowledge and disappear entirely before sound philosophy, which sees in them only the expression of our ignorance of the true causes.

Present events are connected with preceding ones by a tie based upon the evident principle that a thing cannot occur without a cause which produces it. This axiom, known by the name of *the principle of sufficient reason*,[2] extends even to actions which are considered indifferent; the freest will is unable without a determinate motive force to give them birth. . . . The contrary opinion is an illusion of the mind, which . . . believes that choice is determined of itself and without motives.

We ought then to regard the present state of the universe as the effect of its anterior state and as the cause of the one which is to follow. Given for one instant an intelligence which could comprehend all the forces by which nature is animated and the respective situation of the beings who compose it—an intelligence sufficiently vast to submit these data to analysis—it would embrace in the same formula the movements of the greatest bodies of the universe and those of the lightest atom; for it, nothing would be uncertain and the future, as the past, would be present to its eyes. The human mind offers, in the perfection which it has been able to give astronomy, a feeble idea of this intelligence. Its discoveries in mechanics and geometry, added to that of universal gravity, have enabled it to comprehend in the same analytical expressions the past and future states of the system of the world. . . .

Let us recall that formerly, and at no remote epoch, an unusual rain or an extreme drought, a comet having in train a very long tail, the eclipses, the aurora borealis, and in general all the unusual phenomena were regarded as so many signs of celestial wrath. Heaven was invoked in order to avert their baneful influence.... The knowledge of the laws of the system of the world acquired in the interval ... dissipated the fears begotten by the ignorance of the true relationship of man to the universe.

The curve described by a simple molecule of air or vapor is regulated in a manner just as certain as the planetary orbit; the only difference between them is that which comes from our ignorance.

Probability is relative, in part to our ignorance, in part to our knowledge....

It is to the influence of the opinion of those whom the multitude judges best informed and to whom it has been accustomed to give its confidence in regard to the most important matters of life that the propagation of those errors is due which in times of ignorance have covered the face of the earth. Magic and Astrology offer us two great examples.

Laplace's faith in humanity's progress toward certain knowledge of all future events, no matter how minute, is shattered by the development of quantum theory. In subsequent chapters, we will see how twentieth-century physicists explicitly reject Laplace's assertion that the only difference between microscopic and planetary phenomena "is that which comes from our ignorance."

Laplace made some philosophical errors of omission besides this mistaken prognostication with respect to the march of science. Laplace simply ignored Hume's critique as presented in the *Treatise*.[3] He specifically stipulated that the principle of sufficient reason is evident and universal. The problems with this thesis were well known, and a philosophical discussion of these issues would have made Laplace's faith in scientific progress less dogmatic and more persuasive.

Laplace had a specific notion of the progress of scientific knowledge. He saw it as marching toward perfect powers of prediction and retrodiction, a goal now seen as unattainable. Although quantum theory is inconsistent with this goal, it is nevertheless a successful development in empirical science. Even if absolute determinism has been abandoned, twentieth-century physics expands the scope of scientific knowledge.

Laplace could perhaps support the new physics since humanity has gained further ground in banishing primitive notions of animism. Others see quantum theory and subsequent developments as opening the door for a reunification of the spiritual and physical, the one and the many. We will resume this discussion in Chapters 10 and 12.

In the last chapter we examined the notions of Boltzmann and Gibbs regarding the illusory nature of time's directional flow. Laplace also understands the symmetry of forward and reverse temporal directions in the laws of physics. Laplace's demon has both past and future "present to its eyes." The mechanical laws of physics are in this sense the eternal present which governs the seeming past and future. Gibbs and Boltzmann, however, explain one asymmetry between past and future by showing how the future tends to be more disorganized and chaotic then the past. One way to understand this is as a violation of Laplace's postulate of perfect retrodiction. If the future is characterized by random, entropic disorganization, then it becomes difficult to gauge how these organizations became the way they are. For example, once a vapor is released into a room from a particular location, say a bottle placed in one corner, it will subsequently mix with the rest of the air in the room in such a way as to make it impossible to determine that it came from a particular location.

This is not the usual, commonsense sort of asymmetry we associate with time. For us, the act of prediction, not retrodiction, is the more difficult. Ilya Prigogine (see Chapter 10), among others, comments on this disparity between theory and experience, and we will see how this theme helps inspire philosophers and scientists to continue to collaborate.

The Evolution of Positivism and the Obsolescence of Ontology

Auguste Comte defined the school of thought known as positivism, as we saw in Chapter 5. This doctrine evolved significantly in the succeeding century, and in this section we examine the positivism of Ernst Mach. Mach was an Austrian physicist who lived from 1838 until 1916. He is commonly known for the Mach numbers used to give the speed of objects in ratio to the speed of sound. He preceded Boltzmann (see previous chapter) as professor of philosophy at the University of Vienna.

Mach's positivism shares with Comte's the emphasis on what is immediately observable. While Comte saw a hierarchy of science based on positive confirmation and evidence, Mach believed that all science could be reduced to a study of sensory phenomena. His view that science and philosophy should go no farther than what is empirically revealed by the senses led him to abandon metaphysics and ontology. Einstein numbered himself among those heavily influenced by the positivism of Mach. The following are selections from his *The Analysis of the Sensations* (five editions published from 1885 to 1906).[4]

I. INTRODUCTORY REMARKS:

ANTIMETAPHYSICAL

The great results achieved by physical science in modern times—results not restricted to its own sphere but embracing that of other sciences which employ its help—have brought it about that physical ways of thinking and physical modes of procedure enjoy on all hands unwonted prominence, and that the greatest expectations are associated with their application. In keeping with this drift of modern inquiry, the physiology of the senses . . . has also assumed an almost exclusively physical character. This tendency must appear to us as not altogether appropriate, when we reflect that physics, despite its considerable development, nevertheless constitutes but a portion of a *larger* collective body of knowledge, and that it is unable, with its intellectual implements, created for limited and special purposes, to exhaust all the subject-matter in question. Without renouncing the support of physics, it is possible for the physiology of the senses, not only to pursue its own course of development, but also to afford physical science itself a powerful assistance. The following simple considerations will serve to illustrate this relation between the two.

2.

Colors, sounds, temperatures, pressures, spaces, times, and so forth, are connected with one another in manifold ways; and with them are associated dispositions of mind, feelings, and volitions. Out of this fabric, that which is relatively more fixed and permanent stands prominently forth, and engraves itself on the memory, and expresses itself in language. Relatively greater permanency is exhibited, first, by certain complexes of colors, sounds, pressures, and so forth, functionally connected in time and space, which therefore receive special names, and are called bodies. Absolutely permanent such complexes are not.

My table is now brightly, now dimly lighted. Its temperature varies. It may receive an ink stain. One of its legs may be broken. It may be repaired, polished, and replaced part by part. But for me, it remains the table at which I daily write. . . .

My coat may receive a stain, a tear. My very manner of expressing this shows that we are concerned here with a sum-total of permanency, to which the new element is subsequently taken away.

Our greater intimacy with this sum-total of permanency, and the preponderance of its importance for me as contrasted with the changeable element, impel us to the partly instinctive, partly voluntary and conscious economy of mental presentation and designation in ordinary thought and speech. . . .

Further, that complex of memories, moods, and feelings, joined to a particular body (the human body), which is called the "I" or "Ego," manifests itself as relatively permanent. . . .

The apparent permanence of the ego consists chiefly in the single fact of its continuity, in the slowness of its changes. . . . There can hardly be greater difference in the egos of different people, than occur in the course of years in one person. . . .

The ego is as little absolutely permanent as are bodies. That which we so much dread in death, the annihilation of our permanency, actually occurs in life in abundant measure. . . .

A body is one and unchangeable only so long as it is unnecessary to consider its details. Thus, both the earth and a billiard ball are spheres, if we are willing to neglect all deviations from the spherical form, and if greater precision is not necessary. . . .

Man is pre-eminently endowed with the power of voluntarily and consciously determining his own point of view . . . he can rise to the most general abstractions or bury himself in the minutest particulars. . . .

Colors, sounds, and the odors of bodies are evanescent. But their tangibility, as a sort of constant nucleus, not readily susceptible of annihilation, remains behind; appearing as the vehicle of the more fugitive properties attached to it. Habit, thus, keeps our thought firmly attached to this central nucleus. . . .

A common and popular way of thinking and speaking is to contrast "appearance" with "reality." A pencil held in front of us in the air is seen by us as straight; dip it into the water, and we see it crooked. In the latter case we say that the pencil *appears* crooked, but is in *reality* straight. But what justifies us in declaring one fact than another to be the reality, and degrading the other to the level of appearance. . . . Precisely because of its environment the pencil dipped in water is optically crooked; but it is tactually and metrically straight. . . . To be sure, our expectation is deceived when, not paying sufficient attention to the conditions, and substituting for one another different cases of the combination, we fall into the error of expecting what we are accustomed to, although the case may be an unusual one. The facts are not to blame for that. In these cases, to speak of "appearance" may have a practical meaning, but it cannot have a scientific meaning. . . .

. . . The assertion, then, is correct that the world consists only of our sensations. In which case we have knowledge *only* of sensations.

Thus, perceptions, presentations, volitions, and emotions, in short, the whole inner and outer world, are put together . . . out of a small number of elements. Usually, these elements are called sensations. But as vestiges of a one-sided theory inhere in that term, we prefer to speak simply of elements. . . . The aim of all research is to ascertain the mode of connexion of these elements.

Bodies do not produce sensations, but complexes of elements (complexes of sensations) make up bodies. . . . [A]ll bodies are but thought-symbols for complexes of elements (complexes of sensations). . . .

For us, therefore, the world does not consist of mysterious entities, which by their interaction with another, equally mysterious entity, the ego, produce sensations. For us, colors, sounds . . . are provisionally the ultimate elements it is our business to investigate. It is precisely in this that the exploration of reality consists. In this investigation we must not allow ourselves to be impeded by such abridgements and delimitations as body, ego, matter, spirit, etc.

We can see some commonalities between the views of Mach and Heraclitus (see Chapter 1). Mach proclaimed that permanence is nominal. He claimed that the substantial bodies we presume to exist are really only place-holders for collections of sensations. Like Heraclitus, Mach viewed evanescence and perishing as the primary characteristics of the world. Mach was driven to this view because of his empiricism, which strives to preserve a privileged place for the data of science.

Mach's theory of sensations was intended to displace the dualism of Descartes as well as the monism of Leibniz. Instead of investigating substance and their inherent properties, Mach was concerned with "connexions" between the elements of sense phenomena. He attempted to preserve the practical distinction between appearance and reality without bifurcating the study of reality. We will see a different form of a monism of experience in studying the psychology of William James in the next section. While Mach views an empiricism of sensation as establishing the priority of a scientific study of sensation, others such as William James and John Dewey take the approach that empiricism is not equivalent to scientism.

The scientism in Mach's doctrine is evident when he makes the claim that "'appearance' may have a practical meaning, but it cannot have a scientific meaning." Here Mach assumes that science is more than a practical art, and that practical appeal is not the fundamental arbiter of reality. Science is presumed to be the true access to knowledge. The world of the physicist and the world of the physiologist are the systematic ways to pursue an "exploration of reality."

In order for science to describe all of reality, Mach realizes that dualism must be subsumed. Thus, appearance, or subjective experience, and the objective natural world of physics were unified in Mach's "elements" of reality. For Mach, there was no fundamental mind/matter distinction, only a study of sensations. In the next section, we see how the rise of psychology also played a role in overcoming dualism and taking science into areas formerly reserved for philosophy.

The Development of Psychology and the Replacement of Metaphysics of Mind

Positivist prescriptions would be of little use in subsuming the philosophical world if there remained an essence of mind or spirit which was unassailable in physical or physiological terms. And while biology and medicine continued to make great strides in understanding and affecting the living organism, some new approaches were necessary to make inroads into the realm of consciousness. Thus, a new discipline, psychology, emerged at the end of the nineteenth century as a science of healing and description of the mind.

In this section, we will treat two very different perspectives on this new science: William James' philosophical pragmatism and Sigmund Freud's pioneering work in psychoanalysis. James saw a role for both psychology and philosophy in overcoming dualism, and he sought a better, more scientific, and more practical theory of consciousness than one which posits that mental substance is an irreducible component of reality. Freud was less interested in addressing philosophical concerns directly, but his theories have important consequences for philosophy in the postmodern era.

Psychology and Pragmatism

William James, an American psychologist and philosopher, published his *Principles of Psychology* in 1890. James was interested in establishing a foothold for modern science within philosophical questions of mental phenomena. James viewed this as a prerequisite for progress in both science and philosophy, since he saw dualism as a mistaken, semimystical notion that rendered the experience of consciousness inaccessible to scientific study or philosophical critique. He was born in 1842 and died in 1910. Sigmund Freud's work in Vienna emphasized techniques that physicians could use in keeping with medical scientific practice to heal the pathology of the psyche. Freud was born in 1856 and died in 1939.

The implications of the rise of psychology are monumental, both for science and philosophy. In bringing mental phenomena under the scientific umbrella, dualistic tendencies were subsumed. By having a detailed science of mental phenomena—including consciousness, reasoning, impulse, and ideas—a more realistic and complex psychological account of intelligence emerges. This detailed picture undercuts simplistic early modern epistemology. That is, the realm of ideas, consciousness, and rationality are revealed to be both more primitively animalistic and more complex than Descartes believed.

The following are excerpts from James' *The Principles of Psychology*,[5] and *Essays in Radical Empiricism*.[6]

THE PRINCIPLES OF PSYCHOLOGY

PSYCHOLOGY IS A NATURAL SCIENCE

That is, the mind which the psychologist studies is the mind of distinct individuals inhabiting definite portions of a real space and of a real time. . . . "Mind," in his mouth, is only a class name for *minds*. . . .

To the psychologist, then, the minds he studies are *objects*, in a world of other objects. Even when he introspectively analyzes his own mind, and tells what he finds there, he talks about it in an objective way. He says, for instance, that under certain circumstances the color gray appears to him green, and calls the appearance an illusion. . . . In making this critical judgement, the psychologist stands as much outside of the perception which he criticizes as he does of the color. Both are his objects.

It is highly important that this natural-science point of view. should be understood at the outset. Otherwise more may be demanded of the psychologist that he ought to be expected to perform. . . .

Introspective Observation is what we have to rely on first and foremost and always. The word introspection . . . means, of course, the looking into our own minds and reporting what we there discover. *Every one agrees that we there discover states of consciousness.* . . . All people unhesitatingly believe that they feel themselves thinking. . . . *I regard this belief as the most fundamental of all the postulates of Psychology,* and shall dismiss all curious inquiries about its certainty as too metaphysical for the scope of this book. . . .

The inaccuracy of introspective observation has been made a subject of debate. . . .

Some authors take the high ground here and claim for it a sort of infallibility, [e.g.] Brentano:

"The phenomena inwardly apprehended are true in themselves. . . . Who, then, can deny that in this a great superiority of Psychology over the other physical sciences comes to light? . . . No one can doubt whether the psychic condition he apprehends in himself *be,* and be *so.* . . ."[7]

Others have gone to the opposite extreme, and maintained that we can have no introspective cognition of our own minds at all. A deliverance of Auguste Comte . . . seems . . . indispensable here.

Philosophers, says Comte, have "in these latter days imagined themselves able to distinguish . . . two sorts of observation of equal importance, one external, the other internal . . . this pretended direct contemplation of the mind by itself is a pure illusion . . . For by whom shall the observation of these be made?" . . .

Where now does the truth lie? . . . Even the writers who insist upon the absolute veracity of our immediate inner apprehension of a conscious state have to contrast with this the fallibility of our memory or observation of it. . . . But which mode of consciousness of it is that which the psychologist must depend on? If the *having* feelings or thoughts in their immediacy were enough, babies in the cradle would be psychologists, and infallible ones. But the psychologist must not only *have* his mental states . . . he must report them. . . . Whilst alive they are their own property; it is only *post-mortem* that they become his prey.

ESSAYS IN RADICAL EMPIRICISM

DOES "CONSCIOUSNESS" EXIST?[8]

"THOUGHTS" and "things" are names for two sorts of object, which common sense will always find contrasted and will always practically oppose to each other. Philosophy, reflecting on the contrast, has varied in the past in her explanations of it, and may be expected to vary in the future. At first, "spirit and matter," "soul and body," stood for a pair of equipollent substances quite on a par in weight and interest. . . .

I believe that "consciousness," when once it has evaporated to [an] estate of pure diaphaneity, is on the point of disappearing altogether. It is the name of a nonentity, and has no right to a place among first principles. Those who still cling to it are clinging to a mere echo, the faint rumor left behind by the disappearing "soul" upon the air of philosophy. During the past year, I have read a number of articles whose authors seemed just on the point of abandoning the notion of consciousness. . . . But they were not quite radical enough, not quite daring enough in their negations. For twenty years past I have mistrusted "consciousness" as an entity; for seven or eight years past I have suggested its non-existence to my students, and tried to give them its pragmatic equivalent in realities of experience. It seems to me that the hour is ripe for it to be openly and universally discarded.

To deny plumly that "consciousness" exists seems so absurd on the face of it—for undeniably "thoughts" do exist—that I fear some readers will follow me no farther. Let me then immediately explain that I mean only to deny that the word stands for an entity, but to insist most emphatically that it does stand for a function. There is, I mean, no aboriginal stuff or quality of being, contrasted with that of which material objects are made, out of which our thoughts of them are made; but there is a function in experience which thoughts perform, and for the performance of which this quality of being is invoked. That function is *knowing*. "Consciousness" is supposed necessary to explain the fact that things not only are, but get reported, are known. Whoever blots out the notion of consciousness from his list of first principles must still provide in some way for that function's being carried on. . . .

My thesis is that if we start with the supposition that there is only one primal stuff or material in the world, a stuff of which everything is composed, and if we call that stuff "pure experience," the knowing can easily be explained as a particular sort of relation towards one another into which portions of pure experience may enter. The relation itself is a part of pure experience; one of its "terms" becomes the subject or bearer of the knowledge . . . the other becomes the object known. This will need much explanation before it can be understood. . . . the word consciousness to-day does no more than signalize the fact that experience is indefeasibly dualistic in structure. It means that not subject, not object, but object-plus-subject is the minimum that can actually be.

Thus . . . we should have to admit consciousness as an "epistemological" necessity, even if we had no direct evidence of its being there.

But in addition to this, we are supposed by almost every one to have an immediate consciousness of consciousness itself. When the world of outer fact ceases to be materially present, and we merely recall it in memory, or fancy it, the consciousness is believed to stand out and to be felt as a kind of impalpable inner flowing, which, once known in this sort of experience, may equally be detected in presentations of the outer world. "The moment we try to fix our attention upon consciousness and to see *what*, distinctly, it is," says a recent writer, "it seems to vanish. It seems as if we had before us a mere emptiness. When we try to introspect the sensation of blue, all we can see is the blue; the other element is as if it were diaphanous. Yet it *can* be distinguished, if we look attentively enough, and know that there is something to look for."[9]

. . . This supposes that the consciousness is one element, moment, factor—call it what you like—of an experience of essentially dualistic inner constitution, from which, if you abstract the content, the consciousness will remain revealed to its own eye. Experience, at this rate, would be much like a paint of which the world pictures were made. Paint has a dual constitution, involving, as it does, a menstruum[10] (oil, size or what not) and a mass of content in the form of pigment suspended therein. We can get the pure menstruum by letting the pigment settle, and the pure pigment by pouring off the size or oil. We operate here by physical subtraction; and the usual view is, that by mental subtraction we can separate the two factors of experience in an analogous way—not isolating them entirely, but distinguishing them enough to know that they are two.

II

Now my contention is exactly the reverse of this. *Experience, I believe, has no such inner duplicity; and the separation of it into consciousness and content comes, not by way of subtraction, but by way of addition*—the addition, to a given concrete piece of it, other sets of experiences, in connection with which severally its use or function may be of two different kinds. The paint will also serve here as an illustration. In a pot in a paintshop, along with other paints, it serves in its entirety as so much saleable matter. Spread on a canvas, with other paints around it, it represents, on the contrary, a feature in a picture and performs a spiritual function. Just so, I maintain, does a given undivided portion of experience, taken in one context of associates, play the part of a knower, of a state of mind, of "consciousness"; while in a different context the same undivided bit of experience plays the part of a thing known, of an objective "content." In a word, in one group it figures as a thought, in another group as a thing. And, since it can figure in both groups simultaneously we have every right to speak of it as subjective and objective, both at once. The dualism . . . is still preserved in this account, but reinterpreted, so that, instead of being mysterious and elusive, it becomes verifiable and concrete. It is an affair of relations, it falls outside, not inside, the single experience considered, and can always be particularized and defined. . . .

If the reader will take his own experiences, he will see what I mean. Let him begin with a perceptual experience, the "presentation," so called, of a physical object, his actual field of vision, the room he sits in, with the book he is reading as its centre; and let him for the present treat this complex object in the common-sense way as being "really" what it seems to be, namely, a collection of physical things cut out from an environing world of other physical things with which these physical things have actual or potential relations. Now at the same time it is just *those self-same things* which his mind, as we say, perceives; and the whole philosophy of perception from Democritus's time downwards has just been one long wrangle over the paradox that what is evidently one reality should be in two places at once, both in outer space and in a person's mind. . . .

The puzzle of how the one identical room can be in two places is at bottom just the puzzle of how one identical point can be on two lines. It can, if it be situated at their intersection; and similarly, if the "pure experience" of the room were a place of intersection of two processes, which connected it with different groups of associates respectively, it could be counted twice. . . .

Well, the experience is a member of diverse processes that can be followed away from it along entirely different lines. The one self-identical thing has so many relations to the rest of experience that you can take it in disparate systems of association, and treat it as belong-ing with opposite contexts. In one of these contexts it is your "field of consciousness"; in another it is "the room in which you sit," . . .

One of them is the reader's personal biography, the other is the history of the house of which the room is part. . . .

As "subjective" we say that the experience represents; as "objec-tive" it is represented. What represents and what is represented is here numerically the same; but we must remember that no dualism of being represented and representing resides in the experience *per se.* . . .

First of all, this will be asked: "If experience has not 'conscious' existence, if it be not partly made of 'consciousness,' of what then is it made? Matter we know, and thought we know, and conscious con-tent we know, but neutral and simple 'pure experience' is something we know not at all. Say *what* it consists of—for it must consist of something—or be willing to give it up!"

To this challenge the reply is easy. Although for fluency's sake I myself spoke early in this article of a stuff of pure experience, I have now to say that there is no *general* stuff of which experience at large is made. There are as many stuffs as there are "natures" in the things experienced. If you ask what any one bit of pure experience is made of, the answer is always the same: "It is made of *that,* of just what ap-pears, of space, of intensity, of flatness, brownness, heaviness, or what not." . . .

The next objection is more formidable, in fact it sounds quite crushing when one hears it first.

"If it be the self-same piece of pure experience, taken twice over, that serves now as thought and now as thing"—so the objection runs—"how comes it that its attributes should differ so fundamen-tally in the two takings. As thing, the experience is extended; as thought, it occupies no space or place. As thing, it is red, hard, heavy; but who ever heard of a red, hard or heavy thought? Yet even now you said that an experience is made of just what appears, and what appears is just such adjectives. How can the one experience in its thing function be made of them, consist of them, carry them as its own attributes, while in its thought-function it disowns them and at-tributes them elsewhere. . . ."

Descartes for the first time defined thought as the absolutely un-extended, and later philosophers have accepted the description as cor-rect. But what possible meaning has it to say that, when we think of a foot-rule or a square yard, extension is not attributable to our thought?

Like Mach, James believed that experience furnished the basis for a fundamental theory of reality that had "no inner duplicity." And so, like Mach, James stood in direct opposition to Descartes. James denied that reality was composed of two substances, mental and physical, that shared no common attributes. He attempted to subsume both into a metaphysics of experience and said that experience displays both objective and subjective qualities. Presumably, with a new science of psychology, science could probe not only the objective qualities of experience but the subjective as well. In fact, James explicitly advocated this in his *Principles* when he said the "psychologist stands . . . outside of . . . perception." This "natural-science point of view" is crucial for Jamesian psychology.

John Dewey, a pragmatist and successor to James, takes a similar approach to political and social theory. That is, he advocates a deliberate study of social phenomena in order to use the method and results of science on social problems. We will see more of this pragmatist approach in the next chapter.

Psychoanalysis and the Theory of Mind

Sigmund Freud founded the psychoanalytic school of psychology in Vienna at the turn of the last century. Although many of the theoretical underpinnings of his method were controversial and have been significantly revised by his followers, the techniques he developed were important and beneficial breakthroughs. And the practical effectiveness of psychoanalysis is coherent with the empirical genesis of Freud's ideas. In the following passage from "The History of the Psychoanalytic Movement" we see another inroad science makes into the dimension of mind.[11]

The theory of repression is the pillar upon which the edifice of psychoanalysis rests. It is really the most essential part of it, and yet, it is nothing but the theoretical expression of experience which can be repeatedly observed whenever one analyses a neurotic without the aid of hypnosis. One is then confronted with a resistance which opposes and blocks the analytic work by causing failures of memory. . . . The theoretical value of the fact, that this resistance is connected with amnesia, leads unavoidably to the concept of unconscious psychic activity which is peculiar to psychoanalysis, and distinguishes it markedly from the philosophical speculations about unconscious. It may, therefore, be said that psychoanalytic theory endeavors to explain two experiences, which result in a striking and unexpected manner during the attempt to trace back the morbid symptoms of a neurotic to their source in his life history; viz., the facts of transference and of resistance. . . .

I would energetically oppose any attempt to count the principles of repression and resistance as mere assumptions instead of results of psychoanalysis. Such assumptions of a general psychological and biological nature exist, . . . but the principle of repression is an acquisition of the psychoanalytic work, won by legitimate means, as a theoretical extract from very numerous experiences. . . .

I treated my discoveries as ordinary contributions to science and hoped that others would treat them the same way. But the silence which followed my lectures, the void that formed about my person, . . . made me realize gradually . . . that I could not count upon being treated objectively and with toleration. . . .

I was saved, however, from becoming embittered by a circumstance that does not come to the assistance of all lonely discoverers. . . . [T]he psychoanalytic principles enabled me to understand . . . my environment as a necessary consequence of fundamental analytic theories. If it was true that the connections I had discovered were kept from the knowledge of the patients by inner affective resistances, then these resistances would be sure to manifest themselves also in normal persons as soon as the repressed material is conveyed to them from the outside. It was not strange that they should know how to motivate their affective rejections of my ideas on intellectual grounds. This happened just as often in the patients. . . . The only difference was that with patients, one had the means of bringing pressure to bear in order to induce them to recognize and overcome their resistances. . . . How to force these normal people to examine the subject in a cool and scientifically objective manner was an insoluble problem, the solution of which was best left to time. In the history of science it has often been possible to verify that the very assertion which, at first, called forth only opposition, received recognition a little later without the necessity of bringing forward any new proofs.

Freud set his work apart from "philosophical speculations" and developed his techniques of psychoanalysis based on empirical success in helping neurotic patients. Nevertheless, he is led to some fundamental theories of mind that have philosophical implications. Freud's hypotheses of unconscious psychic activity undermine the method of Cartesian doubt and introspection as well as the evidence for Descartes' metaphysical conclusions. Descartes claimed that the mind is more clearly known than the body and that conscious mental activity, i.e., thinking, is the certain and essential attribute of human existence. Freud removed this certainty from our awareness about ourselves.

Freud claimed that the phenomenon of repression, marked by loss of memory about a previous traumatic event and transference of feeling from that trauma onto another object, shows that we cannot always be confident in our own consciousness. If this is the case, then the certain and indubitable facts that Descartes finds in the *Meditations* would need to be reexamined. During this new investigation, Freud's results could give the Cartesian doubter every reason to doubt his own thinking. Additionally, Cartesian rationalism, the belief that basic truths should be discovered with a natural, conscious, rational faculty was thrown into question. The phenomena of repression is common to the healthy patient as well as to the neurotic, according to the excerpted passage, and as such can affect our conscious mind to the extent that we should be suspicious that we can ever clear ourselves of irrational influences. On some accounts, it is the irrational aspects of the mind that dominate the rational.

Freud's method is at odds with James' as well, since James saw conscious introspection as a valuable tool for psychology. Nevertheless, James agreed that the matter of the veracity of data gained via this method is highly questionable. Both James and Freud sought to take one more metaphysical element from the realm of philosophy and place it under the scrutiny of science. Both saw the traditional philosophical model of consciousness as inaccurate and in need of revision. Such revision was not to come from philosophical speculations but from scientific activity in the new discipline of psychology. We will see late-twentieth-century analogs to this position in Chapter 12.

Philosophy and Religion in the Gaps

William James was a pluralist who did not support the tenets of anything like scientism. He saw the need for both science and philosophy in human inquiry. He simply sought to overcome a barrier to further philosophical and scientific progress in the form of Cartesian Dualism. Nevertheless, his mission to bypass consciousness was adopted by others as a way to avoid metaphysics altogether. A true scientism must avoid enshrining consciousness as a separate substance; omit final causes or purposes from a taxonomy of causation; evade metaphysical theories of the beginning of the universe; and bypass intractable debates about fundamental agents and substrata and their relationship to universal laws of cause and effect. Such issues are part of humanity's "childhood" and "youth," in the words of Comte (see Chapter 5). While this approach is theoretically a viable alternative to philosophical and religious theories of reality, in practice science had some serious gaps to fill before it could fully explain such things as consciousness, the origin of life, the beginning of the universe, or the significance of time.

Thus, metaphysics, whether philosophical or primarily religious, continued to enjoy some breathing room throughout the twentieth century. Gaps in scientific understanding—such as existed between the physical laws of nature and the origins of biological activity governed by evolutionary laws; or between physiological laws and psychological therapies; or between the beginning of the universe and the Newtonian world order; or between theoretical determinism and practical uncertainty about the future—gave speculative philosophers and theologians a domain in which to practice without seriously questioning whether or not modern science spoke truth.

A theology based on such a strategy has been termed The God of the Gaps. That is, whatever science cannot explain is left to God. Philosophical metaphysics repeatedly finds itself in an analogous situation. That is, where science is currently lacking, philosophy can fill in the gaps—whether in the interaction between mind and matter, the origins of life or of the universe, or the meaning of time. Such gaps have become increasingly smaller in the twentieth century, albeit not without significant upheavals in the sciences which previously garnered so much faith in scientific realism. If science continues to make inroads into these areas of inquiry, then neither a philosophy nor a religion of such areas can be a credible theory of reality without denying some form of scientism.

In Chapter 12 we will see some contemporary issues in the tension between scientific and philosophical metaphysics.

Summary

Supporters of speculative philosophic principles such as a divine creator or mental substance find themselves at odds with modern scientism. As the sciences of Newton and Laplace, James and Freud became dated, twentieth-century commentators found room for metaphysics, God, and free will in later cosmology and physics. But this is really not a very different attitude from some of the ones in this chapter since science itself is uncritically accepted as factual and non-metaphysical. Religion and philosophy are left to fill in the gaps.

Another alternative is to show that scientism amounts to a metaphysics which is in some sense unscientific and uncritical.[12] By taking the results of scientific inquiry as fact, critical examination of the foundations, methods, and presuppositions of science is avoided. We saw that Hume, for one, challenges scientism on the grounds that its methods of reasoning are insufficient to ground its assumptions. Others claim that scientism unnecessarily impoverishes human experience. By taking scientific inquiry as the exclusive access to fundamental reality, art, literature, music, and drama are all denied access to important dimensions. Science is furthermore a product of human endeavor, and to take its results as exclusively real is a kind of anthropocentrism. We tackle these themes again in discussing reductionism and contemporary physical realists in later chapters.

While the views of Laplace and Mach on exclusive scientific realism and positivism are antiquated, given that the science of these figures is now dated, it is useful to look at these proponents of scientism to compare with twentieth-century views. Twentieth-century figures will claim that the only mistakes made by Newton, Laplace, and Mach are in the details of the science.

The fact that scientific theory has evolved so much since Laplace and Mach may be evidence against twentieth-century scientism. Newton, Laplace, and Mach all thought that revolutionary "paradigm shifts"[13] in world-views had run their course and that finally humanity was close to ending its search for the nature of reality. Contemporary figures claim to have reasons to believe that their science is in fact close to ending this search, even in the face of such historical counter-examples presented herein.[14] This chapter gives a different historical context to a perspective which still colors the philosophy of science.

Notes

1. Pierre Simon de Laplace, *A Philosophical Essay on Probabilities*, trans. F.W. Truscott and F.L. Emory (New York: Dover Publications, 1951).

2. See comments on the principle of sufficient reason in Chapters 1 and 4.

3. See Chapter 4.

4. Reprinted by permission of Open Court Publishing, a division of Carus Publishing Company, Peru, IL, from *The Analysis of the Sensations and the Relation of the Physical to the Psychical*, 1914, by Ernst Mach.

5. William James, *The Principles of Psychology* (New York: Henry Holt, 1890). Copyright 1981 by the President and Fellows of Harvard College. Reprinted by permission of Harvard University Press.

6. William James, *Essays in Radical Empiricism* (New York: Longmans, Green, 1912).

7. See also Descartes, Meditation II.

8. This essay originally appeared in *The Journal of Philosophy, Psychology, and Scientific Methods*, vol. I, No. 18, September 1, 1904.

9. G.E. Moore: *Mind*, vol. XII, N.S. [1903], 450. [note in original]

10. "Figuratively speaking, consciousness may be said to be the one universal solvent, or menstruum, in which the different concrete kinds of psychic acts and facts are contained, whether in concealed or in obvious form." G.T. Ladd: *Psychology, Descriptive and Explanatory*, 1894, 30. [note in original]

11. Sigmund Freud, "The History of the Psychoanalytic Movement," in *The Basic Writings of Sigmund Freud*, ed. and trans. A.A. Brill (New York: Random House, 1938).

12. Pragmatism takes this view, as does José Ortega y Gasset. See also Burtt (Chapter 7), and A.N. Whitehead's *Science and the Modern World*. The philosophy of Whitehead is discussed in Chapter 10.

13. See Chapter 11 for a discussion of this terminology with respect to philosophy of science.

14. See Weinberg's *Dreams of a Final Theory* (New York: Pantheon Books, 1992) for example.

Suggestions for Further Reading

Davies, Paul. *God and the New Physics* (New York: Simon & Schuster, 1984).

Feigl, Herbert, 'The Mind-Body Problem and the Development of Logical Empiricism," reprinted in Herbert Feigl and May Brodbeck, eds., *Readings in the Philosophy of Science* (New York: Appleton-Century-Crofts, 1953).

James, William, *The Writings of William James*, John J. McDermott, ed. (Chicago: The University of Chicago Press, 1977).

Russell, Bertrand. *Our Knowledge of the External World as a Field for Scientific Method in Philosophy* (London: G. Allen and Unwin, 1926).

Chapter

9

Social, Ethical, and Political Dimensions in Science and Technology

Throughout the nineteenth and twentieth centuries, society struggled to adjust to the effects of the industrial age. The Industrial Revolution was not a consciously engineered transformation and did not follow straightforwardly from the scientific revolution. In fact, it has been argued that practical industry and economics were the primary causes for the seventeenth-century revolution in the sciences.[1] In any case, both modern science and modern industry were part of a similar move in science as well as technology: the application of mechanistic principles and analytic methods to all aspects of human culture. This practice at first produced intellectual fruits and later promised benefits in all of human life. Mechanism and analysis, freed from evaluative encumbrances, were presumed to be a productive method for science, economics, and politics. But the culture which emerged from the Industrial Revolution was not without its problems. Indeed, many saw the industrial age, with raw, global capitalism accompanied by slavery, subjugation of working classes, and environmental disasters, as more ethically problematic than the preceding agrarian and feudal eras.

While social Darwinism was used to justify many of the competitive practices of the nineteenth century, some questioned whether the human and environmental price of modernization was too high. Karl Marx criticized the underlying faith that capitalism is inevitable, natural, and good. Henry David Thoreau's classic *Walden* can be interpreted as a criticism of the imbalance between modern society and nature. Rachel Carson saw environmental and eventually human catastrophes in an exploitive mind-set engendered by some interpretations of the scientific and industrial revolutions. That is, the objective study of nature can lead to the objectification of nature. Such objectification is dangerous if not subject to evaluative scrutiny, according to Carson and other environmentalists. In other human arenas, new scientific and technological methodologies yield impressive results that both critics and supporters of modernism see as positive: sociology, economics, and psychology all emerged as new disciplines in the postindustrial age.

Economics and Utilitarianism

Traditionally, the endeavor to answer questions of social value and utility, the relation between the individual and society, and proper social structure had been the business of philosophy. Thomas Hobbes, a seventeenth-century British philosopher, believed that he had founded the scientific study of politics,[2] and this expansion of scientific method into traditional philosophical subjects continued to occupy British empiricists for some time. During the enlightenment, Adam Smith founded the modern study of economic theory. In the nineteenth century, J.S. Mill followed in the footsteps of other utilitarians—including his father, James Mill—in attempting to bring other ethical issues down to a concrete, scientific level. In this section we will treat the birth of economics and the utilitarian movements, which attempted to apply economic theory to traditional ethical and political questions.

Adam Smith

Adam Smith was a British philosopher and economist credited with establishing the modern approach to economic theory implicated in capitalism. He was born in 1723, and published his *Wealth of Nations* in 1776. His work is seen as a model for justifying economic practice as well as a foil for critics of Western capitalism. Smith died in 1790. The following selections from *The Wealth of Nations* exemplify the more famous aspects of his theories.[3]

AN INQUIRY INTO THE NATURE AND CAUSES OF THE WEALTH OF NATIONS

THE annual labour of every nation is the fund which originally supplies it with all the necessaries and conveniences of life which it annually consumes, and which consist always either in the immediate produce of that labour, or in what is purchased with that produce from other nations.

According therefore as this produce, or what is purchased with it, bears a greater or smaller proportion to the number of those who are to consume it, the nation will be better or worse supplied with all the necessaries and conveniences for which it has occasion. . . .

Among the savage nations of hunters and fishers, every individual who is able to work, is more or less employed in useful labour, and endeavors to provide, as well as he can, the necessaries and conveniences of life, for himself, or such of his family or tribe as are either too old, or too young, or too infirm to go hunting and fishing. Such nations, however, are so miserably poor that, from mere want, they are frequently reduced, or, at least, think themselves reduced, to the necessity sometimes of directly destroying, and sometimes of abandoning their infants, their old people, and those afflicted with lingering diseases, to perish with hunger, or to be devoured by wild beasts. Among civilized and thriving nations, on the contrary, though a great number of people do not labour at all, many of whom consume the produce of ten times, frequently of a hundred times more labour than the greater part of those who work; yet the produce of the whole labour of the society is so great that all are often abundantly supplied, and a workman, even of the lowest and poorest order, if he is frugal and industrious, may enjoy a greater share of the necessaries and conveniences of life than it is possible for any savage to acquire. . . .

Whatever be the actual state of the skill, dexterity, and judgment with which labour is applied in any nation, the abundance or scantiness of its annual supply must depend, during the continuance of that state, upon the proportion between the number of those who are annually employed in useful labour, and that of those who are not so employed. The number of useful and productive labourers, it will hereafter appear, is everywhere in proportion to the quantity of capital stock which is employed in setting them to work, and to the particular way in which it is so employed. . . .

THE greatest improvement in the productive powers of labour, and the greater part of the skill, dexterity, and judgment with which it is anywhere directed, or applied, seem to have been the effects of the division of labour.

The effects of the division of labour, in the general business of society, will be more easily understood by considering in what manner it operates in some particular manufactures. It is commonly supposed to be carried furthest in some very trifling ones; not perhaps that it really is carried further in them than in others of more importance: but in those trifling manufactures which are destined to supply the small wants of but a small number of people, the whole number of workmen must necessarily be small; and those employed in every different branch of the work can often be collected into the same workhouse, and placed at once under the view of the spectator. In those great manufactures, on the contrary, which are destined to supply the great wants of the great body of the people, every different branch of the work employs so great a number of workmen that it is impossible to collect them all into the same workhouse. We can seldom see more, at one time, than those employed in one single branch. Though in such manufactures, therefore, the work may really be divided into a much greater number of parts than in those of a more trifling nature, the division is not near so obvious, and has accordingly been much less observed.

To take an example, therefore, from a very trifling manufacture; but one in which the division of labour has been very often taken notice of, the trade of the pin-maker; a workman not educated to this business (which the division of labour has rendered a distinct trade), nor acquainted with the use of the machinery employed in it (to the invention of which the same division of labour has probably given occasion), could scarce, perhaps, with his utmost industry, make one pin in a day, and certainly could not make twenty. But in the way in which this business is now carried on, not only the whole work is a peculiar trade, but it is divided into a number of branches, of which the greater part are likewise peculiar trades. One man draws out the wire, another straights it, a third cuts it, a fourth points it, a fifth grinds it at the top for receiving, the head; to make the head requires two or three distinct operations; to put it on is a peculiar business, to whiten the pins is another; it is even a trade by itself to put them into the paper; and the important business of making a pin is, in this manner, divided into about eighteen distinct operations, which, in some manufactories, are all performed by distinct hands, though in others the same man will sometimes perform two or three of them. I have seen a small manufactory of this kind where ten men only were employed, and where some of them consequently performed two or three distinct operations. But though they were very poor, and therefore but indifferently accommodated with the necessary machinery, they could, when they exerted themselves, make among them about twelve pounds of pins in a day. There are in a pound upwards of four thousand pins of a middling size. Those ten persons, therefore, could make among them upwards of forty-eight thousand pins in a day. Each person, therefore, making a tenth part of forty-eight thousand pins, might be considered as making four thousand eight hundred pins in a day. But if they had all wrought separately and independently, and without any of them having been educated to this peculiar business, they certainly could not each of them have made twenty, perhaps not one pin in a day; that is, certainly, not the two hundred and fortieth, perhaps not the four thousand eight hundredth part of what they are at present capable of performing, in consequence of a proper division and combination of their different operations.

... The nature of agriculture, indeed, does not admit of so many subdivisions of labour, nor of so complete a separation of one business from another, as manufactures. It is impossible to separate so entirely the business of the grazier from that of the corn-farmer as the trade of the carpenter is commonly separated from that of the smith. The spinner is almost always a distinct person from the weaver; but the ploughman, the harrower, the sower of the seed, and the reaper of the corn, are often the same. The occasions for those different sorts of labour returning with the different seasons of the year, it is impossible that one man should be constantly employed in any one of them. This impossibility of making so complete and entire a separation of all the different branches of labour employed in agriculture is perhaps the reason why the improvement of the productive powers of labour in this art does not always keep pace with their improvement in manufactures. ...

This great increase of the quantity of work which, in consequence of the division of labour, the same number of people are capable of performing, is owing to three different circumstances; first, to the increase of dexterity in every particular workman; secondly, to the saving of the time which is commonly lost in passing from one species of work to another; and lastly, to the invention of a great number of machines which facilitate and abridge labour, and enable one man to do the work of many.

First, the improvement of the dexterity of the workman necessarily increases the quantity of the work he can perform; and the division of labour, by reducing every man's business to some on simple operation, and by making this operation the sole employment of his life, necessarily increased very much dexterity of the workman. A common smith, who, though accustomed to handle the hammer, has never been used to make nails, if upon some particular occasion he is obliged to attempt it, will scarce, I am assured, be able to make above two or three hundred nails in a day, and those to very bad ones. A smith who has been accustomed to make nails, but whose sole or principal business has not been that of a nailer, can seldom with his utmost diligence make more than eight hundred or a thousand nails in a day. I have seen several boys under twenty years of age who had never exercised any other trade but that of making nails, and who, when they exerted themselves, could make, each of them, upwards of two thousand three hundred nails in a day. The making of a nail, however, is by no means one of the simplest operations. The same person blows the bellows, stirs or mends the fire as there is occasion, heats the iron, and forges every part of the nail: in forging the head too he is obliged to change his tools. The different operations into which the making of a pin, or of a metal button, is subdivided, are all of them much more simple, and the dexterity of the person, of whose life it has been the sole business to perform them, is usually much greater. The rapidity with which some of the operations of those manufacturers are performed, exceeds what the human hand could, by those who had never seen them, be supposed capable of acquiring.

Secondly, the advantage which is gained by saving the time commonly lost in passing from one sort of work to another is much greater than we should at first view be apt to imagine it. It is impossible to pass very quickly from one kind of work to another that is carried on in a different place and with quite different tools. A country weaver, who cultivates a small farm, must lose a good deal of time in passing from his loom to the field, and from the field to his loom. When the two trades can be carried on in the same workhouse, the loss of time is no doubt much less. It is even in this case, however, very considerable. A man commonly saunters a little in turning his hand from one sort of employment to another. When he first begins the new work he is seldom very keen and hearty; his mind, as they say, does not go to it, and for some time he rather trifles than applies to good purpose. The habit of sauntering and of indolent careless application, which is naturally, or rather necessarily acquired by every country workman who is obliged to change his work and his tools every half hour, and to apply his hand in twenty different ways almost every day of his life, renders him almost always slothful and lazy, and incapable of any vigorous application even on the most pressing occasions.

Thirdly, and lastly, everybody must be sensible how much labour is facilitated and abridged by the application of proper machinery. It is unnecessary to give any example. I shall only observe, therefore, that the invention of all those machines by which labour is so much facilitated and abridged seems to have been originally owing to the division of labour. Men are much more likely to discover easier and readier methods of attaining any object when the whole attention of their minds is directed towards that single object than when it is dissipated among a great variety of things. . . .

All the improvements in machinery, however, have by no means been the inventions of those who had occasion to use the machines. Many improvements have been made by the ingenuity of the makers of the machines, when to make them became the business of a peculiar trade; and some by that of those who are called philosophers or men of speculation, whose trade it is not to do anything, but to observe everything; and who, upon that account, are often capable of combining together the powers of the most distant and dissimilar objects. In the progress of society, philosophy or speculation becomes, like every other employment, the principal or sole trade and occupation of a particular class of citizens. Like every other employment too, it is subdivided into a great number of different branches, each of which affords occupation to a peculiar tribe or class or philosophers; and this subdivision of employment in philosophy, as well as in every other business, improves dexterity, and saves time. Each individual becomes more expert in his own peculiar branch, more work is done upon the whole, and the quantity of science is considerably increased by it.

It is the great multiplication of the productions of all the different arts, in consequence of the division of labour, which occasions, in a well-governed society, that universal opulence which extends itself to the lowest ranks of the people. Every workman has a great quantity of his own work to dispose of beyond what he himself has occasion for; and every other workman being exactly in the same situation, he is enabled to exchange a great quantity of his own goods for a great quantity, or, what comes to the same thing, for the price of a great quantity of theirs. He supplies them abundantly with what they have occasion for, and they accommodate him as amply with what he has occasion for, and a general plenty diffuses itself through all the different ranks of the society.

The difference of natural talents in different men is, in reality, much less than we are aware of; and the very different genius which appears to distinguish men of different professions, when grown up to maturity, is not upon many occasions so much the cause as the effect of the division of labour. The difference between the most dissimilar characters, between a philosopher and a common street porter, for example, seems to arise not so much from nature as from habit, custom, and education. When they came into the world, and for the first six or eight years of their existence, they were perhaps very much alike, and neither their parents nor playfellows could perceive any remarkable difference. About that age, or soon after, they come to be employed in very different occupations. The difference of talents comes then to be taken notice of, and widens by degrees, till at last the vanity of the philosopher is willing to acknowledge scarce any resemblance. . . .

WHEN the division of labour has been once thoroughly established, it is but a very small part of a man's wants which the produce of his own labour can supply. He supplies the far greater part of them by exchanging that surplus part of the produce of his own labour, which is over and above his own consumption, for such parts of the produce of other men's labour as he has occasion or. Every man thus lives by exchanging, or becomes in some measure a merchant, and the society itself grows to be what is properly a commercial society.

But when the division of labour first began to take place, this power of exchanging must frequently have been very much clogged and embarrassed in its operations. One man, we shall suppose, has more of a certain commodity than he himself has occasion for, while another has less. The former consequently would be glad to dispose of, and the latter to purchase, a part of this superfluity. But if this latter should chance to have nothing that the former stands in need of, no exchange can be made between them. The butcher has more meat in his shop than he himself can consume, and the brewer and the baker would each of them be willing to purchase a part of it. But they have nothing to offer in exchange, except the different productions of their respective trades, and the butcher is already provided with all the bread and beer which he has immediate occasion for. No exchange can, in this case, be made between them. . . .

It is in this manner that money has become in all civilized nations the universal instrument of commerce, by the intervention of which goods of all kinds are bought and sold, or exchanged for one another.

What are the rules which men naturally observe in exchanging them either for money or for one another, I shall now proceed to examine. These rules determine what may be called the relative or exchangeable value of goods.

The word value, it is to be observed, has two different meanings, and sometimes expresses the utility of some particular object, and sometimes the power of purchasing other goods which the possession of that object conveys. The one may be called "value in use"; the other, "value in exchange." The things which have the greatest value in use have frequently little or no value in exchange; and, on the contrary, those which have the greatest value in exchange have frequently little or no value in use. Nothing is more useful than water: but it will purchase scarce anything; scarce anything can be had in exchange for it. A diamond, on the contrary, has scarce any value in use; but a very great quantity of other goods may frequently be had in exchange for it.

EVERY man is rich or poor according to the degree in which he can afford to enjoy the necessaries, conveniences, and amusements of human life. But after the division of labour has once thoroughly taken place, it is but a very small part of these with which a man's own labour can supply him. The far greater part of them he must derive from the labour of other people, and he must be rich or poor according to the quantity of that labour which he can command, or which he can afford to purchase. The value of any commodity, therefore, to the person who possesses it, and who means not to use or consume it himself, but to exchange it for other commodities, is equal to the quantity of labour which it enables him to purchase or command. Labour, therefore, is the real measure of the exchangeable value of all commodities. . . .

Wealth, as Mr. Hobbes says, is power. But the person who either acquires, or succeeds to a great fortune, does not necessarily acquire or succeed to any political power, either civil or military. His fortune may, perhaps, afford him the means of acquiring both, but the mere possession of that fortune does not necessarily convey to him either. The power which that possession immediately and directly conveys to him, is the power of purchasing; a certain command over all the labour, or over all the produce of labour, which is then in the market. His fortune is greater or less, precisely in proportion to the extent of this power; or to the quantity either of other men's labour, or, what is the same thing, of the produce of other men's labour, which it enables him to purchase or command. The exchangeable value of everything must always be precisely equal to the extent of this power which it conveys to its owner.

[E]very individual who employs his capital in the support of domestic industry, necessarily endeavours so to direct that industry that its produce may be of the greatest possible value.

The produce of industry is what it adds to the subject or materials upon which it is employed. In proportion as the value of this produce is great or small, so will likewise to the profits of the employer. But it is only for the sake of profit that any man employs a capital in the support of industry; and he will always, therefore, endeavour to employ it in the support of that industry of which the produce is likely to be of the greatest value, or to exchange for the greatest quantity either of money or of other goods.

But the annual revenue of every society is always precisely equal to the exchangeable value of the whole annual produce of its industry, or rather is precisely the same thing with the exchangeable value. As every individual, therefore, endeavours as much as he can both to employ his capital in the support of domestic industry, and so to direct that industry that its produce may be of the greatest value; every individual necessarily labours to render the annual revenue of the society as great as he can. He generally, indeed, neither intends to promote the public interest, nor knows how much he is promoting it. By preferring the support of domestic to that of foreign industry, he intends only his own security; and by directing that industry in such a manner as its produce may be of the greatest value, he intends only his own gain, and he is in this, as in many other cases, led by an invisible hand to promote an end which was no part of his intention. Nor is it always the worse for the society that it was no part of it. By pursuing his own interest he frequently promotes that of the society more effectually than when he really intends to promote it. I have never known much good done by those who affected to trade for the public good. It is an affectation, indeed, not very common among merchants, and very few words need be employed in dissuading them from it.

What is the species of domestic industry which his capital can employ, and of which the produce is likely to be of the greatest value, every individual, it is evident, can, in his local situation, judge much better than any statesman or lawgiver can do for him. The statesman who should attempt to direct private people in what manner they ought to employ their capitals would not only load himself with a most unnecessary attention, but assume an authority which could safely be trusted, not only to no single person, but to no council or senate whatever, and which would nowhere be so dangerous as in the hands of a man who had folly and presumption enough to fancy himself fit to exercise it.

Smith advocated a society based on specialization and organized into natural divisions of labor. Such a structure will lead to increased wealth, he claimed, and should be allowed to operate freely, with no consciously executed social plan. Although no plan is needed for individual and social good, Smith claimed these will both be attained due to the guiding influence of an "invisible hand," which governs a market geared toward individual profit.

This can be seen as an example of a mechanistic approach to the analysis of society. Smith's theory treats society like a machine, composed of individual parts unconsciously working in an aggregate whole. The greater the efficiency of the parts, the larger the output of the whole. Notions of ultimate plan or purpose are conspicuously absent. In fact, Smith believed it would be dangerous for the state as a whole to intentionally pursue some set of social goods.

John Stuart Mill

John Stuart Mill, born in 1806, was a singular genius whose life spanned the first three quarters of the nineteenth century (he died in 1873). His father, James Mill, was an enthusiastic follower of the utilitarianism of Jeremy Bentham. J.S. Mill shared this enthusiasm and is best known as a champion of utilitarianism in ethics and political philosophy.

Utilitarianism is a generally empiricist philosophy of value that uses individual happiness, or satisfaction, as a measure of social good. In *On Liberty* and *Utilitarianism*, Mill argues that this treatment of ethical and political theory can be used as a foundation for individualism and democracy, as well as a catalyst for humanitarian social reform. Mill advocated taking every individual's situation into account and computing total social value by adding each person's satisfaction or dissatisfaction equally. Such measures of value could be used to decide political and social issues, according to utilitarianism. Mill further argued that this method of aggregate computation of value not only produces the greatest social welfare but also the most individual freedom. The tension between social and individual good has been and continues to be thoroughly discussed, and Mill's resolution is far from definitive.

In any case, utilitarians believed that theirs was a scientific approach to ethics and political theory. By using empirically measurable criteria, such as individual pleasure, satisfaction, or happiness, and a repeatable formula for computing social good, i.e., summing up each individual share, utilitarians believed that they finally had a concrete, precise, objective way to determine social and political issues. Thus, it seemed that the scientific revolution was finally gaining ground in the realm of human affairs, and that questions of justice and value could perhaps be turned over to social and political scientists rather than be left to the musings of philosophers.

Mill's *System of Logic* was intended to be a thorough treatment of the principles of reasoning in the sciences. He included a discussion of the "Moral Sciences" in Book VI. In this section, we see the empiricism of Mill's utilitarianism as well as his confidence that the scientific method could be used successfully in the social and political arenas.[4]

Principles of Evidence and Theories of Method are not to be constructed *a priori*. The laws of our rational faculty ... are only learned by seeing the agent at work. The earlier achievements of science were made without the conscious observation of any Scientific Method. ... But it was only the easier problems which could be thus resolved. ... In scientific investigation, as in all other works of human skill, the way of obtaining the end is seen as it were instinctively by superior minds in some comparatively simple case, and is then, by judicious generalization, adapted to the variety of complex cases. We learn to do a thing in difficult circumstances, by attending to the manner in which we have spontaneously done the same thing in easier ones. ...

Concerning the physical nature of man, as an organized being—though there is still much uncertainty and much controversy ... —there is, however, a considerable body of truths which all who have attended to the subject consider to be fully established. ... But the laws of Mind, and in even a greater degree, those of Society, are so far from having attained a similar state of even partial recognition, that it is still a controversy whether they are capable of becoming subjects of science in the strict sense of the term. ... Here, therefore, if anywhere, the principles laid down in the preceding Books may be expected to be useful. ...

At the threshold of this inquiry we are met by an objection. .....
Are the actions of human beings, like all other natural events, subject to invariable laws? Does that constancy of causation, which is the foundation of every scientific theory ... really obtain among them? ...

The question ... is the celebrated controversy of the freedom of the will. ... The affirmative opinion is commonly called the doctrine of Necessity, as asserting human volitions and actions to be necessary and inevitable. The negative maintains that the will is not determined, like other phenomena, but determines itself. ...

I have already made it sufficiently apparent that the former of these opinions is that which I consider the true one.... The metaphysical theory of free-will ... was invented because the supposed alternative of admitting human actions to be *necessary* was deemed inconsistent with every one's instinctive consciousness, as well as humiliating to the pride and even degrading to the moral nature of man....

Correctly conceived, the doctrine called Philosophical Necessity is simply this: that, given the motives which are present to an individual's mind, and given likewise the character and disposition of the individual, the manner in which he will act might be unerringly inferred.... No one who believed that he knew thoroughly the circumstances of any case, and the characters of the different persons concerned, would hesitate to foretell how all of them would act. Whatever degree of doubt he may feel arises from ... uncertainty.... Nor does this full assurance conflict in the smallest degree with what is called our feeling of freedom.... We may be free, and yet another may have reason to be perfectly certain what use we shall make of our freedom....

But the doctrine of causation, when considered as obtaining between our volitions and their antecedents, is almost universally conceived of involving more than this.... There are few to whom mere constancy of succession appears as a sufficiently stringent bond of union for so peculiar a relation as that of cause and effect. Even if the reason repudiates, the imagination retains, the feeling of some more intimate connection, of some peculiar tie, or mysterious constraint exercised by the antecedent over the consequent. Now this it is which, considered as applying to the human will, conflicts with our consciousness, and revolts our feelings. We are certain that, in the case of our volitions, there is not this mysterious constraint. We know that we are not compelled, as by a magic spell, to obey any particular motive.... But neither is any such mysterious compulsion now supposed, by the best philosophic authorities, to be exercised by any other cause over its effect....

That the free-will metaphysicians, being mostly of the school which rejects Hume's ... analysis of Cause and Effect, should miss their way for want of the light which that analysis afford, can not surprise us....

It is a common notion, or at least it is implied in many common modes of speech, that the thoughts, feelings, and actions of sentient-beings are not a subject of science, in the same strict sense in which this is true of the objects of outward nature. This notion seems to involve some confusion of ideas. . . .

Any facts are fitted, in themselves, to be a subject of science which follow one another according to constant laws, although these laws may not have been discovered. . . . Take, for instance, the most familiar class of meteorological phenomena, those of rain and sunshine. Scientific inquiry has not succeeded in ascertaining the order of antecedence and consequence among these phenomena, so as to be able . . . to predict them with certainty, or even with any high degree of probability. Yet no one doubts the phenomena depend on laws resulting from known ultimate laws. . . .

And this is what is or ought to be meant by those who speak of sciences which are not *exact* sciences. Astronomy was once a science, without being an exact science. . . .

The science of human nature is of this description. It falls far short of the standard of exactness now realized in Astronomy; . . . but there is no reason that it should not be as much a science as . . . Astronomy was. . . . [I]t would have attained the ideal perfection of a science if it enabled us to foretell how an individual will think, feel, or act throughout his life. . . . It needs scarcely be stated that nothing approaching to this can be done. The actions of individuals could not be predicted with scientific accuracy, were it only because we can not foresee the whole of the circumstances in which those individuals will be placed. . . .

What the Mind is, as well as what Matter is, or any other question respecting Things in themselves . . . it would be foreign to the purposes of this treatise to consider. Here . . . we shall . . . understand by the laws of mind those of mental Phenomena. . . .

The subject, then . . . is the uniformities of succession, the laws, whether ultimate or derivative, according to which one mental state succeeds another. . . .

Next, after the science of individual man comes the science of man in society—of the actions of collective masses of mankind, and the various phenomena which constitute social life. . .

No wonder that, when the phenomena of society have so rarely been contemplated in the point of view characteristic of science, the philosophy of society should have made little progress. . . .

All phenomena of society are phenomena of human nature, generated by the action of outward circumstances upon masses of human beings; and if, therefore, the phenomena of human thought, feeling and action are subject to fixed laws, the phenomena of society can not but conform to fixed laws....

Men ... in a state of society are still men; their actions and passions are obedient to the laws of individual human nature. Men are not, when brought together, converted into another kind of substance.... Human beings in society have no properties but those which are derived from, and may be resolved into, the laws of the nature of individual man. In social phenomena the Composition of Causes is the universal law....

The actions and feelings of human beings in the social state, are, no doubt, entirely governed by psychological ... laws.... Supposing, therefore, the laws of human actions and feelings to be sufficiently known, there is no extraordinary difficulty in determining from those laws, the nature of the social effects which any given cause tends to produce. But ... when by attempting to predict what will actually occur in a given case ... we attempt a task to proceed far in which, surpasses the compass of the human faculties....

It is evident ... that Sociology, considered as a system of deductions *a priori*, can not be a science of positive predictions, but only of tendencies ... The aim of practical politics is to surround any given society with the greatest possible number of circumstances of which the tendencies are beneficial, and to remove or counteract ... those of which the tendencies are injurious. A knowledge of the tendencies only ... gives us to a considerable extent this power.

Mill built on the empirical tradition of Hume to argue for a science of mind, society, and politics. He saw the empirical existence of regular phenomena as the basis for laws of cause and effect and, like Hume, disparaged any metaphysical connection between the two. As such, the phenomena of mental and social affairs seemed no different to Mill than that of stars and planets. This is an example of a theory that implies conscious free will is compatible with physical determinism.

Mill had some further simplifying hypotheses in his theories. Mill's social utilitarianism can be seen as the political analog of Boyle's corpuscular mechanism in modern chemistry or metaphysical atomism in ancient Greece. Mill believed that individuals are the atoms or corpuscles of society, and that all social phenomena are derived from the aggregate composition of individual activities. Thus, by understanding the principles of individual thought and action, we can understand or derive the principles of social and political theory. This is similar to Boyle's focus on corpuscles of matter in combination and the Democritean statement that atoms are "bound together in a binding which makes them touch and be contiguous with one another but which does not genuinely produce any other single nature whatever" (see Chapters 1 and 7). This thesis is one that comes under attack from other social theorists, as we see later in this chapter.

Humanitarian Issues

Other philosophers and social scientists did not feel that the emerging scientific approach to economics was sufficient to replace philosophical treatment. Socialists saw ethical problems in emerging industrial capitalism. In this section, we will examine the radical socialism of Karl Marx and the democratic socialism of John Dewey. Both see science as a tool, not an end, of society.

Marx was born in the ancient German town of Trier in 1818 and died in 1883. He studied the working conditions of industrial laborers in Britain over the course of decades, employing a method he derived from Hegel. Hegel's method treats intellectual history, as well as personal development, as a recurring conflict of opposing views resulting in a continual transformation of ideas. Marx brought this method to bear on the study of society and politics in a way he regarded as scientific. Marx claims that he reverses Hegel's emphasis from idealism to materialism. That is, Marx explicitly focuses on the concrete material and economic elements of human existence as crucial for philosophy. The dialectical material method of Marx, based on careful observation, yielded an impressive theory that is no less empirical or scientific than Adam Smith's. This theory highlights significant ethical shortcomings in industrial capitalism, shortcomings which yield some evidence that runs counter to Smith's faith in an "invisible hand."

The following is excerpted from *Capital*, Volume I.[5]

The circulation of commodities is the starting point for capital....
The first distinction between money as money and money as capital is nothing more than a difference in the form of circulation. The direct form of the circulation of commodities is C-M-C, the transformation of commodities into money and the re-conversions of money into commodities: selling in order to buy. But along side this form, we find another form, which is quite distinct from the first:

M-C-M, the transformation of money into commodities, and the reconversion of commodities into money: buying in order to sell. . . .

Now it is evident that the circulatory process M-C-M would be absurd and empty if the intention were, by using this roundabout route, to exchange two equal sums of money. . . .

The change in value of the money which has to be transformed into capital cannot take place in the money itself. . . . Just as little can this change originate in the second act of circulation, the resale of the commodity. . . . The change must therefore take place in the commodity which is bought in the first act. . . . In order to extract value out of the consumption of a commodity, our friend the money owner must be lucky enough to find within the sphere of circulation, on the market, a commodity [which] possesses the peculiar property of being a source of value. . . . The possessor of money does find such a special commodity: . . . labour-power.

. . . On this assumption, labour-power can appear on the market only if, and in so far as, its possessor offers it for sale or sells it as a commodity.

For the transformation of money into capital, therefore, the owner of money must find the free worker available on the commodity-market; and this worker must be free in the double sense that as a free individual he can dispose of his labour . . . and that, on the other hand, he has no other commodity for sale . . . he is free of all the objects needed for the realization of his labour-power.

. . . nature does not produce on the one hand owners of money or commodity, and on the other hand men possessing nothing but their own labour-power. This relation has no basis in natural history. . . . It is clearly the result of past historical development.

The labour process, when it is in the process by which the capitalist consumes labour-power, exhibits two characteristic phenomena.

First, the worker works under the control of the capitalist. . . .

Secondly, the product is the property of the capitalist and not that of the worker, its immediate producer.

Now it is quite possible to imagine, with Adam Smith, that the difference between the . . . social division of labour, and the division in manufacture, is merely subjective, exists merely for the observer, who in the case of manufacture can see at a glance all the numerous operations being performed on one spot, while ... the spreading out of the work over great areas and the great number of people employed in each branch of labour obscure the connection.... The fact [is] that the specialized worker produces no commodities. It is only the common product of all the specialized workers that becomes a commodity. The division of labour within a society is mediated through the purchase and sale of the products of different branches of industry, while the connection between the various partial operations in a workshop is mediated through the sale of the labour-power of several workers to one capitalist, who applies it as combined labour power. The division of labour within manufacture presupposes a concentration of the means of production in the hands of one capitalist.... [I]n the society outside the workshop, the play of chance and caprice results in a motley pattern of distribution of the producers and their means of production among the various branches of social labour.... Division of labour within the workshop implies the undisputed authority of the capitalist over men, who are merely the members of a total mechanism which belongs to him. The division of labour within society brings into contact independent producers of commodities ... just as in the animal kingdom the "war of all against all" more or less preserves the conditions of existence of every species. The same bourgeois consciousness which celebrates the division of labour in the workshop, the lifelong annexation of the worker to a partial operation, and his complete subjection to capital ... denounces with equal vigor every conscious attempt to control and regulate the process of production socially.... It is very characteristic that the enthusiastic apologists of the factory system have nothing more damning to urge against a general organization of labour in society than that it would turn the whole of society into a factory.

If, in the society where the capitalist mode of production prevails, anarchy in the social division of labour and despotism in the manufacturing division of labour mutually condition each other, we find, on the contrary, in those earlier forms of society ... on the one hand, a specimen of the organization of the labour of society in accordance with an approved and authoritative plan....

Those small and extremely ancient Indian communities ... are based on the possession of the land in common, on the blending of agriculture and handicrafts and on an unalterable division of labour, which serves as a fixed plan and basis for action whenever a new community is started.

This analytic, materialistic method eventually led Marx to conclude that the capitalist system is inherently exploitive of the worker and that the system impoverishes all members of society by alienating the laborer from the fruits of labor; furthermore, it engenders overspecialization. Marx quotes a reviewer of *Capital* in its second edition and endorses the view that "the social movement [is] a process of natural history, governed by laws not only independent of human will, consciousness, and intelligence, but rather, on the contrary, determining that will. . . ." This thesis is directly opposed to Mill's emphasis on individualism. Mill believed that the study of society could be reduced to the study of individuals, and that social phenomena were no more than aggregates of individual activities. Marx believed this was mistaken, that society is rather the determining of the individual will rather than the other way around. Nevertheless, he viewed society as amenable to study in terms of objective laws. Marx took the scientific revolutions of modernity to heart in attempting to formulate objective laws of history, economy, and society.

John Dewey, an American philosopher born in 1859, was one of the founders of a school of thought known as *pragmatism*.[6] He was a philosopher almost unparalleled in breadth. His work ran through political, metaphysical, ethical, sociological, psychological, aesthetic, scientific, and epistemological topics, and his writings are vast. He regarded modern science as a powerful tool for the transformation of society, but did not believe the development of scientific thinking nor technological achievement alone could affect such a transformation. Like Marx, he saw the deployment of technology in the Industrial Revolution as perpetuating old political power structures without bringing them into careful critical evaluation. Dewey advocated the scientific study of society and the conscious use of scientific method to improve social conditions. He believed, contrary to Adam Smith, that such improvement would not come automatically, but needed the direct participation of social forces. John Dewey died in 1952. The following selections from *Individualism Old and New* and *The Public and Its Problems* illustrate some of Dewey's evaluations and prescriptions based upon scientific thinking.[7]

INDIVIDUALISM OLD AND NEW

The development of a civilization that is outwardly corporate—or rapidly becoming so—has been accompanied by a submergence of the individual. . . . It may be contended that no one class in the past has the power now possessed by an industrial oligarchy. On the other hand, it may be held that this power of the few is, with respect to genuine individuality, specious; that those who outwardly control are in reality as much carried by forces external to themselves as are the many. . . .

Our prevailing mentality, our "ideology," is said to be that of the "business mind. . . ." Are not the prevailing standards of value those derived from pecuniary success and economic prosperity?

There is no greater sign of the paralysis of the imagination which custom and involvement in immediate detail can induce than the belief, sedulously propagated by some who pride themselves on superior taste, that the machine is itself the source of our troubles. . . . [I]t is hard to think of anything more childish than the animism that puts the blame on machinery. For machinery means . . . power. If we have harnessed this power to the dollar rather than to the enrichment of human life, it is because we have been content to stay within the bounds of traditional aims and values although we are in the possession of a revolutionary transforming instrument.

THE PUBLIC AND ITS PROBLEMS

At present, the application of physical science is rather *to* human concerns than *in* them. That is, external, made in the interests of its consequences for a possessing and acquisitive class. Application *in* life would signify that science was absorbed and distributed; that it was the instrumentality of . . . common understanding and thorough communication. . . . The use of science to regulate industry and trade has gone on steadily. The scientific revolution of the seventeenth century was the precursor to the industrial revolution of the eighteenth and nineteenth. In consequence, man has suffered the impact of an enormously enlarged control of physical energies without any corresponding ability to control himself and his own affairs. Knowledge divided against itself . . . has played its part in generating enslavement of men, women, and children in factories in which they are animated machines to tend inanimate machines. It has maintained sordid slums, flurried and discontented careers, grinding poverty and luxurious wealth, brutal exploitation of nature and man in times of peace and high explosives and noxious gases in times of war. Man, a child in understanding of himself, has placed in his hands physical tools of incalculable power. He plays with them like a child, and whether they work harm or good is largely a matter of accident. . . .

The glorification of "pure" science under such conditions is a rationalization of an escape. . . . The true purity of knowledge exists not when it is uncontaminated by contact with use and service. It is wholly a moral matter, an affair of honesty, impartiality and generous breadth of intent in search and communication. The adulteration of knowledge is due not to its use, but to vested bias and prejudice, to one-sidedness of outlook, to vanity, to conceit of possession and authority, to contempt or disregard of human concern in its use. . . .

While Marx and Dewey wanted to deploy scientific method and scientific achievements for the benefit of society, they also found fault with existing social forms. Smith's analysis of the capitalist system based on profit-oriented markets does not fault this system, but rather subjects it to analysis in order to endorse existing practices. Marx perhaps had the advantage of looking at British society a century after Smith, and he took as additional evidence the abominable working conditions of industrial Britain. This is evidence against Smith's prediction that "a workman, even of the lowest and poorest order, if he is frugal and industrious, may enjoy a greater share of the necessaries and conveniences of life than is possible for any savage to obtain." Marx sought to investigate how capitalism has worked in the opposite direction and found the answer in the very profit system and deployment of capital that Smith praises.

Dewey also wanted to critically and scientifically analyze existing social structures, and found that a true application of science to the problems of society had not been pursued. He claimed that a consciously experimental approach to social issues would yield a different society than that of corporate capitalism. But in order to achieve such change, science and technology would have to be critically examined as means to some good. Thus, the naturalistic fallacy of social Darwinism would need to be overcome. This entails reincorporating science into the world of value and human affairs, and reconnecting objective scientific study with philosophical investigations of purpose, at least in a limited sense. This task is ongoing, and we will see some scientific perspectives on reinvigorating the scientific–philosophical dialogue with respect to humanity in Chapter 12.

Environmentalism

American environmentalism often traces its roots to Henry David Thoreau's 1854 classic *Walden*. Although Thoreau made little or no mention of large-scale environmental disasters in this chronicle of his life in the Massachu-setts woods, his work is a critical evaluation of the imbalance between modernity and the natural environment. Thoreau (1817–1862) compared the frenzied life in pursuit of productivity and progress with one more closely tied with simplicity. In this way, *Walden* is the story of the internal price paid by humanity in order to purchase modern society.[8]

Rachel Carson's 1962 *Silent Spring* is more straightforwardly an impe-tus for late-twentieth-century environmentalism.[9] Carson (1907–1964) speaks directly of the external consequences of modern trends in environ-mental exploitation.

The following are excerpts from each of these works.

WALDEN
OR LIFE IN THE WOODS

WHEN I WROTE the following pages, or rather the bulk of them, I lived alone, in the woods, a mile from any neighbor, in a house which I had built myself, on the shore of Walden Pond, in Concord, Massa-chusetts, and earned my living by the labor of my hands only. I lived there two years and two months. At present I am a sojourner in civ-ilized life again.

I should not obtrude my affairs so much on the notice of my readers if very particular inquiries had not been made by my townsmen concerning my mode of life, which some would call im-pertinent, though they do not appear to me at all impertinent, but, considering the circumstances, very natural and pertinent. Some have asked what I got to eat; if I did not feel lonesome; if I was not afraid; and the like. Others have been curious to learn what por-tion of my income I devoted to charitable purposes; and some, who have large families, how many poor children I maintained. I will therefore ask those of my readers who feel no particular inter-est in me to pardon me if I undertake to answer some of these questions. . . .

I would fain say something, not so much concerning the Chi-nese and Sandwich Islanders as you who read these pages, who are said to live in New England; something about your condition, espe-cially your outward condition or circumstances in this world, in this town, what it is, whether it is necessary that it be as bad as it is, whether it cannot be improved as well as not. I have travelled a good deal in Concord; and everywhere, in shops, and offices, and fields, the inhabitants have appeared to me to be doing penance in a thousand remarkable ways. What I have heard of Bramins sitting exposed to four fires and looking in the face of the sun; or hanging suspended, with their heads downward, over flames; or looking at the heavens over their shoulders "until it becomes impossible for them to resume their natural position, while from the twist of the neck nothing but liquids can pass into the stomach"; or dwelling, chained for life, at the foot of a tree; or measuring with their bodies, like caterpillars, the breadth of vast empires; or standing on one leg on the tops of pillars—even these forms of conscious penance are hardly more incredible and astonishing than the scenes which I daily witness. The twelve labors of Hercules were trifling in comparison with those which my neighbors have undertaken; for they were only twelve, and had an end. . . .

I see young men, my townsmen, whose misfortune it is to have inherited farms, houses, barns, cattle, and farming tools; for these are more easily acquired than got rid of. Better if they had been born in the open pasture and suckled by a wolf, that they might have seen with clearer eyes what field they were called to labor in. Who made them serfs of the soil? Why should they eat their sixty acres, when man is condemned to eat only his peck of dirt? Why should they begin digging their graves as soon as they are born? They have got to live a man's life, pushing all these things before them, and get on as well as they can. How many a poor immortal soul have I met well nigh crushed and smothered under its load, creeping down the road of life, pushing before it a barn seventy-five feet by forty. . . .

But men labor under a mistake. The better part of the man is soon plowed into the soil for compost. By a seeming fate, commonly called necessity, they are employed, as it says in an old book, laying up treasures which moth and rust will corrupt and thieves break through and steal. It is a fool's life, as they will find when they get to the end of it, if not before. . . .

Most men, even in this comparatively free country, through mere ignorance and mistake, are so occupied with the factitious cares and superfluously coarse labors of life that its finer fruits cannot be plucked by them. Their fingers, from excessive toil, are too clumsy and tremble too much for that. Actually, the laboring man has not leisure for a true integrity day by day; he cannot afford to sustain the manliest relations to men; his labor would be depreciated in the market. He has no time to be anything but a machine.

The mass of men lead lives of quiet desperation. What is called resignation is confirmed desperation. From the desperate city you go into the desperate country, and have to console yourself with the bravery of minks and muskrats. A stereotyped but unconscious despair is concealed even under what are called the games and amusements of mankind. There is no play in them, for this comes after work. . . .

Here is life, an experiment to a great extent untried by me; but it does not avail me that they have tried it. If I have any experience which I think valuable, I am sure to reflect that this my Mentors said nothing about. . . .

I cannot believe that our factory system is the best mode by which men may get clothing. The condition of the operatives is becoming every day more like that of the English; and it cannot be wondered at, since, as far as I have heard or observed, the principal object is, not that mankind may be well and honestly clad, but, unquestionably, that the corporations may be enriched. . . .

If it is asserted that civilization is a real advance on the condition of man,—and I think that it is, though only the wise improve their advantages,—it must be shown that it has produced better dwellings without making them more costly; and the cost of a thing is the amount of what I call life which is required to be exchanged for it. . . . An average house in this neighborhood . . . will take from ten to fifteen years of the labourer's life. . . . Would the savage have been wise to exchange his wigwam for a palace on these terms? . . .

When I consider my neighbors, the farmers of Concord . . . I am surprised to learn that [one] cannot at once name a dozen in the town who own their farms free and clear. . . . The man who has actually paid for his farm with labour on it is so rare that every neighbor can point to him. I doubt if there are three such men in Concord. . . .

It is possible to invent a house still more convenient and luxurious than we have, which yet all would admit that man could not afford to pay for. Shall the respectable citizen thus gravely teach, by precept and example, the necessity of the young man's providing a certain number of superfluous glow-shoes, and umbrellas, and empty guest-chambers for empty guests, before he dies?

SILENT SPRING

"A FABLE FOR TOMORROW"

There was once a town in the heart of America where all life seemed to live in harmony with its surroundings. The town lay in the midst of a checkerboard of prosperous farms, with fields of grain and hillsides of orchards where, in spring, white clouds of bloom drifted above the green fields. In autumn, oak and maple and birch set up a blaze of color that flamed and flickered across a backdrop of pines. Then foxes barked in the hills and deer silently crossed the fields, half hidden in the mists of the fall mornings.

Along the roads, laurel, viburnum and alder, great ferns and wildflowers delighted the traveler's eye through much of the year. Even in winter the roadsides were places of beauty, where countless birds came to feed on the berries and on the seed heads of the dried weeds rising above the snow. The countryside was, in fact, famous for the abundance and variety of its bird life, and when the flood of migrants was pouring through in spring and fall people traveled from great distances to observe them. Others came to fish the streams, which flowed clear and cold out of the hills and contained shady pools where trout lay. So it had been from the days many years ago when the first settlers raised their houses, sank their wells, and built their barns.

Then a strange blight crept over the area and everything began to change. Some evil spell had settled on the community: mysterious maladies swept the flocks of chickens; the cattle and sheep sickened and died. Everywhere was a shadow of death. The farmers spoke of much illness among their families. In the town the doctors had become more and more puzzled by new kinds of sickness appearing among their patients. There had been several sudden and unexplained deaths, not only among adults but even among children, who would be stricken suddenly while at play and die within a few hours.

There was a strange stillness. The birds, for example—where had they gone? Many people spoke of them, puzzled and disturbed. The feeding stations in the backyards were deserted. The few birds seen anywhere were moribund; they trembled violently and could not fly. It was a spring without voices. On the mornings that had once throbbed with the dawn chorus of robins, catbirds, doves, jays, wrens, and scores of other bird voices there was now no sound; only silence lay over the fields and woods and marsh.

On the farms the hens brooded, but no chicks hatched. The farmers complained that they were unable to raise any pigs—the litters were small and the young survived only a few days. The apple trees were coming into bloom but no bees droned among the blossoms, so there was no pollination and there would be no fruit.

The roadsides, once so attractive, were now lined with browned and withered vegetation as though swept by fire. These, too, were silent, deserted by all living things. Even the streams were now lifeless. Anglers no longer visited them, for all the fish had died.

In the gutters under the eaves and between the shingles of the roofs, a white granular powder still showed a few patches; some weeks before it had fallen like snow upon the roofs and the lawns, the fields and streams.

No witchcraft, no enemy action had silenced the rebirth of new life in this stricken world. The people had done it themselves.

This town does not actually exist, but it might easily have a thousand counterparts in America or elsewhere in the world. I know of no community that has experienced all the misfortunes I describe. Yet every one of these disasters has actually happened somewhere, and many real communities have already suffered a substantial number of them. A grim specter has crept upon us almost unnoticed, and this imagined tragedy may easily become a stark reality we all shall know.

What has already silenced the voices of spring in countless towns in America? This book is an attempt to explain.

The history of life on earth has been a history of interaction between living things and their surroundings. To a large extent, the physical form and the habits of the earth's vegetation and its animal life have been molded by the environment. Considering the whole span of earthly time, the opposite effect, in which life actually modifies its surroundings, has been relatively slight. Only within the moment of time represented by the present century has one species—man—acquired significant power to alter the nature of his world.

During the past quarter century this power has not only increased to one of disturbing magnitude but it has changed in character. The most alarming of all man's assaults upon the environment is the contamination of air, earth, rivers, and sea with dangerous and even lethal materials. This pollution is for the most part irrecoverable.... In this now universal contamination of the environment, chemicals are the sinister and little recognized partners of radiation in changing the very nature of the world....

It took hundreds of millions of years to produce the life that now inhabits the earth.... Given time—time not in years but in millennia—life adjusts, and a balance has been reached. For time is the essential ingredient; but in the modern world there is no time.

The rapidity of change and the speed with which new situations are created follow the impetuous and heedless pace of man.... Radiation is no longer merely the background radiation of rocks, the bombardment of cosmic rays, the ultraviolet of the sun that have existed before there was any life on earth.... The chemicals to which life is asked to make its adjustment are no longer merely the calcium and silica and copper and all the rest of the minerals washed out of the rocks and carried in rivers to the sea....

Much of the necessary knowledge is now available but we do not use it. We train ecologists in our universities and even employ them in our governmental agencies but we seldom take their advice....

Have we fallen into a mesmerized state that makes us accept as inevitable that which is inferior or detrimental, as though having lost the will or the vision to demand that which is good?

The themes expressed by Thoreau and Carson have been much revised and updated throughout the twentieth century. Carson was primarily concerned with a particular kind of environmental danger, namely, that of chemical pollutants used in agriculture. Later environmentalists are concerned with habitat shrinkage, global warming, human overpopulation, biodiversity, and so forth. Yet from a philosophical perspective, the concern is the same. Carson wonders aloud if modern society has come so far in its mechanistic growth that we have lost the ability to evaluate the consequences of our large-scale activities from an ethical perspective.

Thoreau speaks of the impact made by a modern pursuit of progress on the individual human life. Later ethicists bring issues of family and gender into discussions of material progress and its price. Yet environmentalists from Thoreau onward lament the modern separation between social practice and thoughtful, critical reflection. Such reflection would obviate the idea that modern progress is in all respect superior to a simpler life, according to Thoreau.

New Social Sciences

In the nineteenth century, modern analytic method turned to the study of human social phenomena. With abstract modeling techniques and mathematical analysis, pioneering sociologists had high hopes that definitive answers could be provided for the solution of social problems, although most had realistic views on the difficulty of their task. In this section, we treat a seminal work by the French sociologist Emile Durkheim (1858–1917), *Le Suicide,* and a speculative piece from *Walden Two* by the twentieth-century American psychologist and behaviorist B.F. Skinner.

While psychology turned its attention to the individual as an object of scientific study, sociology took as its subject matter society as a whole. And while no one denied the mutual dependence of the two fields, the treatment of sociology as a separate branch of inquiry is warranted on two counts: first, abstracting the general character and features of society from their dependence on individual members might reveal some patterns more clearly and readily; and second, it could be the case that society itself is not dependent on its collective members treated individually. This might be for the reasons that Marx advocates, namely that the individual will is a product of social phenomena, not vice versa or for the weaker reasons advocated by Durkheim under the banner of social realism. George Simpson, in his preface to Durkheim's *Le Suicide,* characterizes this view as follows: "social realism . . . sees society as an entity greater than the sum of its parts, with its accompanying concepts of collective representations and collective conscience."

Durkheim sees suicide as a social problem, and Simpson tells us, "For Durkheim all ameliorative measures must go to the question of social structure . . . [e.g.,] reintegrating the individual into group life." The following is excerpted from *Le Suicide,* or *Suicide: A Study in Sociology.*[10]

Sociology has been in vogue for some time. Today this word, little known and almost discredited almost a decade ago, is in common use. Representatives of the new science are increasing in number and there is something like a public feeling favorable to it. . . . The progress of a science is proven by the progress toward solution of the problems it treats. It is said to be advancing when laws hitherto unknown are discovered, or when at least new facts are acquired. . . . Unfortunately, there is good reason why sociology does not appear in this light, and this is because the problems it poses are not usually clear-cut. It is still in the stage of system-building and philosophical synthesis. Instead of attempting to cast light on a limited portion of the social field, it prefers brilliant generalities. . . . Such a method . . . can achieve nothing objective. . . . [S]uch large and abrupt generalizations are not capable of any sort of proof. . . .

Believers in the future of the science must, of course, be anxious to put an end to this state of affairs. If it should continue, sociology would soon relapse into its old discredit. . . . Instead of contenting himself with metaphysical reflection on social themes, the sociologist must take as the object of his research groups of facts clearly circumscribed, capable of ready definition, with definite limits, and adhere strictly to them. . . .

It is in this spirit that the work here presented has been conceived. Suicide has been chosen as its subject. . . . [B]y thus restricting the research, one is by no means deprived of broad views and general insights. On the contrary, we think we have established a certain number of propositions concerning marriage, widowhood, family life, religious society, etc., which, if we are not mistaken, are more instructive than the common theories of moralists as to the nature of the conditions or institutions. There will even emerge from our study some suggestions concerning the causes of the general contemporary maladjustment being undergone by European societies and concerning remedies which may relieve it. . . . Suicide as it exists today is precisely one of the forms through which the collective affliction from which we suffer is transmitted; thus it will aid us to understand this. . . .

Sociological method as we practice it rests wholly on the basic principle that social facts must be studied as things, that is, as realities external to the individual. There is no principle for which we have received more criticism; but none is more fundamental. Indubitably for sociology to be possible, it must above all have an object all its own. . . . But if no reality exists outside of individual consciousness, it wholly lacks any material of its own. In that case, the only possible subject of observation is the mental states of the individual. . . . That, however, is the field of psychology. . . . *It is not realized that there can be no sociology unless societies exist, and that societies cannot exist if there are only individuals.* . . .

[T]here will . . . emerge . . . from the pages of this book, so to speak, the impression that the individual is dominated by a moral reality greater than himself: namely, collective reality. When each people is seen to have its own suicide-rate, more constant than that of general mortality, that its growth is in accordance with a coefficient of acceleration characteristic of each society; when it appears that the variations through which it passes at different times of the day, month, year merely reflect the rhythm of social life; and that marriage, divorce, the family, religious society, the army, etc., affect it in accordance with definite laws, some of which may even be numerically expressed—these states and institutions will no longer be regarded simply as characterless, ineffective ideological arrangements. Rather, they will be felt to be real, living, active forces. . . . Thus it will appear more clearly why sociology can and must be objective, since it deals with realities as definite and substantial as those of the psychologist or the biologist.

Like Mill, Durkheim believed that the science of society can be objective, and that metaphysical issues can be avoided. But he was clearly opposed to Mill's idea that "Men . . . in a state of society are still men; their actions and passions are obedient to the laws of individual human nature. Men are not, when brought together, converted into another kind of substance." Durkheim believed that sociology has its own phenomena and laws outside the bounds of psychology.

B. F. Skinner (1904–1990) was a psychologist who belonged to a school of thought known as *behaviorism*. Behaviorism espouses the thesis that external behavior is all there is to an analysis of consciousness. Happiness, fulfillment, stress, and other seemingly internal phenomena can all be gauged objectively on this view by measuring behavioral responses. Furthermore, in order to achieve desired ends, behavior modification is supposedly a sufficient, and exclusive, means.

Behaviorism is a psychological thesis with philosophical implications, and it has natural sociological applications. Skinner's 1948 classic *Walden Two* outlines a Utopian society from a psychological behaviorist perspective. The social plan contains broader themes as well. By advocating an experimental approach to social arrangement, with specific procedures for evaluating the outcome of various experiments, *Walden Two* is a general scientific plan for communal living. It is a fictional work. The behaviorist position is given by the character of Frazier; the narrator is a disgruntled college teacher; and the point of view of traditional philosophy is represented by the character of Castle. The following selection outlines some of the features of Skinner's Utopia.[11]

. . . My new interests in social problems and good will seemed to have exactly no effect whatsoever upon society. I could not see that they were of the slightest value to anyone. Yet I continued to pay for them day after day with a sustained feeling of frustration and depression. . . .

Rogers continued, ". . . I can see your point now. . . . Politics really wouldn't give us the chance we want. You see, we want to *do* something. . . . The politicians guess at all the answers and spend their time persuading people they're right—but they must know they're only guessing, that they haven't really *proved* anything."

This was Frazier's line without any doubt. . . .

". . . You've got to experiment, and *experiment with your own life!* . . . Have you ever heard of a man named Frazier, sir? . . . He was starting a community something like the one you used to talk about." . . .

I reached for a yearbook of my professional society. Frazier was not listed as a member. In a minute or two I had located an issue eight years old. He was there . . . The mailing address in the yearbook was a surprise. . . . The address read: *Walden Two, R.D. I, Canton.* . . .

I began to see the light.

"Walden Two. Walden the Second. Of Course. And quite like Frazier—fancying himself a sort of second Thoreau."

Walden Two was about thirty miles from the largest city in the state. . . . "We have much to see and much to talk about," said Frazier. . . . "Shall we walk down to the pond and then back for a cup of tea?" . . .

"The pond is our own work," he said after a moment. . . . . "One of our medical people took quite an interest in the pond. He has it nicely balanced, he tells me. At first the water was brown and slimy. You can see how clear it is now." Frazier picked up an oar . . . and, with some effort, plunged it straight down. The full length was visible and shining white.

"The main buildings, of course, we put up ourselves. . . . Our community now has nearly a thousand members. If we were not living in the buildings you see before you, we should be occupying some two hundred and fifty dwelling houses and working in a hundred offices, shops, stores, and warehouses." . . .

"One advantage of cooperative housing," Frazier said, "is that we can deal with the weather . . . no wonder the *nouveau* Californian is ecstatic! He has a new birth of freedom. He realizes how often he used to surrender to the inconveniences of a bad night—how many times he was kept from seeing his friends, or from going to the theater or a concert or a party. . . .

"In a community unit of this size, . . . it was feasible to connect all the personal rooms with the common rooms, dining rooms, theater, and library. You can see how we did it from the arrangement of the buildings. All our entertainment, social functions, dinners, and other personal engagements take place as planned. We never have to go out of doors at all." . . .

"The actual achievement is beside the point. The main thing is, we encourage our people to view every habit and custom with an eye to possible improvement. A constantly experimental attitude—that's all we need. Solutions to problems of every sort follow almost miraculously."

I was struck by the absence of large crowds. For some reason, the word "community" had suggested barn-sized halls full of noisy people. . . . I confessed my surprise and Frazier laughed heartily.

"What good are crowds?" he said. . . .

"Some people get a certain thrill from being part of a crowd," said Castle.

"A symptom of loneliness," said Frazier flat. ". . . But why should anyone who isn't starved for friendship or affection enjoy a crowd?"

"You can meet some interesting people, . . ."

"Not efficiently," said Frazier gently. "We have much better arrangements for bringing together compatible people with common interests."

"All goods and services are free. . . . Each of us pays for what he uses with twelve-hundred labor-credits each year—say four credits each workday. We change the value according to the needs of the community. At two hours of work per credit—an eight hour day—we could operate at a handsome profit. . . . The profit system is bad even when the worker gets the profits, because the strain of overwork isn't relieved by even a large reward. . . ."

"Your members work only four hours a day," I said. There was an overtone of outraged virtue in my voice. . . .

"On the average," Frazier replied casually . . . "A credit system also makes it possible to evaluate a job in terms of the willingness of the members to undertake it. . . . Bellamy suggested the principle in *Looking Backward*."

"An unpleasant job like cleaning sewers has a high value, I suppose," I said.

"Exactly. . . . Pleasanter jobs have lower values. . . ."

"What about the knowledge and skill required for many jobs?" said Castle. "Doesn't that interfere with free bidding? Certainly you can't allow just anyone to work as a doctor."

"No, of course not. The principle has to be modified where long training is needed. Still the preferences of the community as a whole determine the final value. . . ."

"I thought as much," said Castle. "Too many of your young members will want to go into interesting lines in spite of the work load. What do you do then?"

"Let them know how many places will be available and let them decide."

"Then you don't offer complete personal freedom, do you?" said Castle, with ill-concealed excitement. "You haven't really solved the conflict between a *laissez-faire* and a planned society."

"I think we have. Yes, but you must know more about our educational system. . . ."

"Our only government is a Board of Planners," said Frazier. "There are six Planners. They may serve ten years but no longer." . . .

"Then members don't vote for them?" said Castle.

"*No*" said Frazier emphatically. . . .

"Then the members have no voice whatsoever," said Castle. . . .

"Nor do they wish to have," said Frazier flatly.

"Communities are usually richer in manpower than in materials or cash, and this has often led to the fatal belief that there is manpower to spare. . . . Utopias usually spring from a rejection of modern life. Our point of view here isn't atavistic, however. We look ahead, not backward, for a better version."

"We want a government based upon a science of human behavior. Nothing short of that will produce permanent social structure. For the first time in history we're ready for it, because we can now deal with human behavior in accordance with simple scientific principles. The trouble with the program of anarchy is that it places too much faith in human nature. . . . I have none at all," said Frazier bluntly, "if you mean that men are naturally good or naturally prepared to get along with each other. We have no truck with philosophies of innate goodness. . . . But we do have faith in our power to change human behavior. We can *make* men adequate for group living—to the satisfaction of everybody."

"We call this ledge the 'Throne'," he said, as he put the glass to his eye. "Practically all of Walden Two can be seen from it." . . .

"It must be a great satisfaction," I said finally. "A world of your own making."

"Yes," he said. "I look upon my world and, behold, it is good." . . .

"You mean you think you're God?" I said, deciding to get it over with.

Frazier snorted in disgust.

"I said there was a curious similarity. . . . The parallel is quite fascinating. Our friend Castle is worried about the conflict between long-range dictatorship and freedom. Doesn't he know he's merely raising the old question of predestination and free will? All that happens is contained in an original plan, yet at every stage the individual seems to be making choices and determining the outcome. The same is true of Walden Two. Our members are practically always doing what they want to do—what they 'choose' to do—but we see to it that they will want to do precisely the things which are best for themselves and the community. Their behavior is determined, yet they're free."

Skinner's Utopia can be looked at as the ultimate scientific approach to social planning. However, not all of the figures in this chapter who advocate an application of science to human society are committed to Skinner's particular vision. Skinner's plan is also heavily influenced by his behaviorism. If external behavior is the only criteria for judging individual and social good, then Skinner's approach, which denies the ultimate reality of subjective experience, is appropriate. His dismissal of notions like free will is part of this denial. This section is just one example of a particularly strong view of behavioral, psychological, social, and physical science in their potential applications to human culture as a whole.

Summary

The intellectual legacy of modernity continues to allow humanity to control itself and its surroundings. Positive and negative effects of this subjugation are pronounced. Social, economic, political, and environmental conditions in the nineteenth and twentieth centuries are a result of scientific and technological achievement, and thus these conditions must be part of a treatment of science and philosophy.

We can understand the rise of economics and social science as an application of the methods of the scientific revolution to new domains. Economics examines individual and social goods with an objective method that seeks to resolve philosophical issues of value into deterministic theories. Social science takes the large-scale phenomena of society as a whole for its objective study. Sociology attempts to discern deterministic laws that apply to societies in order to bring discussions of social structure and organization into the scientific arena.

The political and environmental critiques of society we examined in this chapter seek to bring critical evaluation to bear on the results of scientific, economic, and social progress. Thus, the writings of Marx, Dewey, Thoreau, and Carson can be interpreted as seeking to reconnect philosophical evaluation with objective analysis. We see a tension emerging between those who seek an autonomous status for the objective study of science and society and those who want to introduce a new dialog between philosophy, science, and technology.

Notes

1. See Hadden, *On The Shoulders of Merchants* (Albany: State University of New York Press, 1994) for example. The classic case for this thesis is made in B. Hessen's *The Social Roots of Newton's Principia* (New York: Howard Fertig, 1971).

2. C.B. Macpherson says in his Introduction to *Leviathan*, "Hobbes thought his system of politics a science . . . and he had no modest opinion of his own position as the founder of this new scientific philosophy of politics. . . . [H]e had truly caught the spirit of the new science that was transforming men's understanding of the natural world. This was the spirit of Galileo. . . ." Thomas Hobbes, *Leviathan*, C.B. Macpherson, ed. (New York: Penguin Books, 1985), 10.

3. Adam Smith, *Inquiry into the Nature and Causes of the Wealth of Nations* (1776). (New York: Random House, 1937).

4. John Stuart Mill, *A System of Logic*, Eighth Edition (New York: Harper and Brothers, 1874).

5. Karl Marx, *Capital: A Critique of Political Economy* (New York: Vintage Books, 1977).

6. His predecessor William James coined the term, and Charles Peirce is also regarded as a pragmatist who preceded Dewey.

7. John Dewey, *Individualism Old and New* (New York: Capricorn Books, 1962). John Dewey, *The Public and Its Problems* (Chicago: Swallow Press, 1954).

8. Henry David Thoreau, *Walden* (Princeton, N.J.: Princeton University Press, 1971).

9. "A Fable for Tomorrow," from *Silent Spring* by Rachel Carson. Copyright © 1962 by Rachel L. Carson, renewed 1990 by Roger Christie. Reprinted by permission of Houghton Mifflin Co. All rights reserved.

10. Reprinted with the permission of The Free Press, a division of Simon & Schuster, from Emile Durkheim, *Suicide: A Study in Sociology*, transl. John A. Spaulding and George Simpson (New York: The Free Press, 1951). Copyright 1951. Copyright renewed 1979 by The Free Press.

11. B.F. Skinner, *Walden Two* (New York: Macmillan, 1948). Courtesy of B.F. Skinner Foundation.

Suggestions for Further Reading

Durkheim, Emile. *The Rules of Sociological Method* (New York: The Free Press, 1964).

Feigl, Herbert, and May Brodbeck, eds., "Philosophy of The Social Sciences," Chapter VII of *Readings in the Philosophy of Science* (New York: Appleton-Century-Crofts, 1953).

Hadden, Richard W. *On The Shoulders of Merchants: Exchange and the Mathematical Conception of Nature in Early Modern Europe* (Albany: The State University of New York Press, 1994).

Habermas, Jurgen. *Toward a Rational Society* (Boston: Beacon Press, 1970).

Hobbes, Thomas. *Leviathan,* Ed. C.B. Macpherson. (New York: Penguin Books, 1985).

Huxley, T.H. *Science and Culture* (London: Macmillan and Co., 1882).

Mill, John Stuart. *On Liberty* (Indianapolis, IN: Hackett Publishing Company, 1978).

Mill, John Stuart. *Principles of Political Economy,* 2 vols. (New York: D. Appleton and Company, 1870).

Mill, John Stuart. *Utilitarianism* (Indianapolis, IN: Hackett Publishing Company, 1979).

Russell, Bertrand. *The Impact of Science on Society* (New York: Simon & Schuster, 1953).

Skinner, B.F., "The Operational Analysis of Psychological Terms," reprinted in Herbert Feigl and May Brodbeck, eds., *Readings in the Philosophy of Science* (New York: Appleton-Century-Crofts, 1953).

Weiner, Philip P., ed., *Readings in Philosophy of Science*, Part C. "Method and Problems of the Social Sciences" (New York: Charles Scribner's Sons, 1953).

Some Twentieth-Century Developments in Physical Science

In Chapter 8 we traced the evolution of mechanism in physical science from its height in the early modern period to its augmentation by field theory and statistics in the nineteenth century. Even though Maxwell's equations make no reference to mechanistic hypotheses, Maxwell and others attributed the action of electromagnetic forces and the phenomena of light and heat to the direct activity of mechanical agents in the ether. And the statistical mechanical approach to thermodynamics can be seen to be an isolated study of specific applicability, thus complementing rather than undercutting Newton's deterministic laws of motion. In this chapter, we will see how classical theory and the mechanical world of Boyle, Newton, and Laplace are turned upside down.

One of the means for achieving twentieth-century revolutionary insight is via the very postulate intended to give a mechanistic interpretation to electromagnetic theory. Recall from Chapter 8 that Maxwell believed there was a material substance, the ether, permeating all of space as well as the interior of solid bodies. This substance was supposed to be the medium for the transmission of electromagnetic waves, yet continued investigation into the nature of the ether led Einstein to the conclusion that there was no such thing. In hypothesizing the nonexistence of the ether, the story of special relativity begins. General relativity is an extension of the relativistic notions of space and time to the gravitational arena. This development finally unifies the inertial and gravitational properties of matter in a coherent way, thus solving a mystery left by Newton, as we saw in Chapter 3.

Quantum mechanics extends the statistical approach to apply to all the basic properties of matter in more and more profound ways. With quantum theory, physicists finally abandoned determinism, i.e., certainty of prediction and retrodiction. Even the present is indeterminate, according to quantum mechanics, since basic measurements in microphysics were shown to have an inherent uncertainty. Scientists and philosophers sought meaningful interpretations of this profound result. We will also look at a development in mathematical physics that is seen to have broad philosophical and cultural implications, namely, Chaos theory. Although chaos theory does not supersede or replace quantum or classical theory, it treats randomness and indeterminacy from a different perspective than does the quantum physics of the very small.

Finally, we will look at a metaphysical theory developed during these revolutionary times. A.N. Whitehead's metaphysics of process is an ambitious synthesis of some ideas from relativity, quantum theory, and traditional philosophical theories of reality. Although Whitehead did not specifically embrace any particular scientific theory, and indeed felt compelled to move outside of the bounds of scientific postulates altogether, his metaphysical system shares certain qualities of interrelatedness and ephemeral atomicity found in relativity and quantum theory. Full treatment of Whitehead's difficult and speculative system is beyond the scope of this chapter (and this volume), but a brief excerpt from his work should at least provide a qualitative feel for how science and philosophy influenced each other at the beginning of the twentieth century.

The fact that scientific theories became superseded led some philosophers to question the status of scientific results, as we shall see in more detail in Chapter 11. This chapter focuses on the content of twentieth-century "revolutions" and their direct implications. Although daunting in scope, our treatment here of all these developments in one chapter will illuminate some common themes and interactions, as well as provide balance to the historical treatment in order not to bias this study in favor of more contemporary views.

Special Relativity

In this section we will briefly explore some aspects of the development of the special theory of relativity and its implications. Einstein's paper on the subject was published in 1905, and many figures contributed to the insights of Einstein's astounding synthesis. The acceptance of the theory was mixed and conditioned by nation, community, and the understanding of its implications. While on one level, the entire theory can be derived from the simple postulate that the speed of light is a constant for all frames of reference when such frames are moving uniformly (i.e., not accelerating), its implications are broad.

One of the results leading to the theory was the discovery by Americans Albert Michelson and Edward Morley, published in 1887, that the speed of the earth in the ether (Maxwell's "aether") could not be measured.

Although all observable objects in the cosmos are in motion, physicists from Newton's time until the beginning of the twentieth century held that the ether was a fixed medium for the transmission of light and other electromagnetic phenomena.[1] This fixed medium not only gave a mechanistic picture for electromagnetic field theory and light-wave propagation but also a concrete basis for the idea of absolute space and time. Michelson and Morley showed that the propagation of light waves was identical for light travelling parallel to the earth's motion and perpendicular to its motion. Thus, the motion of the earth made no difference in the transmission of light.

While many physicists viewed this result as a sign that they needed new and more complex theories of light propagation in a material substance, Einstein chose to ignore the concept of ether and its attendant ideas of fixed reference frames. Einstein was thus free to reject the idea that traditional geometric theory was manifest in a concrete aspect of the physical universe. The notions of independent three dimensional space, Euclidean geometry,[2] and absolute spatial and temporal coordinates were abandoned. Special relativity is limited to considerations of uniform, i.e., non-accelerated, motion. General relativity radically extends the scope of this initial reformulation of physical space and time to accelerated motion, including motion accelerated by gravitational fields. We will treat this in a separate section.

Albert Einstein was born in 1879 in Germany and made his home in the United States from 1933 until his death in 1955. His life and personality are the colorful and dramatic source of inspiration for both students and the public at large. Besides his contributions to relativity, he is connected with the development of quantum theory, unification theory, statistical physics, and the development of the atomic bomb. He was awarded the Nobel Prize in 1921 for his work on the photoelectric effect. The following is excerpted from Einstein's extemporaneous speech at Kyoto University in 1922 entitled "How I Created the Theory of Relativity," which he delivered on learning of his Nobel award.[3] It is followed by a popularization of relativity authored by a collaboration between Einstein and Leopold Infeld. Our treatment of special relativity concludes with a selection from Einstein's Russian-born teacher Hermann Minkowski, who lived from 1864 until 1909.

HOW I CREATED THE THEORY OF RELATIVITY

It was more than seventeen years ago that I had an idea of developing the theory of relativity for the first time. While I cannot say exactly where the thought came from, I am certain that it was contained in the problem of the optical properties of moving bodies. Light propagates through the sea of ether, in which the Earth is moving. In other words, the ether is moving with respect to the Earth. I tried to find clear experimental evidence for the flow of the ether in the literature of physics, but in vain.

Then I myself wanted to verify the flow of the ether with respect to the Earth, in other words, the motion of the Earth. When I first thought about this problem, I did not doubt the existence of the ether or the motion of the Earth through it. . . . While I was thinking of this problem in my student years, I came to know the strange result of Michelson's experiment. Soon I came to the conclusion that our idea about the motion of the earth with respect to the ether is incorrect, if we admit Michelson's null result as fact. . . . Since then I have come to believe that the motion of the Earth cannot be detected by any optical experiment, though the Earth is moving around the Sun.

I had a chance to read Lorentz's[4] monograph of 1895. At that time I firmly believed that the electrodynamic equations of Maxwell and Lorentz were correct. Furthermore, the assumption that these equations should hold in the reference frame of the moving body leads to the concept of invariance of the velocity of light, which, however, contradicts the addition rule of velocities used in mechanics.[5]

Why do these two concepts contradict each other? . . . An analysis of the concept of time was my solution. Time cannot be absolutely defined, and there is an inseparable relation between time and signal velocity. With this new concept, I could resolve all the difficulties completely for the first time.

Within five weeks the special theory of relativity was completed. I did not doubt that the new theory was reasonable from a philosophical point of view. I also found the new theory was in agreement with Mach's argument.[6] . . .

The following is excerpted from Einstein and Infeld, *The Evolution of Physics.*[7]

The Galilean relativity principle is valid for mechanical phenomena. The same laws of mechanics apply to all inertial systems moving relative to each other. Is this principle also valid for nonmechanical phenomena, especially those for which the field concepts proved so useful? All problems concentrated around this question immediately bring us to the starting point of the relativity theory.

We remember that the velocity of light *in vacuo*, or in other words, in ether, is 186,000 miles per second and that light is an electromagnetic wave spreading through the ether. The electromagnetic field carries energy which, once emitted from its source, leads an independent existence. For the time being, we shall continue to believe that the ether is a medium through which electromagnetic waves, and thus also light waves, are propagated, even though we are fully aware of the difficulties connected with its mechanical structure.

We are sitting in a closed room so isolated from the external world that no air can enter or escape. If we sit still and talk we are, from the physical point of view, creating sound waves, which spread from their resting source with the velocity of sound in air. . . . Experiment has shown that the velocity of sound in air is the same in all directions, if there is no wind and the air is at rest in the chosen Coordinate System (CS).

Let us now imagine that our room moves uniformly through space. A man outside sees, through the glass walls of the moving room (or train if you prefer) everything which is going on inside. . . . The observer in the room claims: the velocity of sound is, for me, the same in all directions.

The outside observer claims: the velocity of sound, spreading in the moving room and determined in my CS, is not the same in all directions. It is greater than the standard velocity of sound in the direction of the motion of the room and smaller in the opposite direction.

These conclusions are drawn from the classical transformations and can be confirmed by experiment. . . .

We can draw some further conclusions from the theory of sound as a wave propagated through a material medium. One way, though by no means the simplest, of not hearing what someone is saying, is to run, with a velocity greater than that of sound, relative to the air surrounding the speaker. The sound waves produced will then never be able to reach our ears. On the other hand, if we missed an important word which will never be repeated, we must run with a speed greater than that of sound to reach the produced wave to catch the word. . . . A bullet fired from a gun actually moves with a speed greater than that of sound and a man placed on such a bullet would never hear the sound of the shot.

All these examples are of a purely mechanical character and we can now formulate the important questions: could we repeat what has just been said of a sound wave, in the case of a light wave? Do the Galilean relativity principle and the classical transformation apply to mechanical as well as optical and electrical phenomena? . . .

In the case of the sound wave in the room moving uniformly, relative to the outside observer, the following intermediate steps are very essential for our conclusion:

The moving room carries the air in which the sound wave is propagated. The velocities observed in two CS moving uniformly, relative to each other, are connected by the classical transformation.

The corresponding problem for light must be formulated a little differently. The observers in the room are no longer talking, but are sending light signals. . . . The light waves move through the ether just as the sound waves move through the air.

Is the ether carried with the room . . .? If the room is closed, the air inside is forced to move with it. There is obviously no sense in thinking of ether in this way, since all matter is immersed in it and it penetrates everywhere. No doors are closed to ether. . . . It is, however, not beyond us to imagine that the room . . . carries the ether along with it. . . . But we can equally well imagine the opposite: that the room . . . travels through the ether . . . not carrying any part of the medium along but moving through it. In the first picture . . . an analogy with a sound wave is possible and quite similar conclusions can be drawn. In the second . . . [n]o analogy with the sound wave is possible and the conclusions drawn in the case of the sound wave do not hold for a light wave. We could imagine [a] still more complicated possibilit[y]. . . . But there is no reason to discuss the more complicated assumptions before finding out which of the two simpler limiting cases experiment favors.

We shall begin with our first picture and assume, for the present: the ether is carried along by the room. . . . If I turn on the light and its source is rigidly connected with my room, the velocity of the light signal has the well-known experimental value 186,000 miles per second. But the outside observer will notice the motion of the room, and, therefore, that of the source and, since the ether is carried along, his conclusions must be: the velocity of light in my outside CS is different in different directions . . . if the ether is carried along with the room . . . then the velocity of the light must depend on the light source. Light reaching our eyes from a moving light source would have a greater velocity if the motion is toward us and smaller if it away from us.

If our speed were greater than that of light we should be able to run away from the light signal. We could see occurrences from the past by reaching previously sent waves. . . . These conclusions all follow from the assumption that the moving CS carries along the ether and the mechanical transformation laws are valid. . . .

But there is no indication as to the truth of these conclusions. On the contrary, they are contradicted by all observations made with the intention of proving them. There is not the slightest doubt as to the clarity of this verdict. . . . *The velocity of light is always the same in all CS independent of whether or not the emitting source moves, or how it moves.* . . .

We must, therefore, give up the analogy between sound and light waves and turn to the second possibility: that all matter moves through the ether, which takes no part whatever in the motion. This means that we assume the existence of a sea of ether with all CS resting in it, or moving relative to it. . . .

Nature . . . places at our disposal a system moving with fairly high velocity: the earth, in its yearly motion around the sun. If our assumption is correct, then the velocity of light in the direction of the motion of the earth should differ from the velocity of light in an opposite direction. . . . This was done in the famous Michelson-Morley experiment. The result was a verdict of "death" to the theory of a calm ether-sea. . . . No dependence of the speed of light upon direction could be found. . . .

The situation grows more and more serious. Two assumptions have been tried. The first, that moving bodies carry ether along. The fact that the velocity of light does not depend on the motion of the source contradicts this assumption. The second, that there exists one distinguished CS and that moving bodies do not carry the ether but travel through an ever calm ether-sea. If this is so, the Galilean relativity principle is not valid and the speed of light cannot be the same in every CS. Again we are in contradiction with experiment.

. . . Every attempt to explain the electromagnetic phenomena in moving CS with the help of the motion of the ether, motion through the ether, or both these motions, proved unsuccessful.

Thus arose one of the most dramatic situations in the history of science. All assumptions concerning ether led nowhere! . . . Looking back over the development of physics we see that the ether, soon after its birth, became the "*enfant terrible*" of the family of physical substances. First, the construction of a simple mechanical picture of the ether proved to be impossible and was discarded. This caused, to a great extent, the breakdown of the mechanical point of view. Second, we had to give up hope that through the presence of the ether-sea one CS would be distinguished and lead to the recognition of absolute, and not only relative, motion. This would have been the only way, besides carrying the waves, in which ether could mark and justify its existence. All our attempts to make ether real failed. . . . After such bad experiences, this is the moment to forget the ether completely and to try to never mention its name. We shall say: our space has the physical property of transmitting waves, and so omit the use of a word we have decided to avoid.

Let us now write down the facts . . . :

1. The velocity of light in empty space always has its standard value independent of the motion of the source or receiver of light.
2. In two CS moving uniformly, relative to each other, all laws of nature are exactly identical and there is no way of distinguishing absolute uniform motion.

. . . In mechanics, we have seen: If the velocity of a material point is so and so, relative to one CS, then it will be different in another CS moving uniformly, relative to the first. . . . But this transformation law is in contradiction to the constant character of the velocity of light. . . .

The relativity theory begins with these two assumptions. From now on we shall not use the classical transformation because we know that it contradicts our assumptions. . . . It is our intention to draw conclusions from (1) and (2) . . . and find the physical meaning of the results obtained.

Once more, the example of the moving room with outside and inside observers will be used. . . . [A] light signal is emitted from the center of the room and . . . we ask the two men what they expect to observe, assuming only our two principles . . . We quote their answers:

The inside observer: The light signal traveling from the center of the room will reach the walls *simultaneously*, since all the walls are equally distant from the light source and the velocity of light is the same in all directions.

The outside observer: In my system, the velocity of light is exactly the same as in that of the observer moving with the room. It does not matter to me whether or not the light source moves in my CS since its motion does not influence the velocity of light. What I see is a light signal traveling with a standard speed, the same in all directions. One of the walls is trying to escape from and the opposite wall to approach the light signal. Therefore, the escaping wall will be met by the signal a little later than the approaching one....

... Two events, i.e., the two light beams reaching the two walls, are simultaneous for the observer on the inside, but not for the observer on the outside. In classical physics, we had one clock, one time flow, for all observers in all CS ... the relativity theory ... force[s] us to give up this view.... Our task is to understand this consequence.... Let us first answer a simple question.

What is a clock?

The primitive subjective feeling of time flow enables us to order our impressions, to judge that one event takes place earlier, another later. But to show that the time interval between two events is ten seconds, a clock is needed. By the use of a clock the time concept becomes objective....

In classical mechanics it was tacitly assumed that a moving clock does not change its rhythm.... We can well imagine that a moving clock changes its rhythm, so long as the law of this change is the same for all inertial CS....

We can well imagine that not only does a moving clock change its rhythm, but that a moving stick changes its length ... if the velocity of light is the same in all CS, then moving rods must change their length, moving clocks must change their rhythm, and the laws governing these changes are rigorously determined....

The following is from Hermann Minkowski's "Space and Time."[8]

The views of space and time which I wish to lay before you have sprung from the soil of experimental physics, and therein lies their strength. They are radical. Henceforth space by itself, and time by itself, are doomed to fade away into mere shadows, and only a kind of union of the two will preserve an independent reality....

The equations of Newton's mechanics exhibit a two-fold invariance. Their form remains unaltered, firstly, if we subject the underlying system of spatial coordinates to any arbitrary *change of position*; secondly, if we change its state of motion, namely, by imparting to it any *uniform translatory motion*; furthermore, the zero point of time is given no part to play . . . the two invariances are probably rarely mentioned in the same breath. . . . The two groups, side by side, lead their lives entirely apart. Their utterly heterogeneous character may have discouraged any attempt to compound them. But it is precisely when they are compounded that the complete group, as a whole, gives us to think.

We will try to visualize the state of things by the graphic method. Let x, y, z, be rectangular co-ordinates for space, and let t denote time. The objects of our perception invariably include places and times in combination. Nobody has ever noticed a place except at a time, or a time except at a place. . . .

Special relativity posits that space and time are relative to each other. The flow of time is different when relative velocity is involved, and so the temporal character of a situation is dependent upon relative rates of spatial translation. We can summarize these results as follows: (1) The velocity of light is a constant in all inertial (uniformly moving) frames of reference; (2) Hence simultaneity is obsolete; (3) objective time is communicated by light waves; (4) spatial measurements are likewise perceived and transmitted by electromagnetic radiation. These results lead to the conclusion that time and space are variable with respect to the speed of a coordinate system relative to observers.

Moreover, since there is no absolute frame of reference for measuring velocity, then we are forced to admit that space and time are ultimately relative. All of these results follow from ignoring the concept of ether, a concept that was used to give a concrete meaning for absolute space as well as a mechanistic interpretation for the propagation of light waves. Once such an absolute notion is abandoned, the point of view of the observer becomes radically important, and the notions of space and time themselves are looked upon as determinate relations only from a particular observational frame of reference. No longer tenable are Newton's ideas of space without objects, time without events, or either of them without observation; hence Minkowski speaks of "notice" of place and "notice" of time.

Finally, since electromagnetic phenomena are attributed to the space-time continuum itself, the physical geometry of this structure is significant. This geometry does not obey the Galilean transformations—since such conformance would yield variable velocities for light waves in different inertial frames—and therefore space-time is not Euclidean.[9] Special relativity is an astounding theory, built on simple ideas, which captures and transforms popular imagination.

Quantum Theory

Although it is clear that relativistic ideas permeated the beginning of the twentieth century and that Einstein's predecessors and collaborators were crucial for his theory of special relativity, it was Einstein alone who crystallized the theory itself and received the credit for establishing relativity in its accepted form. The development of quantum theory had no such individual champion, but sprang from the conjoint efforts of many in the international physics community at the beginning of the twentieth century.

Werner Heisenberg is one candidate for founder of the theory, but contributions by Einstein, Erwin Schrödinger, Louis De Broglie, Max Planck, Niels Bohr, and Paul Dirac are no less significant. In fact, it was Einstein's work with the photoelectric effect that generated the light quantum, the photon, and produced the famous formulation of the law $E = mc^2$, although in a different context than it was applied in relativity theory. Einstein is perhaps better known for his opposition to quantum theory.[10]

In this section we will treat the explicit stipulations of quantum theory and some of the physical interpretations put forward by its proponents. Quantum theory states that light and other fundamental elements of the universe behave both like waves and like particles, and that there is an inescapable uncertainty concerning the positions and momenta of the most basic constituents of matter and energy. Interpretations of this theory posit that the physical universe is itself dependent on observers for any determinate configuration whatsoever; or that there are many alternative universes representing all possible outcomes of quantum theory uncertainties; or at the very least that the determinism of Laplace and Newton, as well as the mechanism of modern classical physics, are not correct.

The Theory

Werner Heisenberg was born in Würzburg, Germany, in 1901. He announced the famous uncertainty principle in 1927 and continued to develop and popularize physical theory until his death in 1976. The following are selections from Heisenberg's 1932 Nobel Prize in Physics Award Address:[11]

In 1900, through studying the law of black-body radiation, Planck had detected in optical phenomena a discontinuous phenomena totally unknown in classical physics which, a few years later, was most precisely expressed in Einstein's hypothesis of light quanta. The impossibility of harmonizing Maxwellian theory with the pronouncedly visual concepts expressed in the hypothesis of light quanta subsequently compelled research workers to the conclusion that radiation phenomena can only be understood by largely renouncing their immediate visualization.... [T]he element of discontinuity detected in radiation phenomena also plays an important part in material processes.... This circumstance was a fresh argument in support of the assumption that natural phenomena in which Planck's constant plays an important part[12] can be understood only by largely forgoing a visual description of them. Classical Physics seemed to be the limiting case of visualization of a fundamentally unvisualizable microphysics....

According to the basic postulates of quantum theory, an atomic system is capable of assuming discrete, stationary states, and therefore discrete energy values; in terms of the energy of the atom the emission and absorption of light by such a system occurs abruptly, in the form of impulses. On the other hand, the visualizable properties of the emitted radiation are described by a wave field....

[S]tudies have established that the comparison of an atom with a planetary system composed of nucleus and electrons is not the only visual picture of how we can imagine an atom. On the contrary, it is apparently no less correct to compare an atom with a charge cloud....

In classical physics, the aim of research was to investigate objective processes occurring in space and time, and to discover the laws governing their progress from the initial conditions. In classical physics a problem was considered solved when a particular phenomena had been proved to occur objectively in space and time, and it had been shown to obey the general rules of classical physics....

The manner in which the knowledge of each process had been acquired, what observations may possibly have led to its experimental determination, was completely immaterial.... In the quantum theory, however, the situation is completely different. The very fact that the formalism of quantum mechanics cannot be interpreted as visual description of a phenomenon occurring in space and time shows that quantum mechanics is in no way concerned with the objective determination of space-time phenomena. On the contrary, the formalism of quantum mechanics should be used in such a way that the probability for the outcome of a further experiment may be concluded.... [T]he only definite known result to be ascertained after the fullest possible experimental investigation of the system is the probability for a certain outcome of a second experiment.... Whereas in the classical theory the kind of observation has no bearing on the event, in the quantum theory the disturbance associated with each observation has a decisive role.... Closer examination of the formalism shows that between the accuracy with which the location of a particle can be ascertained and the accuracy which its momentum can simultaneously be known, there is a relation according to which the product of the probable errors in the measurement of the location and momentum is invariably at least as large as Planck's constant divided by 4pi.... The experimental determination of whatever space-time events invariably necessitates a fixed frame—say the system of coordinates in which the observer is at rest—to which all measurements are referred. The assumption that this frame is "fixed" implies neglecting its momentum.... The fundamental necessary uncertainty at this point is then transmitted via the measuring apparatus into the atomic event....

The laws of quantum mechanics are basically statistical.... The uncertainty relations alone afford an instance of how in quantum mechanics exact knowledge of one variable can exclude the exact knowledge of another. This complementary relationship between different aspects of one and the same physical process is indeed characteristic of the whole structure of quantum mechanics.... [T]he determination of energetic relations excludes the detailed description of the space-time processes. Similarly, the study of the chemical properties of a molecule is complementary to the study of the motions of the individual electrons.... Finally, the areas of validity of classical and quantum mechanics can be marked off one from the other as follows: Classical physics represents that striving to learn about Nature in which essentially we seek to draw conclusions about objective processes from observation and so ignore the consideration of the influences which every observation has on the object to be observed; classical physics, therefore, has its limits at the point from which the influence of the observation can no longer be ignored. Conversely, quantum mechanics makes possible the treatment of atomic processes by partially forgoing their space-time description and objectification.

Heisenberg refers to a "complementary" relationship between different aspects of a physical process. Specifically, this principle of complementarity states that there is an inverse, or complementary, relationship between the precision with which we can measure the position, on the one hand, and the momentum, on the other hand, of any given body. When one is determined with absolute precision, the other is entirely uncertain. This once and for all shatters Laplace's hope that "given ... an intelligence which could comprehend all the forces by which nature is animated and the respective situation of the beings who compose it. . . ." the future and the past would be the objects of perfect knowledge, including "movements . . . of the lightest atom".[13] Physics was seen to contain an inherent uncertainty that defies absolute determination.

Heisenberg can hardly avoid presenting the theory without delving into some physical interpretation. However, Heisenberg's suggestion that observation and experiment interact to produce uncertainty is tame compared to other interpretations of quantum mechanics. In the next section we consider varying understandings of the quantum revolution in physics.

The Interpretations

The significance of the physical theories of quantum physics is still under debate. One of the ways in which physicists and philosophers join this debate is already familiar to us: they dispute whether or not scientific theory is significantly descriptive of fundamental reality. If physical theory is taken to be a description of real elements of the universe, then the significance of quantum theory is quite profound.

If we take for granted a certain amount of scientific realism for a moment (although we may still suspend judgment about the soundness of scientism as discussed in Chapter 8), then the following interpreters of quantum theory would present the implications of the new physics for our understanding of the universe. They range from a reinterpretation of causality, to a reformulation of the notion of objectivity, to a rich tapestry of multiversal existence.

The following is from Max Planck's "The Concept of Causality in Physics."[14]

In the fight currently raging about the meaning and validity of the Law of Causality in modern physics, every attempt to clarify the conflicting opinions must begin with the statement that in this connection everything depends on a clear understanding of the sense in which the word "causality" is used in the science of physics. To be sure, it is agreed *a priori* that whenever a reference is made to a "causal relationship" between two successive events or occurrences, this term is understood to designate a certain regular connection between them, calling the earlier one the *cause*, and the latter one the *effect*. But the question is: What constitutes this specific type of connection?

Is there any infallible sign in nature to indicate that a happening in nature is causally determined by another?

It follows from the numerous inquiries heretofore undertaken into this question that the best and safest way to approach a clear answer is to relate the question to the possibility of making accurate predictions. In fact, there can be no more incontestable way to prove the causal relationship between any two events than to demonstrate that from the occurrence of one it is always possible to infer in advance the occurrence of the other. . . .

Therefore, I want to base all our subsequent considerations on the following simple proposition, equally applicable outside the realm of physics: "*An occurrence is causally determined if it can be predicted with certainty.*" Of course, this sentence is meant to express only that the possibility of making an accurate prediction for the future constitutes an infallible criterion of the presence of the causal relationship, but not that it is synonymous with the latter. I need to mention merely the well known example that we can predict with a certainty while it is still day the coming of the night, yet this does not make day the cause of night.

But conversely, it also often happens that we assume the presence of a causal relationship even in cases where there is no question at all of the possibility of making accurate predictions. Just think of weather forecasts . . . yet there is hardly any trained meteorologist who does not consider the weather to be causally determined. All these considerations indicate that in order to find the right clues to the concept of causality we must go still a little deeper.

In the case of weather forecasts, the thought suggests itself that their unreliability is due merely to the size and complicated nature of the . . . atmosphere. If we single out . . . a cubic foot of air . . . we will be far more likely to make accurate predictions. . . . However, if we observe things still a little more closely, we shall soon reach a very remarkable conclusion. Simple as we make the conditions, and precise as our measuring instruments may be, we shall never succeed in calculating in advance the results of the measurements with an absolute accuracy. . . .

Thus, all the above cited experiences force us to recognize the following principle as a firmly established fact: *It is never possible to predict a physical occurrence with unlimited precision.* . . . [W]e find ourselves facing an unavoidable dilemma: We may elect *either* to adhere literally to the exact wording of our basic proposition in which case there cannot exist even one single instance in nature where a causal relationship would have to be assumed to prevail—*or* to subject that basic proposition to a certain modification, so designed to provide room for the presupposition of strict causality.

A number of contemporary physicists and philosophers have chosen the first alternative. I shall refer to them here as *indeterminists*. They claim that genuine causality . . . actually does not exist. . . . [T]he indeterminist discovers a statistical root in every law of physics, including the law of gravity and of electrical attraction: he regards them one and all as . . . possessing only an approximate validity for individual instances. . . .

Actually, physical science has developed up to now on the very opposite foundation. It chose the *second* one of the two alternatives mentioned above: In order to be able to maintain the full and absolute validity of the law of causality, it modified slightly the basic proposition. . . . Thus, theoretical physics considers as an occurrence not an actual individual process of measurement . . . but a certain, merely theoretical process; and in this manner it replaces the sense world, as given to us directly by our sense organs (or alternatively, by measuring instruments which serve us as sharpened sense organs), by another world, the world picture of physics, which is conceptual in structure, arbitrary to a certain degree, created for the purpose of getting away from the uncertainty involved in every individual measurement and for making possible a precise interrelation of concepts.

Consequently, every measurable physical magnitude, every length, every time interval, every mass . . . has a double meaning, according as we regard it as directly given by some measurement, or conceive of it as translated into the world picture of physics. [I]n the world picture of physics it stands for a certain mathematical symbol, which lends itself to manipulation according to quite definite, precise rules. . . .

It is absolutely untrue, although it is often asserted, that the world picture of physics contains . . . directly observable magnitudes only. On the contrary, directly observable magnitudes are not found at all in the world picture. It contains symbols only. In fact, the world picture even contains constituents which have only a very indirect significance . . . or no significance at all, such as ether waves, partial vibrations, frames of reference, etc. Primarily, such constituents play the part of dead weight or ballast, but they are incorporated because of the decisive advantage assured by the introduction of the world picture—that it permits us to carry through a strict determinism.

Of course, the world picture always remains a mere auxiliary concept. It is self evident that in the last analysis, the things that really matter, are the occurrences in the sense world and the greatest possible accuracy in predicting them. In classical physics this is achieved as follows: First, an object found in the sense world ... is symbolically represented in some measured condition.... Similarly, suitable symbols are substituted in the framework of the world picture for external influences which operate subsequently on the object.... The behavior of the structure is then unambiguously determined for all times for these data....

While in the sense world the prediction of an occurrence is always associated with a certain element of uncertainty, in the world picture of physics all occurrences follow one another in accordance with precisely definable laws—they are strictly determined causally....

Classical physics was but little concerned with ... uncertainty.... [Determinists] who ... look for a rule behind every irregularity, were led to the problem of basing a theory of the gas laws on the premise that the collision of two individual molecules is determined in a strict causal manner. The solution of this problem was the life work of Ludwig Boltzmann, and it represents one of the most beautiful triumphs of theoretic research....

Such outstanding achievements seemed to justify the hope that the world picture of classical physics would in principle accomplish its task.... But the introduction of the elementary quantum of action destroyed this hope at one blow and for good.

The so-called Uncertainty Principle ... asserts that ... when one magnitude is ascertained with absolute accuracy, the other one remains absolutely indefinite.

It is evident that this principle fundamentally precludes the possibility of translating into the sense world with an arbitrary degree of accuracy, the simultaneous values of the coordinates and momenta of material points ... this circumstance constitutes a difficulty with respect to ... the principle of causality.... However, upon closer scrutiny, this conclusion—founded on a confusion of the world picture with the sense world—proves a rash one, to say the very least. For there is another, more logical way out of this difficulty ... namely, the assumption that the attempt to determine simultaneously both the coordinates and momentum of a material point is physically completely meaningless....

The new world picture of quantum mechanics is a product of the need to find a way of reconciling the quantum of action with the principle of strict determinism. For this purpose ... the material point ... had to be deprived of its basic, elementary character; it was resolved into a system of material waves. These material waves constitute the primary elements of the new world picture. ...

In general, the laws of material waves are basically different from those of the classical mechanics of material points. However, the point of central importance is the function characterizing the material waves ... is fully determined. ...

We thus see that the principle of determinism is as strictly valid in the world picture of quantum mechanics as in that of classical physics. ...

Properly speaking, ... our considerations ... have demonstrated that an adherence to a strictly causal outlook—always taking the word causal in the modified sense explained previously—is by no means excluded from the viewpoint of even modern physics, though its necessity can never be proved either *a priori* or *a posteriori*. Nevertheless ... it could be maintained that a relation possessing such profound significance as the causal connection between two successive events represents ought to be independent by its very nature from the human intellect which is considering it. Instead, we have not only linked at the outset the concept of causality to ... the ability of man to predict an occurrence; but we have been able to carry through the deterministic viewpoint only with the expedient of replacing the directly given sense world by the world picture of physics, that is, by a provisional and alterable creation of the human power of the imagination. ...

[E]very prediction presupposes someone who does the predicting. Therefore, in the following discussion we shall direct our attention ... to the predicting subject. ... [T]he actual impossibility of predicting even a single occurrence accurately in classical as well as in quantum physics appears to be a natural consequence of the circumstance that man with his sense organs and measuring instruments is himself a part of nature. ...

[D]evotion to science was, consciously or unconsciously, a matter of faith—a matter of serene faith in a rational world order. ... But the plain fact that we are able, at least to a certain degree, to subject future natural occurrences to our thought processes and to bend them to our will, would be a totally incomprehensible mystery, did it not permit us to surmise at least a certain harmony between the external world and the human intellect. ...

In conclusion we may therefore say: The law of causality is neither true nor false. It is rather a heuristic principle, a signpost. ...

Planck replaces the determinism of trajectories and solid bodies with a determinism of wave equations. These equations give no more than the probabilities of finding particular quanta at given locations, and so Planck asks the physicist to be content with a puzzling sort of determinism: a determinism of probability. Furthermore, this determinism is limited to the world-picture of physics, a realm of human imagination. This can be seen to be similar to Hume's claim in Chapter 4: cause and effect exist only insofar as human beings need to make inferences. We explore some methodological implications of the idea that the world of physics is entirely a construction of the human mind in the next chapter.

The following are selections from Heisenberg's *Physics and Philosophy*, Chapter 3, outlining the Copenhagen interpretation of quantum theory.[15] Roughly, this interpretation takes its cue from the indeterminacy of quantum events until their observation, and gives the observer a crucial role in quantum mechanics.

***

The Copenhagen interpretation of quantum theory starts from a paradox. Any experiment in physics, whether it refers to the phenomena of daily life or atomic events, is to be described in the terms of classical physics. . . . Still the application of these concepts is limited by the relations of uncertainty. . . .

For a better understanding of this paradox it is useful to compare the procedures for the theoretical interpretation of an experiment in classical physics and in quantum theory. In Newton's mechanics, for instance, . . . [t]he result of observation is translated into mathematics. Then the equations of motion are used to derive from these values . . . the values . . . of any other properties of the system at a later time, and in this way the astronomer can predict . . . , for instance, . . . the exact time for an eclipse of the moon.

In quantum theory the procedure is slightly different. We could, for instance, be interested in the motion of an electron . . . and determine, by some kind of observation, the initial position and velocity of the electron. But this determination will not be accurate. . . . A probability function is written down which represents the experimental situation. . . .

When the probability function in quantum theory has been determined at the initial time from the observation, one can from the laws of quantum theory calculate the probability function at any later time. . . . It should be emphasized, however, that the probability function does not in itself represent a course of events in the course of time. It represents a tendency for events and our knowledge of events. The probability function can be connected with reality only if one essential condition is fulfilled: if a new measurement is made to determine a certain property of the system. . . . The result of the measurement again will be stated in terms of classical physics.

Therefore, the theoretical interpretation of an experiment requires three distinct steps: (1) the translation of the initial experimental situation into a probability function: (2) the following up of this function in the course of time; (3) the statement of new measurement to be made of the system. . . . It is only in the third step that we change over again from the "possible" to the "actual." . . .

For many experiments it is more convenient to speak of matter waves; for instance, of stationary matter waves around the atomic nucleus. . . . Therefore, Bohr advocated the use of both pictures, which he called "complementary" to each other. The two pictures are of course mutually exclusive, because a certain thing cannot at the same time be a particle (i.e., a substance confined to a very small volume) and a wave (i.e., a field spread out over a large space). . . . The observation . . . enforces the description in space and time. . . .

A real difficulty . . . arises, however, when one asks the famous question: But what happens "really" in an atomic event? . . . [It] looks as if we meant to say: what happens depends on our way of observing it or on the fact that we observe it. . . .

Now, this is a very strange result, since it seems to indicate that the observation plays a decisive role in the event and that the reality varies, depending on whether we observe it or not. To make this point clearer we have to analyze the process of observation more closely.

To begin with, it is important to remember that in natural science we are not interested in the universe as a whole, including ourselves, but we direct our attention to some part of the universe and make that the object of our studies. . . .

When we . . . come to the next observation . . . it is very important to realize that our object has to be in contact with the other part of the world, namely the experimental arrangement. . . . This means that the equation of motion for the probability function does now contain the influence of the interaction with the measuring device. This influence introduces a new element of uncertainty . . . , and since the device is connected with the rest of the world, it contains in fact the uncertainties of the microscopic structure of the whole world. . . .

The observation itself changes the probability function discontinuously; it selects of all possible events the actual one that has taken place. Since through the observation our knowledge of the system has changed discontinuously, its mathematical representation also has undergone the discontinuous change and we speak of a "quantum jump." . . .

Therefore, the transition from the "possible" to the "actual" takes place during the act of observation. . . .

To what extent, then, have we finally come to an objective description of the world, especially of the atomic world? In classical physics science started from the belief—or should we say from the illusion?—that we could describe the world or at least parts of the world without any reference to ourselves. . . .

The development of quantum theory gives physicists pause for speculation. Some interpret the theory as giving a dual nature to all physical objects: that of waves and of particles. Some interpret the theory to state that there is a fundamental indeterminacy in nature, and that antiquated views of causation must be refined. Others claim that the human observer and all of the world must be included in any description of the smallest phenomena.

An alternative interpretation, put forward by Hugh Everett, John Wheeler, and Bryce DeWitt, states that the indeterminacy and uncertainty stipulated by quantum theory is resolved in determined, certain behavior of a "multiverse." That is, for every possible outcome of a measurement or prediction, an actual universe exists to give it reality. In other words, the universe is continually branching off into alternative realities whenever quantum uncertainties and possibilities arise. This interpretation is more speculative than most, and it is correspondingly regarded more suspiciously than others. In any case, quantum theory is yet again an example of how scientific theory engenders a reformulation of ideas of humanity and its place in the universe.

General Relativity

In order to begin to understand the theory of general relativity, it will be helpful to compare it with special relativity. Special relativity is a theory of the dynamics of systems moving uniformly. It is limited to non-accelerating and non-gravitational frames of reference. General relativity seeks to treat the dynamics of systems, taking into account that they may be accelerating or in a gravitational field. Although it has been written that special relativity could only be understood by a handful of people,[16] in fact its simplicity and elegance, as well as its implications, are fairly easily grasped—especially when compared to the complexities of quantum theory. General relativity also bears more resemblance to a theory that is not fully comprehensible to any but the highly initiated, and it is as difficult as it is profound.

We saw how special relativity posits that space, time, and their derivative concepts of simultaneity, distance, and duration are relative notions. In this section we will briefly explore how general relativity posits that space and matter are also relative to each other and our interpretations of them. The unification of the inertial and gravitational properties of matter, so elusive to modern[17] physics, is realized in Einstein's complex visualization of the field of space, time, matter, and energy. In this section we will touch on some issues of general relativity which may be elucidated without the sophisticated mathematical formulations (including a new form of calculus[18]) that are crucial for their full understanding.

The following are additional selections from Einstein's "How I Created the Theory of Relativity" address in Kyoto, Japan:

My first thought on the general theory of relativity was conceived . . . in 1907. The idea occurred suddenly. I was dissatisfied with the special theory of relativity, since the theory was restricted to frames of reference moving with constant velocity relative to each other and could not be applied to the general motion of a reference frame. I struggled to remove this restriction, and wanted to formulate the problem in the general case.

. . . I came to realize that all the natural laws except the law of gravity could be discussed within the framework of the special theory of relativity. I wanted to find out the reason for this, but I could not attain this goal easily.

The most unsatisfactory was the following: Although the relationship between inertia and energy was explicitly given by the special theory of relativity, the relationship between inertia and weight, or the energy of the gravitational field, was not clearly elucidated. I felt that this problem could not be resolved within the framework of the special theory of relativity.

The breakthrough came suddenly one day. I was sitting on a chair in my patent office in Bern. Suddenly a thought struck me: If a man falls freely, he would not feel his own weight. I was taken aback. This simple thought experiment made a deep impression on me. This led to the theory of gravity. I continued my thought. A falling man is accelerated. Then what he feels and judges is happening in the accelerated frame of reference. I decided to extend the theory of relativity to the reference frame with acceleration. I felt that in so doing I could solve the problem of gravity at the same time. A falling man does not feel his own weight because in his frame of reference there is a new gravitational field which cancels the gravitational field due to the earth. In the accelerated frame of reference, we need a new gravitational field. . . .

Ernst Mach was a person who insisted on the idea that systems that have acceleration with respect to each other are equivalent. This idea contradicts Euclidean geometry, since in the frame of reference with acceleration Euclidean geometry cannot be applied. Describing the physical laws without reference to geometry is similar to describing our thoughts without words. . . . I hit upon the idea that the surface theory of Karl Friedrich Gauss might be the key. . . . I did not know that Bernhard Riemann had discussed the foundation of geometry deeply. . . . I found that the foundations of geometry had deep physical meaning in this problem. . . .

I would like . . . to mention the problem of cosmology. This problem is related to the geometry of the universe and time. . . . I solved the problem . . . by imposing an invariance on the boundary condition for the gravitational equations. I finally eliminated the boundary by considering the Universe to be a closed system. As a result, inertia emerges as a property of interacting matter and it should vanish if there were no matter to interact with. I believe that with this result the general theory can satisfactorily be understood epistemologically. . . .

Einstein gives us the following useful insight in his "Nobel Prize in Physics Award address, 1921":[19]

Already Newton recognized that the law of inertia is unsatisfactory. . . . It makes the observable material bodies responsible for gravitational behavior . . . yet indicates no material cause. . . .

[General relativity] . . . eliminates the distinction between inertial and gravitational effects. It amounts to stipulating that, apart from the arbitrariness governed by the free choice of coordinates, the [universal gravitational] field shall be completely determined by the matter. . . .

The following are selections from Einstein's "Geometry and Experience" from *Sidelights on Relativity*.[20]

How can it be that mathematics, being after all a product of human thought which is independent of experience, is so admirably appropriate to the objects of reality? Is human reason, then, without experience, merely by taking thought, able to fathom the properties of real things.

In my opinion the answer to this question is briefly this:—As far as the laws of mathematics refer to reality, they are not certain; and as far as they are certain, they do not refer to reality. . . .

Let us for a moment consider from this point of view any axiom of geometry, for instance, the following:—Through two points in space there always passes one and only one straight line. How is this axiom to be interpreted in the older sense and in the more modern sense?

The older interpretation:—Every one knows what a straight line is, and what a point is. Whether this knowledge springs from an ability of the human mind or from experience, from some collaboration of the two or from some other source, is not for the mathematician to decide. He leaves the question to the philosopher. Being based upon this knowledge, which precedes all mathematics, the axiom stated above is, like all other axioms, self-evident. . . .

The more modern interpretation:—Geometry treats of entities which are denoted by the words straight line, point, etc. These entities do not take for granted any knowledge or intuition whatever, but they presuppose only the validity of the axioms, such as the one stated above, which are to be taken in a purely formal sense, i.e. as void of all content of intuition or experience. These axioms are free creations of the human mind.

Yet on the other hand it is certain that mathematics generally, and particularly geometry, owes its existence to the need which was felt of learning something about the relations of real things to one another. . . . It is clear that the system of concepts of axiomatic geometry alone cannot make any assertions as to the relations of real objects of this kind. . . . To accomplish this, we need . . . add the proposition:—Solid bodies are related, with respect to their possible dispositions, as are bodies in Euclidean geometry of three dimensions. . . .

Geometry thus completed is evidently a natural science; we may in fact regard it as the most ancient branch of physics. . . . We call this completed geometry "practical geometry." The question whether the practical geometry of the universe is Euclidean or not has a clear meaning, and its answer can only be furnished by experience. . . .

[I]f we admit non-inert systems we must abandon Euclidean geometry.

Can we picture to ourselves a three-dimensional universe which is finite, yet unbounded?

The usual answer to this question is "No," but that is not the right answer. The purpose of the following remarks is to show that the answer should be "Yes. . . ."

What do we wish to express when we say that our space is infinite? Nothing more than that we might lay any number of bodies of equal sizes side by side without ever filling space. . . .

Another example of the infinite continuum is the plane. On a plane surface we may lay squares of cardboard so that each side of any square has the side of another square adjacent to it. The construction is never diminished; we can always go on laying squares. . . . Accordingly we say that the plane is an infinite continuum of two dimensions, and space is an infinite continuum of three dimensions. . . .

Now take an example of an infinite continuum which is finite, but unbounded. We imagine the surface of a large globe, and a quantity of small paper disks, all of the same size. We place one of the discs anywhere on the surface of the globe. If we move the disk about, anywhere we like, on the surface of the globe, we do not come across a limit or a boundary anywhere on our journey. . . . Moreover, the spherical surface is a finite continuum. For if we stick the paper disks on the globe, so that no disc overlaps another, the surface of the globe will become . . . full. . . . Further, the spherical surface is a non-Euclidean continuum of two dimensions. . . . This can be shown in the following way. Place a paper disc on the spherical surface, and around it in a circle place six more discs . . . and so on. If this construction is made on a plane surface, we have an uninterrupted disposition in which there are six discs touching every other disc. . . . On the spherical surface the construction also seems to promise some success at the outset, and the smaller the radius of the disc in proportion to that of the sphere, the more promising it seems. But as the construction progresses it becomes more and more patent that the disposition of the discs in the manner indicated, without interruption, is not possible. . . . In this way creatures which cannot leave the spherical surface, and cannot even peep out . . . might discover . . . that their two-dimensional "space" is not Euclidean, but spherical space.

From the latest results of the theory of relativity it is probable that our three-dimensional space is also approximately spherical. . . .

Einstein's own analogy here is sometimes confusing. He asks us to imagine space curved like that of a sphere. This requires the introduction of a fourth spatial dimension (not the fourth temporal dimension t suggested by special relativity) in order to picture a medium for space to be curved *in*. Such an addition is not directly implied by the theory itself. General relativity simply states that the geometry of space is affected by matter in such a way that a straight line, the path followed by an object moving with no outside force, has properties other than that depicted by Euclidean geometry. In fact, these properties can account for the gravitational *and* inertial behavior of matter.

We can summarize some of these implications informally as follows: the inertial and gravitational properties of matter are different aspects of the same phenomena, namely, the fact that matter affects spatial geometry. Whether one feels a gravitational acceleration or an inertial resistance to motion is the same sort of property of the interaction between space and matter. Indeed, space is merely our representation of the relationships between material bodies. And furthermore, due to the results of special relativity, space and time are also relative to the configuration of our reference frames with respect to matter and velocity.

These qualitative summations must suffice here, but even at this level it is clear that some fundamental ideas must be revised. Relativity posits new relationships between entities in the universe once thought to be totally independent. Einstein's theories question the status of our perceptions as well as the modeling tools of space, time, geometry, and physical law.

Chaos Theory

Several developments in chemistry, biology, physics, and computer science converged in the mid- to late-twentieth century to generate a new scientific way of thinking. The Russian-born Nobel prizewinner in Chemistry Ilya Prigogine is popularly credited with coalescing these developments into the branch of physical science known as chaos theory. Born out of the same sort of studies that Boltzmann undertook in the nineteenth century,[21] chaos theory models the behavior of various processes in time and uses sophisticated mathematical techniques to try to come to some description of the relationship between our ideas of time and the theories used to model physical systems.

Chaos theory is not directly tied to quantum mechanics or relativity theory. In fact, it is more akin to classical studies of systems, and gains its novelty in a new mathematics of randomness. The second law of thermodynamics was explained by Boltzmann's statistical mechanics, and thus the tendency for spontaneous change toward disorder is understood. Prigogine and other chaos theorists once more tackle the problem of reconciling determinism with irreversibility, mechanism with asymmetric time. But instead of using the entropic process as a model for irreversibility, chaos theory concentrates on emerging patterns like those found in the evolution of life.

The following is a selection from a lecture given by Prigogine at the Jawaharlal Nehru University in New Delhi, December 1982.[22] This remarkable address draws from literature, physics, philosophy, and biology, and presents some insights which we will revisit later.

... the meaning of reality.

This question cannot be dissociated from another one, the meaning of time. To us, time and human existence, and therefore also reality, are concepts which are indissociable. But is this necessarily so? I like to quote the correspondence between Einstein and his old friend Besso. In the later years, Besso comes back again and again to the question of time. What is time? What is irreversibility? Patiently, Einstein answers again and again, irreversibility is an *illusion*, a subjective impression, coming from exceptional initial conditions.

Besso's death only a few months before Einstein's was to interrupt this correspondence. At Besso's death ... Einstein wrote:

Michele has preceded me a little in leaving this strange world. This is not important. For us who are convinced physicists, the distinction between past, present, and future is only an illusion, however persistent.

"Only an illusion." I must confess that this sentence has greatly impressed me. It seems to me that it expresses in an exceptionally striking way the symbolic power of the mind. ...

But how to understand this timeless nature which puts man outside the reality he describes? ... Do we really have to make a tragic choice between a timeless reality which leads to human alienation or an affirmation of time which seems to break with scientific rationality?

Most of European philosophy, from Kant to Whitehead, appears as an attempt to overcome one way or another the necessity of this choice.... None of these attempts has met with more than a mitigated success. As a result, we have seen a progressive decay of "philosophy of nature." I agree completely with Leclerc when he writes:

> In the present century we are suffering the consequences of the separation of science and philosophy which followed upon the triumph of Newtonian physics.... It is not only the dialogue between science and philosophy which has suffered.

... But something very dramatic is happening, something as unexpected as the birth of geometry.... We become progressively more and more conscious of the fact that on levels from elementary particles up to cosmology, science is rediscovering time.... A dialogue between natural sciences, human sciences, including arts and literature, may make a new start and perhaps develop into something as fruitful as it was during the classic period of Greece or during the seventeenth century of Newton and Leibniz....

As you know, the nineteenth century was essentially the century of evolution. Think about Darwin's work in biology, of Hegel in philosophy, or the formulation of the famous entropy law in physics.

Let us start with *Darwin*.... His approach combines *two* elements: on one side, the assumption of spontaneous *fluctuations* in biological species, which through selection from the medium lead to *irreversible* biological evolution. Therefore, his model combines two elements ... the idea of *fluctuations*, or randomness, of stochastic processes, and the idea of evolution, of *irreversibility*. Let us emphasize that on the level of biology this association leads to evolution corresponding to increasing complexity, to self-organization.

This is in complete contrast to the meaning generally associated with the law of *entropy* increase as formulated by Clausius in 1865. The basic element in this law is the distinction between reversible and irreversible processes. Reversible processes do not know any privileged direction of time. You may think about ... planetary motion. On the other hand, irreversible processes involve an arrow of time. If you bring together two liquids, they tend to mix, but the unmixing is not observed as a spontaneous process.... This distinction is taken up in the formulation of the second law ... the entropy (entropy means evolution in Greek) ... can only increase....

It is the lifework of one of the greatest theoretical physicists of all times, Ludwig Boltzmann, to have given a first microscopic interpretation to this increase in entropy.... Again, as with Darwin, evolution and probability, randomness, are closely related. However, Boltzmann's result is different and even contradictory to that of Darwin. Probability will reach its maximum when *uniformity will be achieved*.... Therefore, the approach to equilibrium corresponds to ... forgetting of initial structures, in contrast to Darwin where evolution means creation of new structures.

[H]ow can *Boltzmann and Darwin both be right?* ...

The prototype of classical physics is ... the *description of trajectories* leading a point from position A to position B. Some of the basic characteristics of the dynamical description are its deterministic and *reversible character* ... the direction of time does not play any role. Prediction and retrodiction are identical.... [T]here seems to be no place for randomness nor for irreversibility. To some extent, the situation remains the same in quantum theory. Here we do not speak any more about trajectories but about wave functions. Again the wave function evolves according to a reversible deterministic law.

As a consequence, the universe appears as a vast automaton....

It is certain that, whatever our final appreciation of these complex problems, our universe has a pluralistic, complex character. Structures may disappear, like in a diffusion process, but structures may appear, as in biology and, even more clearly, social processes. Some phenomena are, so far as we know, well described by deterministic equations ... but some, like biological evolution, likely involve stochastic[23] processes....

How then to overcome the apparent contradiction between these concepts? We are living in a *single universe* ... we begin to see that irreversibility, life, are inserted into the basic laws, even on a microscopic level.... Today, *we see everywhere the role of irreversible processes.*... The models considered by classical physics appear to us as now to correspond only to limiting situations which we can create artificially....

The *artificial* may be deterministic and reversible. The *natural* contains essential elements of randomness and irreversibility.... This change is so deep that I believe we can really speak about a *new dialogue with nature.*...

[I]t has taken many unexpected developments ... to go from a classic description to the new one which is emerging. In brief, we were looking for all-embracing schemes, for symmetries, for immutable general laws, and we have discovered the mutable, the temporal, the complex.... Quantum theory predicts a *remarkable symmetry* ... between matter and antimatter, but our world does not have this symmetry....

Who could expect that ... the concept of evolution would be applicable to the world as a whole? as matter of fact, astrophysical discoveries ... leave little doubt that the world as a whole has undergone a remarkable evolution.

How then to speak of immutable, eternal laws? We can certainly not speak about laws of life at a moment when there was no life. The very concept of law which emerged at the time of Descartes and Newton, a time of absolute monarchies, has to be revised.

... The classical view ... focused its interest on the transition from order to disorder. Now we find everywhere transitions from disorder to order, processes involving *self-organization* of matter....

[H]ow can we describe the origin of structures, of self-organizations.... What has been shown is that near equilibrium matter indeed conforms to Boltzmann's paradigm; structures are destroyed. If we perturb such a system, the system responds by restoring its initial conditions; such systems are therefore stable.... However, these properties do not extend to far-from-equilibrium systems. The key words here are *"nonlinearity," "instability," "bifurcations."* In brief, this means that if we drive a system sufficiently far from equilibrium, its state may become unstable in respect to perturbation. The exact point at which this happens is called the *bifurcation point.*...

[T]he appearance of bifurcations in the far-from-equilibrium conditions leads to an irreducible stochastic random element on the macroscopic level. Deterministic theories are of no help to permit us to predict which of the branches that arise at the bifurcation point will be followed at the bifurcation point.... Clearly, there is a relation with the role of fluctuations and the Darwinian theory of the origin of species. Again you see why I mentioned before that, in the present perspective, life appears much less isolated, as having much deeper roots in the basic laws of nature....

Irreversibility, as in the theory of Darwin, or also in the theory of Boltzmann, is an even stronger property than randomness. I find this quite natural. Indeed, what could irreversibility mean in a deterministic concept of the universe in which tomorrow is already potentially present today? Irreversibility presupposes a universe in which there are limitations in the prediction of the future ... irreversibility is not a universal property [emphasis omitted—ed.] However, the world as a whole seems to belong to these complex systems, intrinsically random, for which irreversibility is meaningful....

This description of nature, in which order is generated out of chaos *through nonequilibrium conditions* produced by our cosmological environment, leads to a physics that is quite similar in its spirit to the world of "processes" imagined by Whitehead. It leads us to conceive matter as active, as in a continuous state of becoming. This picture deviates significantly from the classical description of physics. . . . It is a momentous step to go away from the royal road opened by Newton, Maxwell, and Einstein. . . .

We have seen that time in the sense of duration, of irreversibility, is basically related to the role of randomness, in full accord with the brilliant intuition of Boltzmann. . . .

As we are able to find the roots of time in nature, time ceases to be the concept which separates men from nature. It now expresses our belonging to nature, not our alienation. . . . With this conclusion the problem of human values, of ethics, expectation, even of art takes on new form. We may now see music with its elements of expectation, of improvisation, with its arrow of time as an allegory of becoming, of physics. . . . It is this moment with its incertitudes, its open questions, but also its hopes for a more integrated human world, which I have tried to describe in this lecture.

Chaos theory is a new model for viewing natural phenomena as disparate as earthquakes, physiology, hydrodynamics, meteorology, and biological evolution. Prigogine claims chaos theory will engender a new understanding of physics as process and time as fundamentally imbedded in the universe. He hopes this will inspire a revolution which will displace the atemporal, objective, universal theories of Newton.

Chaos theory is further productive of a new mathematical geometry of fractals, fractional dimensions which serve as representations of complexity. This development is intimately tied to technological advances in computer science. And if Prigogine is correct, these technological, mathematical, and physical discoveries will entail new human dialogues within nature.

Metaphysical Serendipity: Process Philosophy

In the last section, Prigogine made mention of the process philosophy of British mathematician and philosopher Alfred North Whitehead (1861–1947). Whitehead's view of reality is closely tied with the twentieth-century revolutions in physical science. And although he takes his cue from developments in relativity and quantum theory, he does not presume, as do some of the authors we have discussed, that these scientific theories are the final goal of our inquiries into reality.

Instead, Whitehead proposes a metaphysics of process that rests firmly within the tradition of speculative philosophy. We can view Whitehead's process metaphysics as the twentieth-century analog of Leibniz's metaphysical monadology treated in Chapter 4. Both of these theories spring from the insights of contemporaneous scientific theories but do not hesitate to move beyond technical science.

Whitehead correspondingly has a different understanding of the relationship between science and humanity than his seventeenth- and eighteenth-century counterparts do. In this section, we will briefly look at some features of Whitehead's metaphysics as stated in *Process and Reality*.[24] His views of science in human life and human history are given in *Science and the Modern World*, an excellent treatment very much in the spirit of the present volume.

PROCESS AND REALITY

[H]ow shallow, puny, and imperfect are the efforts to sound the depths in the nature of things. In philosophical discussion, the merest hint of dogmatic certainty is folly....

[N]ecessity in universality means that there is an essence to the universe which forbids relationships beyond itself, as a violation of its rationality. Speculative philosophy seeks that essence....

Philosophers can never hope to finally formulate ... metaphysical first principles. Weakness of insight and deficiencies of language stand in the way inexorably. Words and phrases ... remain metaphors mutely appealing for an imaginative leap.

The difficulty has its seat in the empirical side of philosophy. Our datum is the actual world, including ourselves; and this actual world spreads itself out for observation.... [T]he discovery of metaphysics, the method of pinning down thought to the strict systematization of detailed discrimination, already affected by antecedent observation, breaks down. The collapse of the method of rigid empiricism is not confined to metaphysics.... In natural science, this rigid method is the Baconian method of induction, a method which, if consistently pursued, would have left science where it found it.... The true method of discovery is like the flight of an aeroplane. It starts from the ground of particular observation; it makes a flight in the thin air of imagination; and it lands again for observation rendered acute by rational interpretation....

The field of a special science is confined to one genus of facts, in the sense that no statements are made respecting facts which lie outside that genus. . . . the special sciences, therefore, deal with topics which lie open to easy inspection and are readily expressed by words.

The study of philosophy is a voyage towards the larger generalities. For this reason in the infancy of science, when the main stress lay in the discovery of the most general ideas . . . philosophy was not sharply distinguished from science. To this day, a new science with any substantial novelty in its notions is considered to be in some way peculiarly philosophical. In their later stages . . . most sciences accept without question the general notions in terms of which they develop. . . . In such periods scientists repudiate philosophy; Newton, justly satisfied with his principles, disclaimed metaphysics. . . .

One chapter in the history of culture is concerned with the growth of generalities. In such a chapter it is seen that the older generalities, like the older hills, are worn down and diminished in height, surpassed by younger rivals.

Thus one aim of philosophy is to challenge the half-truths constituting the scientific first principles. . . .

[T]he understanding of the immediate brute fact requires its metaphysical interpretation as an item in a world with some systematic relation to it.

"Actual entities"—also termed "actual occasions"—are the final real things of which the world is made up. There is no going behind the actual entities to find anything more real. They differ among themselves: God is an actual entity, and so is the most trivial puff of existence in far off empty space. . . . The final facts are, all alike, actual entities; and these actual entities are drops of experience, complex and interdependent. . . .

"Creativity" is the universal . . . characterizing ultimate matter of fact. . . . It lies in the nature of things. . . . Creativity is the principle of *novelty*. An actual occasion is a novel entity diverse from any entity in the "many" which it unifies. . . .

The actual world is a process, and . . . the process is the becoming of actual entities. Thus actual entities are creatures. . . .

[E]very item in the universe is involved in each [process]. In other words, it belongs to the nature of "being" that it is a potential for every "becoming." This is the "principle of relativity." . . .

It is fundamental to the metaphysical doctrine of the philosophy of organism, that the notion of an actual entity as the unchanging subject of change is completely abandoned. An actual entity is at once the subject of experiencing and the superject of its experiences. . . .

The ancient doctrine that "no one crosses the same river twice" is extended. No thinker thinks twice . . . no subject experiences twice. . . .

Whitehead here proposes a universe of process, of becoming, of experience. No longer are we concerned with the substances which form the subjects and objects of experience, say mind and matter, observer and spatial objects. Process philosophy posits a metaphysics of actual entities that are their own experiences. There is no dualism of experiencer and experiencing. All concepts, such as space, time, matter, mind, are the elements of relative experience, relative to each other and the occasion of their experience, without independent existence. To deny this independent existence is not to denigrate space or time, mind or matter; it is rather to acknowledge them as ultimate building blocks of the universe since all reality is such as this.

This philosophical metaphysics is coherent with the scientific metaphysics of the twentieth century. Both seek to replace concepts like absolute space and time, as well as solid bodies and deterministic relations. Such notions are inherent in classical physics but find no place in twentieth-century physical theory. Correspondingly, they are not present in process philosophy. While Whitehead significantly augments the world picture of science to make it into an abstract metaphysical theory in the tradition of speculative philosophy, he makes his metaphysics coherent with the physics of Heisenberg, Einstein, and the other founders of contemporary physical theory.

Summary

In the twentieth century, classical paradigms break down. New, astounding, captivating theories, both simple and complex, replace the physics of Newton and Maxwell. As we saw in Chapter 4, the metaphysics of modernity anticipated and responded to the seventeenth-century revolution in science. We now see that a similar phenomena occurs in the twentieth century.

Twentieth-century transformations do not stop with these few subjects, and the legacy of quantum theory and relativity continues to lend new insights into physics. Quantum electrodynamics uses both quantum theory and relativity in mapping fundamental interactions. And grand unification theory uses quantum physics and new high-energy technology to carry on in the spirit of Maxwell by striving to unify all forces of nature into one coherent explanation.

Although the beginning of the twentieth century saw physicists in world-shaking dilemmas that caused them to rethink the very essence of science, the end of the century bears witness to a renewed confidence in the status and results of modern science. As quantum theory and special relativity were applied consistently to more and more difficult and esoteric problems in physics, the new physics accumulated theoretical and empirical victories. Many seemingly intractable problems remain, and some physicists are unhappy with the status of physical interpretation in general during this century, as we will see in Chapter 12. Yet many thinkers in the latter half of the twentieth century see contemporary physics as the ultimate world-view.

Twentieth-century scepticism is reflected in the philosophies of science expressed by Popper, Kuhn, Feyerabend, and others, as we shall see in the next chapter. The renewed confidence is seen in the mutual support disparate fields of physics now lend each other, e.g., quantum theory, big bang cosmology, and grand unification theory. Steven Weinberg, to name one example, sees victory for a science of reductionism and the end of fundamental paradigm shifts in his *Dreams of A Final Theory* (see Chapter 12).

This view is somewhat surprising, given the history of science even in this century. And we have seen that some scientists, Prigogine among them, look forward to new revolutions and new reformulations of the roles of science in human culture. Perhaps the student of history—after having become acquainted with scientific developments through vehicles such as this text—can appreciate that similar claims to final scientific victory in the nineteenth century were premature, to say the least.

Notes

1. Newton himself believed that light was corpuscular and that light particles were emitted from a source and could travel through empty space. However, Newton thought that space was pervaded by some medium that acted as the agent for gravitational interaction (see Chapter 3).

2. Euclidean space is that derived from Euclid's five postulates, four of which are definitional and uncontroversial. The fifth, known as the parallel postulate, states that given a line and a point not on that line, in the plane defined by these there is exactly one line through the given point parallel to the given line. From this hypothesis we derive many substantive geometric results, e.g., that the sum of the angles in a triangle is equal to two right angles, that only three regular polygons will completely cover a plane, and so forth.

3. Reprinted with permission from Einstein, "How I Created the Theory of Relativity," Y.A. Ono transl., *Physics Today*, Vol. 35 #8, August 1982, pp. 45–47. Copyright 1982, American Institute of Physics.

4. Lorentz Hendrick (1853–1928) was the mathematician who devised transformations to describe the phenomena of spatial and temporal geometry with respect to velocity.

5. This rule, anticipated by Galileo and Galilean relativity (discussed in Chapter 3), states that in order to find the velocity of a moving object in a given reference frame, say a baseball thrown on a ship, take the velocity of the frame in which the baseball is thrown, the ship, and add the velocity of the baseball to get the perceived velocity from, say, the dock.

6. It is not known at the time of this writing whether or not Einstein is speaking of philosophical features of Mach's view analogous to those presented in Chapter 7; in fact, it is doubtful.

7. Albert Einstein and Leopold Infeld, *The Evolution of Physics* (New York: Simon & Schuster, 1938). J.H. Weaver attributes all writing to the Polish physicist Leopold Infeld. See *The World of Physics*, Volume II (New York: Simon & Schuster, 1987).

8. Reprinted in J.H. Weaver's *World of Physics*, Volume II.

9. The details of this have been omitted in favor of a nontechnical presentation. The further non-Euclidean properties of space-time are given by General Relativity, discussed later in this chapter.

10. "God does not play dice with the world," responded Einstein to Heisenberg's uncertainty principle.

11. Werner Heisenberg, "The Nobel Prize in Physics Award Address," Copyright The Nobel Foundation, 1932. Used by permission.

12. The physics of the very small.

13. See Chapter 8.

14. Max Planck, "The Concept of Causality in Physics, excerpted from *Scientific Autobiography and Other Papers*, Taynar, trans. (New York: The Philosophical Library, 1949).

15. Excerpts as submitted from *Physics and Philosophy* by Werner Heisenberg. Copyright © 1958 by Werner Heisenberg. Reprinted by permission of HarperCollins Publishers, Inc.

16. See Weaver, p. 102, for example.

17. See Chapter 3, Newton's claim that "the cause of gravity is what I do not pretend to know."

18. The pioneering of tensor calculus as well as other mathematics of transformation along with relativity theory can be seen as analogous to the original advent of calculus in Newton's time.

19. This address was actually given in 1923, two years after the prize was awarded.

20. Albert Einstein, "Geometry and Experience," *Sidelights on Relativity* (London: Methuen, 1921).

21. See Chapter 7.

22. Ilya Prigogine, "Only an Illusion," *The Tanner Lectures on Human Values*, University of Utah Press and Cambridge University Press, 1984.

23. Loosely, we can understand this term as synonymous with random.

24. Reprinted with the permission of Simon & Schuster from *Process and Reality*, Corrected Edition by Alfred North Whitehead. Copyright 1929 by Macmillan Publishing Company; copyright renewed, copyright 1957 by Evelyn Whitehead. Copyright 1978 by the Free Press. David Ray Griffin and Donald W. Sherburne, eds. (New York: The Free Press, 1978).

Suggestions for Further Reading

Browning, Douglas, and William Meyers, eds., *Philosophers of Process*, 2nd ed. (New York: Fordham University Press, 1998).

Dirac, Paul. *The Development of Quantum Theory* (New York: Wiley and Sons, 1971).

Gleick, James. *Chaos: Making a New Science* (New York: Penguin Books, 1987).

Gleick, James. *Genius: The Life and Times of Richard Feynman* (New York: Pantheon Books, 1992).

Heisenberg, Werner. *Physics and Beyond* (New York: Harper and Row, 1971).

Munitz, Milton K. ed., *Theories of the Universe*, "Modern Theories of the Universe" (Glencoe, IL: The Free Press, 1957).

Nicolis, G., and I. Prigogine. *Self Organization in Non-Equilibrium Systems* (New York: Wiley and Sons, 1977).

Prigogine, Ilya. *Order out of Chaos: Man's New Dialog with Nature* (New York: Bantam Books, 1984).

Schlipp, Paul Arthur. *Albert Einstein: Philosopher Scientist* (Evanston, IL: Library of Living Philosophers, 1949).

Weaver, Jefferson Hane, *The World of Physics*, Volume II (New York: Simon & Schuster, 1987).

Weiner, Philip P., ed., *Readings in Philosophy of Science*, Part A, "Foundations of Mathematical and Physical Science" (New York: Charles Scribner's Sons, 1953).

Whitehead, A.N., *Science and the Modern World* (New York: The Free Press, 1925).

Twentieth-Century Views on Scientific Method

In Chapter 5 we saw how the seventeenth-century revolution in physical theory was the catalyst for scientists and philosophers to study scientific method in general. A similar phenomenon takes place in the twentieth century on the heels of the revolutions in physical theory presented in the previous chapter. In addition, philosophers and scientists have evolutionary theory and statistical mechanics to consider, as well as the influence of science on the world at large. In this chapter we will examine some classic writings of the twentieth century on scientific method. And as in Chapter 5, we will again see that views on method have implications for the status of science as well as assumptions about the metaphysics, or ultimate reality, which relates to science.

Construction

Pierre Dühem was a brilliant physicist as well as an eminent historian and philosopher of science. Born in Paris in 1861, he practiced in the field of "energetics," developing mathematical theories concerning the energies of physical systems. Of all the scientific developments presented in this text, Dühem was most familiar with those at the end of Chapter 7, namely, electromagnetic theory and statistical mechanics. While he greatly admired the work of Maxwell and Gibbs, he rejected the mechanical interpretations of their theories. Dühem believed that the aim of physical theory was abstract axiomatic theory, not mechanical, "visual" interpretation.

Dühem's reasons for this rejection are somewhat surprising. Instead of favoring abstract theory because of its advantages as a certain basis for explaining reality, he reasons in the opposite direction. He claims that physical theory is not dependent on metaphysics and that physics has no access to some "unveiled" reality. Thus, he rejects the idea that science can explain what actually happens in any real situation. Dühem favors mathematical theory only because it serves as the most simple, succinct, and general summary of what we can observe through experiment.

The Aim and Structure of Physical Theory was first published in 1906, hence written at the beginning of the relativistic and quantum mechanical revolutions in physics. Although Dühem was not directly acquainted with Einstein's hypothesis of the photon nor later developments in quantum theory, his ideas run counter to those of quantum theory mechanics. He preferred theory that does not posit the existence of atomic structures or subatomic building blocks as ontological entities. Such theory is too dependent on a theory of reality, and thus violates his prescribed separation between physics and metaphysics. Rather, he saw no need for hypothetical objects to hold the qualities and relations of physics. Instead, Dühem believed that these relations can be formalized in axiomatic mathematical systems that speak only of the relations themselves, not any more fundamental structures which those relations might describe or explain. Dühem died in 1916. The following are selections from *The Aim and Structure of Physical Theory*.[1]

The first question we should face is: What is the aim of a physical theory? To this question diverse answers have been made, but all of them may be reduced to two main principles:

"A physical theory," certain logicians have replied, "has for its object the *explanation* of a group of laws experimentally established."

"A physical theory," other thinkers have said, "is an abstract system whose aim is to *summarize* and *classify logically* a group of experimental laws without claiming to explain these laws...."

We begin with the first, which regards a physical theory as an explanation.

But first, what is an explanation?

To explain ... is to strip reality of the appearances covering it like a veil, in order to see the bare reality itself....

For example, string or wind instruments have produced sounds to which we have listened closely and which we have heard become stronger, weaker, higher or lower in a thousand nuances productive in us of auditory sensations and musical emotions; such are the acoustic facts.

... The experimental laws of acoustics aim at the enunciation of fixed relations among ... general notions. A law, for example, teaches us what relation exists between the dimension of two strings of the same metal which yield two sounds of the same pitch or two sounds an octave apart.

But these notions—sound, intensity, pitch, etc.—depict to our reason no more than the general characteristics of our sound perceptions; these notions get us to know sound as it is in relation to us, not as it is by itself. . . . This reality whose external veil alone appears to us is made known to us by theories of acoustics. The latter are to teach us that . . . there is in reality a very small and very rapid periodic motion. . . . Acoustic theories are therefore explanations.

The explanation which acoustic theories give of experimental laws governing sound claims to give us certainty; it can in a great many cases make us see with our own eyes the motions to which it attributes these phenomena, and feel them with our fingers.

Most often we find that physical theory cannot attain that degree of perfection . . . for it cannot render accessible to the senses the reality it proclaims. . . . It is then content with proving that all our perceptions are produced *as if* the reality were what it asserts; such a theory is a hypothetical explanation.

Let us, for example, take the phenomena observed with the sense of sight. The rational analysis of these phenomena leads us to conceive certain abstract and general notions expressing the properties we come across . . . color, brightness, etc. . . . Experimental laws of optics make us acquainted with fixed relations among these abstract and general notions. . . .

Of these experimental laws the vibratory theory of light gives a hypothetical explanation. It supposes that all the bodies we see . . . are immersed in an . . . unobservable medium called the ether. To this ether certain mechanical properties are attributed; the theory states that all simple light is a transverse vibration . . . of this ether . . . and without enabling us to perceive the ether . . . the theory tries to prove that its postulates entail consequences agreeing at every point with . . . experimental optics.

. . . For such an inquiry to make sense or to be at all possible, we must first of all regard as certain the following affirmation: Under the sensible appearances, which are revealed in our perceptions, there is a reality distinct from these appearances. . . .

Therefore, *if the aim of physical theories is to explain experimental laws, theoretical physics is not an autonomous science; it is subordinate to metaphysics. . . .*

There is no thinker who does not wish for the science he cultivates a growth as calm and as regular as that of mathematics....
Now, to make physical theories depend on metaphysics is surely not
the way to let them enjoy the privilege of universal consent.... None
of the systems of thought arising in different eras or the contemporary systems born of different schools will appear more profoundly
distinct, more sharply separated, more violently opposed to one another, than those in the field of metaphysics....

The great cosmological schools, the Aristotelian, the Newtonian,
the atomistic, and the Cartesian, may be arranged in an order such
that each admits the existence in matter of a smaller number of essential properties than the preceding schools are willing to admit....

[A]ll the cosmological schools other than the Aristotelian have
agreed in attacking the latter for the arsenal of qualities stored in substantial form....

Could not this criticism be nearly always applied to the scold-
ing school itself? ... [N]o metaphysics gives instruction exact enough
or detailed enough to make it possible to derive all the elements of a
physical theory from it ... physical theory ... always appeals to
propositions which the metaphysical system has not furnished and
which consequently remain mysteries for the partisans of that system.
At the root of the explanations it claims to give there always lies the
unexplained....

These thoughts ... lead us quite naturally to ask the following
two questions:

Could we not assign an aim to physical theory that would render it *autonomous*? Based on principles which do not arise from any
metaphysical doctrine, physical theory might be judged in its own
terms without including the opinions of physicists who depend on
the philosophical schools to which they may belong.

Could we not conceive a method which might be *sufficient* for
the construction of a physical theory? Consistent with its own definition the theory would employ no principle and have no recourse to
any procedure which it could not legitimately use....

A physical theory is not an explanation. It is a system of mathematical propositions, deduced from a small number of principles,
which aim to represent as simply, as completely, and as exactly as
possible a set of experimental laws.

In order to start making this definition somewhat more precise,
let us characterize the four successive operations through which a
physical theory is formed:

1. Among the physical properties which we set ourselves to represent, we select those we regard as simple properties, so that the others will supposedly be groupings or combinations of them. We make them correspond to a certain group of mathematical symbols. . . . These mathematical symbols have no connection of any intrinsic nature with the properties they represent; they bear only the relation of sign to thing signified. Through the methods of measurement we can make each state of a physical property correspond to a value of the representative symbol.

2. We connect the different sorts of magnitudes, thus introduced, by means of a small number of propositions, which will serve as principles in our deductions. These principles may be called hypotheses . . . but they do not claim in any manner to state real relations among the real properties of bodies. These hypotheses may then be formed in an arbitrary way. The only absolutely impassable barrier which limits this arbitrariness is logical contradiction. . . .

3. The diverse principles or hypotheses of a theory are combined together according to the rules of mathematical analysis. . . . The magnitudes in which the calculations bear are not claimed to be physical realities, and the principles [the scientist] employs in his deductions are not given as stating real relations . . . therefore it matters little whether the operations he performs do or do not correspond to real or conceivable physical transformations. . . .

4. The various consequences thus drawn from the hypotheses may be translated into as many judgements bearing on the physical properties of bodies. . . . These judgements are compared with the experimental laws which the theory is intended to represent. If they agree with these laws to the degree of approximation corresponding to the measuring procedures employed, thetheory has attained its goal, and is said to be a good theory; if not, it is a bad theory, and it must be modified or rejected.

Thus a true theory is not a theory which gives an explanation of physical appearances in conformity with reality; it is a theory which represents in a satisfactory manner a group of experimental laws. . . . *Agreement with experiment is the sole criterion of truth for a physical theory.*

... of what use is such a theory? ... What do physicists gain by replacing the laws which experimental method furnishes directly with a system of mathematical propositions representing those laws?

First of all, instead of a great number of laws offering themselves as independent of one another ... physical theory substitutes a very small number of ... fundamental hypotheses.... Such condensing of a multitude of laws into a small number of principles affords enormous relief to the human mind....

Theory is not solely an economical representation of experimental laws; it is also a *classification* of these laws.... Theory gives us, so to speak, the table of contents and the chapter headings under which the science to be studied will be methodically divided.... These classifications make knowledge more convenient to use and safe to apply. Consider those utility cabinets where tools for the same purpose lie side by side, and where partitions logically separate instruments not designed for the same task: the worker's hand quickly grasps, without fumbling or mistake, the tools needed....

Order, wherever it reigns, brings beauty with it. Theory not only renders the group of physical laws it represents easier to handle, more convenient, and more useful, but also more beautiful.

It is impossible to follow the march of one of the great theories of physics ... without being charmed by the beauty of such a construction, without feeling keenly that such a creation of the human mind is truly a work of art....

This esthetic emotion is not the only reaction that is produced by a theory arriving at a high degree of perfection. It persuades us also to see a natural classification in a theory....

The neat way in which each experimental law finds its place in the classification created by the physicist ... persuade[s] us in an overwhelming manner that such a classification is not purely artificial.... Without being able to explain our conviction, but also without being able to get rid of it, we see in the exact ordering of this system the mark by which a natural classification is recognized....

The physicist who sees in every theory an explanation is convinced that he has grasped ... the proper and intimate basis....

Of course, we do not share these illusions.... But when, after much groping, we see in the plan ... drawn by ... hypotheses a vast domain ... become ordered and organized, it is impossible for us to believe that this order and this organization are not the reflected image of real order and organization....

> Thus, physical theory never gives us the explanation of experimental laws; it never reveals realities hiding under the sensible appearances; but the more complete it becomes, the more we apprehend that the logical order in which theory orders experimental laws is the reflection of an ontological order. . . .

We see many philosophical themes running through these passages, combining in different ways at the beginning of the twentieth century. In some ways, Dühem recollects Hume. Dühem denies that the mathematical, logical, and necessary certainty in physical theory corresponds to reality or is in any way external to the human mind. Dühem's theory is also consistent with Planck's idea that physics describes a world-picture that contains "symbols only," that it is a picture that is entirely formal, abstract, and symbolic. Even in Dühem's discussion of natural classification, it is the human mind that is persuaded of the ontological order, and the mind acquires a "conviction" that is inexplicable and outside the bounds of scientific or philosophical analysis.

We also see positivism in Dühem's search for classification and disavowal of metaphysics. Dühem explicitly invokes Mach in his praise for the intellectual economy of abstract theory and its ability to serve as a taxonomy for experimental laws.[2] Dühem's science does not include a claim of physical explanation, however, unlike the positivist who claims to explore reality[3] via scientific method. Dühem seeks only economy and utility. In this, he agrees with Galen's empiricists (Chapter 1) against the dogmatists of theory.

And we see again that methodological prescription is connected with metaphysical status. Dühem explicitly carves out a niche for physical theory as autonomous from metaphysics. He realizes that to do so requires the specification of a method that makes no claim to explanation of or derivation from reality. And so although the relationship he seeks between science and metaphysics is one of independence, both his method and his defense of it require a discussion of the metaphysical aspects, or lack thereof, in scientific theory. We will see different versions of methodological and metaphysical relationships in the following sections.

Dühem's method will be called *constructivism*. Constructivism claims that physical theory is invented, created, or constructed in order to economically and elegantly represent experimental results. There is no direct explanation or description involved. Dühem's specific method is rather flexible due to his constructivist thesis. The only impediment to creative theorization is "logical contradiction." Correspondence with reality, immediate confirmation, explanatory power, or other criteria for evaluation of theory are not relevant for Dühem. Nevertheless, Dühem believes that theory and experiment are mutually supportive.

Thus Dühem's approach to scientific method is positive. He sees the goal of physical theory as "agreement with experiment." And although he can have no methodological, scientific, or even philosophical justification for his view of logical order revealing ontological order, this transcendent relationship is also positive. Hence Dühem is often identified with the positivists. In the next section, we see an entirely different view of scientific methodology.

Corroboration and Falsification

Karl Popper was born in Vienna in 1902 and practiced philosophy in Vienna, New Zealand, and London. He was knighted in 1965 while serving as Professor of Logic and Scientific Method at the London School of Economics. Popper did not view the aim of science as the arbitrary construction of logical theory that in the end agrees with experimental law. Constructivism has two problems, according to Popper. First, he viewed this arbitrary basis as a door through which pseudoscience can intrude into the proper domain of science. Second, such arbitrary theorizing can interfere with the progress of science at crucial periods. Furthermore, Popper did not judge the merits of scientific theory by its agreement with experiment but rather by its potential for disagreement. Karl Popper died in 1994.

The following are selections from *The Logic of Scientific Discovery*.[4]

... the most important and most exciting problems of epistemology must remain completely invisible to those who confine themselves to analysing ordinary or common-sense knowledge. . . .

I wish to refer here to only one example of the kind of problem I have in mind: the problem of the *growth* of our knowledge. A little reflection will show that most problems connected with the growth of our knowledge must necessarily transcend any study which is confined to common-sense knowledge as opposed to scientific knowledge. For the most important way in which common-sense knowledge grows is, precisely, by turning into scientific knowledge. . . .

... purely metaphysical ideas—and therefore philosophical ideas—have been of the greatest importance. . . . From Thales to

Einstein, from ancient atomism to Descartes' speculation about matter, from the speculations of Gilbert and Newton and Leibniz ... to those of Faraday and Einstein, metaphysical ideas have shown the way. ...

A scientist, whether theorist or experimenter, puts forward statements, or systems of statements, and tests them step by step. In the field of empirical sciences ... he ... tests them against experience by observation and experiment.

I suggest that it is the task of the logic of scientific discovery ... to analyse the method of the empirical sciences. ...

According to a widely accepted view ... the empirical sciences can be characterized by the fact that they use "*inductive methods.* ..."

Now it is far from obvious, from a logical point of view, that we are justified in inferring universal statements from singular ones ... no matter how many instances of white swans we may have observed, this does not justify the conclusion that all swans are white.

The question whether inductive inferences are justified, or under what conditions, is known as *the problem of induction.* ...

Yet if we want to find a way of justifying inductive inferences, we must first of all try to establish a *principle of induction* ... "this principle," says Reichenbach, "determines the truth of scientific theories. ... Without it, clearly, science would no longer have the right to distinguish its theories from the fanciful and arbitrary creations of the poet's mind. ..."[5]

That inconsistencies may easily arise in connection with the principle of induction should have been clear from the work of Hume. ... For the principle of induction must be a universal statement in its turn. Thus if we try to regard its truth as known from experience, then the very same problems which occasioned its introduction will arise all over again. ...

Kant tried to force his way out of this difficulty by taking the principle of induction (which he formulated as "the principle of causation") to be "*a priori* valid." But I do not think that his ingenious attempt to provide *a priori* justification for synthetic statements was successful.

My own view is that the various difficulties of inductive logic here sketched are insurmountable. ... ·

The theory developed in the following pages ... might be described as the theory of *the deductive method of testing,* or as the view that a hypothesis can only be empirically *tested*—and only *after* it has been advanced. ...

The initial stage, the act of conceiving or inventing a theory, seems to me to neither call for logical analysis nor to be susceptible of it. The question how it happens that a new idea occurs to a man ... may be of great interest to empirical psychology; but it is irrelevant to the logical analysis of scientific knowledge. This latter is concerned ... only with questions of *justification or validity*. ...

... we want to reconstruct rationally the *subsequent tests* whereby the inspiration may be discovered to be a discovery, or becomes known to be knowledge. ...

the testing of the theory [is] by way of empirical applications of the conclusions which can be derived from it. ... [W]e seek a decision as regards ... derived statements by comparing them with the results of practical applications and experiments. If this decision is positive, ... then the theory has, for the time being, passed its test: we have found no reason to discard it. But if the decision is negative, or, in other words, if the conclusions have been *falsified*, then their falsification also falsifies the theory from which they were logically deduced.

It should be noticed that a positive decision can only temporarily support the theory, for subsequent negative decisions can always overthrow it. So long as a theory withstands detailed and severe tests ... we may say that it ... is *"corroborated"* by past experience. ...

Of the many objections which are likely to be raised against the view here advanced, the most serious is perhaps the following. In rejecting the method of induction ... I remove the barriers which separate science from metaphysical speculation. ...

The problem of finding a criterion which would enable us to distinguish ... empirical sciences ... I call *the problem of demarcation.*

... the main reason why epistemologists with empiricist leanings tend to pin their faith to the "method of induction" seems to be their belief that this method alone can provide a suitable criterion of demarcation. This applies especially to those empiricists who follow the flag of "positivism. ..."

Positivists usually interpret the problem of demarcation ... as if it were a problem of natural science. Instead of taking it as their task to propose a suitable convention, they believe they have to discover a difference, existing in the nature of things, as it were, between empirical science on the one hand and metaphysics on the other. They are constantly trying to prove that metaphysics by its very nature is nothing but nonsensical twaddle—"sophistry and illusion," as Hume says, which we should "commit to the flames. ..."[6]

The words "meaningless" and "nonsensical" convey, and are meant to convey, a derogatory evaluation; and there is no doubt that what the positivists really want to achieve is not so much a successful demarcation as the final overthrow and the annihilation of metaphysics. However this may be, we find that each time the positivists tried to say more clearly what "meaningful" meant, the attempt led to the same result . . . the criterion of demarcation of their *inductive logic*. . . .

My criterion of demarcation will . . . have to be regarded as a *proposal for an agreement or convention*. . . .

Thus anyone who envisages a system of absolutely certain, irrevocable true statements as the end and purpose of science will certainly reject the proposals I shall make. . . . But I hope that my proposals may be acceptable to those who value not only logical rigor but also freedom from dogmatism; who seek practical applicability, but are even more attracted by the adventure of science, and by discoveries which again and again confront us with new and unexpected questions. . . .

The criterion of demarcation inherent in inductive logic . . . is equivalent to the requirement that all statements of empirical science . . . must be capable of being finally decided, with respect to their truth *and* falsity. . . .

Now in my view there is no such thing as induction. Thus inference to theories, . . . "verified by experience," is logically inadmissible. Theories are, therefore, *never* empirically verifiable . . . we must choose a criterion of demarcation which allows us to admit to the domain of empirical science even statements which cannot be verified.

But I shall certainly admit a system as empirical or scientific only if it is capable of being *tested* by experience. These considerations suggest that not the *verifiability* but the *falsifiability* of a system is to be criterion of demarcation. In other words: I shall not require of a scientific system that it shall be capable of being singled out, once and for all, in a positive sense; but I shall require that its logical form shall be such that it can be singled out, by means of empirical tests, in a negative sense: *it must be possible for an empirical scientific system to be refuted by experience.*

. . . It might be said that . . . it is . . . impossible, for various reasons, that any theoretical system should ever be conclusively falsified. For it is always possible to find some way of evading falsification, for example, by introducing *ad hoc* and auxiliary hypothesis. . . . It is even possible without logical inconsistency to adopt the position of simply refusing to acknowledge the falsifying experience whatsoever. . . .

I must admit the justice of this criticism; but ... I am going to propose that the *empirical method* shall be characterized as a method that excludes ... ways of evading falsification. ... [W]hat characterizes the empirical method is its manner of exposing to falsification, in every conceivable way, the system to be tested. Its aim is not to save the lives of untenable systems but, on the contrary, to select the one which is by comparison the fittest, by exposing them all to the fiercest struggle for survival.

The controversial question whether philosophy exists, or has any right to exist, is almost as old as philosophy itself. Time and again an entirely new philosophical movement arises which finally unmasks the old philosophical problems as pseudo-problems, and which confronts the wicked nonsense of philosophy with the good sense of meaningful, positive, empirical science. And time and again do the despised defenders of "traditional philosophy" try to explain to the leaders of the latest ... assault that the main problem of philosophy is the critical analysis of the appeal to authority of "experience"—precisely that "experience" which every latest discoverer of positivism is, as ever, artlessly taking for granted. ...

Methodological rules are here regarded as *conventions*. They might be described as the rules of the game of empirical science. ... The game of science is, in principle, without end. He who decides one day that scientific statements do not call for any further test, and that they can be regarded as finally verified, retires from the game. ...

... [from note, p. 59] our ordinary language is full of theories; ... observation is always *observation in light of theories*; ... it is only the inductivist prejudice which leads people to think that there could be a phenomenal language, free of theories. ... [end of note]

Whether philosophers will regard these methodological investigations as belonging to philosophy is, I fear, very doubtful. ... Yet it may be worth mentioning ... that not a few doctrines which are metaphysical, and thus certainly philosophical, could be interpreted as typical hypostatizations of methodological rules. An example of this ... is called "the principle of causality". ... It might indeed be said that the majority of the problems of theoretical philosophy, and the most interesting ones, can be re-interpreted ... as problems of method.

The "principle of causality" is the assertion that any event whatsoever *can* be causally explained—that it *can* be deductively predicted. According to the way in which one interprets the word "can" in this assertion, it will either be tautological (analytic) or else an assertion about reality (synthetic).[7] For if "can" means that it is always logically possible to construct a causal explanation, then the assertion is tautological, since for any prediction we can always find universal statements and initial conditions from which the prediction is derivable. (Whether these . . . have been tested . . . is another question.) If, however, "can" is meant to signify that the world is governed by strict laws . . . then the assertion is admittedly synthetic. But in this case it is *not falsifiable*. . . . I shall, therefore, neither adopt nor reject the "principle of causality. . . ."

. . . a severe test of a system presupposes that it is at the time sufficiently definite and final in form to make it impossible for new assumptions to be smuggled in. In other words, the system must be formulated sufficiently clearly . . . to make every new assumption easily recognizable. . . . This, I believe, is the reason why the form of a rigorous system is aimed at: It is the form of a so-called "*axiomatized system*. . . ."

Objections are bound to be raised against my proposal . . . by those who are influenced by the school of thought known as "conventionalism. . . ."[8] The source of the conventionalist philosophy would seem to be wonder at the . . . *simplicity* . . . as revealed by the laws of physics. . . . [T]he conventionalist treats this simplicity as our own creation. . . . Only the *laws of nature* are simple; and these, the conventionalist holds, are our own free creation. . . . For the conventionalist, theoretical natural science is . . . merely a logical construction. . . . It is not the properties of the world which determine this construction; on the contrary it is . . . an artificial world. . . . It is only of *this* world which science speaks.

According to this conventionalist point of view, laws of nature are not falsifiable by observation; for they are needed to determine what an observation . . . is. It is these laws, laid down by us, which form the indispensable basis for the regulation of our clocks, and the correction of our . . . measuring-rods. A clock is called "accurate" and a measuring rod "rigid" only if the movements measured with the help of these . . . satisfy the axioms . . . which we have decided to adopt. . . .

[P]eriods when science develops slowly will give little occasion for conflict—unless purely academic—to arise between scientists inclined towards conventionalism and others. . . . It will be quite otherwise in a time of crisis. Whenever the "classical" system of the day is threatened by the results of new experiments which might be interpreted as falsifications ... the system will appear unshaken to the conventionalist. He will explain away the inconsistencies ... by blaming our inadequate mastery of the system. Or he will eliminate them by suggesting *ad hoc* the adoption of certain ... hypotheses, or perhaps corrections to our measuring instruments.

In such times of crisis this conflict will become acute. We, and those who share our attitude, will hope to make new discoveries. ... But ... in the eyes of the conventionalist one principle only can help us to select a system as the chosen one from among other possible systems: it is the principles of selecting the simplest system ... which of course means in practice the "classical" system of the day. ...

Only with reference to methods applied ... is it at all possible to ask whether we are dealing with a conventionalist or an empirical theory. The only way to avoid conventionalism is by making a *decision*: the decision not to apply its methods. We decide that if our system is threatened we will never save it by any kind of conventionalist stratagem. ...

[W]e can utter no scientific statement that does not go far beyond what can be known with certainty "on the basis of immediate experience ..." The statement, "Here is a glass of water" cannot be verified by any observational experience. The reason is that the universals which appear in it cannot be correlated with any specific sense-experience. ... By the word "glass," for example, we denote physical bodies which exhibit certain law-like behavior, and the same holds for the word "water."

[I]f I am ordered: "Record what you are now experiencing" I shall hardly know how to obey this ambiguous order. Am I to report that I am writing; that I hear a bell ringing; a newsboy shouting; a loudspeaker droning; or am I to report, perhaps, that these noises irritate me? And even if the order could be obeyed: however rich a collection of statements might be assembled in this way, it could never add up to a *science*. A science needs points of view, and theoretical problems.

Popper's work was truly a milestone in twentieth-century philosophy of science. Positivism, already on the decline, was dealt a severe blow by Popper's revitalization of Hume's arguments. And yet Popper attempted, in the spirit of the mission of the positivists, to distinguish science from metaphysics and pseudoscience, and to explain the growth and development of scientific knowledge. His focus on method was widely adopted by subsequent philosophers of science. And the depth of Popper's analysis, including his admission of many weak points of his theory, is a model for philosophic method as well.

Although Popper sought to demarcate science from metaphysics, he also wished to retrieve metaphysics from the wastebin, claiming it is not "meaningless." And contrary to Dühem, Popper sees metaphysics as playing a role in both scientific discovery and empirical observation and test. Metaphysical commitments are important for guiding observation, research, and evaluation of theory. This reinvigoration of metaphysics is important for the critical works that follow.

Again, Popper realized the importance of methodological study for larger results in both science and philosophy. He claimed that method can be reinterpreted as a primary focus for philosophical study, and that many traditional metaphysical problems are in fact methodological in nature. The problem of causality, long a field for metaphysical speculation, is avoided by Popper's method. Popper neither admitted nor denied a principle of causality, but decided that such a principle is irrelevant due to methodological considerations, namely that it is either tautological[9] or impossible to falsify conclusively.

Popper admitted that there were grave difficulties in his method of falsifying theory by experiment. Science can, and sometimes does, proceed in bad faith by adopting *ad hoc* hypotheses, i.e., extraneous definitions and principles not contained within the original theory and designed exclusively to save a theory from falsification. Moreover, in some cases, scientists can simply deny falsifying evidence. To counter these problems, Popper asked us to make a decision, to act by convention, and proceed in good faith by seeking, rather than avoiding, rigorous test.

Another category of problem is perhaps more serious. Popper realized that all our observations, especially scientific experiments and applications, are governed by implicit theory. If such is the case, how can observations, which are dependent on a particular theory or framework, provide the falsifying ammunition for this same theory or framework? This difficulty was seized on by the next two authors we discuss in this chapter and was exploited by them to show that Popper's insights, while profound and productive, were perhaps still naive and inadequate to explain the dramatic changes in scientific theory throughout the history of science.

Revolution

Thomas Kuhn, an American born in 1922 and trained as a professional physicist, attempted a historical analysis of scientific revolutions and intended to describe scientific method as it is actually practiced before, during, and after such revolutions. He found Popper's methodology to be factually inaccurate as well as philosophically inadequate, partly for the reasons that are described in the previous section and that Popper himself was aware of. The inadequacy of Popper's method, according to Kuhn, is that it is actually impossible to implement. Experiments, observations, and applications of theory are too tied to what Kuhn calls the accepted "paradigm," or mind-set, that produced the theory to yield falsifying instances.

The outcome of Kuhn's analysis is not only the disparagement of Popperian method but also the destruction of the offered "criterion of demarcation" that separates science from metaphysics. Instead, Kuhn recognized that both physical theory and metaphysical assumptions form part of a paradigm that controls scientific progress as well as scientific revolution and upheaval. And instead of attempting to describe the history of science as a process of growth, Kuhn saw revolution, refutation, and even regression in the history of science.

Like most methodologists, Kuhn understood that the methodological project is tied to questions of epistemology and metaphysics. Kuhn opposed the positivistic separation of metaphysics from scientific methodology, much like Popper. However, Kuhn was at odds with Popper on several counts. Recall that Popper believed fundamentally in the idea that scientific knowledge is progressive and cumulative. Indeed, Popper's primary motivation for investigating scientific knowledge was to show how knowledge can grow. Kuhn believed that this was a simplistic interpretation of the history of science. Kuhn sought to diagnose the global epistemological and metaphysical assumptions that are found in these mistaken prescriptions for science. And in so doing, he outlines a different, more radical, creative view of the relationship between science and human knowledge, science and reality.

The following are selections from *The Structure of Scientific Revolutions*, first published in 1962.[10] Thomas Kuhn died in 1996.

History, if viewed as a repository for more than anecdote or chronology, could produce a decisive transformation in the image of science by which we are now possessed. That image has previously been drawn, even by scientists themselves, mainly from the study of finished scientific achievements as these are recorded in the classics and, more recently, in the textbooks from which each new scientific generation learns to practice its trade. . . . [A] concept of science drawn from them is no more likely to fit the enterprise that produced them than an image of a national culture drawn from a tourist brochure. . . . This essay . . . is a sketch of the quite different concept of science that can emerge from the historical record of the research activity itself.

Even from history, however, that new concept will not be forthcoming if historical data continue to be sought and scrutinized mainly to answer questions posed by the unhistorical stereotype drawn from science texts. Those texts have, for example, often seemed to imply that the content of science is uniquely exemplified by the observations, laws, and theories described in their pages. Almost as regularly, the same books have been read as saying that scientific methods are simply the ones illustrated by the manipulative techniques used in gathering textbook data. . . . The result has been a concept of science with profound implications about its nature and development.

If science is the . . . facts, theories, and methods collected in current texts, then . . . [s]cientific development becomes the piecemeal process by which these items have been added . . . to the ever growing stockpile that constitutes scientific technique and knowledge. . . .

In recent years, however, a few historians of science have been finding it more and more difficult to fulfill the function that the concept of development-by-accumulation assigns to them. As chroniclers of an incremental process, they discover that additional research makes it harder, not easier, to answer questions like: When was oxygen first discovered? Who first conceived of energy conservation? Increasingly, a few of them suspect that these are simply the wrong sorts of questions to ask. Perhaps science does not develop by the accumulations of individual discoveries and inventions. Simultaneously, these same historians confront growing difficulties in distinguishing the "scientific" component of past observation and belief from . . . "error" and "superstition." The more carefully they study, say, Aristotelian dynamics . . . the more certain they feel that those once current views of nature were, as a whole, neither less scientific nor more the product of human idiosyncrasy than those current today. . . . That . . . however, makes it difficult to see scientific development as a process of accretion. The same historical research that displays difficulties in isolating individual inventions and discoveries gives ground for profound doubts about the cumulative process through which . . . science [was] thought to have been compounded.

[T]he early developmental stages of most sciences have been characterized by continual competition between a number of distinct views of nature, each partially derived from, and all roughly compatible with, the dictates of scientific observation and method. What differentiated these various schools was not one or another failure of method—they were all scientific—but what we shall come to call their incommensurable ways of seeing the world and of practicing science in it. Observation and experience can and must drastically restrict the range of admissible scientific belief, else there would be no science. But they cannot alone determine a particular body of such belief. An apparently arbitrary element, compounded of personal and historical accident, is always a formative ingredient of the beliefs espoused by a given scientific community. . . .

Effective research scarcely begins before a scientific community thinks it has acquired firm answers to questions like the following: What are the fundamental entities of which the universe is composed? How do these interact with each other and the senses? What questions may legitimately be asked about such entities and what techniques employed in seeking solutions? . . . When examining normal science . . . we shall want finally to describe research as a strenuous and devoted attempt to force nature into the conceptual boxes supplied by professional education. . . .

Normal science, the activity in which most scientists inevitably spend almost all their time, is predicated on the assumption that the scientific community knows what the world is like. . . . Nevertheless, so long as those commitments retain an element of the arbitrary, the very nature of normal research ensures that novelty shall not be suppressed for very long . . . revealing an anomaly that cannot, despite repeated effort, be aligned with professional expectation. . . . [N]ormal science repeatedly goes astray. And when it does—when, that is, the profession can no longer evade anomalies that subvert the existing tradition of scientific practice—then begin the extraordinary investigations that lead to . . . scientific revolutions.

The most obvious examples of scientific revolutions are those famous episodes . . . associated with the names of Copernicus, Newton, Lavoisier, and Einstein. . . . Each [episode] necessitated the community's rejection of time-honored scientific theory in favor of another incompatible with it. Each produced a consequent shift in the problems available for scientific scrutiny and in the standards by which the profession determined what should count as admissible problem or as a legitimate problem-solution. And each transformed the scientific imagination in ways that we shall ultimately need to describe as a transformation of the world within which scientific work was done. Such changes . . . are the defining characteristics of scientific revolution.

These changes . . . can also be retrieved from the study of many other episodes that were not so obviously revolutionary. . . . For the far smaller professional group affected by them, Maxwell's equations were as revolutionary as Einstein's. . . . That is why a new theory, however special its range of application, is seldom or never just an increment to what is already known. Its assimilation requires reconstruction of prior theory and re-evaluation of prior fact. . . .

The commitments that govern normal science specify not only what sorts of entities it does contain, but also, by implication, those that it does not. It follows . . . that a discovery like that of oxygen or X-rays does not simply add one more item to the population of the scientist's world . . . the unexpected discovery is not simply factual in its import . . . the scientist's world is qualitatively transformed . . . by novelties of either fact or theory.

In this essay, "normal science" means research firmly based upon one or more past scientific achievements, achievements that some particular scientific community acknowledges for a time as supplying the foundation for its further practice. Today, such achievements are recounted, though seldom in their original form, by science textbooks . . . many of the famous classics of science fulfilled a similar function. Aristotle's *Physica* . . . Newton's *Principia*. . . . They were able to do so because they shared two essential characteristics. Their achievement was sufficiently unprecedented . . . [and] open-ended.

Achievements that share these two characteristics I shall henceforth refer to as "paradigms," a term that relates closely to "normal science." By choosing it, I mean to suggest that some accepted examples of actual scientific practice . . . provide models from which spring particular coherent traditions. . . . Men whose research is based on shared paradigms are committed to the same rules and standards for scientific practice. That commitment and the apparent consensus it produces are prerequisite for normal science, i.e., for the genesis and continuation of a particular research tradition. . . .

Today's physics textbooks tell the student that light is photons, i.e., quantum mechanical entities that exhibit some characteristics of waves and some of particles. Research proceeds accordingly. . . . That characterization of light is, however, scarcely half a century old. Before it was developed by Planck, Einstein, and others early in this century, physics texts taught that light was transverse wave motion. . . .

Nor was wave theory the first to be embraced by almost all practitioners of optical science. During the eighteenth century the paradigm for this field was provided by Newton's *Opticks,* which taught that light was material corpuscles. At that time physicists sought as evidence, as the early wave theorists had not, of the pressure exerted by light particles impinging on solid bodies. . . .

[B]etween remote antiquity and the end of the seventeenth century . . . there were a number of competing schools and subschools, most of them espousing one variant or another of Epicurean, Aristotelian, or Platonic theory. One group took light to be particles emanating from material bodies; for another it was the modification of the medium that intervened between the body and the eye; still another explained light in terms of an interaction in the medium with an emanation of the eye. . . . Each of the corresponding schools derived strength from its relation to some particular metaphysic, and each emphasized, as paradigmatic observations, the particular cluster of optical phenomena that its own theory could do most to explain. Other observations were dealt with by *ad hoc* elaborations, or they remained outstanding problems for further research.

At various times all these schools made significant contributions to the body of concepts . . . from which Newton drew the first nearly uniformly accepted paradigm. . . . Those men were scientists. Yet anyone examining a survey of philosophical optics before Newton may well conclude that, though the field's practitioners were scientists, the net result of their activity was something less than science. Being able to take no common body of belief for granted, each writer . . . felt forced to build his field anew from its foundations. . . .

History also suggests, however, some reasons for the difficulties encountered on that road. In the absence of a paradigm or some candidate for paradigm, all of the facts that could possibly pertain to the development of a given science are likely to seem equally relevant. As a result, early fact finding is a far more nearly random activity. . . . The resulting pool of facts contains those accessible to casual observation and experiment together with some of the more esoteric data retrievable from established crafts. . . .

But though this sort of fact-collecting has been essential to the origin of many significant sciences, anyone who has examined, for example, . . . Baconian natural histories of the seventeenth century will discover that it produces a morass. One somehow hesitates to call the literature that results scientific. The Baconian "histories" of heat, color, wind, mining, and so on, are filled with information, some of it recondite. But they juxtapose facts that will later prove revealing (e.g., heating by mixture) with others (e.g., the warmth of dung-heaps) that will for some time remain too complex to be integrated with theory at all. In addition, since any description must be partial, the typical natural history often omits from its immensely circum-stantial accounts just those details that later scientists will find sources of important illumination. . . .

When the individual scientists can take a paradigm for granted, he need no longer, in his major works, attempt to build his field anew, starting from principles and justifying the use of each concept introduced . . . the creative scientists can . . . concentrate exclusively upon the subtlest and most esoteric aspects of the natural phenom-ena that concern his group. And as he does this, his research com-muniques will begin to change in ways whose evolution has been too little studied but whose modern end products are obvious to all and oppressive to many. . . .

Today in the sciences, books are usually either texts or retro-spective reflections upon one aspect or another of the scientific life. The scientist who writes one is more likely to find his professional reputation impaired than enhanced.

The success of a paradigm—whether Aristotle's analysis of mo-tion, Ptolemy's computations of planetary position . . . or Maxwells' mathematization of the electromagnetic field—is at the start largely a promise of success in selected and still incomplete examples. . . .

Mopping-up operations are what engage most scientists throughout their careers. They constitute what I am here calling normal science. Closely examined, whether historically or in the contemporary laboratory, that enterprise seems an attempt to force nature into the preformed and relatively inflexible box that the para-digm supplies. . . .

By focusing attention upon a small range of relatively esoteric problems, the paradigm forces scientists to investigate some part of nature in detail and depth that would otherwise be unimaginable. . . . Synchrotons and radio telescopes are only the most recent examples of the lengths to which research workers will go if a paradigm assures them that the facts they seek are important. From Tycho Brahe to E. O. Lawrence, some scientists have acquired great reputations, not from any novelty of their discoveries, but from the precision, relia-bility, and scope of the methods they developed for the redetermina-tion of previously known fact.

A second unusual but smaller class of factual determination is directed to those facts that, though often without much intrinsic interest, can be compared directly with predictions from the paradigm theory ... there are seldom many areas in which scientific theory, particularly if it is cast in predominantly mathematical form, can be directly compared with nature. No more than three such areas are even yet accessible to Einstein's general theory of relativity.[11]

... that attempt to demonstrate agreement is a second type of normal experimental work, and it is even more obviously dependant than the first upon a paradigm.

A third class of experiments and observations exhausts, I think, the fact-gathering activities of normal science. It consists of empirical work undertaken to articulate the paradigm theory, resolving some of its residual ambiguities and permitting solutions of problems to which it had previously only drawn attention. ...

Perhaps the most striking feature of the normal research problems we have just encountered is how little they aim to produce major novelties. .... [T]hen why are these problems undertaken at all? ... Bringing a normal research problem to a conclusion is achieving the anticipated result in a new way, and it requires the solution of all sorts of complex instrumental, conceptual, and mathematical puzzles. The man who succeeds proves himself an expert puzzle-solver, and the challenge of the puzzle is an important part of what usually drives him on. ...

Though intrinsic value is no criterion for a puzzle, the assured existence of a solution is.

... one of the things a scientific community acquires with a paradigm is a criterion for choosing problems that, while the paradigm is taken for granted, can be assumed to have solutions. To a great extent these are the only problems that the community will admit as scientific or encourage its members to undertake. Other problems, including many that had previously been standard, are rejected as metaphysical. ...

The scientific enterprise as a whole does from time to time prove useful, open up new territory, display order, and test long-accepted belief. Nevertheless, *the individual* engaged on a normal research problem *is almost never doing any one of these things*. Once engaged, his motivation ... is the conviction that, if only he is skillful enough, he will succeed in solving a puzzle that no one before has solved or solved so well. ...

Throughout the eighteenth century those scientists who tried to derive the observed motion of the moon from Newton's laws of motion and gravitation consistently failed to do so. As a result, some of them suggested replacing the inverse square law with a law that deviated from it at small distances. To do that, however, would have been to change the paradigm, to define a new puzzle, and not solve the old one. In the event, scientists preserved the rules until, in 1750, one of them discovered how they could be successfully applied. . . .

Less local and temporary, though still not unchanging characteristics of science, are the higher level, quasi-metaphysical commitments that historical study so regularly displays. After about 1630, for example, and particularly after . . . Descartes . . . most physical scientists assumed that the universe was composed of microscopic corpuscles and that all natural phenomena could be explained in terms of corpuscular shape, size, motion, and interaction. That nest of commitments proved to be both metaphysical and methodological. As metaphysical, it told scientists what sorts of entities the universe did and did not contain: there was only shaped matter in motion. As methodological, it told them what ultimate laws and fundamental explanations must be like: laws must specify corpuscular motion and interaction, and explanation must reduce any given natural phenomenon to corpuscular action under these laws. . . .

The existence of this strong network of commitments—conceptual, theoretical, instrumental, and methodological—is a principal source of the metaphor that relates normal science to puzzle solving. Because it provides rules that tell the practitioner of a mature specialty what both the world and his science are like, he can concentrate with assurance upon the esoteric problems that these rules and existing knowledge define. . . .

Scientists can agree that a Newton, Lavoisier, Maxwell, or Einstein has produced an apparently permanent solution to a group of outstanding problems and still disagree . . . about the particular abstract characteristics that make those solutions. . . . They can, that is, agree in their *identification* of a paradigm without agreeing on, or even attempting to produce, a full *interpretation* or *rationalization* of it. . . . The coherence displayed by the research tradition . . . may not imply the existence of an underlying body of rules . . . that additional historical or philosophical investigation might uncover. . . . Paradigms may be prior to, and more binding, and more complete than any set of rules for research that could be unequivocally abstracted from them.... [D]eep debates over legitimate methods, problems, and standards of solution, ... though almost non-existent during periods of normal science, ... recur regularly just before and during scientific revolutions, the period when paradigms are first under attack and then subject to change.... The transition from Newtonian to quantum mechanics evoked many debates about both the nature and standards of physics, some of which still continue.[12]...

Normal science, the puzzle solving activity we have just examined, is a highly cumulative enterprise, eminently successful in its aim, in the steady extension of the scope and precision of scientific knowledge. In all these respects it fits with great precision the most usual image of scientific work. Yet one standard is missing. Normal science does not aim at novelties of fact or theory and, when successful, finds none. New and unsuspected phenomena are, however repeatedly uncovered by scientific research, and radical new theories have again and again been invented....

Discovery commences with the awareness of anomaly, i.e., with the recognition that nature has somehow violated the paradigm-induced expectations that govern normal science. It then continues with a more or less extended exploration of the area of anomaly. And it closes only when the paradigm theory has been adjusted so that the anomalous has become the expected. Assimilating a new sort of fact demands more than additive of adjustment of theory, and until that adjustment is completed—until the scientist has learned to see nature in a different way—the new fact is not quite a scientific fact at all.

... we need a new vocabulary and concepts for analyzing ... discovery.... Though undoubtedly correct, the sentence, "Oxygen was discovered," misleads by suggesting that discovering something is a single simple act assimilable to our usual (and also questionable) concept of seeing. That is why we so readily assume that discovering, like seeing or touching, should be unequivocally attributable to an individual and to a moment in time.[13] But the latter attribution is impossible and the former often is as well ... because discovering a new sort of phenomenon is necessarily a complex event, one which involves recognizing both *that* something is and *what* it is....

In science ... novelty emerges only with difficulty, manifested by resistance, against a background provided by expectation....

[N]ovelty ordinarily emerges only for the man who, knowing *with precision* what he should expect, is able to recognize that something has gone wrong. Anomaly appears only against the background provided by the paradigm. . . .

Galileo's contributions to the study of motion depended closely upon difficulties discovered in Aristotle's theory by scholastic critics. . . . Thermodynamics was born from the collision of two nineteenth century physical theories, and quantum mechanics from a variety of difficulties surrounding black-body radiation, specific heats, and the photoelectric effect. Furthermore, in all these cases . . . the awareness of anomaly had lasted so long and penetrated so deep that one can appropriately describe the fields affected by it as in a state of growing crisis. . . .

Consider . . . the late nineteenth century crisis in physics that prepared the way for the emergence of relativity theory. One root of that crisis can be traced to the late seventeenth century when a number of natural philosophers, most notably Leibniz, criticized Newton's retention of an updated version of the classic conception of absolute space. They were very nearly, though never quite, able to show that absolute positions and absolute motions were without any function at all in Newton's system, and they did succeed in hinting at the considerable aesthetic appeal a fully relativistic conception of space and motion would later come to display. But their critique was purely logical. . . . [T]hey did not dream that transition to a relativistic system could have observational consequences. . . . As a result, their views died with them during the early decades of the eighteenth century. . . .

The technical problems to which a relativistic philosophy of space was ultimately to be related began to enter normal science with the acceptance of the wave theory of light after about 1815, though they evoked no crisis until the 1890's. If light is wave motion propagated in a mechanical ether governed by Newton's Laws, then both celestial observation and terrestrial experiment become potentially capable of detecting drift through the ether . . . and the detection of ether drift . . . became a recognized problem for normal science. Much special equipment was built to resolve it. That equipment, however, detected no observable drift, and the problem was therefore transferred from the experimentalists to the theoreticians. During the central decades of the century, Fresnel, Stokes, and others devised numerous articulations of ether theory designed to explain the failure of observable drift. Each of these articulations assumed that a moving body drags some fraction of the ether with it. And each was sufficiently successful to explain the negative results . . . including the famous experiment of Michelson and Morley. . . .

The situation changed again only with the gradual acceptance of Maxwell's electromagnetic theory. . . . Maxwell himself was a Newtonian who believed that light and electromagnetism in general were due to viable displacements of the particles of a mechanical ether[14]. . . .

Maxwell's discussion of the electromagnetic behavior of bodies in motion had made no reference to ether drag, and it proved very difficult to introduce such drag into his theory. . . . The years after 1890 therefore witnessed a long series of attempts, both experimental and theoretical, to detect motion with respect to ether and to work ether drag into Maxwell's theory. . . . The former were uniformly unsuccessful . . ., the latter produced a number of promising results . . . but they . . . finally resulted in just that proliferation of competing theories that we have previously found to be the concomitant of crisis. It is against this historical setting that Einstein's special theory of relativity emerged in 1905. . . .

Though [scientists] may begin to lose faith and then to consider alternatives, they do not renounce the paradigm that has led them to a crisis. They do not, that is, treat anomalies as counter-instances, though in the vocabulary of philosophy of science that is what they are. . . . No process yet disclosed by the historical study of scientific development at all resembles the methodological stereotype of falsification by direct comparison with nature.

. . . [D]efenders will do what we have already seen scientists doing when confronted by anomaly. They will devise numerous articulations and *ad hoc* modifications of their theory in order to eliminate the apparent conflict. . . . [T]hese epistemological counterinstances . . . will . . . help to permit the emergence of new and different analysis of science within which they are no longer a source of trouble. Furthermore . . . these anomalies will then no longer seem to be simply facts. From a new theory of scientific knowledge, they may instead seem very much like tautologies, statements of situations that could not conceivably have been otherwise.

It has often been observed, for example, that Newton's second law of motion, though it took centuries of difficult factual and theoretical research to achieve, behaves for those committed to Newton's theory very much like a purely logical statement that no amount of observation could refute.[15] . . .

To reject one paradigm without simultaneously substituting another is to reject science itself. . . .

The early attacks upon the resistant problem will have followed the paradigm rules quite closely. But with continuing resistance, more and more of the attacks upon it will have involved some minor or not so minor articulations of the paradigm . . . the rules of normal science become increasingly blurred. . . .

When acute, this situation is sometimes recognized by the scientists involved. . . . Einstein . . . wrote . . . , "It was as if the ground had been pulled out from under one, with no firm foundation to be seen anywhere, upon which one could have built."[16] And Wolfgang Pauli, . . . in the months before Heisenberg's paper on matrix mechanics . . . wrote to a friend, "At the moment physics is again terribly confused. In any case, it is too difficult for me, and I wish I had been a movie comedian or something of the sort and had never heard of physics. . . ."

And . . ., more than in any other part of the post-paradigm development of science, [the scientist] will look almost like our most prevalent image of the scientist. He will, in the first place, often seem a man searching at random, trying experiments just to see what will happen, looking for an effect whose nature he cannot quite guess. Simultaneously, . . . the scientist in crisis will constantly try to generate speculative theories, that, if successful, may disclose the road to a new paradigm and, if unsuccessful, can be surrendered with relative ease. . . .

[T]he new paradigm, or a sufficient hint to permit later articulation, emerges all at once, sometimes in the middle of the night, in the mind of the man deeply immersed in crisis. What the nature of that final stage is—how an individual invents (or finds he has invented) a new way of giving order to data now all assembled—must here remain inscrutable and may be permanently so. . . .

When paradigms enter, as they must, into a debate about paradigm choice, their role is necessarily circular. Each group uses its own paradigm to argue in that paradigm's defense.

The resulting circularity does not . . . make the arguments wrong. . . . The man who premises a paradigm when arguing in its defense can nonetheless provide a clear example of what scientific practice will be like for those who adopt the new view of nature. . . . Yet, whatever its force, the status of the circular argument is only that of persuasion. It cannot be made logically or even probabilistically compelling for those who refuse to step into the circle. . . .

In principle, a new phenomenon might emerge without reflecting destructively upon any part of past scientific practice ... scientific development would be genuinely cumulative.... Of course, science ... might have developed in that fully cumulative manner. Many people believe that it did so, and most still seem to suppose that cumulation is at least the ideal that historical development would display if only it had not so often been distorted by human idiosyncrasy ... the view of science-as-cumulation is entangled with a dominant epistemology that takes knowledge to be a construction placed directly upon raw sense data by the mind. ...

The man who is striving to solve a problem defined by existing knowledge is not, however, just looking around. He knows what he wants to achieve, and he designs his instruments accordingly. Unanticipated novelty, the new discovery, can emerge only to the extent that his anticipations prove wrong. ... But if new theories are called forth to resolve anomalies in the relation of an existing theory to nature, then the successful new theory must somewhere permit predictions that are different from those derived from its predecessor. That difference could not occur if the two were logically compatible. ...

[C]ontemporary interpretation ... would restrict the range and meaning of an accepted theory so that it could not possibly conflict with any later theory that made predictions about some of the same natural phenomena. ... [T]hese objections can be developed as follows. Relativistic dynamics cannot have shown Newtonian dynamics to be wrong, for Newtonian dynamics is still used with great success by most engineers and, in selected applications, by many physicists. ... If Einsteinian science seems to make Newtonian dynamics wrong, that is only because some Newtonians were so incautious as to claim that Newtonian theory yielded entirely precise results or that it was valid at very high relative velocities. Since they could not have had any evidence for such claims, they betrayed the standards of science when they made them. In so far as Newtonian theory was ever a truly scientific theory, it still is. Only extravagant claims for the theory ... can have been shown by Einstein to be wrong. ...

But to save theories in this way, their range of application must be restricted to those phenomena and to that precision of observation with which the experimental evidence in hand already deals ... such a limitation prohibits the scientists from claiming to speak "scientifically" about any phenomenon not already observed. ... [T]he result of accepting [these prohibitions] would be the end of the research through which science may develop further.... If positivistic restrictions are taken literally, the mechanism that tells the scientific community what problems may lead to fundamental change must cease to function.... Is it really any wonder that the price of significant scientific advance is a commitment that runs the risk of being wrong?

... paradigm debates always involve the question: Which problems is it more significant to have solved ...? Something even more fundamental than standards and values is, however, also at stake. I have so far argued only that paradigms are constitutive of science. Now I wish to display a sense in which they are constitutive of nature as well. ...

Can it conceivably be an accident, for example, that Western astronomers first saw change in the previously immutable heavens during the half-century after Copernicus' new paradigm was first proposed? The Chinese, whose cosmological beliefs did not preclude celestial change, had recorded the appearance of many new stars in the heavens at a much earlier date.... Using traditional instruments, some as simple as a piece of thread, late sixteenth century astronomers repeatedly discovered that comets wandered at will through the space previously reserved for the immutable planets and stars. The very ease and rapidity with which astronomers saw new things when looking at old objects with old instruments may make us wish to say that, after Copernicus, astronomers lived in a different world. ...

Since remote antiquity most people have seen one or another heavy body swinging back and forth on a string or chain until it finally comes to rest. To the Aristotelians, who believed that a heavy body is moved by its own nature from a higher position to a state of natural rest at a lower one, the swinging body was simply falling with difficulty. Constrained by the chain, it could achieve rest at its low point only after a torturous motion and a considerable time. Galileo, on the other hand, looking at the swinging body, saw a pendulum, a body that almost succeeded in repeating the same motion over and over again ad infinitum. And having seen that much, Galileo observed other properties as well and constructed many of the most significant and original parts of his new dynamics around them.... Until that ... paradigm was invented, there were no pendulums, but only swinging stones, for the scientist to see. Pendulums were brought into existence by something very like a paradigm-induced gestalt switch. ...

Many readers will surely want to say that what changes with a paradigm is only the scientist interpretation of observations that themselves are fixed once and for all by the nature of the environment and of the perceptual apparatus. . . . On this view . . . Aristotle and Galileo both saw pendulums, but they differed in their interpretations of what they both had seen.

Let me say at once that this very usual view . . . can be neither all wrong nor a mere mistake. Rather it is an essential part of a philosophical paradigm initiated by Descartes and developed at the same time as Newtonian dynamics. That paradigm has served both science and philosophy well. Its exploitation, like that of dynamics itself, has been fruitful of a fundamental understanding that perhaps could not have been achieved in any other way. But as the example of Newtonian dynamics also indicates, even the most striking past success provides no guarantee that crisis can be indefinitely postponed. Today, research in parts of philosophy, psychology, linguistics, and even art history, all converge to suggest that the traditional paradigm is somehow askew. That failure to fit is also made increasingly apparent by the historical study of science to which most of our attention is . . . directed here.

Scientists are not, of course, the only group that tends to see its discipline's past as developing linearly toward its present. The temptation to rewrite history backward is both omnipresent and perennial. But scientists are more affected by the temptation to rewrite history, partly because the results of scientific research show no obvious dependence upon historical context of the inquiry, and partly because, except during crisis and revolution, the scientist's contemporary position seems so stable. . . .

Kuhn claimed that it is wrong to interpret science as a progressive "march" (to use Dühem's characterization) toward expanded knowledge. Primarily, he believed that revolutionary paradigm shifts in scientific practice rendered prerevolutionary science incommensurable with postrevolutionary science. That is, scientists are working in a different world with a different language, and they are working toward different goals with different criteria for success after a revolution. All of these differences make translation from prerevolutionary to postrevolutionary science difficult, if not impossible, and obviate the idea that scientific knowledge is an edifice built on the foundations and structure of previous epochs.

Furthermore, he believed that the idea that scientific knowledge grows cumulatively is itself tied to a particular philosophical and scientific paradigm. This paradigm ushered in the seventeenth-century revolution in physical science, and it served this revolution well. Kuhn claimed that this mind-set was "initiated by Descartes" and is a result of a particular epistemological view. Recall that Descartes and Galileo separated the world into the physical realm of objects and the mental arena of subjective qualities. This leads to the idea that the physical world is fixed and unchanging while interpretations are fallible and in need of revision. In our march toward certainty, scientific theories are revised to make them correspond to an external, objective, physical reality, according to this view.

This paradigm worked well for classical physics, but it is in need of revision in light of twentieth-century physical theory. Indeed, Planck, Heisenberg, and others have said that quantum theory resulted from the recognition of the fact that the observer cannot be omitted from even the most objective study of physical phenomena. And if this is the case for science, then why not for philosophy? Thus, Kuhn presents his critical methodology of science as a catalyst for revolution in philosophy.

There is a certain irony in presenting Kuhn's view in a text like this one. After all, this text, like those Kuhn analyzes in his discussions of science texts, succumbs to the temptation to "rewrite history," as any edited version of history must do. Furthermore, the presentation herein is tied to a paradigm, one that views complex and interdependent relationships between dominant philosophical and scientific themes throughout history. Kuhn has foreshadowed such irony in his discussions of Cartesian epistemology and its relationship to Newtonian dynamics, and in his claim that both are being overthrown in the twentieth century. In fact, *The Structure of Scientific Revolutions* has itself become a canonical text for a new paradigm in philosophy of science.

A true historical analysis of method, according to Kuhn, actually displaces objective methodological study. He claimed that in actual scientific practice, "paradigms may be prior to, and more binding" than methodological rules. Certainly, he claimed that Popper's "stereotype of falsification" has not been evident in any historical episode in scientific history. If Kuhn is right, perhaps we should de-emphasize abstract method in favor of more historically and culturally sensitive analysis. The next section explores this theme to the full.

For all of Kuhn's radical ideas, he has significant agreements with his predecessors. Kuhn agrees with Popper on the impossibility of analyzing the psychology of discovery. He also talks of "scientific advance" and the risk of theories being "wrong." This underlying realism and latent progressivism is perhaps a sign that Kuhn has not provoked a full revolution, but only pointed out a crisis state in philosophy of science. In any case, the influence of Kuhn's work has been immense. The next view takes Kuhnian analysis a step further and prescribes more radical views on method in science and philosophy.

Anarchy

Paul Feyerabend takes historical analysis and radical criticism a step further in *Against Method: Outline of an Anarchistic Theory of Knowledge*. While historical analysis might seem a natural approach to a philosophical discussion of scientific method and results, such an approach violates some cherished principles both in philosophy of science and philosophy as a whole. First, it seems to blur the lines between descriptive and prescriptive analysis. Philosophers of science might claim they are not trying to describe what scientists actually do, but prescribe how we can judge and understand scientific theory and practice. Popper is a clear example here. He does not seek to describe the psychological processes that lead to a discovery (what he has called elsewhere "the context of discovery") but rather to offer criteria that are helpful in the judgement of scientific systems (what he has called "the context of justification").

This distinction is closely linked to the subject/object split set up during the modern scientific and philosophical revolution, and itself is perhaps too caught up in the underlying assumptions of science to be held as an a priori distinction in a discussion of scientific method. (Kuhn also realizes similar problems with traditional philosophy of science, e.g., his discussion of Cartesian epistemology and its ties to scientific practice.)

Second, historical analysis, if carried to the extreme, can spill into personal and political dimensions that are often viewed as outside the bounds of proper philosophical argument in general. For example, the *ad hominem* fallacy, the fallacy of arguing against the person rather than the theory, is supposed to be off-limits to serious philosophy. In the preceding section, we saw how Kuhn tried to justify his interest in historical analysis and do battle with the subject/object distinction. Paul Feyerabend understands this as well, and he is further willing to extend his philosophical discussions to personal and political dimensions. Indeed, he sees "anarchistic" method, in both science and philosophy, as the best route to humane progress for science, society, and the individual thinker.

The following are selections from *Against Method.*[17]

History is full of "accidents and conjectures and curious juxtapositions of events"....[18] Are we really to believe that the naive and simple-minded rules which methodologists take as their guide are capable of accounting for such a "maze of interactions"?[19] And is it not clear that successful *participation* in a process of this kind is possible only for a ruthless opportunist who is not tied to any particular philosophy and who adopts whatever procedure seems to fit the occasion?

This is indeed the conclusion that has been drawn by intelligent and thoughtful observers.... "The external conditions," writes Einstein, "which are set for [the scientist] by the facts of experience do not permit him to let himself be too much restricted, in the construction of his conceptual world, by the adherence to an epistemological system. He therefore, must appear to the systematic epistemologist as a type of unscrupulous opportunist...."[20]

This being the case, the history of science will be as complex, chaotic, full of mistakes, and entertaining as are the minds of those who invented them. Conversely, a little brainwashing will go a long way in making the history of science duller, simpler, more uniform, more "objective" and more easily accessible to treatment by strict and unchangeable rules.

Scientific education as we know it today has precisely this aim. It simplifies "science" by simplifying its participants: first, a domain of research is defined. The domain is separated from the rest of history (physics, for example, is separated from metaphysics and from theology) and given a "logic" of its own. A thorough training in such a "logic" then conditions those working in the domain; it makes *their actions* more uniform and it freezes large parts of the *historical process* as well.... Stable "facts" arise and persevere despite the vicissitudes of history ... a scientific education as described above (and as practised in our schools) cannot be reconciled with a humanitarian attitude. It is in conflict "with the cultivation of individuality which alone produces, or can produce, well developed human beings"; it "maims by compression, like a Chinese lady's foot, every part of human nature which stands out prominently, and tends to make a person markedly different in outline"[21] from the ideals of rationality that happen to be fashionable in the sciences, or in the philosophy of science....

The idea of a method that contains firm, unchanging, and absolutely binding principles for conducting the business of science meets considerable difficulty when confronted with the results of historical research. We find then, that there is not a single rule, however plausible, and however firmly grounded in epistemology, that is not violated at some time or other. It becomes apparent that such violations are not accidental events, they are not the results of insufficient knowledge or of inattention which might have been avoided. On the contrary we see that they are necessary for progress. Indeed, one of the most striking features of recent discussions in the history and philosophy of science is the realization that events and developments, such as the invention of atomism in antiquity, the Copernican revolution, the rise of modern atomism ... ocurred only because some thinkers either *decided* not to be bound by certain "obvious" methodological rules, or because they simply *unwittingly broke* them.

This liberal practice, I repeat, is not just a *fact* of the history of science. It is both reasonable and *absolutely necessary* for the growth of knowledge. More specifically, one can show the following: given any rule, however "fundamental" or "necessary" for science, there are always circumstances when it is advisable not only to ignore this rule, but to adopt its opposite. For example, there are circumstances when it is advisable to introduce ... *ad hoc* hypotheses, or hypotheses which contradict well-established and generally accepted experimental results, or hypotheses whose content is smaller than the content of the existing and empirically adequate alternative, or self-inconsistent hypotheses, and so on....

There are even circumstances—and they occur rather frequently—when *argument* loses its forward-looking aspect and becomes a hindrance to progress. Nobody would claim that the teaching of *small children* is exclusively a matter of argument ... and almost everyone agrees that what looks like the result of reason—the mastery of language, ... logical ability—is due partly to indoctrination and partly to a process of *growth* that proceeds with the force of natural law. And where arguments *do* seem to have an effect, this is much more often due to their *physical repetition* than to their *semantic content....*

That interests, forces, propaganda and brainwashing techniques play a much greater role than is commonly believed in the growth of our knowledge and in the growth of science, can also be seen from an analysis of the *relation between idea and action*. It is often taken for granted that a clear and distinct understanding of new ideas precedes, and should precede, their formulation and their institutional expression. (An investigation starts with a problem, says Popper.) *First* we have an idea . . . *then* we act. . . . Yet this is certainly not the way in which small children develop. They use words, they combine them, they play with them, until they grasp a meaning that has so far been beyond their reach. And the initial playful activity is an essential prerequisite of the final act of understanding. . . .

For an empiricist, "progress" will mean transition to a theory that provides direct empirical tests. . . . Some people believe quantum theory to be a theory of this kind. For others, "progress" may mean unification and harmony. . . . This is how Einstein viewed the general theory of relativity. *And my thesis is that anarchism helps to achieve progress in any one of the senses one cares to choose.* Even a law-and-order science will succeed only if anarchistic moves are occasionally allowed to take place. . . .

A scientist who wishes to maximize the empirical content of the views he holds and who wants to understand them as clearly as he possibly can must therefore introduce other views; that is, he must adopt a *pluralistic methodology.* He must compare ideas with other ideas . . . and he must try to improve rather than discard the views that have failed the competition. . . . Knowledge so conceived is not a series of self consistent theories that converges towards an ideal view; it is not a gradual approach to the truth. It is rather an ever increasing *ocean of mutually incompatible (and perhaps even incommensurable) alternatives,* each single theory . . . each myth that is part of the collection forcing the others into greater articulation and all of them contributing, via this process of competition, to the development of our consciousness.

. . . observational reports, experimental results, "factual" statements, either *contain* theoretical assumptions or *assert* them by the manner in which they are used. . . . Thus our habit of saying "the table is brown" when we view it under normal circumstances . . . but "the table seems to be brown" when . . . lighting conditions are poor . . . expresses the belief that some of our sensory impressions are veridical while others are not. We also take for granted that the material medium between the object and us exerts no distorting influence. . . .

[W]e need a set of alternative assumptions, or, as these assumptions will be quite general, constituting, as it were, an alternative world, *we need a dream-world in order to discover the features of the real world we think we inhabit* (and which may actually be just another dream-world). The first step in our criticism of familiar concepts and procedures . . . must be to break the circle. . . . We must invent a new conceptual system that suspends, or clashes with the most carefully established principles . . .[22]

[T]he case of the consistency condition can be dealt with. . . . It is well known . . . that Newton's theory is inconsistent with Galileo's . . . ; that statistical thermodynamics is inconsistent with the second law of phenomenological theory; . . . and so on. . . .

Now it seems to me that these brief considerations, although leading to an interesting and tactical criticism of the consistency condition, . . . do not yet go to the heart of the matter. . . . [A] defender of the consistency condition might point out . . . that . . . The exclusion of alternatives is . . . simply a measure of expediency: their invention not only does not help, it even hinders progress by absorbing time and manpower that could be devoted to better things. . . . This is how a practicing scientist will defend his concentration on a single theory. . . .[23]

But . . . facts and theories are much more intimately connected. . . . Not only is the description of every single fact dependent on *some* theory . . . , but there may also exist facts which cannot be unearthed except with the help of alternatives to the theory to be tested, and which become unavailable as soon as such alternatives are excluded. . . .

This being the case, the invention and articulation of alternatives may have to precede the production of refuting facts. . . .

Assume that physicists have adopted, either consciously or unconsciously, the idea of the uniqueness of complementarity[24] and that they elaborate the orthodox point of view and refuse to consider alternatives . . . Now if it is true . . . that many facts become available only with the help of alternatives, then the refusal to consider them *will result in the elimination of potentially refuting facts as well.* . . . The chances for the consideration of alternatives are now very slight indeed. The final success of the fundamental assumptions of quantum theory, and of the idea of complementarity, seems to be assured.

At the same time it is evident, on the basis of our considerations, that this appearance of success *cannot in the least be regarded as a sign of the truth and correspondence with nature.* Quite the contrary, the suspicion arises that the absence of major difficulties is a result of the decrease of empirical content brought about by the elimination of alternatives. . . . Its "success" is *entirely man-made* . . . all contact with the world has been lost. . . . How can we possibly test, or improve upon, the truth of a theory if it is built in such a manner that any conceivable event can be described in terms of its principles? . . . This,

I think, is the most decisive argument against any method that encourages uniformity . . . It enforces an unenlightened conformism, . . . it leads to a deterioration of intellectual capabilities, . . . it destroys the most precious gift of the young—their tremendous power of imagination. . . .

[A]lternatives . . . may be taken from the past as well. . . . The whole history of a subject is utilized in the attempt to improve its most recent and most "advanced" stage. The separation between the history of a science, its philosophy and the science itself dissolves into thin air and so does the separation between science and non-science. . . .

An . . . interesting example is the revival of traditional medicine in Communist China. We start with a familiar development: a great country with great traditions is subjected to Western domination and is exploited in the customary way. A new generation recognizes or thinks it recognizes the material and intellectual superiority of the West and traces it back to science. Science is imported, taught, and pushes aside all traditional elements. Scientific chauvinism triumphs. . . . Things incompatible with the results must be eliminated. Old style doctors, for example, must either be removed from medical practice, or they must be re-educated. Herbal medicine, acupuncture. . . . and the underlying philosophy are a thing of the past, no longer to be taken seriously. This was the attitude up to about 1954 when . . . the ministry of health started a campaign for the revival of traditional medicine. No doubt the campaign was politically inspired. . . . But it provided the counterforce that was needed to . . . make a plurality . . . of views possible.

Now this . . . has led to the most interesting and puzzling discoveries both in China and the West and to the realization that there are effects and means of diagnosis which modern medicine cannot repeat and for which it has no explanation. . . .

Pluralism of theories and metaphysical views is not only important for methodology, it is an essential part of a humanitarian outlook. Progressive educators have always tried to develop the individuality of their pupils. . . . Such an education, however, has very often seemed to be a futile exercise in day-dreaming. For is it not necessary to prepare the young for life *as it actually is*? Does this not mean that they must learn *one particular set of views* to the exclusion of everything else? . . . this need not happen. It is possible to *retain* what one might call the freedom of artistic creation *and use it to the full,* not just as a road of escape but as a necessary means for discovering and perhaps even changing the features of the world we live in. . . .

No single theory ever agrees with all the known facts in its domain. . . . [A] theory . . . inconsistent not with a recondite fact . . . but with circumstances which are easily noticed and which are familiar to everyone . . . is Parmenides' theory of the unchanging and homogeneous One. . . . The theory has much in its favor, and plays a role even today, for example in the general theory of relativity. Used in an undeveloped form by Anaximander, it led to the insight repeated by Heisenburg . . . that the basic substance, or basic elements of the universe, cannot obey the same laws as the visible elements. . . .

[N]atural interpretations[25] have been regarded either as *a priori* suppositions of science, or as *prejudices* which must be removed. . . . The first view is that of Kant. . . . the second view is due to Bacon. . . . Galileo is one of those rare thinkers who neither wants forever to retain natural interpretations nor altogether eliminate them. . . . He insists upon a critical discussion to decide which natural interpretation can be kept and which must be replaced. . . . The argument from falling stones[26] seems to refute the Copernican view. This may be due to an inherent disadvantage of Copernicanism; but it may also be due to the presence of natural interpretations which are in need of improvement. . . .

Galileo replaces one natural interpretation by a very different and as yet (1630) at least partly unnatural interpretation. How does he proceed? How does he manage to introduce absurd . . . assumptions, such as the assertion that the earth moves, and yet get them a just and alternative hearing? . . . Galileo uses *propaganda.* . . . [T]he experience on which Galileo wants to base the Copernican view is nothing but the result of his own fertile imagination . . . it has been *invented.* . . .

Galileo urges us to "remember" . . . "There remains observable only that part in which neither the tower nor we are participants" . . . "transfer this argument to the whirling of the earth and to the rock placed on top of the tower, whose motion you cannot discern because, in common with the rock, you possess from the earth that motion which is required for following the tower . . . the circular portion of the motion which is common to the stone and the eye continues to be imperceptible. The straight motion alone is sensible. . . ."

[E]xperience now ceases to be the unchangeable fundament which it is both in common sense and in the Aristotelian philosophy. The attempt to support Copernicus makes experience "fluid" in the very same manner in which it makes the heavens fluid. . . . An empiricist who starts from experience . . . now loses the very ground on which he stands. . . .

We can now add that it leads to the invention of a *new kind of experience* that is not only more sophisticated *but also far more speculative* than is the experience of Aristotle or of common sense. . . . [O]ne may say that *Galileo invents an experience that has metaphysical ingredients.* . . .

Let it be noted, incidentally, that Galileo's procedure drastically reduces the content of dynamics. Aristotelian dynamics was a general theory of change, comprising locomotion, quantitative change, generation and corruption. . . . Galileo's dynamics and its successors deal with *locomotion* only, and here again just with locomotion of *matter*.

Galileo prevails because of his style and his clever techniques of persuasion, because he writes in Italian rather than Latin, and because he appeals to people who are temperamentally opposed to the old ideas and the standards of learning connected with them. . . .

It is obvious that . . . a new world view will take a long time appearing, and that we may never succeed in formulating it in its entirety. . . . This need to *wait*, and to *ignore* large masses of critical observations and measurements, is hardly ever discussed in our methodologies. Disregarding the possibility that a new physics or a new astronomy might have to be judged by a new theory of knowledge . . . scientists at once confront it with the *status quo* and announce triumphantly "it is not in agreement with facts and received principles". . . . How shall we proceed in order to bring about . . . a fair comparison?

The first step is clear: we must *retain* the new cosmology until it has been supplemented by the necessary auxiliary sciences. . . . We may, of course, try to explain our action, . . . but we cannot support such an explanation by a single objective reason. Whatever explanation we give is nothing but a *verbal gesture*, a gentle invitation to participate in the development of a new philosophy. . . .

[A]llegiance to the new ideas will have to be brought about by means other than arguments. It will have to be brought about *by irrational means* such as propaganda, emotion, *ad hoc* hypotheses. . . .

The similarity with the arts which has often been asserted arises at ... this point. Once it has been realized that close empirical fit is no virtue and that it must be relaxed in times of change, then style, elegance of expression, simplicity of presentation, tension of plot and narrative, and seductiveness of content become important features of our knowledge. ... They create and maintain interest in a theory that ... would be inferior to its rivals when judged by the customary standards. It is in this context that much of Galileo's work should be seen. ...

Is it not clear that our beautiful and shining methodologies which demand from us that we concentrate on theories of high empirical content, which implore us to take ... refutations seriously ... would give extremely bad advice in the circumstances? ...

Galileo, who was convinced of the truth of the Copernican view and who did not share the ... belief in a stable experience, looked for new kinds of fact which might support Copernicus and still be acceptable to all. Such facts he obtained in two different ways. First, by the invention of the telescope, which changed the sensory core of everyday experience ... and by his principle of relativity and his dynamics which changed its conceptual components. ...

[A] comprehensive empirical theory of motion is replaced by a much narrower theory ..., just as "empirical" experience is replaced by an experience that contains speculative elements. This, I suggest, was the actual procedure followed by Galileo. Proceeding in this way, he exhibited style, a sense of humor, an elasticity and elegance, and an awareness of the valuable weaknesses of human thinking. ... Here is an almost inexhaustible source of material for methodological speculation and, much more importantly, for the recovery of those features of knowledge which not only inform, but which also delight us. ...

The idea that science can, and should, be run according to fixed and universal rules, is both unrealistic and pernicious. It is *unrealistic,* for it takes too simple a view of the talents of man and of the circumstances which encourage, or cause, their development. And it is *pernicious,* for the attempt to enforce the rules is bound to increase our professional qualifications at the expense of our humanity. In addition, the idea is detrimental to science, for it neglects the complex and historical conditions which influence scientific change. It makes our science less adaptable and more dogmatic: every methodological rule is associated with cosmological assumptions, so that using the rule we take it for granted that the assumptions are correct. ...

In this last passage Feyerabend makes it clear that he is not simply describing what actually happens in history, but he is in fact analyzing the good and valuable components of scientific method. He is not simply discussing something like the psychological "context of discovery," but prescribing anarchism as the proper method for justifying and improving scientific knowledge. He views a proper scientific methodology as incorporating both description and prescription, and finds that this realistic approach favors pluralism and anarchy. Feyerabend claims that separating the history of science from the study of science is naive and simplistic. Methodologies which do not take into account historical description are detrimental characterizations of the process of science, on this view.

In his analysis, Feyerabend takes some of Kuhn's work for granted. Feyerabend agrees with Kuhn's description of the bulk of scientific work: both contend that most research is constrained by inarticulate assumptions. But the "paradigm" driven "normal science" of Kuhn is the target for much of Feyerabend's criticisms. Feyerabend believes such normal science is not a benign part of the evolution of science but an obstacle to overcome—by any means necessary.

In order to enrich science, according to Feyerabend, the scientist cannot wait for the development of an anomaly. Such anomalies may never arise in the absence of "invention and articulation of alternatives." Scientists should propose such articulations much like artists create works of art. Even Dühem's "barrier" of "logical contradiction" should not be an impediment. Inconsistent theories, as well as self-inconsistent hypotheses, have a place in Feyerabend's process of scientific development.

In proposing his "anarchistic theory of knowledge," Feyerabend understands, as did his predecessors, that there is a relationship between method and metaphysics, between scientific procedure and the status of scientific results. Underlying his criticism is a strong version of empiricism which relies on an unstable, fluid, human-influenced picture of empirical fact. As such, his metaphysics as well as his scientific laws are not timeless, stable, or entirely objective. This is another example of how twentieth-century philosophy must do battle with the legacy of Descartes, since Cartesian metaphysics claims to deliver just such stability, objectivity, and certainty.

Summary

Dühem set the stage for speculation on two fronts. He proposed a model for scientific method and the status of scientific results; and he explored the relationships between science and philosophy, physics and metaphysics. He did so in his constructivism, which undercut a naive interpretation of science as a simple description of physical fact. Such realism is the basis for much popular belief in the truth of science. Traditional positivism attempted to ground this realism by admitting only positive, "verifiable" experience into the domain of scientific theory and test. Constructivism, the thesis that science is in large part an arbitrary practice, insists on positive agreement but posits a more radical transformation between the world of experience and scientific models of physics.

It is perhaps as if a Kuhnian revolution in philosophy of science itself takes place in the twentieth century. With bold speculation, yet clinging to many tenets of positivism, Dühem proposed a new relationship (with some similarities to Hume's theories) between science and reality, between humanity and science, between scientific fact and metaphysical theory. Popper abandons yet more tenets of prevailing positivism, although still largely in keeping with many dominant Western ideas on the position of science within intellectual endeavor. Scientific achievement holds a preeminent place in the minds of Popperians as the primary way knowledge achieves growth. This privileged position should be objectively established by methodological rules, according to Popper.

Kuhn, on the other hand, questioned this long-held belief in the position of science within Western culture. He attempted to bring in focus the dependence between the prevailing epistemological notions in the West (Cartesianism, positivism, and progressivism, among others) and various biases in favor of scientific advance and the status of scientific results. He also brings a historical perspective to bear on philosophy of science and takes the process of scientific revolution as a recurring theme. Kuhn has the advantage of working in a time when revolution in science is obvious, and a study of the historical context of the twentieth-century revolutions in physical science informs much of his analysis.

Feyerabend attempts to complete the revolution by dissuading us from prescribing any method whatsoever to scientific practice, arguing as he does that philosophy of science has become ossified and out of touch with the facts of scientific history as well as the value of scientific knowledge. In the end, neither Dühem's consistency, nor Popper's survival of the fittest empirical falsification, nor Kuhn's normal science evade criticism. The history presented in these four sections illustrates a fertile period for criticism and reflection in philosophy of science.

Notes

1. Pierre Dühem, *The Aim and Structure of Physical Theory.* Copyright 1954 by Princeton University Press; renewed 1982. Reprinted by permission of Princeton University Press.
2. Dühem, p. 21; see also translator's note in this passage.
3. See Mach, Chapter 8, for example.
4. Karl Popper, *The Logic of Scientific Discovery* (New York: Harper and Row, 1959). Reprinted by permission of the Estate of Sir Karl Popper.
5. Hans Reichenbach, *Erkenntis,* Vol. I, 1930, p. 186 [note in original].

6. David Hume, *Enquiry Concerning Human Understanding*, Antony Flew, ed. (LaSalle, IL: Open Court Publishing Co., 1988).

7. See Kant, Chapter 4.

8. The chief representatives of the school are Poincare and Dühem [note in original].

9. That is, trivially true or true by definition, as the equation a = a, for example.

10. Thomas S. Kuhn, *The Structure of Scientific Revolutions*, The University of Chicago Press, 1970. Reprinted by permission of The University of Chicago Press.

11. The only long-standing check point still generally recognized is the precession of Mercury's perihelion. The red shift in the spectrum of light from distant stars can be derived from considerations more elementary than general relativity, and the same may be possible for the bending of light around the sun . . . [note in original].

12. See Chapter 10.

13. For a parallel discussion of seeing, which relates to Kuhn's logic here, see *Consciousness Explained* by Daniel C. Dennett (treated in Chapter 12).

14. See Chapter 7.

15. See also Einstein's statement in Chapter 10 "redefining" spacial geometry as simply the ability of space-time to propagate light.

16. Schlipp, *Albert Einstein: Philosopher Scientist* (Evanston, Illinois: The Library of Living Philosophers, 1949) 45 [note in original].

17. Paul Feyerabend, *Against Method: Outline of an Anarchistic Theory of Knowledge* (New York and London: New Left Books, 1975). Reprinted by permission of Verso.

18. Lenin, *Selected Works*, Vol. 3 (London: M. Lawrence, Ltd. 1967), 401 [note in original]

19. Herbert Butterfield, *The Whig Interpretation of History* (New York: Norton, 1965), 25 [note in original]

20. Albert Einstein, *Albert Einstein: Philosopher Scientist*, ed. P.A. Schlipp (Evanston, IL: Library of Living Philosophers, 1949) 683f [note in original]

21. John Stuart Mill, "On Liberty", *The Philosophy of John Stuart Mill*, ed. Marshall Cohen (New York: Modern Library, 1961), p. 258 [note in original].

22. This method recalls Descartes.

23. Thomas Kuhn, *Structure of Scientific Revolutions* [note in original].

24. That is, the idea that only something like the complementing relationship between precision in measuring position and precision in measuring momentum specified in the uncertainty principle can be true in microphysical theory.

25. "Mental operations" (Bacon) connected to sensory impressions. See Chapter 4.

26. See Chapter 3.

Suggestions for Further Reading

Carnap, Rudolf, "Empiricism, Semantics, and Ontology," in his *Philosophical Foundations of Physics* (New York: Basic Books, 1966).

Kourany, Janet A., *Scientific Knowledge* (Belmont, CA: Wadsworth, 1987).

Hempel, Carl, and Paul Oppenheim, "Logic of Explanation" in *Readings in Analytical Philosophy*, Ed. by Hans Regnell (Stockholm: Laromedelsforlagen, 1971).

Reichenbach, Hans, *The Rise of Scientific Philosophy* (Berkeley, CA: The University of California Press, 1951).

Science and Philosophy
at the Turn of the Millennium

This final chapter will be devoted to musings by the author on some trends in popular scientific and philosophical literature at the end of the twentieth century. We will look at how some themes presented throughout this book are influencing science, philosophy, and the popular perception of the search for truth. Instead of long excerpts intended to stand on their own merits with only summary and introductory commentary, these themes will be developed with only brief citations and references where appropriate.

Twentieth-century physics has achieved greater theoretical coherence and empirical corroboration in the last decades. Not surprisingly, this success has had a large impact on the scientific and philosophical community. Some scientists feel that physics is finally on the right track and see no radical "paradigm shifts" in the future. We will examine the current paradigm and the views of scientists and philosophers interested in this way of thinking.

Additionally, some philosophers believe that answers to traditional metaphysical questions may be within reach of modern scientists. Specifically, Cartesianism is again under attack, accompanied by much hope of final resolution to the mind/body problem as well as an objective analysis of mind itself. Philosophers and scientists draw from biological and mathematical sciences (including computer science) to aid in this endeavor. Although these theorists use new and updated theories from physics, biology, mathematics, and philosophy, their mission is a traditional modern analytical quest. That is, in the spirit of Descartes, Newton, and Kant, philosophers and scientists see science as a cumulative analytical task appropriate for subsuming all aspects of experience of the world.

Of course, postmodernism is not without its influences. In Chapter 11 we saw an example of a postmodern analysis of scientific theory in Feyerabend's *Against Method.* Kuhn also sees much less objectivity in the scientific arena than do many practicing scientists. Both see scientific practice as crucially embedded in a social, cultural, and historical context. Both see limitations as well as new potential in this relative state of scientific knowledge. And there are clear implications in both views for the interaction between individual subjective mind and objective scientific law. We will look at another school of thought, including the work of Larry Laudan, that takes the cultural aspects of science seriously.

There are also those who question the new paradigm under which science operates. Briefly, I will describe this paradigm as employing elements of evolutionary, quantum, relativistic, and mathematical theory to establish a mind-set for scientific practice. This characterization will be necessarily flawed and vastly inappropriate for universal application to all scientists or even most scientific fields, but it can serve as a backdrop for considering criticisms of this paradigm. If any of these elements is in need of radical revision, then philosophy, science, and the world-views that emanate from them will be overthrown.

Finally, we will look at how perennial themes—dating from the Presocratics through Newton and Galileo, Descartes and Hume—play a role in these discussions. In doing so we may come full circle in the history of science and philosophy, but we may discover that old questions take on new dimensions and find that we are able to revisit familiar issues with new clarity. Such a model is proposed for philosophy by José Ortega y Gasset,[1] and it may be appropriate for looking at the history of philosophy and science as well. I contend, along with Popper, that traditional philosophy will always have a role in calling for the examination of elements of experience that scientists, philosophers, and the world at large recurrently take for granted.

The Scientific Faith

Many popular treatments attempt to explain the universe and its history in terms of twentieth-century science.[2] Such explanations take for granted a certain scientific realism as well as a particular scientific world-view. I will attempt to characterize this world-view briefly.

The modern doctrine of antecedent causation is a premise for physicists who try to explain the world in terms of its origins, although the concept of causation has been modified to include considerations from quantum theory as well as statistical mechanics. An original "big bang" occurred approximately fourteen to sixteen billion years ago, and this event is responsible for the universe as we know it, according to this view. In keeping with the spirit of statistical mechanics as well as evolutionary theory, the current state of the universe is not given any privileged position, and it is not assumed that the entities and physical structures we are familiar with now are anything more than phases in a cosmic developmental process. This process is not intentional and is grander in scope than human experience or human history. As such, this world view supports objectivity and realism in modern science.

Quantum mechanics seems to impose some limits on objective analysis, however. We explored some of these aspects, such as nondeterministic theories of causation, the discovery that it is impossible to obtain arbitrarily precise measurements, and so forth, in Chapter 10. But these difficulties that appear on the surface of quantum theory are taken to be of a lower order than scientific understanding as a whole. That is, science can proceed to find out the laws, equations, and causes for events in the world, although these laws and causes take a different shape than that of classical physics (see Planck's commentary in Chapter 10). Such laws basically rely on the success of quantum mechanics, quantum electrodynamics, and relativity theory to form the basic postulates for physics. These elements combine to form a provocative world-view.

The quantum-relativistic paradigm, augmented by new mathematical theories, e.g., Chaos theory (see Chapter 10), takes on the universe. In so doing, scientists expand scientific knowledge into the nanoscopic world of microphysics, the limits of space and time in the cosmos, and the interactions with complex substances in physical chemistry. If we can describe the laws of physics from the big bang to the end of time, from the subatomic singularity to the black hole, from the existence of matter to the existence of life, then the universe will finally be within the realm of understanding of human beings. Early success in these areas leads Steven Weinberg to speculate that a final scientific theory is within our grasp. In *Dreams of a Final Theory*, he skillfully defends this bold claim for popular audiences.

In order to make such a claim, we need at least two key components. First we need Scientific Realism, the claim that the entities and relations described by scientific theory are real. Weinberg claims that he, like most scientists, holds "a rough and ready realism, a belief in the objective reality of the ingredients of our scientific theories." We have seen several figures who deny this, and others who are simply sceptical, i.e., they withhold judgment. Hume, for example, claims that the assumption of law-like behavior in external reality is entirely a human invention. Dühem claims that science is an arbitrary construction. Other sceptics include empiricists like Galen and Popper, who see little role for a claim of scientific realism in a debate about scientific practice.

Second, we need reductionism, the claim that all phenomena is based upon a foundation of entities and relations within a scientific description of reality. Weinberg takes this a step further and claims that such a description will be one taken from theoretical physics. Weinberg weakens this claim somewhat by stating that everything is not ultimately reducible to physical law in a simple or deterministic way. Rather, he claims that the phenomena of history, literature, art, emotion, and other human experiences, as well as chemistry, psychology, economics, and other sciences, must be described with reference to physical theory. On the other hand, physical theory can be described without reference to these other arenas, thus establishing physics as more basic. For these and other reasons, he believes there is a natural "arrow of explanation" that points to theoretical physics.

Since physical theory has achieved such remarkable success within the quantum-relativistic paradigm, Weinberg concludes that we can now say that a final theory of the universe is, in principle, possible and that we are on the right track. We have unified forces in nature under a single explanation. We have enhanced our understanding of cosmology, chemistry, geology, medicine, and even anthropology with quantum theory. Quantum electrodynamics takes quantum relativistic analysis to new understandings about time, space, and matter. And with considerably more work, but work that falls under Kuhn's description of "normal science," we can, in principle, achieve a final physical theory, according to Weinberg. He makes no claims regarding the ultimate shape of this theory, but he expresses confidence in the beauty and adequacy of many parts of the theoretical physics of his own time.

Now, such a bold claim is not without its weaknesses. Some, already mentioned, lie in the claim to scientific realism in the first place. Others lie in a claim to reductionism. Feyerabend and others who will be discussed claim that physical theory *cannot* be described independently of, say, history, politics, or anthropology. And in any case, the reductionist assumptions, by their very nature, can find no ground in a purely scientific justification. They are, as should be apparent, components of a *metaphysics* of science. Many practicing scientists may find such a metaphysics appealing, empirically fruitful, even promising. However, they can give no independent, paradigm-neutral reasons for the truth of this metaphysics. Nevertheless, such a belief may well hold sway in the coming decades, at least within the scientific community.

Although scientists may find no reason to doubt this overall faith, historians and philosophers perhaps should. We have seen other attempts at reductionism, e.g., in the positivism of Mach. Mach's reductionism is not to physical theory, however, but to psychology or a science of perception. Such a reductionism was not so much overthrown as abandoned. We have also seen confidence in the timelessness of certain paradigms that eventually must be replaced, e.g., classical mechanics. And recall that Aristotelian physics embodied a unified theory of qualitative change, hierarchy of substance, and evaluative natural processes. It was a theory of such power and scope that it held sway in the West for centuries and yet succumbed, not to incremental building on top of preexisting foundations but to the revolutionary sweep of new sciences.

Weinberg has potential responses for these criticisms, some of which are dealt with in his work, and the fact that he makes his assumptions explicit is a credit to his foray into philosophy of science. Indeed, his view may be the prevailing one for some time. Yet its value is probably in its provocative nature rather than in its accurate prediction.

Other popular works of prominent scientists do not make their reductionist, realist, or unificationist views explicit. Hawking's *A Brief History of Time*[3] is one example. Even some philosophers are not as candid as Weinberg, which is far less excusable. In the next section, we will examine some efforts to formulate a final theory of mind.

Science and Mind

Similarly, but with more eclectic methods, philosophers and scientists have attacked the problem of mind. *The Mind's New Science*, by Howard Gardner,[4] *The Emperor's New Mind*, by Roger Penrose,[5] and *Consciousness Explained*, by Daniel C. Dennett[6] are but three examples of popular works from the 1980s and 1990s that bring new scientific, mathematical, and philosophical perspectives to bear on the legacy of Descartes. Of these, Dennett's has been the most popular and is perhaps the most direct in its claim to transcend the mind/body dilemma.

Most philosophical treatments of the science of mind attempt to bring a paradigm shift to bear on the problems of dualism, or an analysis of mind. Most philosophers and scientists realize that if an investigation of mental existence begins as Descartes' does, and follows a Cartesian method, then the viewpoints of the *Meditations* are hard to evade. And if evaded in these terms, dualism is simply replaced by physicalism or idealism. That is, physicalism denies the existence of mental substance and attempts to reduce both objective physical phenomena and the phenomena of consciousness to material entities and interactions. Idealism, a rather unpopular thesis among scientists, denies the existence of physical substance and instead characterizes reality exclusively as an aspect of mind. If these alternatives are to be avoided, then Descartes' project must be approached from a different perspective.

There are many possible routes to a new stance regarding the project of "explaining" the mind. First, we can abandon Descartes' mission of certainty or indubitability. Second, we can deny the existence of truths so clear and distinct that they can be recognized intuitively by our rational faculty.

Third, closely related to the second, we can attempt a more in-depth analysis of our experience, both of mental operations and external sensations.

Dennett takes the third strategy. In doing so, however, he realizes he must bring to light many tacit assumptions in the philosophy and science of mind—assumptions that are perhaps largely the result of the Cartesian legacy that led to dualism in the first place. Primarily, according to Dennett, most philosophers, scientists, or inquisitive laypersons take for granted that there *is* a subject of experience. That is, investigation usually begins by attempting to explain the relationship between subject and object, mind and matter, not to discern the fundamental nature of reality. Descartes himself may be the source of this assumption, and if so, then his *cogito, ergo sum* is simply a restatement of this premise, namely, the subject exists as a subject of experience.

Dennett claims that there are psychological, chemical, and biological contexts that make this assumption unnecessary. Dennett prefers to treat the assumption of a self as a rationalization, an *ex post facto* postulate that comes *after* experience, not as an indubitable accompaniment to experience. The self is a story we tell ourselves, according to this view. Sensations, impressions, memories, imaginary thoughts, and illusions are all complex processes that are smeared over rather long spans of time. The brain gathers and collects different parts of experience in different places, altering memory, triggering reactions, producing "mental images," and so forth. There is no one locus of such processes. In analyzing these experiences scientifically, and by paying particular attention to the clock, certain experiments show that our description of experience after the fact does not match the processes of perception, memory, or imagination. And it is but a trivial step from this point to hypothesize that the self, the monadic subject of experience, is just an attribute of this description, not of the experience itself.

If this is the case, then the self emerges over time from a complex of physical processes. It no longer makes sense to say "I think" as an unanalyzable, atomic sentence. Nor "I doubt"; neither "I feel"; likewise "I imagine." All these statements have little to do with the process of perceiving, remembering, reacting, or formulating thoughts. But when such statements are taken as the given facts of experience, they lead the philosopher into the morass and mysteries of dualism. This explanation for consciousness is ingeniously presented in a delightful manner by Dennett, and it is well supported by his gathering together of results from modern scientific experiments and everyday experience. It is not entirely original, however, as Dennett realizes. Laplace held a view that equates mind with physical processes, for example. And since the explosion of twentieth-century computer technology, many scientists have believed that an explanation of mind may be within reach of modern scientific theory.

Computers have given some philosophers hope that objective modeling and scientific method may yield up the mysteries of subjectivity. Dennett uses computational analogies throughout his work, for example. Yet in order for computer science to be relevant to philosophy of mind, we must understand how studying machines can be enlightening for theorists interested in mental phenomena. A classic case for this idea is Newell and Simon's "Computer Science as Empirical Inquiry."[7] This work incorporates computer science into the mechanistic and empirical tradition of modern scientific inquiry. They further assert that such empirical inquiry is informative with respect to the human mind. In other works, such as *Human Problem Solving*,[8] they assert that "thinking can be explained by means of an information processing theory." They characterize the relevance of computer science as providing the means to construct an abstract model for both human thinking and computer behavior, and do not assert that human beings are in fact computers. Nevertheless, they are persuaded that the advances in artificial intelligence and other computational fields may someday provide adequate models for human mental operations. Following in the footsteps of Newell and Simon are theorists like Dennett and Douglas R. Hofstadter,[9] who have much confidence in the relevance of computer science to a study of mind.

Others are not so sure that an explanation of consciousness is at hand. Roger Penrose has doubts about the ability of twentieth-century science to understand mind, and he has put forward a different program in his popular works concerning mind, physics, and computers. We have seen the foreshadowing of some of these views in studying Chaos theory (Chapter 10). Chaos theory deals with unpredictable, nondeterministic phenomena that emerge from complex physical systems in highly unstable situations. Ilya Prigogine and others depict surprising difficulties within classical physics with regard to the modern mission of reduction, mechanistic explanation, and physical modeling. Penrose claims that when quantum mechanics and relativity are put into the mix, the crisis in physical interpretation of both microscopic and macroscopic phenomena, including the physical understanding of the mind, becomes more acute.

It is not that Penrose believes that physical or mathematical theories have no bearing on reality. Penrose is, rather, a self-confessed Platonist. He believes sophisticated understanding of logical, mathematical, and physical theories actually puts us in touch with ultimate reality. He simply does not believe we have achieved a sufficient level of sophistication. He states in *The Emperor's New Mind*, for example, that "it is our present lack of understanding of the fundamental laws of physics that prevents us from coming to grips with the concept of 'mind' in physical or logical terms."[10] Part of the problem, according to Penrose, lies with quantum mechanics. Much of the flavor of quantum theory is reflected in the current logical, algorithmic, and digital thinking in computer science. Underneath the picture of a digital computer, the sort of computer that is in almost universal use and the sort of machine practically all philosophers are talking about when they speak in computational metaphors, paradigms, or analyses, is a *discrete model.* That is, the ones and zeros of a digital computer, the basic bits of information, are, according to Penrose, the *quanta* of information as we currently understand computational models.

He admits that there are crucial differences between digital and quantum theory, namely, the former lacks the uncertainty principle. But he believes that the uncertainty principle, along with the analogous complementarity and duality of quantum phenomena, is simply a stage through which physics will pass in time to a more "complete" (in Einstein's words) physical theory. The various interpretations of quantum theory, from the many worlds hypotheses to radical determination by subjective observation (see Chapter 10), are examples of the problems that quantum theory brings with it. Penrose claims that a new physics will transcend these esoteric difficulties.

He sees a new physics, with an evolved (or replaced) quantum hypothesis, incorporating more wholistic approaches as well as new mathematical insights, as the avenue to something like Weinberg's final theory. Such a theory is in principle possible, but not immediately within our grasp. Something like a revolutionary "paradigm shift" will need to occur in order to bring forth the physics for the next millennium. One of the facets of such a paradigm shift might give meaning to humanity's place in the universe. Penrose and others see many puzzles and enigmas associated with our existence in the face of the sterile, even biologically hostile, theories of space and matter found in quantum theory, statistical mechanics, and modern cosmology. Yet empirical evidence, including our own existence and success in understanding the world, seems to indicate that the presence of intelligent biological life in the universe may be part of some as yet unknown relationship between the basic components of the universe. In physics, this is known as "the anthropic principle," and Penrose hopes that a new physical theory may treat this principle less as an anomaly and more as a fundamental relation in a new mathematical physics. Such a physics may then tackle the problem of mind, according to Penrose. We will treat the anthropic principle in a later section of this chapter.

We have briefly discussed examples of views that try to explain mind on the one hand and reinvigorate some of the enigmas of the science of mind on the other hand. Yet both the explanations and reinvigorations of mind share similar traits. Both assume that science and mathematics can be discussed independently of and prior to mind and that some version of scientific realism is correct. This is a weaker version of scientific realism than the reductionism of Weinberg. Penrose, Dennett, Newell, and Simon may not accept the reductionist claim regarding mind, but they take mind, and indeed any of the phenomena that inhabit our reality, to be amenable to objective inquiry.

This stance opposes that of either Hume or Dühem, for example. That is, instead of taking science to be only a creation of the human mind, scientific realists take science as an independently applicable body of objective knowledge or procedures that can be brought to bear on the phenomenon of mind. And while this may be promising in some contexts, it is perhaps not philosophically or scientifically justified in its entirety.

Such a project assumes not merely the results of modern science, but a *metaphysical* theory as well. Roughly, this metaphysical theory is scientific realism, anticonstructivism (see Chapter 11), and belief in the universal applicability of objective analysis. We have already labeled this metaphysics as *scientism* (see Chapter 8). It is the same metaphysical theory brought out in the previous section, without reductionism. Other metaphysical theories may be equally tenable, at least in some contexts. One of these contexts is reading Descartes' *Meditations*, for example. Most thoughtful readers, including Dennett, are struck by the power of Descartes' work. This power is simply the ability to take the reader to a different context than that of modern psychology, biology, chemistry, and physics. The exercise of entertaining the hypotheses and methods of the *Meditations* actually produces dualism as a valid experience. While it may be true that a committed scientific realist can be convinced of Dennett's explanation of the self as rationalization, this will never eradicate the experience of wonder produced by a careful reading of *Meditations on First Philosophy*.

Such an experience, even if it is "artificially" produced, can be a different starting point for a metaphysics of experience. Scientism could be potentially informed by this dualistic metaphysics, and in fact has to a large extent been motivated by it, if only at times to overcome it. Nevertheless, Dennett's engaging work brings scientism to new and current positions within the traditional scientific/philosophical relationship.

If Dennett is correct, or even if he is taken sufficiently seriously, then vast areas of philosophy and culture will be affected. Most Western ethical, political, and social theories all involve the postulate of a self. If such a postulate is misguided, or at least not necessarily true, then these theories, from considerations of political individualism to ethical obligation to religious salvation, must be critically reevaluated. And, as Feyerabend has said of similar situations in scientific and philosophical history (see Chapter 11), such a reexamination in light of possible alternative theories is bound to enrich our understanding of our own intellectual heritage. Thus, even an assault on dualism that produces limited success will be productive. And even a stubbornly resistant dualism, one that recurrently survives attempts to transcend the mind/body problem, will continue to enrich the philosophical and scientific dialogue.

Scientific and Philosophical Discord

Despite my own misgivings about the reductionist project and the possibility of explaining mind once and for all, either by contemporary theory as Dennett proposes or through a new science as Penrose suggests, many philosophers and scientists see these and similar projects as the driving force behind scientific and philosophical interaction. Other scientists and philosophers see grave difficulties ahead for science, as we know it, and its place in society. In this section, we will treat critical examinations of science from a scientific and a philosophical perspective.

Scientific Discord

The scientific community is far from having unanimity regarding any one, basic world-view, however. In the beginning of the twentieth century, Einstein vigorously opposed the adoption of quantum theory. Some of his objections and formulations have been incorporated in scientific literature, and one of the phenomena he predicted, known as the Einstein-Podolsky-Rosen (EPR) paradox, has been fruitful of numerous theoretical and experimental achievements. We will examine the EPR result in the next section.

Other scientists and philosophers have risen to challenge the current paradigm in physical science and have exposed some serious anomalies in physical theory. For example, although progress is currently being made on this problem, modern cosmological theory cannot account for the fact that the theoretical age of the universe is less than the calculated age of some of its own stars. Eric J. Lerner's *The Big Bang Never Happened*[11] uses this and other anomalies to argue for a reexamination of big bang theory. He claims its problems, and the attempts for their resolution, are due in part to a predominant attitude in professional and popular science to try to coerce nature into a particular world-view.

Such a world-view attempts to provide ultimate causes for phenomena in the universe via a model of primordial causation that is largely compatible with many religious views of creation. Big bang theory relates too closely to religious ideas of creation, according to Lerner, and certainly physicists from Einstein to Hawking use God as a metaphor for physics. This tendency promotes the idea that physical theory is consistent with religious metaphysics. We saw one example of this paradigm in Chapter 2: Aquinas viewed Aristotelian cosmology and Christian teaching as mutually reenforcing truths, and this doctrine was an impediment for scientific progress. A similar paradigm in the twentieth century, even if liberally interpreted to include progressive inquiry and revision, could yield problems in a purely scientific inquiry. According to Lerner it already has.

The age problem is but one anomaly in cosmology. Another is the mass of the universe. Big bang cosmologists can calculate the overall mass of the universe given their assumptions that it originated from the explosion of a primordial singularity. This estimation is done based on the assumption that the current motions of the galaxies are a result of this explosion (along with other subsequent forces that tend to drive apart matter), coupled with the effect of a cosmic deceleration caused by the gravitational attraction between all of the matter in the universe. But this calculation resists correlation with empirical observation.

Astronomical observation suggests that the universe in fact seems to be much less massive than theoretical calculations predict. Thus, some mass is missing from our observations if cosmological theory is correct. This "missing mass" has given rise to many theoretical explanations and new empirical searches. Some physicists suggest that there are many more "black holes" than we are aware of. Black holes are singularities of densely packed matter that cannot be directly detected because not even light can escape their gravitational fields. Other theorists hypothesize about "dark matter," a different kind of matter that does not radiate like most of the material we know and hence is difficult to detect.[12] Indeed, in this light, some of these hypotheses look like the *ad hoc* components of Popper's bad-faith science. In any case, many basic cosmological questions are far from settled, and may pose more than "normal science" puzzles. Instead, they may be "anomalies" waiting to provoke a crisis in contemporary cosmology (see Kuhn, Chapter 11).

The Specter of Relativism

Other theorists see problems with science from a philosophical perspective. While some scientists, such as Weinberg, claim to see little of relevance for scientific practice in the speculations and criticisms of philosophers, they are at least concerned about the place of science in society from the perspective of allocation of research funds. Other scientists may be more concerned with both the perception of growth and the possibility of progress in scientific history. Larry Laudan attempts to salvage the concept of scientific progress from the relativistic morass many see as the legacy of Kuhn and Feyerabend (see Chapter 11).

While Kuhn speaks at times of progress within his model of revolutionary paradigm shifts, many see Kuhnian theory as a threat to the notion of the growth of scientific knowledge. This is because of the incommensurability of both theoretical and experimental results in scientific practice across paradigms. That is, since revolutions cause older paradigms to be overthrown and replaced by new ones, resulting in a gestalt shift in the way scientists see the world, it is difficult to speak of a new paradigm making any kind of objective progress over the old. It is more like scientists after a revolution are speaking a new language and working with new ideas that cannot be completely translated into the old, and vice versa. Thus, the results of pre- and post-revolutionary science cannot be objectively compared against one another.

An anarchistic theory of knowledge has similar problems. Although Feyerabend makes many claims about anarchy and its necessity for progress, it is difficult to see how such progress can be measured without any methodological standards. Laudan, in *Progress and Its Problems: Toward a Theory of Scientific Growth*[13] (as well as in *Relativism and Science*, among other works) tackles this problem. He sees historical and cultural analysis as crucial for understanding any scientific milieu, but believes in scientific progress. Specifically, he thinks such "progressiveness" can be defined in culturally (or paradigm) neutral terms, and as such can be used as a criterion for improving scientific method.

He accepts, with Kuhn, that "evaluation of theories is a comparative matter. . . . Absolute measures of the empirical or conceptual credentials of a theory are of no significance." He also identifies with Kuhn's basic model of using some context of embeddedness to analyze scientific practice, but replaces Kuhn's paradigm with his own formulation of a research tradition.

The idea of the research tradition is supposed to be more flexible than the paradigm of Kuhn's work. Kuhn's paradigms must be overthrown in a revolutionary manner since they are resistant to falsification or correction. By contrast, Laudan sees the context of scientific practice as more flexible and evolutionary. In a related fashion, Laudan puts less emphasis on revolution, since he sees adaptation of science progressing continually within the guidelines of a research tradition. Consequently, he sees no need to bifurcate scientific practice into "normal" and "revolutionary" periods.

However, Laudan views the context of the research tradition as providing some of the same features of a paradigm. There is "an ontology, which specifies, in a general way, the types of fundamental entities which exist in the domain or domains within which the research tradition is embedded."[14] There is also an assumption "about the appropriate methods to be used for investigating the problems and constructing theories in that domain."[15] But a research tradition need not be overthrown to make "revolutionary" progress.

For example, Maxwell was working within a mechanistic research tradition (see Chapter 8) and believed in a mechanical medium, the ether, through which electromagnetic interaction operated. Nonetheless, his work showed the way out of mechanism toward field-oriented theory. As such, this period in history is regarded more properly as evolutionary rather than revolutionary, according to Laudan. Different research traditions can mix and mingle, influencing each other. Laudan says, "Research traditions . . . are historical creatures. They are created and articulated within a particular intellectual milieu, they aid in the generation of specific theories—and like all other historical institutions—they wax and wane. Just as surely as research traditions are born and thrive, so they die. . . ."[16] "We should speak . . . of a *natural evolution in the research tradition*,"[17] suggests Laudan.

And yet, despite the historical relativism of research traditions, we can measure their progress, according to Laudan. We do this objectively, but in the terms of the tradition itself. We can measure "the general progress of a research tradition. . . . by comparing the adequacy of the sets of theories which constitute the oldest and those which constitute the most recent versions of the research tradition;" and "the rate of progress of a research tradition"[18] by measuring the change in problem-solving adequacy of the research tradition within a given time span. The problems are taken from those specified in the tradition itself.

This gives us a way to measure the progress of a tradition, and hence provides the ability to choose between traditions based on their progressiveness, thus avoiding the incommensurability problem of Kuhn and the methodological black hole of Feyerabend. Laudan's theory stands or falls with the results of historical analysis, however. That is, if his evolutionary, rather than revolutionary, model is more accurate, then we have a candidate for describing the growth of scientific knowledge. Science proceeds by choosing theories and traditions which increase progressiveness. If, however, revolution and incommensurability are more accurate, it is difficult to avoid the more radical relativism of Kuhn and Feyerabend. The exercise of proceeding through this text may give the reader a flavor of such analysis.

Laudan's attempt to measure progress in relative terms yet salvage commensurability may satisfy many who want to give science a privileged status within the Western tradition. Certainly it has, as a matter of fact, occupied such a place in many interpretations of intellectual history. The question of the ultimate justification of this privileged status is, like the question of progress in science, a philosophical question with metaphysical and methodological components. Answering it in a historically, scientifically, and philosophically neutral manner may be in principle impossible. Perhaps, however, the reader can delve into his or her own experiences in studying the theories in this text. Does entertaining Aristotelian (or Newtonian, for that matter) physical and cosmological assumptions feel like taking a step backward to a less progressive state of scientific history? Or does it feel more like visiting a foreign land in which all scientific (and many other) ideas seem alien, mysterious, and difficult for a stranger to fathom? The former experience would tend to support Laudan (and Weinberg), the latter to support Kuhn. For my part, I think the latter experience is more interesting and aesthetic, and so I do not evade or discard it.[19] These feelings are by no means decisive, nor on some accounts even philosophically relevant. But given the difficulty of detached, objective analysis, they may at least be inspiring, if not informative.

In any case, philosophers who take science seriously must wrestle with the specter of relativism that is the legacy of Kuhnian analysis. Scientists themselves have been stung by this issue. Certainly the thrust of many of Weinberg's arguments can be interpreted as an attempt to educate the public on the fundamental status he feels science must have in society, and thus to secure a recognition of this status by way of allocation of resources. A rough and ready realism coupled with a need for superb talent, highly trained staffs, and elaborate equipment are not compatible with scientific relativism. If there is no absolute notion of progress in science, nor any agreement that science works toward more basic modes of explanation than, say, history or anthropology, then physicists might have to be content with the same level of funding that these other disciplines obtain. This is at least one reason the scientific community must recurrently deal with the relativistic challenge.

In this section we have seen that both the content of modern science and its status in society are undergoing much critical analysis at the end of the twentieth century. Perhaps this alone is some evidence against the proximity of a final theory. Yet if scientism, including scientific realism, is correct, such subjective and anthropocentric concerns are of little use in evaluating the results of scientific practice.

Roles for Philosophy: Perennial Themes Revisited

If the scientists we discussed earlier in this chapter are correct, philosophers will have little to occupy them in the coming millennium. But as discussed in the preceding section, science and philosophy have some rather large unresolved problems. Some of these problems bring us back to the themes presented in Chapters 1 and 2. Indeed, throughout the presentation in this text we have seen scientists and philosophers revisiting issues of the past. In this chapter, we will see some examples of philosophical and scientific interaction that take us back two-and-a-half millennia, and which could inform humanity in the next.

An Anthropic Universe?

This section takes us back to Chapter 2 and a reinvigoration of some of the themes of Aristotelian cosmology. Since the seventeenth-century revolution in physical science, there has been no scientific grounding for the idea that humanity's place in the universe is special in any meaningful way. Furthermore, the concept of purpose and meaning in the universe has been a subject for speculation more in philosophy than in science. Yet certain discoveries in chemistry, elementary particle physics, cosmology, and biology lead some scientists back to the question of purpose and meaning in the universe from a scientific perspective.

Recall that Aristotle postulated a purposive natural world, in which the universe, as well as natural processes within the universe, aim at final goods. This notion of final causation was at the root of Aristotle's ordered cosmos and purposive dynamics. The cosmos was arranged into spheres of ascending perfection, with the higher spheres embodying increasing divinity with their distance from the earthly sphere. In the age of Copernicus, Galileo, and Newton, it was found that heavenly matter did not display any more perfection than that of the earth. Furthermore, a nongeocentric picture of the universe served as a better model for astronomy than did Aristotle's picture of concentric spheres surrounding the earth. Laws of inertia, motion, and gravitation within a model of antecedent causation became more powerful scientific theories than a theory of final causes. Such discoveries displaced humanity from a privileged position in the universe as well as discredited anthropocentric ideas of a universe of purpose. Other scientific achievements affirmed the tangential place humanity would occupy in a modern scientific world-view. Darwin showed that the existence of the human species could be explained by a struggle for survival and adaptation compatible with notions of antecedent causation, and that human beings were thus simply another of the currently existing species that had exhibited one or another adaptive advantages. Boltzmann claimed that the current cosmic epoch, inhabited by high degrees of order in cosmological organization as well as biological life, is a brief episode in the random unfolding of a universe of increasing entropy. Time itself seemed to lose meaning in such an explanation.

Yet Boltzmann's model gave rise to certain apparent puzzles. Given that human life is not special in any scientific sense, how is it that we find ourselves in existence? A statistical survey of all of the possible universes seems to indicate that such existence is almost impossible. That is, if the universe differed in any of its fundamental parameters, e.g., in its mass, energy, magnitudes of fundamental constants, ratio of fundamental particles, and so forth, the existence of life at *any* epoch in its evolution would have been ruled out. Is there some connection between these parameters that we have yet to discover? Is this connection some sort of scientific explanation for the existence of life? And since such a connection would be a fundamental relation in the makeup of the universe, would its articulation give a special place, and hence perhaps meaning, to life in the universe?

Answering affirmatively to these questions may be warranted, even from a purely objective statistical stance. The suspicion that these issues are scientifically significant has been called the *anthropic principle*. Basically, the anthropic principle is the suspicion that some fundamental aspects of the universe are bound up with the possibility of the existence of life—even of consciousness—in the universe. As we have seen, Penrose believes this is a fact that modern physics as we know it cannot account for.[20] As such, if the anthropic principle becomes a genuine problem for physics, it could provoke a profound shift in science in the coming age.

The anthropic principle comes in many forms, however, and is worth examining in its own right. A superb investigation is found in *The Anthropic Cosmological Principle* by John D. Barrow and Frank J. Tipler.[21] One version of this principle appears in contemplating the results of physicists like Boltzmann as well as modern cosmological theory. Modern cosmological theory puts the age of the universe at somewhere around fourteen to sixteen billion years, and its size in comparison with that of the solar system is almost unimaginably vast. These empirical results, together with the theoretical speculations of Boltzmann (see Chapter 8) and others, indicate that the zone of our living world is trivial in size and duration when compared with that of the universe as a whole. This inspires in some a sense of wonder that we exist at all, and this wonder contributes to the feeling that humanity may be the result of some cosmic necessity rather than a hugely improbable accident. Yet elementary particle physics and big bang cosmology dictate that the universe would *have* to be of a given size, composition, and age in order for the elements of which we are composed to exist. So though we may wonder at the scale and significance of the spot we occupy in a vast universe, it really is dictated by physical law. That is, in order for any biological beings to observe any universe at all, it would have to be one of approximately the age and size as ours.

This version of the cosmological principle is known as the *weak cosmological principle*. It is weak in that it simply constrains the parameters of any universe that we could possibly observe. And since we *are* observing one, there is a certain necessity to its composition. This version of the anthropic principle does not dictate any special necessity for the existence of life and consciousness, only that if such existence occurs, certain features of the universe must obtain.[22]

The *strong cosmological principle* is derived from empirical results that seem to give more force to the idea that this particular universe, i.e., one in which there are observers, is more than just an arbitrary, random occurrence. Furthermore, this universe seems strangely conducive to life. "It was found that there exist a number of unlikely coincidences between numbers of enormous magnitudes that are, superficially, completely independent;

moreover, these coincidences appear essential to the existence of carbon-based observers in the Universe. So numerous and unlikely did these coincidences seem that [B.] Carter proposed a stronger version of the Anthropic Principle . . . : that the Universe *must* be such 'as to admit the creation of observers within it at some stage.'"[23] Understanding the nature of this necessity, this *must*, poses a problem for both physicists and philosophers. Current physical theory, as we have stated, regards the relevant constants of nature as independent. If there is a fundamental relation between them as yet undiscovered, a physical interpretation of this necessity, then it is of fundamental significance for physicists to investigate this relation.[24]

Philosophers have long wrestled with the issue of the possibilities and necessities associated with considering alternative universes. What does the idea of alternative universes actually mean? Some philosophers have put these alternatives into the mind of God, speculating that a creator chose this particular universe from a number of possibilities. This choice, which philosophers and physicists alike have tried to characterize as either constrained in some way or free, again binds up a notion of value with the natural world. For God presumably would choose a universe based on some judgement of which one would be better. Thus, the universe, including our existence, is given both meaning and value in this highly speculative scheme.

Other philosophers, and physicists for that matter, assign a more potentially concrete meaning to this discussion of necessity and possibility. It is conceivable, according to this view, that this universe is just one of a multitude of universes existing in a vast multiverse of space and time. David Bohm, for example, uses the metaphor of a cosmic ocean in which "'the big bang' is to be regarded as actually just a 'little ripple.'"[25] In the next section we will see how his ideas in this regard are connected with issues of wholism in modern physics. In any case, viewing this universe as simply a local phenomenon, either in space, time, or both, within a much more vast universe gives the idea of possible universes a concrete meaning. These possible universes do not simply exist in metaphysical speculation, alternative philosophical theories, or the mind of God, but rather in reality. As such, the unlikely coincidences we see in the fundamental constants, the very relationships that make life possible, are in fact just coincidences within our local region of a universe of expanded scope.

If this is the case, then perhaps the strong cosmological principle reduces to the weak cosmological principle. That is, we observe a local region (still of immense proportions when compared with our world) of space, time, matter, and energy, that exhibits fundamental constants whose relation permits life simply because such an observation is necessitated by the fact of observation itself. Other regions of the universe exhibit other relations, but there are no observers within them. We should no more wonder at our measurements of these unlikely coincidences than we should wonder at the size and age of our local region of the universe. Both are necessitated not by some basic property of the universe—or the choice of a creator—but by the fact that this region happens to have observers in it.

Although this is one potential way to dissolve the strong anthropic principle, it borders on the purely speculative. While it is conceivable that some derivative aspects of such a theory may impact physical theory or experiment, such impact is not on the immediate horizon.[26] Hence, there is some circumstantial evidence from a strictly scientific point of view for the strong anthropic principle. This version of the cosmological principle is reminiscent of Aristotelian teleology. That is, if the universe is necessarily conducive to life—perhaps even consciousness—then it is a small step to say that its design or purpose is to produce such life. According to this view, our existence may be bound up with a teleological explanation of the universe in terms of final causes.[27]

Thus, the mechanism of Galileo, Newton, Boyle, Laplace, and Boltzmann (Chapters 3, 7, and 8) may be as outdated as the classical mechanics to which it gave rise. The history of science and philosophy returns again to the question of meaning, this time on a grander scale and with more sophisticated techniques. The legacy of Aristotle not only provides a powerful mode of explanation but also a world-view that, in one form or another, continues to motivate scientific interpretation. Again, the issue of meaning creeps into science in the seemingly inexpungible task of interpreting scientific theory.

Some scientists see a new type of physics emerging that can transcend both mechanism and final causation. This sort of theory would account for the anthropic principle as well as the objectively detached physics of Einstein, Boltzmann, and the dominant scientific tradition. Penrose believes such a new science is indicated by certain problems in quantum theory and the anthropic principle. Other physicists have not hesitated to engage in similar speculation. In the next section we will see how this line of reasoning takes us even further back in our cycle of examining the interpenetrations of science and philosophy.

Wholism and Modern Physics

In the last section we saw how Aristotelian themes re-emerge in late-twentieth-century science. In this section we will see how Presocratic ideas continue to inform science, and may point the way for a new scientific paradigm in the next millennium. In Chapter 1, we examined the theories of Parmenides, who believed that existence was related to thinking. He stipulated that contemplating this relationship would show that the universe is indeed One, whole, and undivided. Heraclitus agreed that the universe is One, but while Parmenides believed that this One was unchanging, Heraclitus saw change and flux as the basic character of the world. From this point, let us engage in a seeming digression into a puzzling issue in modern physics that leads some scientists to turn again to Presocratic notions.

Ever since the onset and successful deployment of quantum mechanics, based on the quantum hypothesis and the uncertainty principle, some physicists have rebelled against its adoption. Einstein was its most famous critic during the first half of the twentieth century, and in 1935 he published, along with Podolsky and Rosen, an article in *Physical Review* entitled "Can a Quantum Mechanical Description of Physical Reality Be Considered Complete?"[28] In this article, the authors show that under certain conditions, quantum theory dictates exceptions to the laws of special relativity. Recall that the uncertainty principle entails a complementary relationship between the position and momentum of a particle under investigation (see Chapter 10). That is, when one of these attributes has been determined precisely, the other is entirely uncertain, or indeterminate. Due to the complementarity inherent in the uncertainty principle, in some systems properly correlated and then separated without affecting this prior correlation, measurements of some attributes of the system must simultaneously affect attributes of other parts of the system, even though the parts be separated by arbitrary distances. Einstein believed this showed that quantum theory must be false.

Subsequent work on this problem, notably by John Bell and later by David Bohm, showed that the puzzle was deeply imbedded within quantum theory. Bell showed that quantum mechanics entailed some very nonmechanical results. Namely, quantum theory must be *non-local*, that is, it must contain variables, attributes, and entities that are not isolable to fixed locations or mechanistic interaction. Over finite spaces, perturbations and measurements of parts of any quantum system simultaneously affect other parts of the system, exceeding any possible speed of mechanical interaction. These results have since been experimentally corroborated.[29]

This sort of "trans-luminal" (faster than light) interaction is not seen to strictly violate relativity theory or lead to any time-travel paradoxes (see Chapter 10). This is because the effects are essentially random and cannot be used to carry any sort of information about the future back to the past, and so forth. Yet there is a puzzling "connectedness" behind this aspect of quantum theory that violates both the spirit of relativity and quantum theory itself. This connectedness is not any sort of mechanistic interaction, nor is it the result of an electromagnetic field, nor is it the result of spacial geometry being influenced by the presence of matter or energy. None of these modes of explanation, that is, neither quantum mechanics nor special or general relativity, do anything to help understand or interpret this effect.

This leads some physicists to follow Einstein, at least in spirit. While they do not believe that quantum theory is incorrect or mistaken as far as it goes, they do believe that the EPR paradox, as the result has been called, could be used to point the way to a physics that gives a more complete or deeper explanation than twentieth-century physical theory. David Bohm, who has worked extensively in this area, is one of these scientists. In *Wholeness and the Implicate Order*,[30] he attempts an ambitious mission that I will here interpret as a synthesis of Parmenides, Heraclitus, Einstein, Planck, and Heisenberg.

We saw in Chapter 10 that Whitehead, for one, took twentieth-century science as a cue to construct a speculative metaphysics of relatedness, flux, and interpenetration. While I will not attempt to describe his process of construction, it may be said that quantum theory was reflected in the flux and overall atomism of his theory, while relativity was modeled in the interconnectivity, interaction, and relatedness of the theory. Throughout, however, *Process and Reality* is primarily atomistic. That is, Whitehead begins with basic building blocks, his "basic ontological entities" to construct reality. This atomism is coherent with the spirit of quantum theory.

While physicists have wrestled, mostly unsuccessfully, with the task of uniting relativity and quantum theory, Whitehead may be said to have achieved some moderate success at the metaphysical level. Penrose and Bohm believe the task is misguided, and that what is needed is a new theory that transcends both. They especially find fault with the atomism of quantum theory. The quantum postulate is basically an atomic postulate (see Democritus, Chapter 1). Physicists, in their attempted syntheses, have largely sought after a quantum explanation of general relativity, for example, theories of quantum gravity and quantum space-time. Both Penrose and Bohm believe that it is quantum mechanics itself that must be explained as a derivative result of a new theory, and that such a theory may look more like general relativity than quantum theory.

Specifically, the theme of such a new physics, according to Bohm, would be wholism. That is, undividedness, connectedness, and interpenetration would be basic to a new physics, not atomistic quanta. As such, this new physics would capture the spirit of the unity found in the general relativistic idea of a field of space-time, matter, and energy (see Chapter 10). However, such a physics would explain not only gravity, spacial geometry, electromagnetic phenomena, and temporal/spacial interrelatedness, but also all of the other forces and phenomena of nature, including the EPR-Bell result. In addition, the connectedness between consciousness and physical experiment hinted at by the Copenhagen interpretation of quantum theory (see Chapter 10) would also be embodied in a new physics. This new physics, transcending ideas of relativity, quantum theory, space, time, matter, and a bifurcated reality of physical objects, would emphasize an interconnectedness more profound than that of general relativity. In particular, consistent with the EPR-Bell result, the "enfolding" effects of such a universe would not be bound by the speed of light.

In this, Bohm harkens back to Parmenides. Bohm sees a universe that is One, undivided, and whole. He specifically mentions Parmenides and his disciple Zeno in arguing for the fullness of space.[31] Bohm sees such a fullness as arising from a background of radiation and gravitational energy that permeates the entire universe, which on some counts exceeds the usually calculated energy and mass of the universe by many factors of ten (even producing infinite energy, according to some calculations). This spacial plenitude is merely a manifestation of wholeness, however. A full understanding of this wholeness awaits a new physics, according to Bohm.

Unlike Parmenides, and in keeping with Heraclitus, Bohm sees the wholeness as constantly changing and "enfolding" into itself, upon itself, transforming itself. Parmenides viewed this as impossible, since in thought when one contemplates change, there must be at least two things, the old and the new. Bohm regards thought as yet another aspect of this wholeness, not necessarily indicative of its total structure. In this, he regards the anthropic principle as an example of an "Implicate Order" in the wholeness of the universe. The two versions of the anthropic principle can be summarized by saying that (1) conscious thought and observation necessitate that the universe be of such and such a character (weak), and (2) the universe is constructed so as to create thought, consciousness, and observation, which in turn are necessary to produce the reality of some physical processes (strong). That the universe acts to produce thought and thought necessitates the universe is an example of the undividedness between these dimensions of reality as a whole. All of this should be explained scientifically, according to Bohm, when we see beyond big bang theory, quantum and fundamental particle physics, and the relativistic problems in the EPR-Bell result.

According to Bohm, the failure to see this is a result of some classical ideas of Newton, Galileo, and Descartes. Since the revolution wrought by these philosophers and scientists was immensely fruitful, contemporary physics has not yet been able to free itself from its metaphors and methods. Focus is still on analysis into building blocks, isolated dimensions, and independent parameters. These are the methods Descartes, Galileo, and Newton (among others) used so successfully to defeat Aristotelianism. And these were the very methods needed to overcome Aristotle, since, according to

Bohm, Aristotle held that "the universe is to be regarded as a single living organism."[32] We have seen the power of the ordered cosmological and metaphysical theories of Aristotle, and if entrenched Aristotelianism needed to be revised, even overthrown, then it is natural that new methods would need to be deployed. This is a proper way to proceed when couched in the appropriate historical context, but these methods may have outlived their usefulness. Indeed, this method of analysis has dominated well after the downfall of the mechanical dynamics it produced.

For all the nondeterminism of quantum theory, the unified fields of electromagnetic and relativity theory, and the atemporal views of statistical mechanics, physics still operates under the assumptions that analysis into parts is the proper method. This analysis proceeds either to produce fundamental building blocks or independent dimensions of description. Most unificationists assume interaction is basically quantum mechanical, although not traditionally deterministic. This thinking, according to Bohm, leads to all of the paradoxes and problems of modern physics: the EPR-Bell result; cosmological riddles such as the Anthropic Principle; a seemingly never-ending analysis into more and more quantized, atomistic, "fundamental" particles; and various competing interpretations of the uncertainty principle that many scientists either ignore or find unsatisfying. While these anomalies, puzzles, and quests cannot themselves be said to be wrong-headed or misguided, attempts to tackle them with Cartesian and Newtonian thinking will only postpone scientific progress, according to Bohm. Like Kuhn, Feyerabend, and Penrose, Bohm sees value in a scientific process that continually forces revolution and transformation, and which is productive of and influenced by radical philosophical ideas.

Wholeness and the Implicate Order is an exercise in metaphysics. In the spirit of Whitehead, it is informed by its contemporary science. Bohm brings many scientific facts to bear in his favor, but his arguments are basically metaphysical, and as yet they can find little ground in scientific investigation.

Summary

Could science and philosophy converge on these issues, yielding, if not a final physical theory, perhaps a final theory of physical and philosophical components? I suggest this will not be the case. As Kuhn, Einstein, Heisenberg, and others have pointed out, philosophical ideas are inspirational for scientific change. Dühem, among others, recognized that philosophy is never a discipline of unanimity. And if philosophy cannot be presumed to converge upon a final theory, metaphysics will always available for external criticism of scientific practice. As Popper has said, philosophers must continually reflect on "experience" that both the scientific and the philosophic communities periodically take for granted. And as perennial themes in science and philosophy are revisited, philosophical dialogue is enriched with new perspectives and perhaps greater precision, while methodological criticisms are reinvigorated with each new scientific and philosophic interaction.

A recurring theme we have not touched upon within the body of the text is one of self-evaluation. All serious philosophers and scientists must come to grips with the preconceived ideas they bring to their own disciplines. Descartes advocated the method of doubt to purge such contaminants from his investigation. Bacon, Comte, and Mach recommended reporting and systematizing raw sense data. Popper advocated focusing on empirical testability rather than rational justification. These and other purgative methods were seen to be incomplete, assuming as they did other preconceptions about experience and its relation to thought and science. Kuhn and Laudan advocate embracing such preconceptions, giving them a just place in a method of scientific progress. In so doing, they in turn are products of their own time, since the post-modern and contemporary periods are full of theories of social relativism as well as practical attempts to deglorify the past.

Indeed, self-evaluation is a never-ending process. Neither scientists nor philosophers can ever be sure that they are not carrying some historical baggage that has lost its potency. The only assurance is that both science and philosophy are products of history, and each carries with it the influence of the past. In order to evaluate whether this influence has outlived its usefulness, historical awareness must be brought to the fore, and in this process of evaluation, alternatives to the *status quo* must be proposed. Both science and philosophy must continually offer such alternatives to each other, and a final, ahistorical answer to the questions of philosophy and science in this context is unlikely. In this, human endeavor mirrors a physics and metaphysics of process and change. If transformation is a fundamental component of reality, then perhaps it is just that the disciplines of philosophy and science should mirror this aspect in their own continuing and interpenetrating attempts to answer some of the most profoundly important questions:

> What is the nature of the world?
>
> What are we, that experience the universe?
>
> What is experience?

Notes

1. José Ortega y Gasset, *What is Philosophy?* (New York: W. W. Norton, 1960).

2. Steven Weinberg's *The First Three Minutes* (New York: Basic Books, 1977) is his precursor to a work we will consider in this chapter: *Dreams of a Final Theory* (New York: Pantheon, 1992). Both combine the success of a "standard model" in physics with

reductionism and scientific realism in sweeping ways to apply to problems as diverse as "Genesis" (in Weinberg's words, see the preface to *The First Three Minutes*), the meaning of life, and the future of the cosmos, science, and humanity. Hawking's *A Brief History of Time* follows a similar pattern. Another, Dennett's *Consciousness Explained*, has a different area of application but relies on similar views on the content and status of modern science. Dennett's work will be treated in a subsequent section.

3. Stephen Hawking, *A Brief History of Time* (New York: Bantam, 1992).

4. Howard Gardner, *The Mind's New Science* (New York: HarperCollins, 1985).

5. Roger Penrose, *The Emperor's New Mind* (Oxford University Press, 1989).

6. Daniel C. Dennett, *Consciousness Explained* (Boston: Little, Brown, 1991).

7. Allen Newell and Herbert A. Simon, "Computer Science as Empirical Inquiry," *Communications of the ACM* 19, no. 3, 1976: 113–126.

8. Allen Newell and Herbert A. Simon, *Human Problem Solving* (New York: Prentice-Hall, 1972), 5.

9. Author of *Godel, Escher, Bach: an eternal golden braid* (New York: Basic Books, 1979), and coauthor, with Dennett, of *The Mind's I* (New York: Basic Books, 1981).

10. Page 4. This is one of his earlier, and still most popular, books on the subject.

11. Eric J. Lerner, *The Big Bang Never Happened* (New York: Vintage Books, 1992).

12. These particular cosmological problems may be dated by the time of publication of this text. However, there will likely be other provocative anomalies, such as the mysteriously powerful emissions of radiation recently observed, that theoreticians must cope with in good faith and that sceptics can use to criticize the standard model.

13. Larry Laudan, *Progress and Its Problems: Toward a Theory of Scientific Growth* (Berkeley, CA: UC Press, 1977).

14. Laudan, *Progress and Its Problems*, 79.

15. Ibid., 81.

16. Ibid., 95.

17. Ibid., 98. Emphasis in original.

18. Ibid., 98–101.

19. Aesthetic criteria are important for Weinberg (as well as Dühem and many others). And so if aesthetic appeal is a measure of success, then a more aesthetic approach to the history and philosophy of science may be more successful than a "boring" one (as Feyerabend would say).

20. However, Weinberg, for one, disagrees (see 220–225 of *Dreams of a Final Theory*).

21. John D. Barrow and Frank J. Tipler, *The Anthropic Cosmological Principle* (Oxford, England: Oxford University Press, 1988).

22. See Barrow and Tipler, 4–5.

23. M.S. Longair, ed., *Confrontation of Cosmological Theories with Observation* (Dordrecht: Reidel, 1974), 291.

24. This differs from the unification of observer and experiment in quantum theory. While quantum theory and the uncertainty principle establish that experimental apparatus and the process of observation cannot be effectively separated from the phenomenon under investigation, Barrow and Tipler point out that a living observer plays no special role, and that a photographic plate could serve the same purpose. While Penrose believes this interpenetration between observation and event is related to the anthropic principle, they are on the surface different areas of scientific interpretation.

25. David Bohm, *Wholeness and the Implicate Order* (London and New York: Routledge, 1980), 192.

26. Another highly provocative approach to the anthropic principle involves using it against the very science that produced it. In other words, we should be highly suspicious of a scientific "tradition," "paradigm," or set of theories and practices that confirms some of our most cherished metaphysical views. The mere fact that this agreement obtains is not evidence for the truth of the metaphysics, but rather evidence against the validity of the scientific practice. It is an indication that our scientific practice has been contaminated by non-scientific ideas, and again that science has simply found what it was looking for and succeeded, to some degree, in forcing nature into the box that it had already selected. This is in fact not progress, but bad-faith scientific practice, according to some. This type of argument relies on the characterization of science provided by Kuhn, Feyerabend, and others, and is deployed to some extent by Lerner in *The Big Bang Never Happened*, as we have seen. According to Lerner, there *is* in fact some evidence against the big bang, single universe model, but it is being systematically overlooked or coerced by the current paradigm (see also previous discussion of Lerner).

27. Barrow and Tipler, Chapter 3.

28. Albert Einstein, B. Podolsky, and N. Rosen, "Can a Quantum Mechanical Description of Physical Reality Be Considered Complete?" *Physical Review* Vol. 47, 1935, 777–780.

29. Lucien Hardy, *Physical Review Letters* 68 (1992): 2981–2988.

30. David Bohm, *Wholeness and the Implicate Order* (New York and London: Routledge, 1981).

31. Ibid., 191.

32. Ibid., 113.

Suggestions for Further Reading

Davies, Paul. *Other Worlds* (New York: Simon & Schuster, 1980).

Davies, Paul. *God and the New Physics* (New York: Simon & Schuster, 1983).

Donovan, Arthur, Laudan, Larry, and Laudan, Rachel, eds. *Scrutinizing Science: Empirical Studies of Scientific Change* (Boston: Kluwer Academic Publishers, 1988).

Hawking, Stephen. *A Brief History of Time* (New York: Bantam, 1992).

Herbert, Nick. *Quantum Reality* (New York: Doubleday, 1985).

Rae, Alistair. *Quantum Physics: Illusion or Reality?* (Cambridge University Press, 1986.)

Stapp, Henry P. *Mind, Matter, and Quantum Mechanics* (Springer-Verlag, 1993).

Weinberg, Steven. *The First Three Minutes* (New York: Basic Books, 1977).

Conclusion

At the beginning of this inquiry, I likened the study of the history of philosophy and science to the experience of observing the growth of consciousness in a child. This metaphor has much romantic appeal and is productive of some helpful analogies, although like all metaphors it is not without its problems.

This picture is helpful because it encourages a student of intellectual history to approach the process with an open mind and to be flexible in proceeding toward expectations. As any parent knows, the process of child rearing teaches us as much about ourselves as it teaches the child about the world. And in this text, we can see not only how humanity has developed through various stages of intellectual history but also where our notions of the world and knowledge about it come from. Popular ideas such as the cumulative view of scientific growth have a specific origin in particular metaphysical views. And beliefs in mechanical causation are recurrently popular and problematic. At some stages, the very notion of mechanism can permeate an entire culture, from science and technology to psychology and politics. These ideas, furthermore, do not always produce the results that are intended. This also has a direct parallel in the process of child development.

But the notion that human history is a process of growth is extremely loaded. We saw positivists deploy this idea in attempting to dismiss metaphysics and religion. This particular belief in scientific progress is dated at best, discredited at worst. And the idea that knowledge grows cumulatively is controversial. Thus, the parallel between scientific history from ancient to modern times and individual development from infancy to adulthood seems to break down.

Yet I suggest that this does not necessarily represent a breakdown in our metaphor. The history of science and philosophy has passed through many phases, some seemingly cyclical, others entirely novel. Mechanism and determinism seem to cycle with anthropocentrism and wholism, for example. On the other hand, there do seem to be progressive phases in the discovery of our place in the universe, at least physically. We continue to discover that our world is one of minute dimension in space and time compared with cosmic existence, and these discoveries have progressed from geocentrism to heliocentrism to modern cosmology. These facts could lend some support to the metaphor. However, if some twentieth-century philosophers of science are correct, these phases and cycles cannot be judged independently as periods of growth but must be evaluated on their own terms within their own cultures. If this is the case, does this mean that the process of individual growth and development is fundamentally different, since we tend to judge the process of child development by its results from an adult perspective?

The answer to this last question should be: no. Anyone who is intimately involved in child care knows that as much is lost as is gained in the maturation process. The innocence and wonder, the genuineness and inquisitiveness of small children become sacrificed to worldly experience, and this sacrifice is something to lament. In addition, the quickness of intellect and sympathetic character that come naturally to children is dulled, seemingly inevitably, by the developmental process. While this process results in individuals and societies that are more empowered to survive in and master their surroundings, it does not come without cost. Thus, the end result is not a cumulative gain that is in all senses superior to its beginning. Similarly, the history of science and philosophy is not necessarily one of cumulative growth and mastery, yielding greater sophistication without sacrifice. ·

These picturesque notions should be suspect simply because of their emotional appeal. Yet they are intended to serve as invitations rather than final descriptions. For if the wonder of childhood is lost in the adult, it need not be permanently so. An adult has the opportunity to rediscover this state by passionately and sympathetically involving himself or herself with the growth of a child. And the student of ideas has the ability to recapture some of the unity, simplicity, and grace of the past by studying the development of history with an open mind.

Index